STRUCTURED PROGRAMMING
in PL/I and PL/C

STRUCTURED PROGRAMMING
in PL/I and PL/C

PETER ABEL

British Columbia Institute of Technology

RESTON PUBLISHING COMPANY, INC.
A Prentice-Hall Company
Reston, Virginia

Library of Congress Cataloging in Publication Data

Abel, Peter, 1932-
   Structured programming in PL/1 and PL/C.

   Includes index.
   1. PL/1 (Computer program language) 2. PL/C (Com-
puter program language) 3. Structured programming.
I. Title
QA76.73.P25A23   001.64'24   81-5201
ISBN 0-8359-7120-1   AACR2
ISBN 0-8359-7119-8

10   9   8   7   6   5   4   3   2   1

Printed in the United States of America

CONTENTS

PREFACE

APPROACH

Structured Programming in PL/I and PL/C offers a new and original approach to learning the PL/I language. The most elementary features of PL/I are introduced first with simple program examples. After only two chapters of PL/I (Chapters 3 and 4), students are able to write a simple program by concentrating on only the statements necessary for its completion and by temporarily using the simple GET LIST and PUT LIST statements for input/output. The text adds new features and concepts gradually with program examples, and consequently students are never overwhelmed by a topic.

Structured programming is introduced early. Even before formally discussing the topic, the text adopts and illustrates structured programming features: indentation of code, meaningful names, and organization into main logic and subsidiary sections. By the time Chapter 10 formally describes structured programming, students are already accustomed to its features.

An objective of this text is to provide a tool for problem solving. Subjects are introduced and program examples are designed to solve practical problems that students and professional programmers are likely to encounter.

A problem in current PL/I texts is omission of specific topics. Thus, one book omits programming strategy and style, another omits business programming requirements, and another omits file organization methods. Ideally one text should cover all of these essential topics, and *Structured Programming in PL/I and PL/C* does just this.

ORGANIZATION

Chapters 1 and 2 contain introductory material on computers and programming that is intended for students who have had no prior computer programming course. Chapters 3 through 9 cover the basics of PL/I, representing 80 percent or more of standard program coding. Chapter 10 is concerned with programming style and the use of the CALL statement in structured programming. From this point on, readers can study the chapters in various sequences. Chapters 11 through 13 are designed especially for the computer science specialist, whereas Chapters 14 through 17 are designed for the business programmer; however, users would be wise to study both parts. The following chart indicates the relationships of the chapters:

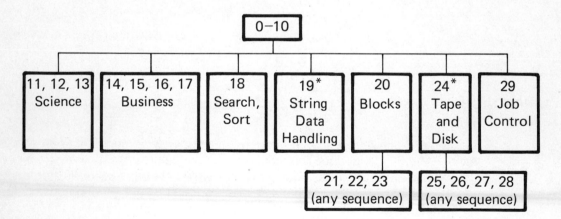

PL/I DIFFERENCES

There are a number of PL/I versions that vary largely because of differences in computer operating systems. Basically, there is a PL/I-D Subset version, PL/I-F, the DOS PL/I Optimizer, the OS PL/I Optimizer, and special versions such as PL/C. This text indicates differences among the versions in the relevant sections.

*Because chapters 19 and 24 use structures extensively, you should cover chapters 15 and 16 first.

The main differences is the definition of files (data sets). The differences, however, constitute only a small portion of a PL/I program, and students should be able to easily adapt the material in this text to their own compiler version.

This text is not intended to replace the manufacturers' PL/I reference texts. Users of IBM PL/I should have access to the *IBM PL/I Reference Manual and PL/I Programmer's Guide* for unique and specialized features. Users of PL/C should have access to the *PL/C reference manual.*

NOTATIONS USED IN THIS TEXT

In this text and in the PL/I manuals, left and right parentheses (. . .) enclose a list of one or more required entries. A pair of square brackets [. . .] means that the enclosed entry or entries is optional and may be omitted. For example:

PUT LIST (data-name); You must code a "data-name" within parentheses.
END [program-name]; You may optionally code a "program-name" with no parentheses.

Words in uppercase letters such as PUT, LIST, and END are PL/I keywords that must be used as shown. Words in lowercase letters imply a user-defined name.

ACKNOWLEDGEMENTS

The author is grateful for the assistance and cooperation of all those who contributed typing, reviews, and suggestions and to IBM for permission to reproduce some of their copyrighted material. The following materials are printed with permission, and with modifications, from publications copyrighted in 1972, 1976, and 1978 by International Business Machines Corporation as IBM form numbers GC20-1648, GC20-1850, GC33-0009, and GC20-1649: Figures 1-3, 24-2, Appendix B, Appendix D, and Appendix F.

PART I

PROGRAMMING FUNDAMENTALS

CHAPTER 1

COMPUTER PRINCIPLES

OBJECTIVES

To explain the internal characteristics of the digital computer, input/output devices, and the role of the stored program.

INTRODUCTION

The purpose of computers is to produce answers that are both faster and more accurate than manual calculations. The two classes of computers are analog and digital. An *analog* computer measures physical variables such as rotation speed, water pressure, and electric current and includes speedometers, steam pressure gauges, and barometers. A *digital* computer works with digits to perform calculations. Whereas the analog computer is designed to perform one function, the digital computer may solve many problems. The digital computer uses a *stored program,* which is a set of instructions that the computer executes. When one stored program has completed processing, another program can replace it to work on a different problem. This text uses the term *computer* to mean the common digital computer.

In the 1940s, research scientists developed the modern digital computer using the stored program that would solve complex problems by means of fast, accurate calculations. Since that time, the computer has made its impact in two main areas: scientific and business. The scientific programmer uses the computer to perform calculations for applications such as the design of bridges and buildings, simulation models of the national economy, and statistical studies of the population. The business programmer uses the computer to process and control large volumes of data. Common business applications include payroll, billing, sales analysis, production control, airline reservations, and inventory control. In addition, government agencies require many reports relating, for example, to pensions, income tax, and depreciation.

A computer has the ability to process data in the form of alphabetic characters and numeric values and can perform arithmetic and make comparisons. Assume, for example, that a computer installation maintains data about inventory items on disk storage. The record for each item contains item number, item name, quantity-on-hand, and unit-cost. If programmed accordingly, the computer can read each inventory record and calculate the value of each item (quantity times unit-cost). It can also add the total of all item values and print a final total. But the computer has significant limitations: it can process only data with which it is provided, and only according to the instruction steps with which it is programmed.

Some of the advantages that the computer provides are as follows:

- Solutions and reports that otherwise may be impossible to achieve.
- Better control over business activity and industrial processes.
- Faster answers, which give better return on investment and better control over data. For example, computers can help minimize a company's investment in inventory or notify customers who are late in paying their accounts.
- More accurate answers and, consequently, a more reliable base for decision making.

These advantages are not easily achieved. The computer is no panacea for the problems of business and industry. Its success depends on considerable planning, experience, effort, and skill, involving the cooperation of many people.

THE COMPUTER SYSTEM

Since the first primitive models, computers have evolved radically and although there are many manufacturers and types, their basic structure remains the same. Figure 1-1 illustrates the four main components: input/output, main storage, arithmetic/logic, and control. Arithmetic/logic and control together form what is called the *Central Processing Unit (CPU)*.

Input/Output

In order to access new data, the computer "reads" data into its main storage from input devices such as terminals and disk storage. Also, in order to communicate its results to the user, the computer "writes" data from storage onto devices such as printers and magnetic tape.

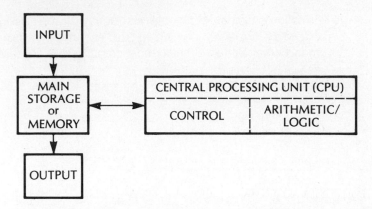

FIGURE 1-1. Basic Computer Components.

Main Storage, or Memory

A computer program is written to solve a specific problem. The program consists of *instructions* (such as read, add, and compare) and *data* (numbers used in calculations, and areas to develop answers and to read input data). The instructions and data areas may be read or *loaded* from punched cards, terminal, or disk into the computer storage and become the *stored program* that reads input data, makes calculations, and writes output according to the program instructions. Figure 1-2 illustrates a possible organization of program areas in main storage.

An instruction may require only a few locations, whereas an area for data may require one location or hundreds. Each storage location (*byte*) has a specific address (numbered consecutively from location 0, the first location), so that the control unit can locate stored instructions and data as required.

The size of storage varies considerably by computer model, from as little as a few thousand storage positions (bytes) to millions. Storage size in an installation depends on the volume of data and the complexity of the problems. The amount of available main storage is expressed in sizes such as 16K, 32K, 64K, up to sizes as large as 1000K, where K = 1024 bytes.

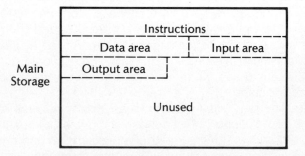

FIGURE 1–2 Map of Program in Main Storage.

The following simple example is typical of the way most computers work. The example adds the number 025 to 250. Assume that 025 is in locations 2338, 2339, and 2340 and that 250 is in locations 2263, 2264, and 2265:

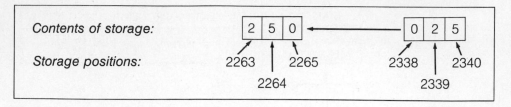

Assume that an add operation is the letter A. The instruction to add the contents of locations 2338–2340 to the contents of locations 2263–2265 would be

Locations 2263–2265 would now contain 275. Locations 2338–2340 would still contain 025, unchanged by the Add operation. This instruction itself would require nine storage locations consisting of an *operation* and two *operands*. The operation (A) tells the computer what function to perform, whereas the operands (2263 and 2338) specify which storage locations to process.

Programming in which main storage locations are directly referenced by number is known as the *machine language* level. But few people today code in machine language. Programming languages like PL/I are designed to use statements that are similar to the English language, and a special translator program converts the PL/I instructions to machine language.

The Central Processing Unit (CPU)

The CPU consists of two main units: an *arithmetic/logical unit* and a *control unit.* The *arithmetic/logical unit* performs addition, subtraction, multiplication, division, shifting, and moving. Its capability of logic enables a programmer to code instructions that can compare one value in storage to another and permits a program to change the sequence of instruction execution. The *control unit* directs and coordinates the computer system. It controls arithmetic/logic, input/output units, the transfer of data into and out of main storage, and the location of data and instructions to be executed.

The time required to transfer data is known as *access time,* which is measured in thousandths of a second (milliseconds), millionths (microseconds), or even billionths (nanoseconds). The type and complexity of arithmetic/logic circuitry and the access time vary considerably by computer model.

Instruction Execution

A computer program consists of instructions and data areas, all kept temporarily in main storage during execution. A machine instruction is comprised of at least two parts:

1. *The operation*—The function that the computer is to perform, such as read, add, or move.
2. *The operand(s)*—The address of a data area, of another instruction, or of an input or output unit.

The computer extracts the instruction to be executed from main storage and delivers it to the CPU. For example, the operation could be Read (the operation) data from a specific disk drive (the operand) into a main storage area (operand-2). An Add operation, for example, adds the contents of one main storage location (operand-2) to the contents of another location (operand-1), using the arithmetic unit.

The CPU extracts instructions one at a time sequentially from main storage until encountering an instruction that specifies a *branch* operation. A branch operation directs the sequence of execution to some other instruction in the program that is not in the regular sequence. For example, an instruction may be a Compare (IF) operation that checks an arithmetic field for its sign (plus or minus) using the Logical Unit. If the sign is plus, control is to branch to some other instruction in the program, and if minus, control is to continue with the next sequential instruction following the compare operation.

Input Units

Input units are used to enter data into the computer's main storage. The most commonly used input devices are as follows:

*   Typewriter or visual display terminals—for input of data or for inquiry about the current status of stored data.
*   Card readers—for reading punched cards that originate from keypunch devices or computer output. Typical speed is 600–1200 cards per minute.
*   Magnetic tape drives—for reading magnetic tape, which is similar to that used in a home music system and which can store millions of bytes of data on a reel.
*   Disk storage devices—for reading flat, spinning disks that are similar to phonograph records and that contain millions of bytes of data stored in circular tracks.

- Optical Character Recognition (OCR) devices—for reading computer-printed documents, such as a customer's telephone bill.
- Magnetic Ink Character Recognition (MICR) devices—for reading encoded checks in the banking industry.

Data is entered into the device through some applicable medium. For example, a terminal "reads" the characters entered on a terminal keyboard, and a disk drive "reads" data stored as magnetized bits on a rotating disk. In addition to providing input data to the system, magnetic tape and disk devices have another important use: storage of large quantities of data.

Output Units

Output devices provide information from the computer's main storage. The computer directs the output device to record and "write" data from main storage, for example, to print information on printed forms. Common output devices include the following:

- Line printers—for printing reports. There are many different types of line printers, but all have certain common features. Printing speeds range from a few hundred to several thousand lines per minute.
- Typewriter or visual display terminals—to provide the status of records and computations either at the computer or at remote locations.
- Magnetic tape—for recording data files, such as customer records, or to act as temporary storage used for intermediary results.
- Disk storage devices—for recording data files, such as customer records, or to act as temporary storage. Many computer systems store (or *catalog*) programs on disk for ready execution.
- Computer Output Microfilm (COM) devices—for producing microfilm.

PUNCHED CARDS

The main card format is the common 80-column card measuring 7⅜ by 3¼ inches, punched with rectangular holes. As shown in Figure 1-3, the common 80-column card contains twelve punching positions (rows). The rows are divided into two areas: *numeric* rows numbered 1 through 9, and *zone* rows called 12, 11, and 0 (the 12-zone is the topmost punch, the 11-zone next, then the 0-zone, and 1 through to 9 to the bottom). The 0 is either numeric or zone, depending on how it is used. A single punch (0 through 9) in a column represents the ten digits. A combination of two punches in the same column (a multipunch), one a zone and one numeric, represents alphabetic characters. The letters A through I use the 12-zone with numeric 1 through 9 respectively. The letters J through R

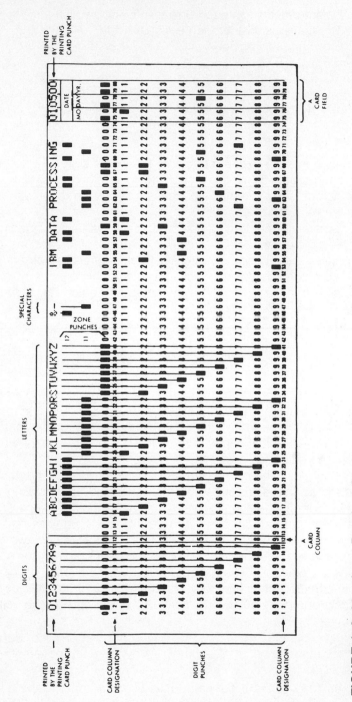

FIGURE 1–3 80-column Punched Card.

9

use the 11-zone with numeric 1 through 9 respectively, and letters S through Z use the zero-zone with numeric 2 through 9 respectively:

Letter	Zone	Digit
A–I	12	1–9
J–R	11	1–9
S–Z	0	2–9

A single punch in the 11-zone represents the minus sign (−), and the 12-zone represents the plus sign (+), although the plus sign is seldom used. A unique combination of two or three multipunches in a column represents special characters, such as *, $, and %.

Punched cards enter the reading unit of the card reader one at a time. The reading unit senses the presence of the holes by photoelectric cells and "reads" a card by translating a punched hole into electronic-signals, which are sent to the computer. The entire 80 columns, including blank columns if any, are read into an 80-byte area in main storage. The punched characters are represented in main storage by bytes of specific bit values.

LINE PRINTER

Line printers vary considerably in print speed, from a few hundred to several thousand lines per minute. Many can print 60 or more different characters, including the numbers 0 through 9, letters A through Z, and special characters such as $, #, *, and +. Typical printers can print 10 characters to the inch, and 120, 132, or 144 characters on a line.

The paper used for printing is called *continuous forms*. The forms are perforated horizontally so that each sheet can be separated after printing. Manufacturers supply the forms in various sizes, such as 11 and 15 inches wide and 11 inches long. Printing at six lines per inch permits up to 60 lines of print per page. The forms are available in single-part or, with carbon inserts, two or more parts. Some forms are preprinted according to the user's design for a special purpose, such as customer bills. Other forms, called *stock tab forms* or *continuous printout,* contain only horizontal lines or bars; these are general purpose forms for use in a variety of reports but are not normally issued outside the company.

DATA ENTRY DEVICES

Data entry devices record the initial data to be used for input to the computer system. Common transactions that are recorded for data entry include customer sales and payments, changes to employee pay rates, statistical samplings, and

PL/I program instructions. Common data entry devices include key-to-tape, key-to-cassette, key-to-diskette, and key-to-disk. The latter provide advantages in variable record length, speed, flexible formats, and ease of correction. Any one may be particularly economical for processing large volumes of data.

Data to be entered usually consists of *records,* such as payments from customers. The record is subdivided into various related *fields* of data, such as customer number, amount of payment, and date paid. A collection of related records comprises a *file* or *data set,* such as all customer payment records for a day.

Keypunch Machine

An operator punches data in the form of rectangular holes into cards by means of a keypunch machine. The operator places blank cards in a hopper and punches the cards on a keyboard similar to that of a typewriter. Cards are punched from left to right, columns 1 through 80.

Punched cards may still be economical when processing a small-to-medium volume of data, requiring only a few keypunch devices and not requiring great speed. Operators can easily rearrange records and add or delete records. But the punched card does have certain inherent drawbacks. The keypunching step is relatively slow, and the cards require considerable manual handling, are easily damaged, and cannot be easily reused.

Key-to-tape

The first key-to-tape devices were introduced in 1965 and permitted an operator to "write" data directly onto a standard reel of ½-inch magnetic tape. An operator can easily transfer a completed tape reel to a computer, which reads the data directly from the tape into main storage for processing.

Key-to-cassette

Operators key data onto a tape cassette, usually about 2½ by 4 inches and small enough to facilitate easy handling and mailing. The tape can store about 200,000 characters and is particularly suited for use in a branch office for transmitting transactions to a central office. Key-to-cassette is otherwise similar to tape, but is easier to mail and store.

Key-to-diskette

The diskette or *floppy disk* is a recordlike disk 8 inches in diameter, which can store about 240,000 characters of data. It is often used to transmit data over a transmission line from a branch office directly into a computer in a central office.

In some installations, an operator keys onto diskette and then enters the diskette data directly through a diskette reader into the computer.

Key-to-disk (Multistation Systems)

In *multistation* systems, the keying devices are connected to a single minicomputer that writes the data onto disk and is dedicated to handling only the key-to-disk devices. The minicomputer contains a stored program that provides useful "editing" or validating of input data, error detection, and a variety of statistical and production figures. An operator can periodically copy the disk data records onto a tape reel and send it to the central computer for processing.

Terminal Entry

Terminal devices, such as a typewriter terminal, a video display, or a cash register, may be directly connected to the computer system on-line. An entry that an operator keys in to the terminal is read directly into the computer's main storage, where a program immediately processes the entry. The computer program both receives data from a terminal and transmits information to a terminal.

BINARY NUMBER SYSTEM

The basic numbering system of computers is binary format. A decimal (base-10) number has ten digits (0 through 9), but a binary (base-2) number has two: 0 and 1. For any number system, the position of a digit determines the value. Consider the decimal number 1111:

$$\text{decimal } 1111$$
$$= (1 \times 10^3) + (1 \times 10^2) + (1 \times 10^1) + (1 \times 10^0)$$
$$= 1000 \quad\quad + 100 \quad\quad + 10 \quad\quad + 1$$

Instead of base-ten, a binary number uses the base of two. Consider the same number, 1111, this time expressed as binary:

$$\text{binary } 1111$$
$$= \text{decimal } (1 \times 2^3) + (1 \times 2^2) + (1 \times 2^1) + (1 \times 2^0)$$
$$= 8 \quad\quad\quad\quad\quad + 4 \quad\quad + 2 \quad\quad + 1$$
$$= 15 \quad\quad\quad\quad (\text{or } 2^4 - 1)$$

As another example, the value of the decimal number 1010 is determined as follows:

decimal 1010

$= (1 \times 10^3) + (0 \times 10^2) + (1 \times 10^1) + (0 \times 10^0)$

$= 1000 \quad\quad + 0 \quad\quad\quad + 10 \quad\quad\quad + 0$

A decimal digit zero, as shown, has no value, nor has a binary digit zero. The same number 1010 expressed in binary is as follows:

binary 1010

$= $ decimal $(1 \times 2^3) + (0 \times 2^2) + (1 \times 2^1) + (0 \times 2^0)$

$= 8 \quad\quad\quad\quad\quad\quad + 0 \quad\quad\quad + 2 \quad\quad\quad + 0$

$= 10 \quad\quad\quad\quad\quad$ (decimal)

In this way, a binary number using only digits 0 and 1 can represent any decimal value. The computer represents the two possible 0 and 1 values as "off" or "on" conditions. This simplicity makes binary the important fundamental numbering system of computers.

BITS

A storage location, called a *byte,* consists of a specified number of *bits* (an abbreviation for *binary digit*). A bit can be related to a binary digit, since a bit can be "off" (zero) or "on" (one). Assume a computer in which each byte consists of four bits to represent data:

8	4	2	1
0	0	0	0

A storage location (byte)

All bits off (0000) means zero. If only the bit numbered 1 (the rightmost one) is on (0001), the value in the location is 1. If only bit 2 is on (0010), the value is 2. Both bits 1 and 2 on (0011) represent the value 3. Combinations of bits provide values 1 through 9.

Actually, each byte has one extra bit called a *parity bit* that is not used to represent data. On the typical computer, each byte must have *odd parity* so that the number of bits "on" is an odd number. For example, the value in a byte is 7: bits 4, 2, and 1 are on. Because the number of bits is odd, the computer sets the parity bit off:

Parity bit

off ⟶

P	8	4	2	1
0	0	1	1	1

Assume that the value in a byte is 9: bits 8 and 1 are on. To force odd parity, the computer sets the parity bit on:

Parity bit	P	8	4	2	1
on ————————→	1	1	0	0	1

It sometimes happens, although rarely, that an "on" bit condition is somehow "lost" and becomes "off". When processing the contents of a byte, the computer automatically checks the parity. If the parity is even, the computer signals a warning and stops processing; the computer may require servicing. Setting bits on and off is an entirely automatic process over which a programmer has no control.

A reference to bit capacity does not normally include the parity bit. Thus, the previous example would be a "four-bit" code. Some computers use a six-bit code, some a seven-bit code, and others an eight-bit code. The more bits, the more characters a byte can represent. For example, a seven-bit code can represent 2^7 or 128 different characters, and an eight-bit code can represent 2^8 or 256 characters. PL/I programmers only occasionally need to be concerned with the bit format of their computer.

BYTES

The basic building block of main storage on the IBM 370 series is the byte, which represents a single storage location. Each byte consists of nine bits, of which eight bits represent data and the ninth bit ensures odd parity. The eight data bits are "split" into two portions of four bits (half-bytes), a *zone* and a *numeric* portion:

		Byte						
		½-byte				*½-byte*		
Bits:	0	0	0	0	0	0	0	0
Value:	8	4	2	1	8	4	2	1
Portion:		Zone				Numeric		

The value represented in a byte varies from zero (all bits OFF, 0000 0000) through 255 (all bits ON, 1111 1111). The CPU normally executes a program by accessing bytes or groups of bytes.

Each group of 1,024 bytes is called 1K. Addressable storage varies from a minimum of 8,192 (8K) bytes to a maximum of 16,777,216 (16,384K) bytes.

DATA FORMATS

Bytes in main storage may represent instructions or data:

1. *Instructions.* A 370 machine instruction is always 2, 4, or 6 bytes, depending on the type of instruction.
2. *Data.* Although some instructions can access bits or half-bytes, a byte is considered the smallest data length. Data may be defined so that it is represented in bytes as Character or arithmetic format.
   Character Format. A character field requires one byte for each character. The eight bits in a byte can represent 256 (2^8) possible characters, including the letters A through Z, the numbers 1 through 9, and special characters such as $ or * or &. For example, the ON bits 1100 0001 represent the letter A, and 1111 0001 represents the number 1. The character code is called the *extended binary-coded-decimal-interchange code* (*EBCDIC*) and is shown in detail in Appendix E. Character format is for descriptive information only and is not intended for arithmetic processing.

Arithmetic data

There are three types of arithmetic data:

1. *Decimal, or packed, format.* For ordinary decimal arithmetic, the digits 0 through 9 are "packed" two digits per byte. The sign (+ or −) requires a ½-byte on the right; for example, the value 125 would require two bytes: 12/5 + /.
2. *Binary format.* For binary arithmetic, addressing, and special features, each bit represents a binary 0 or 1. For example, the binary value 0100 0111 equals the decimal value 71.
3. *Floating-point format.* For representation and processing of extremely small or large values.

Note that to represent the value '1,' character format requires a full byte (1111 0001), packed format requires a half-byte (0001), and binary format requires one bit (1).

HEXADECIMAL REPRESENTATION

The hexadecimal numbering system uses base-16. Hexadecimal (or *hex*) numbers are 0 through 9 and A through F, for the decimal values 0–15. *Hexadecimal numbers are used to represent the contents of storage.* Hexadecimal is only a

BINARY	DECIMAL	HEXADECIMAL	BINARY	DECIMAL	HEXADECIMAL
0000	0	0	1000	8	8
0001	1	1	1001	9	9
0010	2	2	1010	10	A
0011	3	3	1011	11	B
0100	4	4	1100	12	C
0101	5	5	1101	13	D
0110	6	6	1110	14	E
0111	7	7	1111	15	F

FIGURE 1–4 Binary, Decimal, and Hex Representation.

representation of storage—at no time does the computer actually work in base-16 as such. One hex digit depicts four bits of a byte, and two hex digits represent all eight bits in a byte, one hex digit for the zone portion and one for the numeric portion of a byte. Figure 1–4 lists the equivalent decimal, binary, and hexadecimal numbers.

Two hex digits can represent the contents of any storage location, regardless of the data format that it contains. For example, a byte contains the character 'A.' The binary representation of 'A' in main storage is 1100 0001 for which the hex representation is 'C1,' or as commonly notated, X'C1.' Thus, if an input record contains the letter A in a certain position, when read into storage, it appears in a byte as 1100 0001, and the representation of its contents is either character A or X'C1'. A blank is a true character, with binary format 0100 0000, and hex representation X'40.'

There are only about 60 different print characters, but there is no way to represent each of the 256 possible combinations of bits in a byte as a single character. Assume that a byte contains the packed digits 4 and 5. The binary representation of the byte's contents is 0100 0101. Although there is no single character that can represent this 8-bit code, two hex digits can represent it as X'45'.

A byte used for binary data could contain 0101 1011 (which equals decimal value 91). The hexadecimal representation is X'5B'. In this way, hex format can represent all data formats, such as character, packed, and binary, one hex digit for each half-byte (four bits). The computer Supervisor and the Assembler language both use hex extensively to represent the contents of storage, although only the programmer knows that the specific contents of bytes and fields are in a particular format.

GENERAL-PURPOSE REGISTERS

The 370-type computers have 16 general-purpose registers (GPR's) that are special circuitry. Each register consists of 32 bits. The two main uses of registers are as follows:

1. Addressing storage positions, by means of *base displacement addressing*. Every reference to a location in main storage is by means of a "base address" in a register and a "displacement" from that address. This feature is important to a programmer using Assembler, but not to one using PL/I.
2. Performing binary arithmetic in the registers, done at extremely high speed.

PROBLEMS

1–1. Distinguish between an analog and a digital computer.

1–2. What are the basic components of a digital computer? What is the function of each one?

1–3. Distinguish between instructions and data.

1–4. What holes are punched in a card for the letters COMPUTER?

1–5. Define the following:
   (a) Stored program   (d) Record
   (b) Access time   (e) File, or data set
   (c) Field   (f) Alphanumeric data

1–6. What is the decimal value of binary (a) 1110, (b) 11001, (c) 101101?

1–7. What is a bit? What is a bit's relationship to a byte?

1–8. The left four bits of a byte are the _____portion; the right four bits are the _____portion. The ninth bit is called _____; what is its purpose?

1–9. What are the three types of arithmetic data?

1–10. What is the purpose of hexadecimal representation?

1–11. Give the hexadecimal representation for the following binary vales:
   (a) 1110, (b) 0101 1101, (c) 1011 0011, (d) 1111 0010 1100 1110.

1–12. Convert the following decimal values to hexadecimal (refer to Appendix F):
   (a) 10, (b) 16, (c) 24, (d) 32, (e) 275, (f) 2048, (g) 4096.

1–13. Convert the following hex values to decimal:
   (a) F, (b) 10, (c) 2D, (d) 4F, (e) 80, (f) 800, (g) 1000.

1–14. Show the bit configuration and the hexadecimal representation for the following:
   (a) PL/I, (b) IBM, (c) 256, (d) $1,235.26, (e) THE END (including the blank).

CHAPTER 2

PROGRAMMING PRINCIPLES

OBJECTIVES
To cover the principles of program translation
and proper logic.

INTRODUCTION

Chapter 1 covered computer *hardware,* the physical components of a computer system. This chapter is concerned with *software,* the operating system and compiler programs that the manufacturer supplies and the programs that users write for their own purposes. The material in this chapter is basically appropriate to any computer in any language.

OPERATING SYSTEMS

An *operating system* is a set of programs that the computer manufacturer supplies. The operating system handles the various *jobs* that need to be run, such as payroll earnings, customer bills, and depreciation accounting. The heart of the operating system is the *Supervisor,* a program that resides permanently in main storage, as shown in Figure 2–1. If a program that is executing has trouble and "crashes," the Supervisor takes control of the computer and terminates the pro-

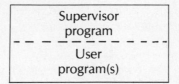

FIGURE 2–1 Supervisor Program in Main Storage.

gram. The Supervisor then arranges for the next program to run. Some of the functions of a typical Supervisor are as follows:

- Handles the steps between jobs.
- Loads programs into main storage for execution.
- Performs job accounting of the time taken for each program to execute.
- Determines priority for the programs waiting for execution.
- Checks for requests from users at visual display terminals.
- Provides error diagnostics and error recovery where possible.

Programmers and operators notify the Supervisor of what action to perform by means of *job control,* punched cards, or entries keyed into a terminal. Typical requests are to "compile" a PL/I program, to execute a program, or to sort data records on a disk file. Job control entries are coded in *Job Control Language (JCL).*

THE APPROACH TO PROGRAMMING

Programming is more than simply coding instructions for the computer to execute. Usually there are three steps: analysis, design, and coding.

Analysis

The first step, analysis, consists of interviewing people concerned with the problem, studying input data to be processed, and designing the output required. If other programs use the same input or require the output, then the new program must integrate with the present system.

Design

The second step involves the design of the program logic in which you depict the solution to the problem. It is common to draw a *flowchart,* a pictorial representation of the program's flow of logic, or write *pseudocode,* showing the steps that the program coding is to take. A later section describes pseudocode and flowcharting in detail.

Coding

You next code the program based on the preceding analysis and design, carefully following the design logic to avoid making errors in coding. After coding the program, you should *desk-check* by carefully reviewing the coding and tracing some imaginary data through the program logic. This practice minimizes program errors.

PROGRAM TRANSLATION

Machine Language

Each computer comes equipped with a set of executable machine instructions that may vary by manufacturer and model. Instructions include, for example, read input data, move data in storage, add, subtract, compare, and print.

A computer executes only machine language instructions that are loaded as a program from disk storage into main storage (the stored program). The Add instruction in the previous chapter is an example of machine language—the *operands* reference the addresses of storage locations by number. Programmers wrote in this basic level on the earliest computers. Machine language, however, is far too complex and detailed for normal programming. Consequently, manufacturers supply *symbolic languages* to facilitate programming: assembler languages and compiler languages.

Assembler Language

Manufacturers supply a "low-level" language, called Assembler. An Assembler language is more like a written language; each operation has an unique name, such as ADD, MPY, and MOVE. After you code a program, you can use the Assembler translator program to *assemble* or translate the assembler instructions into machine language. The Assembler translator supplies addresses for instructions and the various data fields in computer storage. Most Assembler languages also provide *macro-instructions* that cause the Assembler program to generate two or more instructions for each macro coded. Although far simpler than machine language, coding in Assembler language requires an intimate knowledge of the computer operation and is still laborious and time consuming. Assembler language is also usually unique to a particular manufacturer. As a result, changing computers may require rewriting all the Assembler programs.

Compiler Language

To overcome the disadvantages of the Assembler level, manufacturers supply compiler, or "high-level," languages. These are coded entirely as a series of macro-instructions, so that when a program *compiles,* the compiler translates each statement into one or more low-level instructions.

Compiler languages such as PL/I consist of macro-instructions that are easy to remember and code and that generate large Assembler routines requiring no knowledge of either Assembler or machine language. For example, the formula to calculate the distance between two points is as follows:

$$d = \sqrt{(x_2\text{-}x_1)^2 + (y_2\text{-}y_1)^2}$$

In PL/I, you could code the formula with a statement such as

```
DIST = SQRT ( (X2-X1)**2 + (Y2-Y1)**2 ) ;
```

The disadvantages of compiler languages are that

1. They generate considerably more code than a comparable Assembler program and thus use more storage.
2. They generally execute more slowly, although not always noticeably.
3. There are some specialized functions that only Assembler can adequately perform, although PL/I can handle almost anything you may ever reasonably require.

Although there are over 300 different compiler languages that have been spawned since the beginning of the computer age, there are only a few that are universally in use. Compiler languages other than PL/I include the following:

*   FORTRAN (Formula Translator), one of the earliest languages for programming engineering and scientific problems and still popular today.
*   ALGOL (Algorithmic Language), another scientific language, used mostly in Europe.
*   COBOL (Common Business Oriented Language), an early language designed to solve business problems and still widely used.
*   BASIC (Beginners' All-purpose Symbolic Instruction Code), a language chiefly dedicated to the use of computer terminals.
*   RPG (Report Program Generator), used primarily on small computers to produce business reports.
*   APL (A Programming Language), based on mathematical notation and used for scientific problem solving on terminals.
*   PASCAL, a general-purpose language designed to be simple and efficient for teaching computer science and in use on many microcomputers.

PL/I Compilation

The PL/I compiler performs the following:

*   Accounts for the amount of storage required for instructions and data and assigns storage positions to them.
*   Translates the source program into machine language (object code).
*   Supplies diagnostics for programming errors, such as invalid use of an instruction, and spelling errors.
*   Prints the original symbolic coding that is useful in "debugging" the program and in making subsequent changes.
*   Writes the machine language object program, usually onto disk, for use when the program is to be executed.

PROGRAM DESIGN

In order to design a computer program, you must know the following:

1. *What is the required output?* One of the first steps in programming is knowing the required output data and its design. The program may display output information on a visual display terminal, record it on tape or disk, or print it on a line printer.
2. *What is the required input?* You will have to determine if the data required in calculations is already stored on some available input device, or if it can be entered through a data entry device.
3. *Given the available input, what processing must the program perform to achieve the required output?* This step involves solving *how* to translate the available input data into output information.

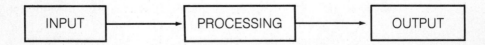

The three states—input, processing, and output—are the essence of the computer program and are usually first solved in general terms before coding by means of a *program flowchart, decision tables,* or *pseudocode.*

This text uses flowcharts and pseudocode extensively to illustrate the logic of program design. The particular advantage of pseudocode and flowcharting is that they do not require an intimate knowledge of a programming language, but only familiarity with the basic computer operations.

PSEUDOCODE

Pseudocode is a shorthand method that involves writing a skeleton of the program logic and is independent of any language and its unique rules. Consequently, anyone familiar with what a computer can do—read input, perform caculations, make tests, and write output—should be able to understand the pseudocode.

FLOWCHARTS

A flowchart consists of standard symbols that are drawn to trace the logic of the solution to the problem. Each symbol portrays executable operations, such as test or add, that the program is to perform. (You need not draw symbols for nonexecutable statements, such as those that define data areas.)

Many programmers prefer to rough out their initial flowchart solution because there are always errors and oversights discovered once they begin coding. However, the final flowchart should be clear and legible, preferably In pencil. Most manufacturers supply a plastic flowchart template. The most commonly used flowchart symbols and their use are as follows:

SYMBOL   MEANING

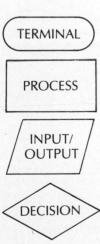

Indicates the initial entry to, or the final exit from, the program (or subroutine).

Indicates one or more processing instructions, such as move, add, subtract, etc.

Used to represent an input or an output operation, such as Read a Disk record, or Write a Printer record.

Used for logical decision-making. The symbol may have two or three exits. Example, branch to one instruction if a value is negative, and to another if positive.

On-page connector, used to indicate that the program flow links to a routine elsewhere on the same page. The other routine also has a connector, both containing the same unique letter. The connector is used if a straight line cannot easily be drawn to the next symbol.

Off-page connector, used to indicate that the program links to a routine on a different page. The other routine also has an off-page connector. Both have a common unique letter and a page number.

Subroutine symbol to denote that program control exits here to a subroutine and returns.

The symbols provide for all possible computer operations: read input, make logical tests, perform arithmetic, move data, and write results. All narrative within a flow-chart symbol is simple and clear, free from any technical terminology. In effect, anyone can read a flowchart, and it is suited to any computer language. It is acceptable to use abbreviations and to combine operations in one symbol where they are related. As a rule, the flow of logic through the symbols is vertically *downward* or horizontally to the *right*. To depict a flow of logic upward or to the left, or to clarify the flow in any direction, use an arrowhead (▷). Other than the terminal symbol that denotes the start and the end of the flowchart, every symbol must have a line that provides an entry into the symbol and a line that provides an exit out of it. A flowchart, like a program, should have no "dead ends."

Notation

Commonly accepted pseudocode and flowchart notations include the following:

+	Add	=	Equal
−	Subtract	≠	Not equal
× or *	Multiply	<	Less than
÷ or /	Divide	>	Greater than
**	Exponentiation	:	Compare
EOF	End of File	EOJ	End of Job

EXAMPLE I—READ, PROCESS, AND WRITE

As a simple case, assume a file of inventory records for which we have to produce a report of inventory value (quantity of stock on hand × unit-cost = stock value). For illustration, there is one input record containing stock number, description, quantity, and unit-cost. The record could be on any format—cards, tape, disk, or entered on a terminal. The pseudocode for this example is as follows:

```
Begin;
Read stock record;
Stock value = quantity × unit cost;
Print results;
End.
```

Example 2—Repetitive Processing   **25**

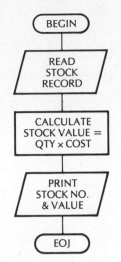

STK. NO.	DESCRIPTION	QTY	UNIT COST

INPUT RECORD:

FIGURE 2–2 Read, Process, and Write.

The program simply reads the input record, multiplies quantity by unit-cost, and prints the required output information. Note that the flowchart in Figure 2–2 has a beginning point, BEGIN, and a termination point, EOJ, to indicate respectively the first and last executable instructions in the program.

EXAMPLE II—REPETITIVE PROCESSING

Since the preceding program processed only one record, it would be easier to perform the calculation manually. An inventory file would normally consist of hundreds or thousands of records, making calculations that are time consuming and prone to errors. The next example illustrates *repetitive processing,* or *looping,* in which the program reads, calculates, prints, and then returns to read the next input record. The program continues in this manner until it has exhausted all the input data. The pseudocode for this example is as follows:

```
Begin;
DO repetitively;
   Read stock record;
   Stock value = quantity × unit-cost;
   Print results.
```

The flowchart in Figure 2–3 and the pseudocode have an important omission: there is no program exit. The program would read past the last record in the input file, and the system would signal that there is an error condition. There must be some provision for terminating when the end of the data is reached. Indeed, for

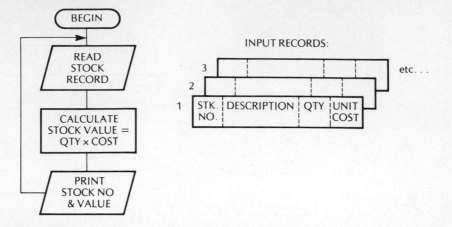

FIGURE 2–3 Repetitive Processing (incomplete).

a loop of any kind, the program must always have some means of exiting. Without an exit, a routine could loop endlessly—a common programming error. In such a case, the computer operator may recognize that the program is looping and can cause the job to terminate. Some computers have a built-in *interval timer* that automatically cancels a program after it has run a specified time.

EXAMPLE III—END-OF-FILE PROCESSING

On a typical computer, the input data is followed by a special end-of-file (EOF) indicator, which varies according to the type of device.

INPUT DEVICE	EOF INDICATION
Punched cards	Following the last data card is a special "job control" record.
Magnetic tape	The last tape record is followed by a special system EOF record.
Disk storage	The last disk record is followed by a record that has a "length" of zero bytes on IBM systems or by an "EOF mark" on some other systems.
Terminal	Typically, the program is coded to ask if there is to be no more data, such as keying in a code number as all zeros, or to reply Y (yes) or N (no) to the query: "Any more input data?"

Except for terminals, the computer operating system automatically tests for the end-of-file record. The system then directly links to your own designated end-of-file address, which in PL/I you define as a special ON ENDFILE statement.

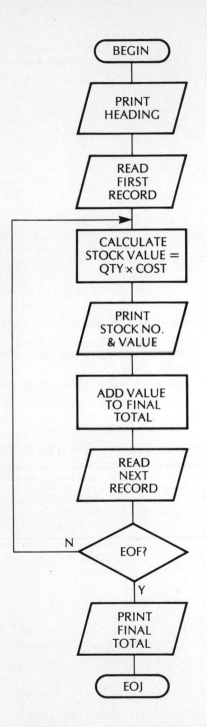

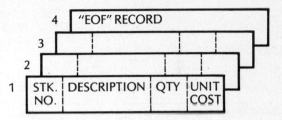

INPUT RECORDS:

FIGURE 2–4 Repetitive Processing and Final Totals.

Let's extend the previous example so that the program prints a page heading at the start and a final total of stock value at the end. The logic involves an initial Read operation and a repetitive loop that processes the input data, prints the results, and reads the next record. If not end-of-file, the logic repeats the loop; if end-of-file, the loop terminates and control drops into printing of final totals. The pseudocode for this logic is as follows:

```
Begin;
Print page heading;
Read the first stock record;
DO repetitively while there is still input data;
    Stock value = quantity × unit-cost;
    Print the results;
    Add stock value to total value;
    Read the next stock record;
End of repetitive loop;
Print total value;
End.
```

The flowchart in Figure 2–4 depicts the end-of-file test immediately after the read operation. The read operation therefore has *two* symbols: the first symbol represents the transfer of data from the input device into main storage, and the second symbol represents the logic test for end-of-file (EOF).

A program that accumulates a total must define an arithmetic field as an accumulator and must initialize it to zero. In PL/I, you can define the field so that it contains an initial zero. The practice of initializing ensures that when a program executes, the field does not contain "garbage" from some previous program that used the same storage locations. You need not show the defining of a field in a flowchart or pseudocode. The rule is draw a symbol to denote all executable instructions, but not for data definition.

It is not absolutely necessary to know the technicalities of computer language to understand flowcharting or pseudocode. However, an insight into the PL/I language will make program logic clearer.

PROBLEMS

2–1. What is the purpose of an operating system?

2–2. Where is the Supervisor stored? What are the main functions of the Supervisor?

2–3. What is job control?

2–4. Distinguish between machine language and symbolic language.

2–5. Distinguish between an assembler language and a compiler language.

2–6. What are the basic functions of the PL/I compiler program?

2–7. Provide pseudocode and a flowchart for the following problem. Input data consists of one employee record containing employee number, employee name, hours worked, and rate-of-pay. The program is to calculate wage (hours × rate) and is to print all input items and the calculated wage.

2–8. Revise Problem 2–7 so that there are any number of input records for employees. At the start, the program is to print a heading, and at the end, the program is to print total hours worked and total wages.

PART II

FUNDAMENTALS OF PL/I

CHAPTER 3

INTRODUCTION TO PL/I

OBJECTIVES
To introduce the basic programming
requirements of PL/I.

INTRODUCTION

Prior to the 1960s, there was a proliferation of programming languages designed for specific purposes. For example, many scientific programmers used FORTRAN, and many business programmers used COBOL (and unfortunately this condition still exists). The languages were quite dissimilar and required considerable expertise to master each one. In 1962, a team comprised of IBM employees and users of IBM computers began to develop a new language that would combine the scientific capability of FORTRAN and ALGOL with the business file-handling capability of COBOL. The new language, called *PL/I* for *Programming Language I* (not very clever), was introduced in 1966.

How well did the team succeed in its objectives? PL/I is a superior language in almost all respects. But, ALGOL, COBOL, and FORTRAN are still in use today, perhaps more used than ever. PL/I has three defects that have prevented it from replacing inferior languages:

1.   The initial versions of PL/I that IBM released were incomplete and full of compiler "bugs." These versions were so bad that many users abandoned PL/I and returned to their less elegant but more capable compilers.

2. PL/I is considered by many to be an IBM language, and few other manufacturers have provided it for their computers. This is a serious handicap in the minicomputer field where many manufacturers compete.

3. PL/I's attempt to be "all things to all men" has made it a large, quite complex language with many specialized but rarely used features. The effect is a language that is not easy to learn in total (but then neither is COBOL easy), and many PL/I versions require a large computer for processing.

However, for any programmer who is willing to learn and who has access to the compiler, PL/I offers a powerful repertoire of instructions that facilitate handling of complex algorithms, tape and disk files, and virtually every feature that only an assembler language can perform. PL/I—perhaps better than any other language—also lends itself well to the important concept of *structured programming.* Further, PL/I is now under the auspices of the American National Standards Institute, which has adopted universal standards for its use; this step should help establish PL/I as a particularly important language in the future.

This chapter examines the basic rules concerning PL/I coding, including the coding sheet format, spacing, comments, character set, keywords, and identifiers.

THE PL/I CODING SHEET

A programming language *syntax* is the rules and punctuation regarding its use. PL/I statements terminate with semicolons and may be coded one or more statements per line, with any number of blanks between statements. This "free-form" approach has its disadvantages, and in fact a PL/I program is easier to debug and maintain if it follows carefully structured rules.

Figure 3–1, explained in detail in the next chapter, illustrates a simple PL/I program coded on a PL/I coding sheet. The program simply defines (DCL) and prints (PUT) four items: TITLE, SCORE1, SCORE2, and SCORE3.

A PL/I statement may appear in any columns between columns 2 and 72 inclusive. PL/I's free-form allows a statement to begin in any of these columns. The compiler ignores any code past column 72; a statement that exceeds column 72 may continue on the next line.

You may code an entire statement, part of one, or more than one statement on a line. Although permitted by the compiler, coding several statements on a line may result in an unintelligible program listing. As a result, this text recommends a practice of coding one statement only per line, beginning in fixed positions, such as

COLUMN	STARTING FIELD
2	Statement labels and Declaratives.
11	Executable statements.
31	Attribute lists for Declaratives.
41	Comments following statements.

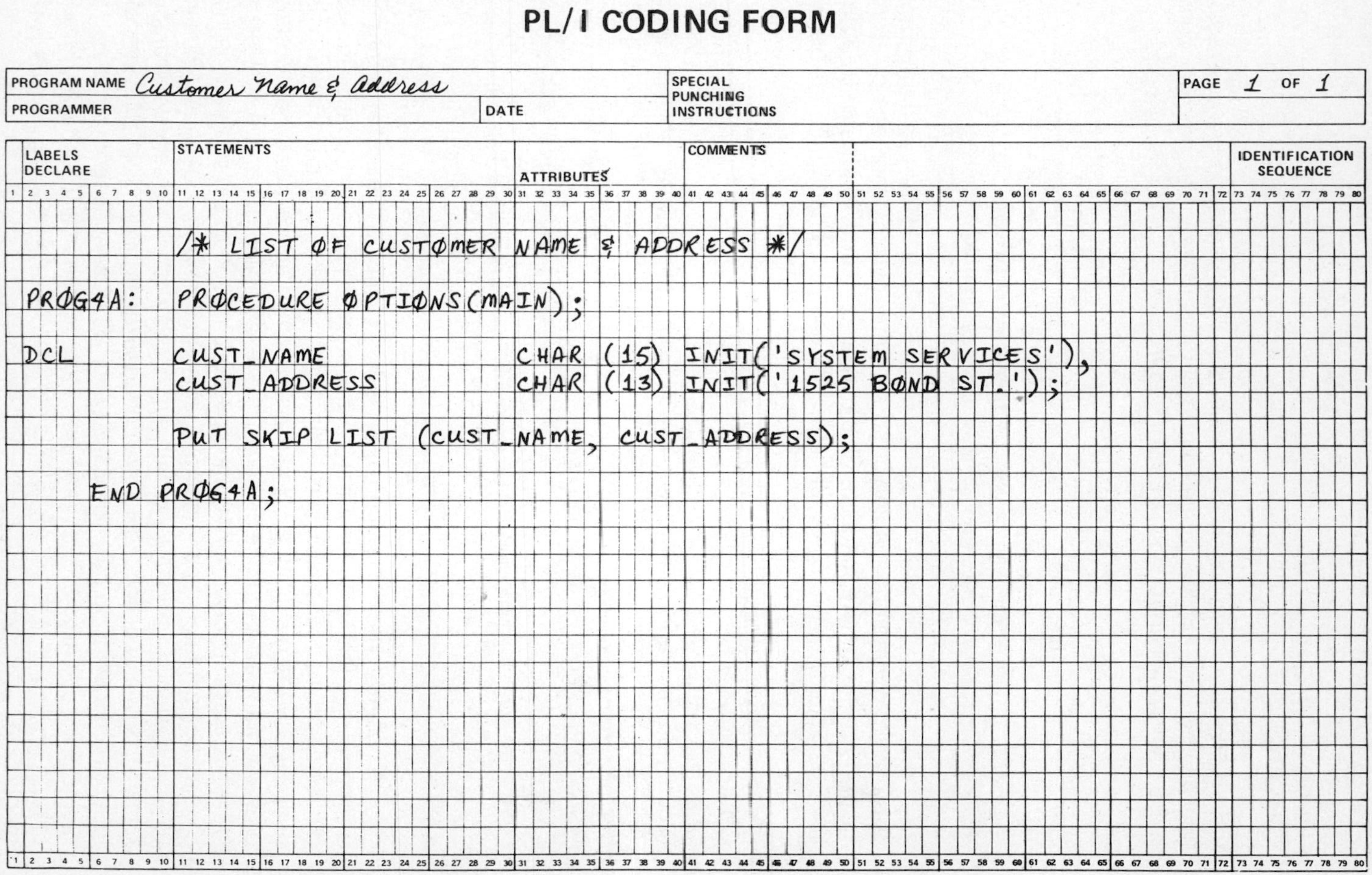

PL/I CODING FORM

PROGRAM NAME *Customer Name & Address*

PROGRAMMER

DATE

SPECIAL PUNCHING INSTRUCTIONS

PAGE 1 OF 1

LABELS DECLARE	STATEMENTS	ATTRIBUTES	COMMENTS	IDENTIFICATION SEQUENCE

```
          /* LIST OF CUSTOMER NAME & ADDRESS */

PROG4A:   PROCEDURE OPTIONS(MAIN);

DCL       CUST_NAME         CHAR (15)  INIT('SYSTEM SERVICES'),
          CUST_ADDRESS      CHAR (13)  INIT('1525 BOND ST.');

          PUT SKIP LIST (CUST_NAME, CUST_ADDRESS);

          END PROG4A;
```

FIGURE 3–1 PL/I Coding Sheet.

Spacing

Column 1 of the coding sheet is reserved for a *forms control character* that facilitates spacing of the compiled program listing (*not* the computer output report). The forms control characters are as follows:

b (blank)	Space one line before printing
0 (zero)	Space two lines before printing
− (minus)	Space three lines before printing
1 (one)	Skip to a new page before printing

The control characters enable you to separate different portions of a program listing to make it more readable. You may also insert blank cards in a program deck or blank lines through a terminal; the compiler "prints" them as blank lines.

Comments

A comment may appear anywhere in a PL/I program between columns 2 through 72. A comment begins with the characters slash/asterisk (/*) and terminates with the characters asterisk/slash (*/) on the same line or on a following line. (In PL/C, restrict comments to one line.) For example:

```
/* CALCULATION OF AVERAGE */ or /* CALCULATION
                OF
            AVERAGE */
```

A comment may appear on a separate line or on a line that already contains a statement (in fact, anywhere that a *blank* position is legal). Because PL/I coding is intended to be reasonably self-explanatory, you may limit comments to general headings and for clarification of logic. As a useful practice, code the *first* statement of a program as a comment because the compiler prints the first statement (whether a comment or not) at the top of each page of the program listing.

Warning: Watch for beginning a comment in column 1 because IBM systems use /* in columns 1 and 2 to indicate *end of compilation*—a serious error. Further, ensure that */ end of comment is not coded to the right of column 72; the compiler ignores any coding in columns 73–80 and will treat succeeding program statements up to the next */ (if any) as part of the comment. In that way, large parts of a program meant to be executable statements can become uncompiled comments.

THE CHARACTER SET

PL/I is designed to handle two character sets—a 60-character set (used in this text), and a 48-character set for printers with fewer characters. Figure 3–2 lists the complete 60- and 48-character sets.

---

10 *digits,* 0 through 9
29 *alphabetic* characters:
    A through Z, letters
          $, dollar sign
          #, number sign (not in the 48-character set)
          @, commercial *at* symbol (not in the 48-character set)

21 *special* characters:

		Coded in 48-character set as
	Blank	
=	Equal sign or assignment symbol	
+	Plus sign	
—	Minus sign	
*	Asterisk or multiply	
/	Slash or divide	
(	Left parenthesis	
)	Right parenthesis	
,	Comma	
.	Decimal point or period	
'	Apostrophe	
%	Percent	//
;	Semi-colon	,.
:	Colon	..
	"Not" symbol	NOT
&	"And" symbol	AND
|	"Or" symbol	OR
>	Greater than	GT
<	Less than	LT
?	Question mark	?
_	Break character or underline	_

FIGURE 3–2 PL/I Character Set.

Certain composite characters differ between the character sets:

60-CHARACTER		48-CHARACTER
<=	Less than or equal	LE
||	Concatenation	CAT
<	Not less than	NL
>	Not greater than	NG
=	Not equal	NE
>=	Greater than or equal	GE
->	Locator qualification	PT

Some of the characters have special uses. For example, the comma, colon, and semicolon are used for punctuation, whereas the plus, minus, asterisk, and slash are used for arithmetic operations.

KEYWORDS

PL/I recognizes certain keywords depending on where they appear in a program. Keywords include statement identifiers, such as PUT to write data and DECLARE to define data, and data attributes, such as DECIMAL and CHARACTER. Most compilers do not reserve these words, although PL/C and the Subset have restrictions. Appendix B gives a complete list of PL/I keywords and their abbreviations.

IDENTIFIERS

You may use any name in a PL/I program, including keywords, with only minor restrictions. A name in PL/I is properly called an identifier to identify names of data areas, statement labels, and keywords. There are two types of identifiers: external and internal.

1. *External Identifier.* An external identifier is one that the system knows and recognizes outside of the PL/I Main Procedure. It is limited to a maximum of seven characters (six in PL/C and the Subset). The first character must be alphabetic (A through Z only) and the rest alphanumeric, excluding the break (—) character. External identifiers include the following:
   - The name of the Main Procedure (the label preceding PROCEDURE OPTIONS(MAIN), for example, PROG25). The Supervisor links to this address to begin execution of the program.
   - The name of an input/output file (or data set), such as a terminal, card

reader, printer, disk, or tape, because the Supervisor handles all input/output outside the program.

- The name of a "subprogram," an external Procedure that is separately compiled from the Main Procedure but must be linked to it.

2. *Internal Identifier.* An internal identifier is one that the program recognizes and is limited to 31 characters in length. The first character must be alphabetic, and the following characters are alphabetic, numeric, and the break character (__). In a name such as RATE-OF-PAY, PL/I treats a hyphen as a minus sign; the name in PL/I would properly be RATE__OF__PAY.

Internal identifiers include the following:

- Names of data areas, such as FACTOR, PRINT__AREA, and TOTAL1.
- Statement labels, such as A20BEGIN and P30HEADING.

If an identifier begins with a digit 0 through 9, the compiler assumes a numeric constant—perhaps incorrectly. To improve program clarity, use names for identifiers that are meaningful.

PROGRAM ORGANIZATION

A PL/I program consists of one or more Procedures. Later chapters describe Procedures in detail, but for now, it is sufficient to know that a PL/I program must consist of at least one Procedure, the MAIN Procedure, coded as

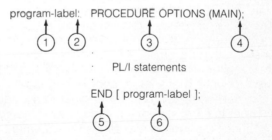

program-label: PROCEDURE OPTIONS (MAIN);

PL/I statements

END [program-label];

1. The program-label is an *external identifier* that tells the operating system the name of this program.
2. All program labels terminate with a colon, either adjacent to the label or with separating blanks.
3. This statement contains the keywords PROCEDURE OPTIONS(MAIN) to tell the compiler that this is the Main (and in this case only) Procedure in the program. The abbreviation for PROCEDURE is PROC. All Procedure statements must have a label. Comments and page spacing statements are the only statements that may precede the PROCEDURE OPTIONS(MAIN) statement.
4. All PL/I statements terminate with a semicolon, either adjacent to the statement or with separating blanks.

5. All Procedures terminate with an END statement. This END indicates the end of both the Procedure and the program.

6. An END statement may optionally be followed by the program-label (point 1 above). If coded, the label must be identical to the original program label. The END statement also terminates with a semicolon.

Note: Labels, names, and elements of a statement are separated by at least one blank, a comma, a colon, or a semicolon, depending on the type of statement.

PROGRAMMING STEPS

The steps to code, compile, and execute a PL/I program are as follows:

1. Coding. Generally, you analyze the problem and solve the logic by means of a flowchart or overall pseudocode. You can then code the program on a coding sheet in the standard columns to facilitate the keying operation.

2. Keying. The coded program may be entered through a terminal or on a keypunch device. Many errors occur because keypunch operators are usually not proficient in PL/I and may have to guess what the careless coding intends. If the coding sheets are punched onto cards, scan the cards for obvious errors, especially punctuation.

3. Compiling. For program testing, arrange test data to thoroughly check out the program logic. Preceding and following the program deck and the test data are job control entries. (Job control is covered in detail in Chapter 29.) The PL/I compiler is typically cataloged on a disk storage device, and the job control loads the compiler program into main storage. The compiler scans your program for errors in spelling and syntax (but not for logic errors), translates valid PL/I statements into Assembler instruction modules, and then reduces these into machine language.

    The compiler lists the original PL/I coding and assigns a *statement number* to each statement. At the end of the compiled printout, the compiler produces diagnostic messages by statement number.

4. Linkage Editing. The Linkage Editor is a program that the manufacturer supplies. If the compilation is successful, then a special job control statement causes the Linkage Editor program to incorporate any necessary precompiled input/output modules and other catalogueed routines. A PL/I program may actually consist of more than one program, and the Linkage Editor resolves addresses that are common between the programs.

5. Execution. The compiled, link-edited program is now ready for execution in machine language. A job control entry causes the program to load into an area in main storage and to begin execution at the first executable instruction.

If the program is to read input data, then you should supply test data, and you should have predetermined results for testing the output from the program.

Output may consist of the following:

- Valid results. The program works, or appears to work, because the limited test data has not tested all possibilities.
- Invalid or incomplete results. You will have to check your program logic to determine why the results are not as expected. Consider also that the input data may be incorrect.
- Error diagnostics. If program execution "crashes," PL/I provides error diagnostics, some of which are automatic and some you must direct. The diagnostics usually (but not always) specify which statement caused the error. A common error is a *data exception* in which the program has attempted arithmetic on a field that does not contain valid arithmetic data.

PROBLEMS

3–1. Based on the PL/I coding sheet:
   (a) What is the purpose of column 1? What are the valid characters that are permitted in column 1?
   (b) What is the purpose of columns 73–80?
   (c) In what column(s) may you begin coding a PL/I statement?

3–2. PL/I comments:
   (a) How do you indicate a comment in a PL/I program?
   (b) What would happen during program compilation if a comment began with a /* in column 1?
   (c) What would happen if a comment ended with a */ in columns 72–73?

3–3. Provide the PL/I symbols for (a) "and," (b) "or," (c) "not," (d) "greater than," and (e) "less than."

3–4. Correct the following PL/I code (there are eight errors):
```
Column 1
      CALC_PROGRAM; PROCEDURE (MAIN):



      END OF CALC_PROGRAM.
```

3–5. What is a keyword?

3–6. Distinguish between an internal identifier and an external identifier.

3–7. Check the validity of the following external identifier names:
   (a) PROG253, (b) PROGRAM8, (c) PROG_25, (d) 25PROG.

3–8. Check the validity of the following internal identifier names:
   (a) TOTAL, (b) SUM_OF_THE_SQUARES, (c) #25, (d) $TOTAL, (e) 25DOLLARS, (f) *TOTAL, (g) RATE-OF-CHANGE.

3–9. What is the Linkage Editor and what are its functions?

CHAPTER 4

DATA DEFINITION

OBJECTIVES

To cover the rules for defining character data, bit data, and arithmetic data.

INTRODUCTION

PL/I not only automatically defines numeric values (see Defaults in a later section), but also permits you to define them explicitly. Explicit definition of data variables provides better control over precision and makes programs easier to maintain. Consequently, many computer installations require explicit declaration of all variables as a standard.

Technically, an *identifier* is the name of a defined field; the data field itself is an *element* (or *scalar*) *variable.* The purpose of a variable is to provide constants, input/output areas, and arithmetic work areas. You may define an identifier with or without an initial constant value. If uninitialized, a variable will contain "garbage"—whatever the bytes contained from the previous program that used the same storage area.

The PL/I statement that defines variables is DECLARE, abbreviated as DCL.

DECLARATIVES

A Declarative is a statement that causes the compiler to reserve an area in storage—a single byte, or a group of bytes that are used to store data. The data may be a permanent constant, such as a report title or a fixed arithmetic constant, or it may be a temporary variable, such as an input area or an accumulator for a total. The programmer designates all the attributes about the declarative—its length and the type of data that it will hold. The general format for the DECLARE statement used to define a data area is

DECLARE   name   attributes   [INITIAL (. . .)]   ;
1   2   ʹ 3   4   5

1. DECLARE is a PL/I keyword that tells the compiler that the following non-executable statement is to reserve an area of storage. The abbreviation is DCL.
2. name is a unique name that you want to assign to a declarative. You define the name only once, but may reference it in the program any number of times. Depending on the type of declarative, the name is either an external identifer, such as the name of a program (limited to seven characters), or an internal identifier, such as the name of a constant (limited to 31 characters).
3. attributes defines the type of data that you expect to store in the defined variable. The basic types of attributes are
   • String Data—Character and Bit nonarithmetic data used mostly for descriptive purposes.
   • Arithmetic data—coded arithmetic (Decimal or Binary base, and Fixed-point or Floating-point scale), used for all arithmetic processing.
4. INITIAL is an optional attribute that enables defining an initial value. Examples are alphabetic titles and an arithmetic rounding factor. The abbreviation is INIT.
5. All PL/I statements end with a semicolon.

Although PL/I allows you to define data anywhere in a program, most programmers conventionally declare data immediately after the PROCEDURE statement.

STRING DATA

There are two types of String data—*Character* and *Bit*. Character data is the common format requiring one character per byte for items such as name, address, and descriptive messages. Bit data is a specialized format that uses eight bits per byte largely for logic testing and "switch" indicators.

Character Data

The purpose of Character data is largely for descriptive reasons, but as a general rule declare as Character all input data that is not to be used for arithmetic purposes. The general format for declaring Character data is

DCL name CHARACTER (ℓ) [INIT ('character-constant')];

The abbreviation for CHARACTER is CHAR, used throughout the rest of the text. You define the length of the variable in bytes as (ℓ). The maximum length is

Subset:	255
PL/C:	255
Full PL/I:	32,767

Omission of (ℓ) causes the compiler to assume a length of (1). An initialized character constant is contained within apostrophes. The constant may contain blanks or any valid alphanumeric or special character. Each character occupies one byte of storage. Some examples of Character data are as follows:

```
DCL   FIELD     CHAR (4) ;
DCL   TITLE     CHAR (7)   INIT ('JUNE 17') ;
DCL   NAME      CHAR (5)   INIT ('JUNE 17') ;
DCL   HEADING   CHAR (9)   INIT ('JUNE 17') ;
DCL   HDG2      CHAR (5)   INIT ('JOE''5') ;
DCL   FLDA      CHAR (4)   INIT ( (2) 'YO' );
```

1. FIELD defines a 4-byte area of storage. The contents of FIELD is initially undefined and may contain "garbage," but you may code statements that "assign" valid Character data to FIELD.

2. TITLE defines a 7-byte area initialized with a 7-character string constant, or *literal,* enclosed in apostrophes. The blank on the right also requires one storage position.

3. NAME defines a 5-byte field initialized with the same 7-byte constant as TITLE. The compiler left-adjusts the constant and truncates the rightmost two characters. Some compilers produce a warning message.

4. HEADING defines a 9-byte field also initialized with the same 7-byte constant as TITLE. The compiler left-adjusts the constant and fills blanks to the right. Note: The compiler fills blanks to the right of any constant shorter than the defined length and does not print a warning.

5. HDG2 specifies a character constant containing an apostrophe. Since apostrophes denote the start and end of a string constant, the compiler must have some way to know when an apostrophe is intended to be included within a string. For this purpose, code two apostrophes to represent one.

6. FLDA uses a *string repetition factor* (2) preceding the constant (YO) that tells the compiler to generate the constant twice (as YOYO) and to store the generated value in the 4-byte field. (PL/C does not support the string repetition factor.)

These declaratives could also be coded with one DCL statement, with commas separating each identifier. This practice generates the same code and is slightly more efficient during program compilation:

```
DCL   FIELD     CHAR (4),
      TITLE     CHAR (7)   INIT ('JUNE 17'),
      NAME      CHAR (5)   INIT ('JUNE 17'),
      ETC ...
```

PL/I's free-format also permits declaring more than one identifier on a line, as

DCL FIELD CHAR(4), TITLE CHAR(7) . . . ;

Coding this way, however, makes locating and changing identifiers more difficult. The common convention of coding one statement per line and indenting all items similarly greatly facilitates program maintenance.

A long INIT character string that exceeds column 72 of the coding sheet must resume in column 2 of the next line, as

Column 2   *Column 72*
DCL COMPANY-NAME CHAR(37) INIT('INTERNATIONAL DATA SYSTEMS CORP
ORATION');

In PL/C, code a long character string as two or more separate DCL statements, each one line.

Bit Data

On 370-type computers, each position (or byte) of storage consists of eight bits. PL/I has the facility to access single bytes or groups of bytes of Character strings and to access single bits or groups of bits of Bit strings. Bit strings have occasional programming use, such as for logic testing for bit "switches," and for representation of bits in a byte for which no character exists. Since there are eight bits per byte, each with two possible values 0 or 1, then the combination of bits is 2^8 = 256. But there are normally only about 60 keyboard and printer characters. The format for declaring Bit data is

DCL name BIT (ℓ) [INIT ('bit-constant'B)];

A Bit constant consists of only the binary digits 0 and 1, enclosed in quotes and followed by the letter B. Bits are stored eight per byte, and often (but not necessarily) the Bit string is a multiple of eight. For most PL/I compilers, the maximum number of bits in a string is 32,767. (The Subset maximum is 64 bits.) Examples of Bit strings are as follows:

```
DCL   BITA      BIT (8)    INIT ('00110110'B),    00110110
      BITB      BIT (8)    INIT ('101'B),         10100000
      BITC      BIT (3)    INIT ('011'B) ;        011
```

1. BITA depicts a Bit string that consists of eight bits, or one byte.
2. BITB is a string of eight bits, of which only three are defined. The compiler left-adjusts the constant and pads five zero bits to the right.
3. BITC defines a 3-bit field. The compiler stores and aligns the 3-bit constant in the leftmost three bits of the byte. Any program reference to BITC is to a 3-bit string.

```
1    PROG4A:   PROCEDURE OPTIONS(MAIN);
2    DCL       CUST_NAME       CHAR(15)   INIT ('SYSTEM SERVICES'),
3              CUST_ADDRESS    CHAR(13)   INIT ('1525 BOND ST.');
4              PUT SKIP LIST (CUST_NAME, CUST_ADDRESS);
5              END PROG4A;
```
Output:

```
                        SYSTEM SERVICES   1525 BOND ST.
        Print position:  1                25
```

FIGURE 4–1. Customer Name and Address.

PROGRAM: DEFINE AND PRINT CUSTOMER NAME AND ADDRESS

Figure 4–1 illustrates a very simple program in five lines that defines and prints customer name and address. The DCL statements define the data; they do not execute. The first (and only) statement that executes is PUT in line 4.

Note the following points:

LINE	EXPLANATION
1	Defines the name of the program as PROG4A and tells the compiler that this is the MAIN (and only) PROCEDURE.
2	Defines and initializes CUST_NAME as a 15-character string constant.
3	Defines and initializes CUST_ADDRESS as a 13-character string constant. Note that a comma separates line 2 and line 3 because the DCL in line 2 also applies to line 3. Line 3 ends with a semicolon because it defines the last declarative.
4	Prints the contents of the two variables specified within parentheses: (CUST_NAME, CUST_ADDRESS). PUT LIST indicates printing on the system printer (or terminal screen if the program is handled that way). SKIP directs the printer to the start of a new line, like the carriage return on a typewriter. The two items print beginning in print positions 1 and 25 respectively.
5	Informs the PL/I compiler that this is the END of PROG4A.

Technically, lines 2 and 3 are one statement, and all PL/I statements end with a semicolon. Distinguish carefully between compilation and execution. The PL/I compiler analyzes the coded statements and converts them to machine-executable code. If the compiler finds no apparent errors, the machine code can execute. In this example, the first executable statement is line 4, PUT, that causes printing of the two named items. The END statement results in termination of program execution and return to the Supervisor program for processing of the next job.

Suggestion: Try coding a similar program using your own name and address and change the CHAR attribute to the appropriate length. Execution of the program requires job control statements preceding and following the program. These vary by PL/I version and installation requirements. You may need a special password from the operations department to gain access to the computer. You may also examine Chapter 29 on Job Control.

ARITHMETIC DATA

There are various types of arithmetic data; the choice of type depends on the particular type of processing. You may specify base, scale, mode, and precision.

Base

The two *bases* available in PL/I for arithmetic data are DECIMAL (base-10) and BINARY (base-2). Decimal base is for common base-10 arithmetic. Binary, although the most efficient for the computer, has specialized uses. Abbreviations are DEC and BIN respectively.

Scale

The two *scales* are fixed-point (FIXED) and floating-point (FLOAT). In fixed-point scale (DECIMAL FIXED and BINARY FIXED), you specify the decimal or binary point, if any. In floating-point scale, the number is followed by an exponent that indicates the position of the assumed decimal or binary point.

Mode

The two *modes* of an arithmetic value are REAL (which expresses a real value) and COMPLEX. The compiler assumes that any declarative has the REAL attribute unless explicitly declared as COMPLEX.

Precision

For fixed-point scale, you specify (p,q), where

1.   p is the number of decimal or binary digits the arithmetic value contains; and

2.   q is an optional entry for the position of the assumed decimal or binary point.

For example, DECIMAL FIXED (5,2) means a base-10 fixed-point value that has five digits of precision, of which two are to the right of the decimal point. In effect, the value is comprised of three integer digits and two fractional digits, such as the number 123.45:

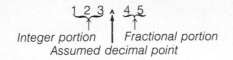

Integer portion | Fractional portion
Assumed decimal point

Omission of q causes the compiler to assume no fractional digits so that the decimal point is to the right of the value. For example, (5) is the same as (5,0).

Sequence of Attributes

Attributes may appear in almost any sequence, but there must be at least one attribute between the declarative name and the precision:

```
Valid:    DCL SUM   FIXED DECIMAL (5,2);
Valid:    DCL SUM   FIXED (5,2) DECIMAL;
Invalid:  DCL SUM   (5,2) DECIMAL FIXED;
```

The latter precision is invalid because it defines the identifier as an *array* (covered in a later section).

The following sections describe DECIMAL FIXED and BINARY FIXED formats. FLOAT format is covered in Chapter 11. Note that an arithmetic constant, unlike a String literal, is not enclosed in apostrophes.

DECIMAL FIXED DATA

Many programs use Decimal Fixed format for ordinary decimal processing. The format uses digits 0 through 9 with an optional sign on the left and an optional decimal point. Omission of a sign implies a positive value, and omission of a decimal point implies that the point is to the right. The 370-type computers store Decimal Fixed as "packed," with each digit and the sign occupying ½ byte, so that − 123.45 is stored in three bytes as 12 34 5 − . The sign, although coded on the left, is stored on the right, and the decimal point is not stored at all. Since a Decimal Fixed field always contains an *odd number* of digits, it is generally more efficient to declare it as an odd number length. The maximum length in most PL/I versions is 15 digits. The format for DECIMAL FIXED data is

```
DCL name DECIMAL FIXED (p,q) [INIT( decimal constant )];
```

where p is the total number of decimal digits (integer and fractional portions), and q is an optional decimal point position. The abbreviation for DECIMAL is DEC but FIXED has no abbreviation.

The following examples illustrate Decimal Fixed variables:

```
DCL   COUNT      DEC FIXED (5),
      AMOUNT     DEC FIXED (5,2) INIT (1.25),
      VALUE      DEC FIXED (5,2) INIT (.125),
      TOTAL      DEC FIXED (7,2) INIT (0),
      NEGATIVE   DEC FIXED (7,2) INIT (-123.45),
      LARGE      DEC FIXED (5,2) INIT (1234.567) ;
```

undefined			
	00	12	5+
	00	01	2+
00	00	00	0+
00	12	34	5-
	23	45	6+

1. COUNT defines an arithmetic field that is five digits long and decimal point assumed to the right. The contents of COUNT is uninitialized and likely contains invalid data.
2. AMOUNT also has 5-digit precision, but two digits are for the fractional portion. The compiler aligns the value according to the defined precision, filling zeros to the left.
3. VALUE defines a constant that contains more fractional digits than the precision allows. The compiler truncates the third fractional digit and aligns on the decimal point according to the expressed precision (5,2).
4. TOTAL illustrates a common practice of initializing an accumulator to zero. The compiler fills zeros to the left and to the right of the decimal point.
5. NEGATIVE is initialized with a negative constant.
6. LARGE contains a serious coding error. The compiler aligns the constant on the decimal point according to the precision. Because the precision is (5,2), the compiler truncates the leftmost and rightmost digits and stores the value as 234.56+. Loss of a leftmost significant digit is a SIZE error, as explained in Chapter 21. The correct precision for 1234.567 is (7,3).

BINARY FIXED DATA

Binary Fixed is the most efficient format for computer processing, but although it has specialized uses, it is often not convenient for normal processing. You use Binary Fixed, for example, for counting and for *subscripts*. The computer stores and processes a Binary Fixed value as a string of zero and one bits, the two possible values for a base-2 digit. For example, you can express a decimal value and a binary value as

$Decimal$: $125_{10} = 1 \times 10^2 + 2 \times 10^1 + 5 \times 10^0 = 100 + 20 + 5 = 125$

$Binary$: $111_2 = 1 \times 2^2 + 1 \times 2^1 + 1 \times 2^0 = 4 + 2 + 1 = 7$

A binary constant consists of a string of binary digits followed by the letter B, as 101101B. On 370-type computers, there are two fixed lengths: 15 and 31 binary digits. The compiler converts any precision expressed as 15 or less to a length of 15 and converts precision of over 15 to 31. 15 or 31 binary digits plus a 1-bit sign give 16 or 32 digits. With 8 bits per byte, the lengths are respectively 2 bytes and 4 bytes.

Binary Fixed maximum and minimum values are as follows:

Digits	Max. Value	Min. Value	Length
15	32,767	− 32,768	Halfword (2 bytes)
31	2,147,483,647	− 2,147,483,648	Fullword (4 bytes)

The format for a Binary Fixed declarative is

DCL name BINARY FIXED (p,q) [INIT(binary or decimal constant)];

where p is the total number of binary digits, and q is an optional binary point position. (The Subset permits only whole numbers with precision (p).) You can initialize Binary Fixed with a binary constant or with a decimal constant that the compiler converts automatically to binary. The following illustrates various declaratives, abbreviated as BIN FIXED:

```
DCL   IT          BIN FIXED (15,0),
      KOUNT       BIN FIXED (15)    INIT (10111B),
      LONG        BIN FIXED (15)    INIT (23),
      MAGIC       BIN FIXED (31,5) INIT (−123.45) ;
```

1. IT defines a BINARY FIXED field of 15 binary digits, with the binary point assumed to the right and no initialized constant. IT initially will contain "garbage." BINARY and FIXED may appear in any sequence.

2. KOUNT initializes with a binary constant 10111B, equivalent to the decimal value 23. The assumed precision is (15,0). The letter B indicates a binary value.

3. LONG initializes with a decimal constant, 23, which the compiler converts to binary 10111. Technically, you can initialize any arithmetic declarative with any arithmetic format such as a decimal value and let the compiler convert it to binary.

4. MAGIC initializes a negative decimal constant in a Binary Fixed declarative with precision (31,5). The precision expresses binary, not decimal, digits. There is a loss of accuracy to the right of the decimal point since five binary digits cannot precisely represent the value .45.

USE OF BLANKS

Generally in PL/I, where you code one blank you may code any number of blanks. A blank (or blanks) separates identifiers from keywords. In the following example, DCL is a keyword and FACTOR is an identifier:

Valid: DCL FACTOR . . . ; (space between DCL and FACTOR)
Invalid: DCLFACTOR . . . ; (no space between DCL and FACTOR)

But punctuation and special characters may be coded with or without leading or trailing blanks:

Valid: PROGRAM : PROCEDURE OPTIONS(MAIN) ;
Valid: PROGRAM:PROCEDURE OPTIONS(MAIN);

FACTORING OF ATTRIBUTES

Often a program contains many variables with identical attributes. Each separate DCL initiates a PL/I compiler routine. In such cases, it is more efficient to code the identifiers within parentheses, called *factoring*. It is possible (and recommended) to factor all types of declaratives whenever possible. The following example gives the three identifiers AMOUNT, VALUE, and TOTAL the same base, scale, precision, and initialization:

DCL (AMOUNT, VALUE, TOTAL) DEC FIXED (7,2) INIT (0) ;

The PL/I compiler stores all declaratives in its own desired sequence at the end of the object program, regardless of where you code them.

PROGRAM: DEFINE AND PRINT DECLARATIVES

Problem Definition

A program is to define three scores, SCORE1, SCORE2, and SCORE3, with initial values and is to print them with a leading title 'SCORES'.

Solution

The program requires a PROCEDURE statement, declaratives for the title and three scores, a print statement, and an END. See Figure 3–1 for the original coding sheet for this example. The statement in Figure 4–2

PUT SKIP LIST (TITLE, SCORE1, SCORE2, SCORE3);

will cause the data items specified in parentheses to print respectively beginning in columns 1, 25, 49, and 73, as follows:

SCORES	27.53	33.76	44.85
1	25	49	73

```
STMT LEV NT

  1     0   PROG4A:   PROCEDURE OPTIONS(MAIN);

  2  1  0   DCL       TITLE         CHAR (6)           INIT ('SCORES');
  3  1  0   DCL       SCORE1        FIXED DEC (5,2)    INIT (27.53) ,
                      SCORE2        FIXED DEC (5,2)    INIT (33.76) ,
                      SCORE3        FIXED DEC (5,2)    INIT (44.85) ;

  4  1  0             PUT SKIP LIST (TITLE, SCORE1, SCORE2, SCORE3) ;
  5  1  0         END PROG4A ;


     Output:-

  SCORES                  27.53              33.76                 44.85
```

FIGURE 4–2 Defining and Printing Declaratives.

Figure 4–2 contains the complete program with executed output. STMT to the left of the program listing indicates the number that the compiler assigns to statements. In effect, since a statement terminates with a semicolon, some statements such as number 3 involve more than one line. LEV (for "level number") and NT (for "nesting") are not important at this point and are explained later. Note the following points:

STATEMENT	EXPLANATION
2	Defines a Character variable containing the literal 'SCORES'.
3	Defines three arithmetic scores with initialized constants. All of the variables in statements 2 and 3 could have been defined with one DCL.
4	Prints the title and the three scores in positions 1, 25, 49, and 73. The blank line between SCORE3 and the PUT statement has nothing to do with program execution; its purpose is clarity to clearly distinguish the end of declaratives.

CROSS-REFERENCE TABLE

After listing the compiled program and any error diagnostics, the compiler prints an "Attribute and Cross-Reference Table" (unless requested not to do so). Figure 4–3 illustrates the cross-reference table produced for the previously compiled program (Figure 4–2). The leftmost column under DCL NO. shows the statement number in which the identifier is defined. The heading ATTRIBUTES AND REFERENCES shows the type of identifier, its attributes, and where it is referenced.

• PROG4A. This identifier is defined in statement 1. It is an EXTERNAL identifier and is an ENTRY point for program execution. The default attributes DEC-

```
ATTRIBUTE AND CROSS-REFERENCE TABLE (FULL)

DCL NO.     IDENTIFIER     ATTRIBUTES AND REFERENCES

1           PROG4A         EXTERNAL ENTRY RETURNS(DECIMAL /* SINGLE */ FLOAT (6))

3           SCORE1         AUTOMATIC ALIGNED INITIAL DECIMAL FIXED (5,2)
                           1,4

3           SCORE2         AUTOMATIC ALIGNED INITIAL DECIMAL FIXED (5,2)
                           1,4

3           SCORE3         AUTOMATIC ALIGNED INITIAL DECIMAL FIXED (5,2)
                           1,4

********    SYSPRINT       EXTERNAL FILE PRINT
                           4

2           TITLE          AUTOMATIC UNALIGNED INITIAL CHARACTER (6)
                           1,4
```

FIGURE 4–3 Cross-Reference Table.

IMAL/SINGLE/FLOAT may be ignored, since the item is not intended for arithmetic.
- SCORE1, SCORE2, and SCORE3. These identifiers are all defined in statement 3, and all have the same attributes. AUTOMATIC and ALIGNED are defaults. The numbers 1,4 indicate that the items are referenced in program statement 4.
- SYSPRINT. This identifier is the name of the printer device. Since a PUT statement references the printer, but the program does not define it, the compiler has assumed SYSPRINT, the standard system printer device. Defaulted attributes are EXTERNAL, FILE, and PRINT. The asterisks under DCL NO. indicate an undeclared identifier.
- TITLE. This identifier is defined in statement 2 and is referenced in statement 4.

This compiler has listed the identifiers in alphabetic sequence to facilitate locating them. The Cross-Reference Table is a useful feature. Be sure to examine it after each compilation to ensure that there are no spelling errors in your program and no unexpected defaults. You can request a cross-reference table under the Optimizing compiler and PL/C with an XREF option in the PROCESS statement (Chapter 29).

DEFAULTS

Occasionally, a program contains a reference to a variable that is intentionally or accidentally not declared. For example:

Statement-1:   DCL AMT DEC FIXED (5,0) ;
Statement-2:   AMNT = 0 ;

Statement-1 defines an arithmetic variable called AMT. Statement-2 is an assignment statement that assigns a zero value to AMNT (spelled incorrectly). The compiler does not treat such "spelling errors" as invalid, but, instead, assumes that the identifier was coded that way on purpose. PL/I is designed to assume default attributes for names that are undeclared or partially declared. The compiler indicates default assumptions in its diagnostics. The compiler always assumes that default variables are numeric, with a base/scale/precision depending on whether the name is undeclared or partially declared.

Identifiers with No Declared Attributes

If an identifier is undeclared, as AMNT in the previous example, the compiler's default assumption is based on the first letter of the identifier:

If the initial letter is I, J, K, L, M, or N, then the attributes become BINARY FIXED (15). For all other beginning letters, the default is DECIMAL FLOAT (6).

For AMNT in the preceding, the compiler creates a variable called AMNT with the attributes DECIMAL FLOAT (6), and Statement-2 assigns a zero value to this variable.

Some programmers let attributes default only for Binary Fixed identifiers. Many installations, however, require that all programmers explicitly define all identifiers for reasons of clarity.

Identifiers with Partially Declared Attributes

PL/I has standard defaults for incomplete declarations. The following defines identifiers with only base or only scale and shows the defaulted attributes:

DECLARATIVE	DEFAULT ATTRIBUTES
AMTA BINARY	BINARY FLOAT (21)
AMTB DECIMAL	DECIMAL FLOAT (6)
AMTC FIXED	DECIMAL FIXED (5)
AMTD FLOAT	DECIMAL FLOAT (6)

Suppose you define a base and precision, but no scale. The default for scale (FIXED or FLOAT) depends on whether you code the precision as (p) or as (p,q):

DECLARATIVE	DEFAULT ATTRIBUTE
AMTE BINARY (15)	BINARY FLOAT (15)
AMTF BINARY (15,5)	BINARY FIXED (15,5)

Other compiler assumptions include REAL (instead of COMPLEX), and IN-TERNAL (instead of EXTERNAL).

Default Statement (Not in PL/C)

PL/I provides a DEFAULT statement that enables you to modify compiler defaults. There is seldom any need even to allow defaults, let alone modify them. But, you may want the compiler to give all constants the STATIC rather than the defaulted AUTOMATIC attribute. The statement

DEFAULT RANGE(*) STATIC ;

tells the compiler to apply the STATIC attribute to *all* identifiers, as indicated by RANGE(*). The statement

DEFAULT RANGE(A:H) DEC FIXED ;

tells the compiler to default the attribute DEC FIXED to all identifiers that begin with the letters A through H and that are not already defined. The standard default precision for DEC FIXED is (5,0). Optimizer compilers also have a VALUE option to cause a default for precisions other than (5,0).

DEBUGGING TIPS

The following are some common programming errors:

- The program name violates rules of external identifiers (too long, or contains the break character).
- PROCEDURE OPTIONS(MAIN) is missing or is spelled incorrectly.
- A statement contains a punctuation error. For example, a colon must follow a program name, and a semicolon must follow statements.
- A declared name violates the rules of internal identifiers (begins with a digit).
- An arithmetic variable has incorrect base, scale, or precision.
- An INIT option contains an error. For example, a Character or Bit literal should be in apostrophes. An arithmetic constant is not in apostrophes and should be the same precision (p,q) as defined.
- The last statement in the program is not END, or its label is not the same as the program name.
- The job was submitted with an error in job control. Possibly the program will not be compiled or listed and you may get only a diagnostic message.

PROBLEMS

4–1. If the following Character declares are valid, depict the generated constant (if any); if invalid, explain why:
   (a) DCL FLDA CHAR ;
   (b) DCL FLDB CHAR (5) INIT (' ') ;
   (c) DCL FLDC CHAR (5) INIT(TOTAL) ;
   (d) DCL FLDD CHAR (5) INIT((2)'TON') ;
   (e) DCL HDG CHAR (12) INIT ('GENERAL MOTORS') ;
   (f) DCL NAME CHAR (7) INIT ('SAM'S') ;

4–2. Define the following Character variables:
   (a) An 8-character field called SAVE, with no initialized constant.
   (b) A field called HEADING containing "VILLA ELECTRONICS."
   (c) A 10-character field called BLANKS containing blanks.
   (d) A field called HEAD2 containing "SAM'S CONSULTANTS."

4–3. Define the following Bit string variables:
   (a) A 1-bit string called EOF containing a zero value.
   (b) An 8-bit string called SAVE containing 10101010.

4–4. Explain how each of the following Decimal Fixed declaratives is invalid:
   (a) DCL AMOUNT-1 DEC FIXED (3) ;
   (b) DCL AMOUNT   FIXED DECIMAL (5) INIT (' ') ;
   (c) DCL AMT3   DEC FIXED (4,2) INIT (123.456) ;
   (d) DCL AMT4   DEC BINARY (5,2) INIT (0) ;
   (e) DCL AMT5,AMT6 DEC FIXED (5,2) ;
   (f) DCL AMT7   DEC FIXED (16) ;

4–5. Define the following as Decimal Fixed variables:
   (a) A 9-digit field called TEMP with decimal point to the right and no initialized constant.
   (b) A field HOURS, of the form xxx.xx, containing zero.
   (c) WAGE, as xxxxx.xx, containing 150 dollars.

4–6. Define the following as Binary Fixed variables:
   (a) A binary field called BINA initialized with the decimal constant 19.
   (b) BINB initialized with the binary digits equivalent to constant 19.
   (c) Correct the error:

DCL AMTBIN BIN FIXED (15) INIT (125B) ;

4–7. Under what circumstances would you typically declare a variable as
   (a) Character?
   (b) Decimal Fixed?
   (c) Binary Fixed?

4–8. Provide default base, scale, and precision for the following Declaratives:

    (a) DCL TOTAL ;

    (b) DCL KOUNT ;

    (c) DCL TOTAL FLOAT ;

    (d) DCL NAME CHAR ;

    (e) DCL TOTAL FIXED ;

    (f)   DCL TOTAL BINARY (10,3) ;

4–9. Explain the effect of the following Declare. (Hint: Note the comma after DEC.)

DCL TOTAL DEC, FIXED (5,2) ;

CHAPTER 5

DATA EXECUTION

OBJECTIVES

To cover the PL/I rules to assign data into variables and to perform arithmetic.

INTRODUCTION

Chapter 4 covered the rules for declaring character and arithmetic variables in storage. This chapter introduces the basic statements necessary for execution of a complete PL/I program. Typical executable statements are the following:

- Read data into storage (the GET or READ statement).
- Process the data within storage (the assignment statement).
- Write the results out of storage onto the printer (the PUT or WRITE statement) or display screen (PUT).

Regardless of where you code Declaratives, the compiler separates them into a separate section of the object program. Execution begins with the first executable statement following the Main Procedure label.

This chapter covers the processing of character and arithmetic data, followed by a sample program that illustrates most of the features covered.

STATEMENTS

In PL/I, there are two types of simple statements: Keyword and Assignment.

1. *Keyword statement,* which contains a keyword identifier that indicates the function of the statement, such as DCL . . . ; GET . . . ; DO . . . ; .
2. *Assignment statement,* which is coded as variable = expression; .

Assignment statements form the topic for the rest of this chapter. Appendix B provides a list of all PL/I keywords and abbreviations.

ASSIGNMENT STATEMENTS

An assignment statement transfers the results of an expression to a receiving ("target") field variable. The basic form is

variable = expression ;

An assignment statement always contains an equal (=) sign that means a transfer or copy of data from one location to another (and does not denote an algebraic equal sign). The *expression* consists of a constant, a variable, or a combination of both. In an expression, a constant is coded the same way as it is initialized in a Declare statement. For example, a character constant must be contained in apostrophes.

Normally, the receiving variable is the same length as (or longer than) the assigning field. As a general rule, you assign data of like attributes, that is, string (character or bit) to string, and arithmetic data to arithmetic. Any transfer between string and arithmetic may cause a *Conversion* error (covered in Chapter 21) and is invalid in the Subset.

STRING ASSIGNMENT STATEMENTS

There are two types of String data: Character and Bit. A Character and Bit String constant (or *literal*) is enclosed in apostrophes.

Character String Assignments

Examples of Character assignments are as follows:

	DCL FIELD CHAR (6);	*Result in FIELD;*
1.	FIELD = 'REPORT';	R E P O R T
2.	FIELD = 'REPORTS';	R E P O R T
3.	FIELD = 'REPO';	R E P O b b
4.	FIELD = ' ';	b b b b b b

1. Assigns a 6-character constant to the 6-byte variable FIELD.
2. Assigns a 7-character constant. At execute-time, the operation truncates the rightmost character (a "STRINGSIZE" error, covered in Chapter 21).
3. Assigns a 4-character string. The operation left-adjusts the constant and fills the rightmost bytes with blanks (a valid operation).
4. Clears FIELD to blanks. It is common to assign a single blank to a character field because of the characteristics of character assignments: The operation inserts the single character (in this case, a blank) on the left and automatically fills blanks to the right.

An apostrophe within the constant is denoted by two apostrophes, as 'SAM''S,' although the compiler reduces the constant to one apostrophe: SAM'S.

Bit String Assignments

A Bit string is enclosed in apostrophes and is followed by the letter B, as '1011'B. Examples of Bit string assignments are as follows:

	DCL BITVAL BIT (8);	RESULT IN BITVAL:
1.	BITVAL = '01011001'B;	01011001
2.	BITVAL = '010110010'B;	01011001
3.	BITVAL = '1'B;	10000000

1. Assigns an 8-bit (literal) string to the 8-bit variable BITVAL, replacing all eight bits.
2. Assigns a 9-bit literal to BITVAL. At execute-time, the operation truncates the rightmost bit (a STRINGSIZE error).
3. Assigns a 1-bit literal to BITVAL. The operation left-adjusts the literal and fills rightmost bits with zeros.

ARITHMETIC ASSIGNMENT STATEMENTS

It is permissible (and sometimes necessary) to assign one arithmetic type to a different type. All arithmetic assignment operations align the variables and constants on the decimal point. The following statements illustrate this:

```
DCL   AMOUNT        DEC FIXED (7,3),
      VALUE         DEC FIXED (5,2) INIT (1.25) ;
      TOTAL         DEC FIXED (5,2),
```

1.   AMOUNT = 0 ;

Clears an arithmetic element to zero. You need not code the constant with the same precision as AMOUNT (0000.000) because the operation fills AMOUNT algebraically with zeros to the left and right of the decimal point.

2.   AMOUNT = VALUE

Assigns the contents of a variable, VALUE, to AMOUNT, aligning on the decimal point.

3.   VALUE = VALUE + 5 ;

Illustrates an arithmetic expression that adds the constant 5 to the contents of VALUE. The arithmetic is performed in a separate PL/I work area, before assignment of the result to VALUE. Note that the constant 5 is treated as 5.00. The next section covers expressions in detail.

Arithmetic Expressions

An arithmetic expression may contain a mixture of variables and constants and is subject to the normal rules of algebra. You may use a variable in an expression only if it contains an *initialized* or *assigned* value.

- Example of *initializing* zeros:

```
DCL AMOUNT DEC FIXED (5,2) INIT (0) ;
AMOUNT = AMOUNT + 25 ;
```

- Example of *assigning* zeros:

```
DCL AMOUNT DEC FIXED (5,2) ;
AMOUNT = 0 ;
AMOUNT = AMOUNT + 25 ;
```

It is permissible to mix arithmetic types in an expression, although it is more efficient if variables have the same base, scale, and decimal-point precision.

Arithmetic Operators

The PL/I arithmetic operators are as follows:

+ Addition
− Subtraction
* Multiplication
/ Division
** Exponentiation

Technically, these are *infix operators* and determine the operation to perform on two operands, such as HOURS * RATE. A *prefix operator* is a plus or minus sign that is associated with and precedes a single operand, such as +TOTAL or −TOTAL (the effect of −TOTAL is a change of its sign).

You may express an exponent as a numeric constant or as a variable. For example, you may code the area of a circle, πr^2, as

PI * R**2

Blanks between identifiers and infix operators are optional. Any part of an expression may be enclosed in parentheses; the operation always executes the contents of parentheses first, starting with the innermost pair of parentheses, if any. Subject to this rule of parentheses, the *priority of operators* is as follows:

1.   ** exponentiation, + prefix, − prefix (performed from right to left in an expression)
2.   * multiplication and / division (performed whichever is first, from left to right in an expression)
3.   + addition and − subtraction (performed whichever is first, from left to right in an expression)

When in doubt or if necessary for clarity, use extra parentheses in an arithmetic expression. If two or more operators are coded at the highest level of priority (exponentiation and prefix operators), they are processed from right to left. For example, in the expression

−AREA**2

exponentiation occurs first and then negation. Also in an expression such as

AREA ** X ** Y

PL/I performs the rightmost exponentiation first as if it were coded

AREA ** (X ** Y)

All other processing is performed from left to right. On execution, the program performs arithmetic in concealed workareas and completely handles alignment of the decimal point. For example, assume the following statements:

```
DCL   PROFIT      DEC FIXED (7,2),
      QTY         DEC FIXED (3,1)   INIT (13.5),
      PRICE       DEC FIXED (5,2)   INIT (3.25),
      COST        DEC FIXED (5,2)   INIT (2.00) ;
                                              RESULT:
  1.  PROFIT = QTY * PRICE - COST ;             41.87
  2.  PROFIT = QTY * (PRICE - COST);            16.87
  3.  PROFIT = QTY * (PRICE - COST) + .005 ;    16.88
  4.  DISTANCE = ( (X2-X1)**2 + (Y2-Y1)**2 ) **.5 ;
```

1. First multiplies the contents of QTY by PRICE (43.875), then subtracts COST, and assigns the result (41.875) into PROFIT as 41.87. (It is valid and normal for an assignment statement to truncate rightmost unwanted fractional digits, although the operation does not round.)

2. First executes the contents of the parentheses (PRICE − COST), which equals 1.25. Multiplying by QTY gives 16.875, assigned to PROFIT as 16.87.

3. Adds a *rounding factor* to the unwanted fractional digit. If the result were negative, you would have to subtract the rounding factor. Another approach is to use the ROUND built-in function (see a later section in this chapter).

4. Assumed to reference valid declaratives, calculates the distance between two points. The operation first calculates X2 − X1 and squares it, Y2 − Y1 and squares it, sums the two results, and then calculates the square root, as an exponent .5. Using the SQRT built-in function is more efficient:

DISTANCE = SQRT ((X2−X1)**2 + (Y2−Y1)**2) ;

A calculation in fixed-point has certain limitations, as described fully in Chapter 21. For example, a fixed-point expression can exceed the limit of the PL/I work area, causing a FIXEDOVERFLOW error condition. Or, an assignment statement may cause loss of a *leftmost* significant digit, causing a SIZE error:

DCL AMOUNT DEC FIXED (5,2) ;   Stored Result:

AMOUNT = 125.00 * 10 ;   250.00   (should be 1250.00)

PROGRAM: CALCULATE AND PRINT MEAN AVERAGE

Problem Definition

A program that defines three scores is to calculate and print the mean average of the scores.

Solution

Figure 4–2 in the previous chapter illustrated defining and printing. The only new features required are a declarative for a variable named AVERAGE, an assignment statement that performs the calculation, and a PUT statement to print the average. Note the following points in the revised program in Figure 5–1:

STATEMENT	EXPLANATION
3	Defines the three scores used for arithmetic (they must contain valid arithmetic data).
4	Defines the variable AVERAGE for the mean average of the three scores. AVERAGE need not contain an INITIAL value because it is not used in an expression, that is, to the right of an equal sign.
5	Assigns the result of the expression directly into AVERAGE, erasing any previous contents.
6	Prints a title and the three scores.
7	Prints a title and the mean average of the three scores.

MULTIPLE ASSIGNMENTS

You may assign an expression to more than one variable in one assignment statement (not in the Subset). The following statement assigns the arithmetic constant zero to each of the specified variables AMOUNT, VALUE, and TOTAL (separated by commas):

```
AMOUNT, VALUE, TOTAL = 0;
```

```
STMT LEV NT

 1    0  PROG5A:  PROCEDURE OPTIONS(MAIN);

 2  1 0  DCL     TITLE1       CHAR(6)        INIT ('SCORES') ,
                 TITLE2       CHAR(7)        INIT ('AVERAGE') ;
 3  1 0  DCL     SCORE1       FIXED DEC (5,2)  INIT (27.53) ,
                 SCORE2       FIXED DEC (5,2)  INIT (33.76) ,
                 SCORE3       FIXED DEC (5,2)  INIT (44.85) ;
 4  1 0  DCL     AVERAGE      FIXED DEC (5,2) ;

 5  1 0          AVERAGE = (SCORE1 + SCORE2 + SCORE3) / 3 ;
 6  1 0          PUT SKIP LIST (TITLE1, SCORE1, SCORE2, SCORE3) ;
 7  1 0          PUT SKIP LIST (TITLE2, AVERAGE) ;
 8  1 0  END PROG5A ;


 Output:-

 SCORES        27.53        33.76        44.85
 AVERAGE       35.38
```

FIGURE 5–1 Calculate and Print Mean Average.

FIXED SCALE PRECISION

The PL/I compiler uses its own concealed work area to process arithmetic expressions. Because Fixed scale is limited to 15 decimal digits and 31 binary digits, a complex expression can easily exceed this limit. The compiler attempts to maintain as much precision after the decimal or binary point as possible. Consequently, an expression containing a number of multiplies and divides can easily cause loss of a leftmost significant digit in the PL/I work area—a FIXEDOVERFLOW error. Solutions to prevent this serious error are as follows:

1. Code the expression in a number of separate statements. For example, a PL/I statement to calculate standard deviation,

    SD = SQRT(((N * SUMSCORESQ) − SUMSCORE**2) / (N * (N−1)));

    could be coded as

    TEMP1 = (N * SUMSCORESQ) − SUMSCORE**2;
    TEMP2 = N * (N − 1);
    SD = SQRT (TEMP1 / TEMP2);

2. Control the precision with the Arithmetic built-in functions ADD, MULTIPLY, and DIVIDE (discussed in detail in Chapter 10).

3. If all else fails, change the scale to floating-point, which provides for a range of values from 10^{-78} to 10^{75} on most compilers.

BUILT-IN FUNCTIONS

Built-in functions are precoded PL/I routines that facilitate handling certain common or specialized conditions that otherwise would be difficult or impossible to process in PL/I. The general format for a built-in function is

$$result = function\ (\ argument\ )\ ;$$

The argument may be a data element or an array, or a structure in a few special cases. The built-in function categories are as follows:

CATEGORY	WHERE COVERED
String Handling	Chapter 19
Stream I/O functions	Chapter 12
Storage Control functions	ADDR, ALLOCATION, EMPTY, NULL, OFFSET, and POINTER; Chapter 23.
Condition Handling	Chapter 21
Asynchronous I/O	COMPLETION and STATUS.
Arithmetic	Chapter 10
Mathematical	Chapter 11
Array Handling	Chapter 8

ROUND BUILT-IN FUNCTION

The ROUND built-in function is generally used to round only fixed-point calculations. Note when rounding binary values: a binary point is not the same as a decimal point. The general format for ROUND is

$$result = ROUND(\ x,\ y\ )\ ;$$

where x is an arithmetic expression to be rounded, according to its absolute value, and y is a decimal integer constant giving the digit position that is to be rounded. The operation adds a 5 to the absolute value of x according to the digit y specified.

There is special provision for rounding either to the *right* or to the *left* of a decimal or binary point:

- A *positive* value y indicates rounding the yth digit to the right of the decimal point. Thus, y = 3 means round at the third digit (add 5 to the fourth). For example,

$$\begin{array}{r} \text{ROUND (123.4567, 3)} \\ \text{implies} \quad 123.4567 \\ +\quad\quad 5 \\ \hline 123.4572 \end{array}$$

- A *zero* value y indicates rounding the first digit to the left of the point. For example

$$\begin{array}{r} \text{ROUND (12345.67, 0)} \\ \text{implies} \quad 12345.67 \\ +\quad\quad 5.00 \\ \hline 12350.67 \end{array}$$

- A *negative* value y indicates rounding the $(y + 1)^{th}$ digit to the left of the decimal point. Thus, y = −2 means round at the third digit from the left (add 5 to the second). For example,

$$\begin{array}{r} \text{ROUND (123456.7, -2)} \\ \text{implies} \quad 123456.7 \\ +\quad\quad 50.0 \\ \hline 123506.7 \end{array}$$

The following program provides an example of arithmetic declaratives, an arithmetic expression, and the ROUND built-in function:

```
PROG5A:    PROCEDURE OPTIONS(MAIN);
   DCL    BALANCE    DEC FIXED (7,2)   INIT (2345.67),
          RATE       DEC FIXED (3,3)   INIT (.125),
          INTEREST   DEC FIXED (7,2) ;
   DCL    ROUND                 BUILTIN;

          INTEREST = ROUND( BALANCE * RATE, 2 ) ;
          PUT LIST (BALANCE, RATE, INTEREST);
   END PROG5A;
```

The effect of the multiply and ROUND is as follows:

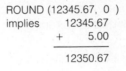

Product:	293.20875
Round:	500
Result:	293.21375

The result stored in INTEREST is 293.21. The PUT statement prints BALANCE, RATE, and INTEREST beginning respectively in positions 1, 25, and 49, as follows:

       2345.67   .125   293.21

CONVERSION OF DATA FORMATS

It is sometimes necessary to assign a data format to a different type, such as fixed-point to floating-point or Binary to Bit. For these statements, the compiler generates special code that involves conversion of data formats. It is valid to assign any arithmetic format, subject to field sizes, to any other arithmetic format. Certain other conversions are invalid, depending on the assigned field and the version of the compiler. Appendix G lists all possible conversions and should be a useful reference when required.

COMPILER DIAGNOSTICS

The PL/I compiler provides diagnostic messages at the end of the compiled listing. There are different levels of diagnostics, depending on the severity of the message. For example, some messages are merely informatory because the compiler has detected a trivial condition that could be improved, whereas other diagnostics are so severe that the compilation must be terminated. The following lists the severity of diagnostics for the DOS Optimizer; other compilers will provide similar messages.

SEVERITY	EXPLANATION OF MESSAGE
I	Informatory. Notifies you of some aspect of the program, generally harmless, that may assist programming.
W	Warning. Warns of a possible program error or a possible failure to achieve full optimization; a correction may help make the program more efficient.
E	Error. Describes an error that the compiler has attempted to correct, probably unsuccessfully.
S	Severe error. Describes an error that the compiler has attempted to correct, probably unsuccessfully.
U	Unrecoverable error. Describes an error that the compiler cannot correct, usually because of an error in the compiler or the system, not the program. The compilation is terminated.

```
STMT LEV NT

   1     0  PROG5B: PROCEDURE OPTION(MAIN) ;

   2  1  0  DCL     TITLE1        CHAR(6)          INIT ('SCORES') ,
              TITLE2        CHAR(7)          INIT ('AVERAGE') ,
       DCL     SCORE1        FIXED DEC (5,2)  INIT (27.53) ,
              SCORE2        FIXED DEC (5,2)  INIT (33.76) ,
              SCORE3        FIXED DEC (5,2)  INIT (44.85) ;
   3  1  0  DCL     AVERAGE       FIXED DEC (5,2) ;

   4  1  0          AVERAGE = (SCORE1 + SCORE2 + SCORE3 / 3 ;
   5  1  0          PUT SKIP LIST (TITLE1, SCORE1, SCORE2, SCORE3) ;
   6  1  0   END PROG5B ;
   7  1  0          PUT SKIP LIST (TITLE3, AVERAGE) ;


COMPILER DIAGNOSTIC MESSAGES OF SEVERITY E AND ABOVE

ERROR ID L   STMT    MESSAGE DESCRIPTION


SEVERE AND ERROR DIAGNOSTIC MESSAGES


IEL0241I S            END OF SOURCE TEXT FOUND BEFORE LOGICAL END OF PROGRAM.
                        1 'END' STATEMENT(S) ASSUMED.
IEL0328I S   1        INVALID OPTION IN 'PROCEDURE' 'BEGIN' OR 'ENTRY' STATEMENT.
                        'OPTION(MAIN)' IGNORED.
IEL0317I S   2        INVALID ATTRIBUTE SPECIFICATION AFTER 'IT ('AVERAGE') ,DCL'.
                        'SCORE1' IGNORED.
IEL0400I E   4        RIGHT PARENTHESIS ASSUMED AFTER 'CORE2 + SCORE3 / 3'.
IEL0289I S   6        LOGICAL END OF PROGRAM FOUND BEFORE END OF SOURCE TEXT.
                        STATEMENT IGNORED.
```

FIGURE 5–2 Compiler Diagnostic Messages.

It is necessary to correct the S and U messages and generally desirable to modify the program to cause the compiler to delete the W and E messages. The PL/C compiler makes a greater effort than PL/I to repair errors, and is more likely to permit execution of a program with serious errors.

Figure 5-2 contains a number of intentional (honest!) errors in order to illustrate compiler diagnostic messages. The diagnostics for the Optimizing compiler are organized according to severity: S and E first together, then W, and finally I. The code numbers beginning with IEL are IBM message numbers that are further explained in an IBM PL/I messages manual, although you should seldom have to reference it.

Severe and Error Diagnostics

STMT	
blank	The compiler complains that "end of source text found before logical end of program." This type of message is typically clarified by a later diagnostic, in this example, statement 6.

STMT	
1	The word OPTION should be OPTIONS—a serious error because the program now contains no MAIN option.
2	Where one DCL statement defines a number of identifiers, you have to determine which identifier is incorrect. In this case, the DCL for SCORE1 should be omitted, or the previous line should end with a semicolon.
4	The compiler has validly corrected a missing right parenthesis.
6	The END statement should be the last statement in the program.

Informatory Messages

```
IEL0533I  I     NO 'DECLARE' STATEMENT(S) FOR 'SCORES',
                'SCORE1','TITLE3','SYSPRINT'.

IEL0430I  I  1  NO 'MAIN' OPTION ON EXTERNAL PROCEDURE.
```

STMT	
blank	This statement lists identifiers for which there are no DCL statements. SCORES appears as an incorrect INIT in statement 2; SCORE1 contains an invalid INIT value; and TITLE3 in statement 7 should be spelled TITLE2—all of these default to DEC FLOAT (6). The compiler assumes that the PUT statements will print using SYSPRINT, the standard printer device.
1	This is a further warning about the MAIN option that was ignored because of a spelling error in OPTIONS. There are situations in which a Procedure may validly omit the MAIN option, but this is not one of them.

One additional error for which there is no diagnostic: SCORE3 is an arithmetic variable that is initialized with a character string (in apostrophes). Although the initialization is incorrect, the compiler converts the character string (inefficiently) to an arithmetic value.

Note: when you analyze the diagnostic messages, also check the cross-reference table for defaults. Often, information in one listing can help explain the other listing.

DEBUGGING TIPS

The following are common errors concerned with assignment statements. The compiler locates *syntactical* errors, those that violate rules of the language. The compiler does not locate *semantic* errors, which follow the rules of the language but use an incorrect instruction or incorrect logic.

- A spelling error in an expression causes the compiler to make an incorrect default.
- An assignment expression is written incorrectly. For example, a Character or Bit literal is not enclosed in apostrophes, or an arithmetic expression uses parentheses incorrectly.
- An assigned value is too long for a receiving field.
- An assignment causes improper conversion between data types.
- An uninitialized arithmetic variable is used as an accumulator. (This error is the first one to suspect when an execution diagnostic signals a "data exception.")
- A ROUND operation specifies rounding at the wrong position or rounds a binary value as if it were a decimal value.

PROBLEMS

5-1. For each of the following, declare a suitable variable and assign to it the required expression:
   (a) The literal DELAWARE ELECTRONICS.
   (b) Blanks to clear a six-byte variable.
   (c) Zeros to clear a seven-digit variable that has two positions to the right of the decimal point.
   (d) Zeros to clear a 15-digit variable that has five positions to the right of the binary point.

5-2. Given the following declaratives, show the result in the receiving field of the following *unrelated* assignment statements (use hexadecimal notation if you know how). Explain if an operation is *invalid*.

```
DCL  TOTAL     DEC FIXED (7, 2),
     SUM       DEC FIXED (5, 2) INIT (1.25),
     AMOUNT    DEC FIXED (5, 2) INIT (5) ;
```

(a) TOTAL = 2.5;
(b) TOTAL = SUM * 100;
(c) AMOUNT = AMOUNT + SUM;
(d) TOTAL = (SUM + 3.75) / 5;
(e) AMOUNT = SUM * 1000;
(f) TOTAL = SUM * 25 + 150;
(g) SUM = SUM + 101B;

5–3. Explain the cause of the error in the following execution statement:

```
DCL   AMNT1      DEC FIXED(5,2) INIT (5),
      TOTAL      DEC FIXED(7,2) INIT (0);
      TOTAL = TOTAL + AMT1;
```

5–4. Your program uses the ROUND built-in function in order to round an arithmetic expression. In its diagnostics, the compiler complains that ROUND is not declared. Explain what the problem is and show how to delete the message.

5–5. The following assignment statement causes a Data Exception error. Explain the cause.

```
DCL   TOTAL      DEC FIXED (7,2),
      AMNT2      DEC FIXED (5,2);
      GET LIST (AMNT2);
      TOTAL = TOTAL + AMNT2;
```

5–6. Code the following as valid PL/I statements. Declarative statements are not required.

(a) $A = \dfrac{1}{3}bh$

(b) $A = 2\pi rh$

(c) $V = \sqrt{x^2 + y^2 + z^2}$

(d) $V = \dfrac{4}{3}\pi r^3$

CHAPTER 6

SIMPLE INPUT/OUTPUT

OBJECTIVES

To describe the requirements for reading and writing data and for repetitive processing.

INTRODUCTION

PL/I supports two main types of input/output: Stream I/O and Record I/O. Stream I/O is mainly used in scientific programming, but it is also useful as a debugging aid. Record I/O is mainly used in business programming, especially for processing tape and disk files.

Stream I/O provides three unique formats: List-Directed, Data-Directed, and Edit-Directed I/O. This chapter introduces List-Directed Stream I/O because its simplicity facilitates quick entry to program writing. Later chapters cover Record I/O and the rest of Stream I/O. GET and PUT LIST, as covered in this text, are suitable for processing on either cards or online terminals.

LIST-DIRECTED INPUT

Although you may submit data in the form of fields on an input record, Stream I/O ignores record boundaries and treats data as a continuous "stream" of input fields. The standard format for List-Directed input is

GET [FILE (filename)] LIST (data-list) ;

Omission of FILE (filename) causes the compiler to assume that SYSIN, the system input device, is to be the input file for this program. The data-list may not be omitted and may include variable names, structure names, array names, and subscripted variables. Data in the input stream may consist of arithmetic constants with decimal point and sign (if required) to the left, and string literals enclosed in apostrophes. All input data items are separated either by a comma or by one or more blank positions on the input "record."

In the following example, an input record contains four data items that the program reads and transfers into four defined variables:

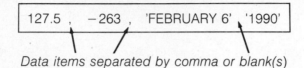

Input record | 127.5 ,   − 263 ,   'FEBRUARY 6' ,'1990' |

Data items separated by comma or blank(s)

```
DCL   PRICE      DEC FIXED (5,2),
      QUANTITY   DEC FIXED (3),
      MONTH      CHAR (12),
      YEAR       CHAR (04) ;

      GET LIST (PRICE, QUANTITY, MONTH, YEAR) ;
```

The GET operation reads each data item and transfers it one at a time from left to right into the variables defined in the data-list. The numeric items 127.5 and − 263 are first converted to Decimal Fixed format and assigned to PRICE and QUANTITY respectively. These are straight assignment statements, with alignment according to the decimal point (if any) in the input field and the precision in the declared variable.

The character items in the input record 'FEBRUARY 6' and '1990' are contained in apostrophes that separate the items. Note that the character string (or literal) may contain blanks. The input data and the data-list match in number and in format. They both contain two numeric items followed by two character items. On completion of the GET operation, the specified variables contain the following:

VARIABLE	CONTENTS
PRICE	127.50 +
QUANTITY	263 −
MONTH	FEBRUARY 6
YEAR	1990

Because input is a "stream," you could also code a separate GET statement for each input item (although less efficient), as:

```
GET LIST ( PRICE ) ;
GET LIST ( QUANTITY ) ;
GET LIST ( MONTH ) ;
GET LIST ( YEAR ) ;
```

If input data were on punched cards, a card could contain all four items, or four cards could contain one item. Either way, the items must be in the correct sequence.

Mismatched Data-List

You must coordinate the GET LIST data-list with the input stream. It is possible to assign input data to the wrong variable, or to assign character data invalidly to an arithmetic variable (and cause a CONVERSION error), or fail to align a decimal point correctly. For example, if PRICE is declared with precision (5,2) but is entered on the input record as 12.345, it is stored as 012.34.

Valid Input Data

The types of input data that may appear in an input stream are as follows:

*   Character strings, enclosed in apostrophes, such as 'BROWNING LABS'
*   Bit strings, enclosed in apostrophes, such as '1011'B
*   Decimal values, such as 123.45 or − 123.45
*   Binary values, such as 1101B (equivalent to 13)
*   Floating-point values, covered in a later chapter

LIST-DIRECTED OUTPUT

Output is also in the form of a stream, and fields print in predetermined positions. The standard format for List-Directed output is

PUT [FILE (filename)] LIST (data-list) ;

Omission of FILE (filename) causes the compiler to assume that SYSPRINT, the standard system printer device, is to be the output device. SYSPRINT assumes 120 print positions and 60 lines per page, unless requested otherwise. The data-list must be included and may contain literals, variables, and expressions that are to be printed. The operation prints the data items from left to right in preset positions 1, 25, 49, 73, and 97 (and in 121 if the print line exceeds 120 positions). The following example illustrates printing three data items:

```
DCL  PRICE    DEC FIXED  (5,2)  INIT  ( − 123.45) ,
     MONTH  CHAR (5)            INIT  ('APRIL') ;

     PUT LIST ( 'VALUES',  PRICE,    MONTH) ;
                   ↑          ↑         ↑
               Character  Arithmetic  Character
                literal    variable   variable
```

Printer position:	VALUES	− 123.45	APRIL
	↑	↑	↑
	1	25	49

The PUT statement inserts the data-list items into the print area from left to right: The character literal 'VALUES' begins in column 1, the arithmetic variable PRICE begins in column 25 (with minus sign to the left and decimal point inserted), and the character variable MONTH begins in column 49. Note that a character literal is enclosed in apostrophes. If the PUT statement were coded with VALUES not in apostrophes, as

```
PUT LIST ( VALUES, PRICE, MONTH );
```

then the compiler would expect to print the *contents* of a variable declared as VALUES—if any.

The first (or only) PUT statement executed always causes the printer to begin at the top of a new page. The previous example could also have been coded with three separate PUT statements, as

```
PUT LIST ( 'VALUES' ) ;
PUT LIST ( PRICE ) ;
PUT LIST ( MONTH ) ;
```

with exactly the same results.

Format Options

There are three format options to control the spacing of lines and the ejecting of forms to a new page: SKIP, LINE, and PAGE. All these options execute before actual printing occurs.

SKIP.   The SKIP option causes spacing of one or more lines, as follows:

```
PUT SKIP LIST    ( . . . ) ; Space 1 line
PUT SKIP(1) LIST ( . . . ) ; Space 1 line
PUT SKIP(0) LIST ( . . . ) ; Space 0 lines
PUT SKIP(3) LIST ( . . . ) ; Space 3 lines
```

SKIP(0) causes printing without spacing, useful, for example, to print a string of underline characters or to reprint the same line for darker emphasis. The maximum SKIP is any number that causes the printer to reach the bottom of a page (the Subset maximum is 3).

Assume the earlier PUT statement that printed the word 'VALUES' and the contents of PRICE and MONTH. Another PUT LIST following, if coded similarly, would enter the next item ('VALUES') in column 73. A common practice is to code the PUT with a SKIP option to force the program to start the next item in column 1 of the next line, as follows:

PUT SKIP LIST ('VALUES', PRICE, MONTH) ;

LINE.   For Stream output, PL/I maintains a *current line counter* and increments it for each line printed or skipped for a page. You can request the printer to skip to a particular line on a page through use of the LINE option, as follows:

PUT LINE(5) LIST (. . .);   or PUT LINE(5);   with no data-list.

The PUT operation skips to line 5 of the page. If the line counter is already past line 5 of the page, the print form is ejected to the next page.

PAGE.   Unless you provide alternate coding, when the bottom of a page is reached (line 60), the forms are automatically ejected to the top of the next page. If you want to eject the forms before reaching line 60, you can use the PAGE option, as follows:

PUT PAGE LIST (. . .);   or PUT PAGE;   with no data-list.

The system resets the current line counter to 1.

If you code PAGE and LINE in the same PUT statement, PAGE executes first. SKIP may not appear in the same PUT statement with PAGE or LINE.

PROGRAM: READING INPUT DATA

Problem Definition

A program is to read three scores from an input record and is to compute their mean average, rounded.

Solution

Use Figure 5–1 from Chapter 5 as a guide. Instead of an INIT option for the declares for the three scores, the program requires a GET LIST statement to read the scores. The GET should read three scores from the input stream into SCORE1,

SCORE2, and SCORE3 respectively. Figure 6–1 gives the complete program. Note the following points:

STATEMENT	EXPLANATION
3	Reads the three scores from input.
4	Sums the three scores into a variable named TOTAL, which is initialized to zero.
5	Calculates the mean average of the three scores (TOTAL / 3) and rounds the result.
6	Prints a title (a literal, 'SCORES') and the three scores.
7	Prints a title (a literal, 'AVERAGE') and the average score.

An overview of program execution is as follows:

```
GET data
Calculate mean average
PUT data
END
```

Input data for this program is:

```
27.53   33.76   44.85
```

```
STMT LEV NT


  1      0   PROG6A:   PROCEDURE OPTIONS(MAIN);

  2   1  0   DCL       (SCORE1,
                        SCORE2,
                        SCORE3)        FIXED DEC (5,2),
                        AVERAGE        FIXED DEC (5,2),
                        TOTAL          FIXED DEC (7,2) INIT (0);


  3   1  0             GET LIST (SCORE1, SCORE2, SCORE3);
  4   1  0             TOTAL = SCORE1 + SCORE2 + SCORE3;
  5   1  0             AVERAGE = ROUND(TOTAL / 3, 2) ;
  6   1  0             PUT SKIP LIST ('SCORES', SCORE1, SCORE2, SCORE3) ;
  7   1  0             PUT SKIP LIST ('AVERAGE', AVERAGE) ;
  8   1  0   END PROG6A;


Output:-

SCORES          27.53              33.76              44.85
AVERAGE         35.38
```

FIGURE 6–1 Input, Calculation, and Output

REPETITIVE PROCESSING

Most programs must be able to process more than one input record. The ideal approach uses the same instructions repetitively to process any number of records. A top-down view of the overall logic is as follows:

GET first data items	Initialize

DO WHILE still input records
    Perform calculations
    PUT results
    GET next data items
END of DO WHILE
	Execute
	    repetitively
	    until
	    no more
	    input data

PUT final totals (if any) END of program	Terminate

Two new PL/I statements are required: ON ENDFILE, which signals the action to be performed when all input records have been processed, and DO WHILE, which controls repetitive processing.

THE ON ENDFILE STATEMENT

When the end of input data is reached, a program usually must take special action. Sometimes the action is as simple as terminating the run; other times the program must first print final totals. Under IBM computers, a special job control card containing a slash/asterisk (/*) in columns 1 and 2 must follow input data. The computer *system* is designed to check for this job statement each time it reads a record and to act on the ON ENDFILE statement. The general format for ON ENDFILE is

ON ENDFILE(filename) action ;

- filename is the name of the input file, called SYSIN up to now.
- action (technically "on-unit") is an assignment statement or a statement that begins with the keyword SIGNAL, CALL, BEGIN, or GO TO.

ON ENDFILE should appear before the first GET in the program. The program executes the ON ENDFILE action only as a result of the computer system encountering the /* job statement following the input data. A program should completely read all input data before terminating, and once it executes ON END-FILE, a program should not attempt to read another record. Either of these actions will cause a system error.

If the action of an ON ENDFILE designates an assignment statement, the program executes the assignment and then resumes with the statement immediately following the GET that encountered end-of-file.

THE DO WHILE STATEMENT

A program is to continue processing *while* there are still input records. The statement used for this purpose is DO WHILE, used as follows :

DO WHILE (expression) ;

END ;

The operation causes repetitive processing of the statements between the DO WHILE and the END until the expression is no longer true. Once this event occurs, the program "drops through" to execute the statement following the END. Of course, an expression may be not true even before the first execution; if so, the program drops past the END without executing the DO WHILE statements at all. (Chapter 7 covers DO WHILE in more detail.)

TOP-DOWN ILLUSTRATION

To control end-of-file and the DO WHILE, a program can define a Bit variable (named EOF below) initialized to '0'B. The following is a skeleton program that reads data items repetitively:

```
PROGREP:
    PROCEDURE OPTIONS(MAIN) ;

    DCL   EOF        BIT(1)     INIT('0'B) ;

        ON ENDFILE(SYSIN) EOF = '1'B ;
        GET LIST ( ... ) ;
        DO WHILE (¬EOF) ;
             .
             PROCESS
             .
             PUT SKIP LIST ( ... ) ;
             GET LIST ( ... ) ;
        END ;

    END PROGREP ;
```

The example program processes each record and repeats the loop until the end-of-file (/*) condition occurs. At that point, the ON ENDFILE statement assigns '1'B to EOF, and program control returns to the statement following the GET (in the DO WHILE). An END immediately follows the GET, and because the DO WHILE condition is no longer true, program control drops through the END of the DO WHILE.

Note that the program must now have *two* END statements: the first END denotes end of the DO WHILE, and the second END denotes end of the program.

PROGRAM: REPETITIVE PROCESSING AND FINAL TOTAL

Problem Definition

Data records contain employee name, hours worked, and rate of pay. There are any number of records in the file. A program is to read each record, calculate wage (hours X rate), and print the final total of wages.

```
 1     0  PROG6B:  PROCEDURE OPTIONS(MAIN) ;

 2  1  0  DCL      EMPNAME            CHAR(20) ;
 3  1  0  DCL      HOURS              DEC FIXED (5,2) ,
                   RATE               DEC FIXED (5,2) ,
                   WAGE               DEC FIXED (7,2) ,
                   TOTALHRS           DEC FIXED (7,2) INIT (0) ,
                   TOTALPAY           DEC FIXED (9,2) INIT (0) ;
 4  1  0  DCL      EOF                BIT (1)         INIT ('0'B) ;

 5  1  0           PUT SKIP LIST ('NAME', '    RATE');
 6  1  0           PUT LIST ('    HOURS', '      WAGE');
 7  1  0           PUT SKIP ;
 8  1  0           ON ENDFILE(SYSIN) EOF = '1'B ;
 9  1  0           GET LIST (EMPNAME, HOURS, RATE) ;

10  1  0           DO WHILE (EOF = '0'B) ;
11  1  1              WAGE = ROUND( HOURS * RATE, 2 ) ;
12  1  1              TOTALHRS = TOTALHRS + HOURS ;
13  1  1              TOTALPAY = TOTALPAY + WAGE ;
14  1  1              PUT SKIP LIST (EMPNAME, RATE, HOURS, WAGE) ;
15  1  1              GET LIST (EMPNAME, HOURS, RATE) ;
16  1  1           END ;

17  1  0           PUT SKIP(2) ;
18  1  0           PUT SKIP LIST (' ', 'TOTAL', TOTALHRS, TOTALPAY) ;
19  1  0           SIGNAL FINISH ;
20  1  0  END PROG6B ;

Output:-

    NAME                RATE            HOURS           WAGE

    AB SMITH            9.25            22.50           208.13
    EP JOHNSON          10.50           10.25           107.63


                        TOTAL           32.75           315.76
```

FIGURE 6-2 Repetitive Processing.

Solution

The program should use DO WHILE for repetitive processing and use ON END-FILE to handle the end-of-file condition. For each input record, the program calculates and prints wage and adds wage to a final wage accumulator. Once all records are processed, the program terminates looping, prints total wages, and ends processing. Figure 6–2 provides the working program and output results.

Input data is as follows:

22.50   9.25   10.25   10.50

Note the following points:

STATEMENT	EXPLANATION
4	Defines EOF as BIT(1), initialized to '0'B, to control action at end-of-data.
5	Prints headings for NAME and HOURS.
6	Prints headings for RATE and WAGE. Because this PUT LIST contains no SKIP option, these headings continue on the same line as the previous PUT.
7	Causes a blank line between the heading line and the printed information that follows.
8	Notifies the program of the action to perform on reaching end-of-data—assigns '1'B to EOF.
9	Gets first employee name, hours, and rate-of-pay. The statement executes only once.
10	Controls repetitive processing—the loop executes as long as EOF contains zero.
11	Calculates and rounds wage.
12	Adds hours to total hours (initialized to zero).
13	Adds wage to total pay (initialized to zero).
14	Prints employee name, rate, hours, and wage.
15	Gets next employee name, hours, and rate. If end-of-data, EOF is set to '1'B and execution of the loop terminates.
16	Establishes the END of the DO WHILE loop—control returns to the start of the DO WHILE loop.
17	Causes spacing of two blank lines.
18	Prints the literal 'TOTAL' and the values for total hours and total pay. The PUT list contains a blank literal so that total hours and pay print under their correct columns.

DEBUGGING TIPS

The following are common errors concerned with input/output and DO WHILE statements:

- A GET data-list must exactly coordinate the contents of the input record with the declared variables. Items must match according to data format (character, arithmetic), precision, and number of items.
- A PUT may not contain SKIP with LINE or PAGE options.
- A DO WHILE may be incorrect because of
  1. Failure to include an END statement. (The compiler will treat the program END as the END of the DO WHILE with curious results, depending on the compiler version.)
  2. Improper use of an EOF Bit value. In the following statements,

      DCL EOF   BIT(1)   INIT ('0'B);

      DO WHILE (EOF = '1'B);

  the EOF condition is not "true." Consequently, the DO WHILE will not execute at all, and the program will drop through to the program END. Defining EOF as any length other than 1 may cause unpredictable results.
- Failure to include an end-of-file (/*) record will cause the program to attempt reading past the end of data. The computer operator or operating system may have to intervene.

PROBLEMS

6–1. What is the effect of the following PUT statements? If invalid, explain.
  - (a) PUT SKIP;
  - (b) PUT PAGE(1);
  - (c) PUT SKIP(5);
  - (d) PUT LINE(3);
  - (e) PUT SKIP PAGE;

6–2. Input Formats. Input records contain items with data that look like the following:

35468 'CONVERTERS' 475   47.32

The values represent respectively part number, part description (up to 25 characters), quantity (maximum is 9999), and unit cost (999.99). Code suitable declaratives and the GET LIST statement.

6–3. Output Format. Assume the same data as Problem 6–2. Code the statement to calculate part value (quantity × cost), the required declarative, and the PUT statement to print the input items and the calculated value. Where does each field begin printing?

6–4. Combine Problems 6–2 and 6–3 into a full working program that prints a heading at the start, processes any number of records, and prints total value at the end. Be sure to space a line after the heading and before the final total.

6–5. Compound Interest. Suppose you were to invest $5,000 at 8% compounded quarterly. What would be the compound amount at the end of five years? The solution is based on the fundamental formula of compound interest:

$$S = P(1 + i)^n$$

where S is the compound amount, P is the original principal, i is the rate per period (8% ÷ 4), and n is the number of periods (5 years compounded quarterly is 20). Consequently

$$S = 5000(1 + .02)^{20}$$
$$= 5000 \times 1.4859474$$
$$= 7{,}429.74 \text{ (rounded)}$$

Code a program that reads input records containing original principal, interest rate per period, and number of periods. Print a heading, the input values, and the calculated amount. Test the program using a variety of different values. Check that the program produces the right answers.

6–6. Depreciation. A program has to calculate depreciation periodically on assets. Input records contain asset number, original cost, estimated scrap value, useful life in years, and depreciation-to-date. Depreciation for the current period is based on the declining balance method:

Current depreciation = R × (cost − depreciation-to-date), and

$$R = 1 - \sqrt[n]{\frac{\text{scrap value}}{\text{cost}}} \quad (n = \text{life in years})$$

Arrange 10 or 12 input records with various values. Scrap value should be less than original cost. Print headings for the report, and print input values and current depreciation for each asset. Suggestion: perform the calculation of current depreciation in two or three steps to avoid a FIXEDOVERFLOW error (see Chapter 21).

CHAPTER 7

PROGRAM LOGIC

OBJECTIVE:
To cover the logic involved in program looping
and decision making.

INTRODUCTION

Up to this chapter, the flow of program control has involved executing one statement immediately after another. Chapter 6 introduced a simple *loop,* which performed a group of statements repetitively until a specified condition was reached. A program may also interrupt the flow of control in order to *branch* to another section of the program. A program must often test if certain conditions exist and direct the control of execution to some other routine. For example:

*   Is an input control code number equal to a specified constant value?
*   Is the customer's current balance owed greater than the credit limit?
*   Is an arithmetic amount, whose square root is to be computed, negative?

The type of comparison depends on the attributes of the data being compared. Normally you compare data of similar attributes. The types are as follows:

1.   *Character.* Comparison of fields is left to right, one byte at a time. A shorter field is extended internally to the right with blanks.

2.   *Bit.* Comparison of fields is left to right, one bit at a time. A shorter field is extended internally to the right with zero bits.

3.   *Arithmetic.* Algebraic comparison of values (for example, a positive value is greater than a negative value). Fields that are of different base, scale, or precision are converted to common attributes.

THE IF STATEMENT

The result of a test is either true or false, and the program can take appropriate action. The PL/I statement that provides for such decision making is the IF statement. Its format is

```
IF expression THEN action-1 ;
         [ ELSE action-2 ; ]     (ELSE action is optional)
```

The expression consists of a comparison using the following *comparison operators:*

=	Equal	¬ =	Not Equal
<	Less Than	¬ <	Not Less Than
>	Greater Than	¬ >	Not Greater Than
> =	Greater Than or Equal	< =	Less Than or Equal

If an expression is *true,* the operation executes the THEN action and bypasses the ELSE action (if any). If an expression is *false,* the operation bypasses the THEN action and executes the ELSE action. If there is no ELSE, the program executes the statement following the IF.

The THEN and ELSE *action* is any single statement, such as another IF, CALL, an assignment statement, a DO-group, GO TO, or a BEGIN block, but not END or PROCEDURE. If there is a THEN action but no ELSE action, you may code the statement with no ELSE, as

```
IF expression THEN action ;
```

or with a "null ELSE" (an ELSE followed immediately by a semicolon), as

```
IF expression THEN action ;
         ELSE ;
```

Example 1—Simple Character String Test

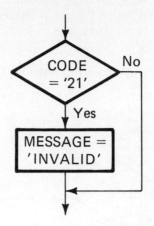

IF CODE = '21' THEN MESSAGE = 'INVALID' ;

The IF expression tests if CODE contains the character constant '21.' If true (='21'), the operation assigns a warning message and continues with the following statement. If false (not '21'), the program continues with the following statement. The ELSE is omitted here because there is no alternate action (although you could code a "null ELSE" as ELSE;).

Example 2—Simple Arithmetic Test

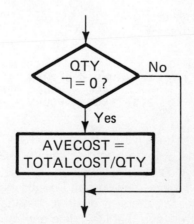

IF QTY ﹁ = 0 THEN AVECOST = TOTALCOST / QTY ;

The IF expression tests if the contents of QTY is not zero. If *true* (not zero), the THEN action calculates average cost and then continues with the next statement (not shown). If *false* (zero), the program bypasses the THEN and goes to the next statement. A null ELSE is optional here as well.

Example 3—IF with an Alternate ELSE Action

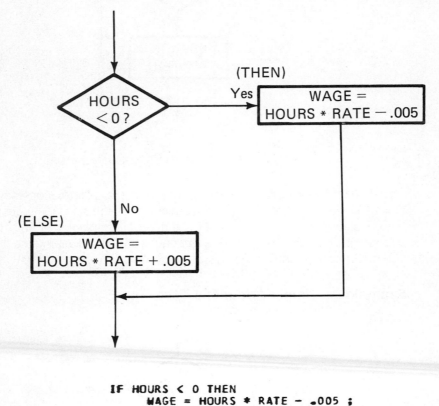

```
IF HOURS < 0 THEN
    WAGE = HOURS * RATE - .005 ;
ELSE WAGE = HOURS * RATE + .005 ;
```

The expression tests if the contents of HOURS is less than zero (negative). If *true* (negative), the THEN action calculates WAGE with negative rounding and then branches *around* the ELSE statement. If *false* (positive), the ELSE action calculates WAGE with positive rounding and continues with the next statement. The word ELSE is necessary here; if omitted, a negative condition would calculate and round negatively and then calculate and round positively!

Example 4—Nested IF's and the Null ELSE

IF statements may be nested within IF statements. An ELSE, if any, matches with the last unmatched THEN. The following checks employee hours worked:

```
IF HOURS <= 40 THEN
        IF HOURS > 0 THEN
                WAGE = HOURS * RATE ;
        ELSE ;
ELSE WAGE = RATE * 40 + (HOURS - 40)* 1.5 * RATE;
```

HOURS WORKED	ACTION
Zero hours or less	Do not calculate pay; bypass.
One to 40 hours	Calculate straight time (hours X rate).
Over 40 hours	Calculate straight time (hours X rate) plus overtime pay (multiply hours in excess of 40 by 1.5).

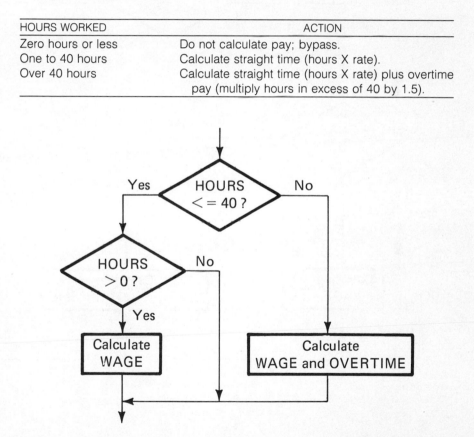

An ELSE matches the immediately preceding unmatched THEN. The example requires the use of a null ELSE; its omission would cause the compiler to assume that the following ELSE matched the preceding THEN, with the unusual results shown in the next example.

Example 5—Omission of a Required ELSE

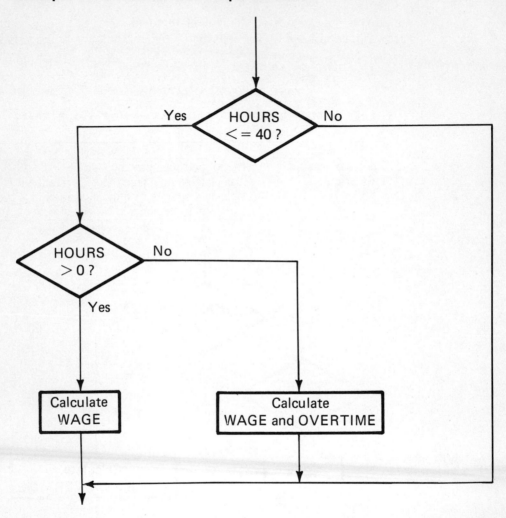

```
IF HOURS <= 40 THEN
     IF HOURS > 0 THEN
          WAGE = HOURS * RATE ;
ELSE WAGE = RATE * 40 + (HOURS-40) * 1.5 * RATE;
```

Invalid: With the null ELSE omitted, the compiler matches the ELSE statement with the previous THEN. An employee who works overtime now receives no pay!

PROGRAM: CALCULATE SALES DISCOUNTS

Problem Definition

A program has to calculate billing amount and discount amount. Input data consists of customer number, quantity, and price. Billing amount equals quantity times price. The discount rate depends on the quantity sold, as follows:

QUANTITY SOLD	DISCOUNT RATE
less than 10	0.00%
11 - 24	2.00
25 - 49	4.00
50 and over	6.00

The amount of discount equals billing amount times discount rate.

Solution

The program can determine the discount rate by testing quantity sold successively for less than 10, less than 25, and less than 50. The program listing appears in Figure 7–1. Note the following points:

STATEMENT	EXPLANATION
5	Prints a heading for customer number, billing amount, and discount.
8	If quantity is less than 10, assigns 0.00 to discount rate.
9	If quantity is less than 25, assigns 0.02 to discount rate.
10	If quantity is less than 50, assigns 0.04 to discount rate.
11	Otherwise assigns 0.06 to discount rate.
12	Calculates billing amount.
13	Calculates discount amount.
14	Prints customer number, billing amount, and discount amount.

Input data is as follows:

CUSTOMER NUMBER	QUANTITY	PRICE
'26342'	27	1.95
'28743'	60	2.50
'29546'	5	10.25
'36299'	20	9.75

```
 1    0   PROG7B:   PROCEDURE OPTIONS(MAIN);
 2   1  0   DCL      CUSTNO              CHAR (5),
                     QTY                 DEC FIXED (5),
                     PRICE               DEC FIXED (5,2),
                     DISC_RATE           DEC FIXED (3,2),
                     BILL_AMT            DEC FIXED (9,2),
                     DISC_AMT            DEC FIXED (7,2);
 3   1  0   DCL      EOF                 BIT (1)   INIT('0'B);

 4   1  0            ON ENDFILE(SYSIN) EOF = '1'B;
 5   1  0            PUT SKIP LIST ('CUST#', '  AMT BILLED', 'AMT DISCOUNT');
 6   1  0            PUT SKIP;
 7   1  0            GET LIST (CUSTNO, QTY, PRICE);

 8   1  0            DO WHILE (¬EOF);
 9   1  1               IF QTY < 10 THEN DISC_RATE = 0.00;
10   1  1               ELSE IF QTY < 25 THEN DISC_RATE = 0.02;
11   1  1                  ELSE IF QTY < 50 THEN DISC_RATE = 0.04;
12   1  1                     ELSE DISC_RATE = 0.06;
13   1  1               BILL_AMT = QTY * PRICE;
14   1  1               DISC_AMT = ROUND(BILL_AMT * DISC_RATE, 2);
15   1  1               PUT SKIP LIST (CUSTNO, BILL_AMT, DISC_AMT);
16   1  1               GET LIST (CUSTNO, QTY, PRICE);
17   1  1            END;

18   1  0      END PROG7B;
```

Output:-

CUST#	AMT BILLED	AMT DISCOUNT
26342	52.65	2.11
28743	150.00	9.00
29546	51.25	0.00
36299	195.00	3.90

FIGURE 7-1 Customer Discounts.

THE DO STATEMENT

There are three types of DO statements: the simple DO-group that follows THEN or ELSE actions, the DO WHILE statement, and the iterative DO-loop.

Type 1—The Simple DO-Group

THEN or ELSE actions permit only one statement, but often an action requires several statements. To delimit a group of statements in a THEN or ELSE clause, you use a DO-group, beginning with a DO statement and terminating with an END.

The following example checks if a salesman has sold an amount greater than $1,000.00. If he has, he receives a commission of $50.00 plus a bonus of 12% of sales over $500.00. If not, he receives a commission of only 8% on sales.

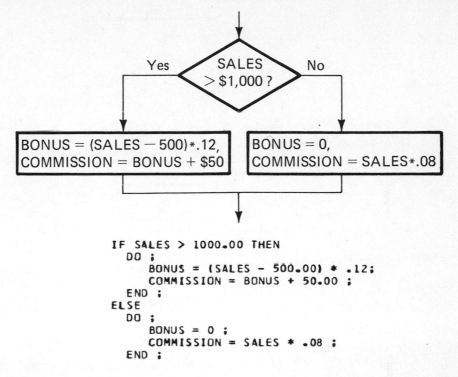

```
IF SALES > 1000.00 THEN
   DO ;
        BONUS = (SALES - 500.00) * .12;
        COMMISSION = BONUS + 50.00 ;
   END ;
ELSE
   DO ;
        BONUS = 0 ;
        COMMISSION = SALES * .08 ;
   END ;
```

Omission of an END such as the last one may cause the compiler to assume that the rest of the program is contained in the ELSE DO action, often with unusual results.

Type 2—DO WHILE

DO WHILE performs a loop as long as the specified expression remains *true* and is an important feature of structured programming:

DO WHILE (element-expression) ;

DO WHILE may be placed anywhere in a program, including after a THEN or an ELSE. The statements between the DO and the END execute repetitively as long as the WHILE expression remains *true*. The WHILE expression may be any valid string or arithmetic expression.

The following program calculates the sum of the digits from 1 through 10 (1 + 2 + 3 . . . + 10):

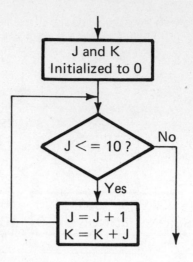

```
PROG7B:    PROCEDURE OPTIONS(MAIN);
     DCL   (J, K)      BIN FIXED (15) INIT (0) ;

           DO WHILE (J <= 10) ;
                J = J + 1 ;
                K = K + J ;
           END ;
           PUT SKIP LIST (J, K);
     END PROG7B;
```

The loop repeats as long as J is less than or equal to 10. When J increments to 10, the value in K becomes 55. Once J reaches 11, it is no longer equal to or less than 10; the program terminates the loop and proceeds to the statement following the END. Output at the end is: 11 and 55.

For iterative loops such as DO WHILE, ensure that there is always some way for the routine to terminate, for if the expression is always found *true,* the program will loop endlessly, as in the following:

```
DCL   J               BIN FIXED (15) INIT (0) ;

      DO WHILE (J ¬= 5) ;
           J = J + 2 ;
      END ;
```

The loop increments J by 2, as 0, 2, 4, 6, ..., and is never equal to 5.

A WHILE condition may be initially *true* as in the following:

```
DCL   K               BIN FIXED (15) ;

      K = 0 ;
      DO WHILE (K ¬= 0) ;
           .
           .
      END ;
```

The WHILE expression is *true* if K is not equal to 0. But since K already contains 0, program control immediately proceeds past the END with no execution of the loop.

Type 3—The Iterative DO-Group (DO-Loop)

An iterative DO-loop executes a group of statements a stated number of times. Like DO WHILE, a DO loop may follow a THEN or an ELSE. The group begins with DO and terminates with END. The previous example used DO WHILE to calculate the sum of the digits from 1 to 10 (1 + 2 + 3 . . . + 10). You could also calculate the sum of digits using an iterative DO-loop:

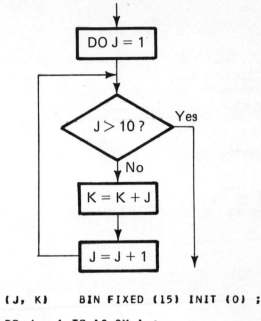

```
DCL   (J, K)     BIN FIXED (15) INIT (0) ;

      DO  J = 1 TO 10 BY 1 ;
         K = K + J ;
      END ;
```

The loop initializes J to 1 and executes repetitively until J exceeds the limit 10. You can also combine types 2 and 3, as

DO I = 1 TO 10 WHILE (AMT > 0) ;

The statement first tests if I > 10 and then if AMT > 0 ; if *either* condition is true, the loop terminates.

Because DO-loops are generally associated with the processing of arrays, a detailed discussion is in Chapter 8.

Nested DO-Statements

A DO-group may contain nested DO-groups, provided that the entire group through to its END is completely nested, as:

```
IF expression-1 THEN
   DO ;
      IF expression-2 THEN
         DO ;
            :
         END ;
      :
   END ;
```

⎱ Nested
⎰ DO-Group

An END refers to the *immediately preceding* DO. Consequently, the first END refers to the second DO, and the second END refers to the first DO. Omission of the first END would cause the compiler to associate the only END with the second DO. The first DO would have no END—an error.

LOGICAL EXPRESSIONS

There are times when a test must determine if two expressions are *both* true or if *either* expression is true. For this purpose, PL/I provides *logical* (or *Boolean*) *operators* & (and) and | (or). Consider the following compound expressions:

EXPRESSION			RESULT
(6 > 5)	&	(3 > 2)	true (both expressions are true)
(6 = 5)	&	(3 > 2)	false (first expression is false)
(6 = 5)			(3 > 2)	true (second expression is true)

If A and B are expressions, then the following table provides all possible results of conditions:

A	B	A & B	A | B
true	true	true	true
true	false	false	true
false	true	false	true
false	false	false	false

For example, the second line of the table reads: If expression-A is true and expression-B is false, then

1.   A & B is false
2.   A | B is true

Priority of Operators

Priority of operators in a compound expression is similar to that for arithmetic expressions. Any arithmetic expression is performed first, then logical operators (>,<, =), then &, and finally |. Consequently,

$$A > B \mid C = D \& E > F$$

is the same as

$$(A > B) \mid ((C = D) \& (E > F))$$

Logical Expressions in IF Statements

An IF statement may contain a *logical expression* using the *bit string operators* & (And) and | (Or) to connect two expressions. For example, the following statement tests if *both* conditions are true, then assign '1' to CODE, otherwise assign '2' to CODE:

```
IF AMT = 0 & COUNT > 25
    THEN CODE = '1' ;
    ELSE CODE = '2' ;
```

The following statement tests if *either* (or both) condition is true, assign '1' to CODE, otherwise assign '2' to CODE:

```
IF AMT = 0 | COUNT > 25
    THEN CODE = '1' ;
    ELSE CODE = '2' ;
```

Although you can often code IF logic several different ways, a good rule is to use the simplest and clearest method. The following two examples are equivalent:

1.   IF with a logical expression:

```
IF AMT = 0 & COUNT > 25 THEN CODE = '1' ;
```

2.   IF with a nested IF:

IF AMT = 0 THEN IF COUNT > 25 THEN CODE = '1' ;

Reversing the Logic

Consider again the logical expression using the & operator:

IF AMT = 0 & COUNT > 25
THEN CODE = '1' ;
ELSE CODE = '2' ;

Suppose you want the *true* condition to assign '2' and the *false* condition to assign '1.' You will have to reverse the comparison operators (from = to ¬ = and from > to ¬ > respectively) and change the logical operator & to | :

IF AMT ¬ = 0 | COUNT ¬ > 25
THEN CODE = '2' ;
ELSE CODE = '1' ;

Satisfy yourself that this change is correct using the following four possibilities for AMT and COUNT:

AMT	COUNT	CODE
0	50	1
0	0	2
1	50	2
1	0	2

BIT STRING LOGIC

A main use of Bit String format is for logical operations. In PL/I, a bit value '1' means *true,* and a bit value '0' means *false.* There are three logical operations (also known as Boolean): AND (&), OR (|), and NOT (¬).

AND

According to Boolean logic, AND means that if *both* compared values are true ('1'), then the result is true ('1'). The four possible AND conditions are as follows:

A	&	B	RESULT
0		0	0
0		1	0
1		0	0
1		1	1

OR

In the case of OR, if *either* compared bit is true ('1') then the result is true. The four possible OR conditions are as follows:

A	|	B	RESULT
0		0	0
0		1	1
1		0	1
1		1	1

NOT

The NOT (¬) operator is used to reverse a bit value. Thus, '0' (false) means ¬'1' (not true), and '1' (true) means ¬ '0' (not false).

Truth Table

A *truth table* involves all possible combinations of values for A and B. Assume that A and B are declared as BIT strings, as

DCL (A, B) BIT (1) ;

The truth table for A and B appears as follows:

1		2		3	4	5	6	7	8
A	B	¬A	¬B	A & B	A | B	¬A & ¬B	¬(A | B)	¬A | ¬B	¬(A & B)
0	0	1	1	0	0	1	1	1	1
0	1	1	0	0	1	0	0	1	1
1	0	0	1	0	1	0	0	1	1
1	1	0	0	1	1	0	0	0	0

- Column 1 establishes the four combinations of 0 and 1 for A and B.
- Column 2 provides the values for ¬A and for ¬B.
- Columns 3 and 4 provide the values for A & B and for A | B respectively.
- Column 5 establishes the values for (¬A & ¬B); that is, the result of ANDing column 2.
- Column 6 establishes the values for ¬(A | B), the result of reversing column 4.
- Column 7 contains the values for ¬A | ¬B, the result of ORing column 2.
- Column 8 contains the value for ¬(A & B), the result of reversing column 3.

Some conclusions based on this analysis:

1.   Since columns 5 and 6 contain identical results, then

$$¬A \& ¬B = ¬(A | B)$$

2.   Since columns 7 and 8 contain identical results, then

$$¬A | ¬B = ¬(A \& B)$$

3.   Since columns 3 and 7 contain opposite results, then

A & B is logically opposite to ¬A | ¬B

4.   Since columns 4 and 5 contain opposite results, then

A | B is logically opposite to ¬A & ¬B

These latter two conclusions explain how you can reverse a logical expression and the THEN/ELSE to obtain the same results, as was illustrated in the preceding section on logical expressions ("Reversing the Logic"). The reversed logic is known as DeMorgan's Rule.

Bit Operations

There are special uses in Bit logic using the comparison operators:

Greater than	>	Not greater than	¬>
Equal	=	Not equal	¬=
Less than	<	Not less than	¬<
Greater than or equal	>=	Less than or equal	<=

You can make a comparison of two values (string or arithmetic) that returns a bit indication of '1' for *true* and '0' for *false*. Consider the following example:

```
DCL   SWITCH          BIT (1),
      FLDA            DEC FIXED (5),
      FLDB            DEC FIXED (5);

      SWITCH = FLDA < FLDB ;
```

The test is if FLDA is less than FLDB (that is, 'true'), then assign the value '1'B to SWITCH. If not less (false), then assign '0'B to SWITCH.

For further extension of true/false conditions for Bit strings, there are three Boolean operations: AND (&), OR (|) and NOT (¬). AND means that if both compared bits are '1', then the result is '1'. OR means that if either or both compared bits are '1', then the result is '1'. All other results are '0'. NOT (¬) is used to reverse the bit value. The following Bit string operations illustrate this:

```
DCL   A           BIT (4),
      B           BIT (4)   INIT ('1100'B),
      C           BIT (4)   INIT ('0110'B) ;

      A = ¬B ;               /*'0011'B */
      A = B & C ;            /*'0100'B */
      A = B | C ;            /*'1110'B */
```

EOF Test.   A common use for the Boolean NOT is in the DO WHILE test for end-of-file. An earlier program tested if an EOF Bit switch contained '0'B, as

```
DCL   EOF       BIT (1)   INIT ('0'B) ;

      ON ENDFILE(SYSIN) EOF = '1'B ;
      DO WHILE (EOF = '0'B) ;
          •
          •
      END ;
```

The example can be changed from testing for '0'B to testing for NOT '1'B, as

```
      DO WHILE (EOF ¬ = '1'B) ;
```

And the WHILE condition can be further simplified as

```
      DO WHILE ( ¬ EOF);
```

which tests "while not end-of-file," or "while EOF does not contain the value '1'B."

PROGRAM: CALCULATION OF UNIT-COST AND REORDER QUANTITY

Problem Definition

Inventory data records contain stock number, quantity, value, reorder point, and reorder quantity. A program is to calculate unit-cost (value ÷ quantity). It also has to check stock numbers between 23000 and 80000: for items within this range, if the quantity is less than the reorder point, the program is to print the reorder quantity. The total value of all stock items is also required.

Solution

The program should be organized with a DO WHILE for looping. An IF statement should check that the quantity is not zero before calculating unit-cost. A compound IF statement can check if the stock is to be reordered. Figure 7–2 provides the program solution and test results. Input data is as follows:

STOCK NUMBER	QUANTITY	VALUE	REORDER POINT	REORDER QUANITITY
'00363'	10	527.30	25	250
'01522'	50	249.63	30	500
'23060'	95	163.80	75	300
'36525'	15	265.27	30	200
'39417'	0	0.00	25	200

Note the following points:

STATEMENT	EXPLANATION
11	Prints the first heading line.
12	Prints the second heading line.
14	Gets the first stock data.
16	If QTY is not equal to zero, calculates unit-cost.
17	If QTY equals zero, cannot calculate unit-cost; assigns it with zero.
18	Determines quanity-to-order for stock numbers greater than 23000 and less than 80000 for which quantity is less than the reorder point.
19	Defines a null ELSE to complete the logic.
20	Assigns zero for items not to be reordered.
21	Adds stock value to total value, used for final total (and initialized to zero).
22	Prints stock information.

```
  1      0   PROG7A:   PROCEDURE OPTIONS(MAIN);

  2   1  0   DCL       SYSIN     FILE INPUT ENV( BUFFERS(2) );
  3   1  0   DCL       SYSPRINT FILE PRINT ENV (BUFFERS(2) );

  4   1  0   DCL       STOCKNO             CHAR (5) ;
  5   1  0   DCL       (QTY,
                       QTY_TO_ORDER,
                       REORDER_PT,
                       REORDER_QTY)        DEC FIXED (5) ;
  6   1  0   DCL       (UNITCOST,
                       VALUE)              DEC FIXED (7,2) ;
  7   1  0   DCL       TOTAL_VALUE         DEC FIXED (9,2) INIT (0);
  8   1  0   DCL       EOF           BIT (1)   INIT ('0') ;

  9   1  0             OPEN FILE(SYSIN), FILE(SYSPRINT);
 10   1  0             ON ENDFILE(SYSIN) EOF = '1'B ;
 11   1  0             PUT SKIP LIST (' ', ' ', 'STOCK REORDER REPORT');
 12   1  0             PUT SKIP LIST ('STOCK NO.', 'QUANTITY',
                             ' UNIT-COST', '     VALUE', ' REORDER');
 13   1  0             PUT SKIP ;
 14   1  0             GET LIST (STOCKNO, QTY, VALUE, REORDER_PT,
                             REORDER_QTY) ;

 15   1  0             DO WHILE (¬EOF) ;
 16   1  1                 IF QTY ¬= 0 THEN
                                UNITCOST = VALUE / QTY ;
 17   1  1                 ELSE UNITCOST = 0 ;
 18   1  1                 IF STOCKNO > '23000' & STOCKNO < '80000' THEN
                              IF QTY < REORDER_PT THEN
                                  QTY_TO_ORDER = REORDER_QTY ;
 19   1  1                   ELSE ;
 20   1  1                 ELSE QTY_TO_ORDER = 0 ;
 21   1  1                 TOTAL_VALUE = TOTAL_VALUE + VALUE ;
 22   1  1                 PUT SKIP LIST (STOCKNO, QTY, UNITCOST,
                                VALUE, QTY_TO_ORDER) ;
 23   1  1                 GET LIST (STOCKNO, QTY, VALUE, REORDER_PT,
                                REORDER_QTY) ;
 24   1  1             END ;

 25   1  0             PUT SKIP(2) LIST
                             (' ', ' ', 'TOTAL VALUE =', TOTAL_VALUE);
 26   1  0             CLOSE FILE(SYSIN), FILE(SYSPRINT) ;
 27   1  0             SIGNAL FINISH ;
 28   1  0       END PROG7A ;
```

Output:-

		STOCK REORDER REPORT		
STOCK NO.	QUANTITY	UNIT-COST	VALUE	REORDER
00363	10	52.73	527.30	0
01522	50	4.99	249.63	0
23060	95	1.72	163.80	0
36525	15	17.68	265.27	200
39417	0	0.00	0.00	200
		TOTAL VALUE =	1206.00	

FIGURE 7–2 Calculation of Unit-Cost.

EXTENDED CONTROL FEATURES: SELECT, DO UNTIL, AND REPEAT

The PL/I Optimizer compilers provide a number of additional features to facilitate structured programming for looping and testing without the use of GO TO statements. The extended features are SELECT, UNTIL, and REPEAT. Another feature, LEAVE, is covered in Chapter 10.

The SELECT Statement

SELECT is a useful substitute for IF. . . THEN . . . ELSE . . . where there is a number of choices to be made. The general format for SELECT is

```
SELECT (expr);
    WHEN (expr-1, expr-2, . . . ) action-1 ;
    WHEN (expr-n, expr-n + 1 . . . ) action-2 ;

        .

    OTHERWISE action-p;
END ;
```

A SELECT statement contains two new clauses: WHEN (one or more) and OTHERWISE (one only), and terminates with END. SELECT first evaluates the expression (expr). It then evaluates the expressions in the WHEN clauses in sequence, comparing each value to the SELECT expression. If a WHEN expression is found equal to the SELECT expression, the program executes the action following the corresponding WHEN clause; the program then discontinues evaluating further expressions in WHEN clauses. If SELECT finds no equal expressions in WHEN clauses, it executes the action in the OTHERWISE clause; OTHERWISE may be a null action (OTHERWISE ;).

Any action may be a simple statement (for example, an assignment, CALL, or DO), a compound statement (IF, ON), a DO-group, SELECT, or BEGIN block. On completion of the action, control normally passes to the statement following the END of the SELECT group.

If you want to perform *comparisons* in the WHEN expressions, you may omit the SELECT expression, as

```
SELECT ;
    WHEN (DIVISOR > 0) ... ;
    WHEN (DIVISOR < 0) ... ;
    OTHERWISE ... ;
END ;
```

Consider the following example that selects the number of days in each month:

```
DCL   MONTH     CHAR (3),
      DAYS      CHAR (2) ;

SELECT (MONTH) ;
      WHEN ('APR', 'JUN', 'SEP', 'NOV') DAYS = '30';
      WHEN ('FEB') DAYS = '28' ;
      OTHERWISE     DAYS = '31' ;
END ;
```

The SELECT expression specifies a character variable, MONTH. The first WHEN clause compares MONTH successively against each expression ('APR', 'JUN', etc.). An equal condition causes the character constant '30' to be assigned to DAYS, and an exit from the SELECT-group, past the END. If all expressions are unequal, the next WHEN clause executes, comparing the contents of MONTH against 'FEB'. Again, an equal condition causes '28' to store in DAYS, and unequal causes execution of the next statement. The OTHERWISE clause simply assigns '31' to DAYS. A more sophisticated solution would account for leap-years, in which the year is evenly divisible by 4 (but not the year 2000).

The DO UNTIL Statement

DO UNTIL, like DO WHILE, performs a loop as long as the specified expression remains true. The general format of DO UNTIL is

DO UNTIL (element-expression);

.
.
.

END;

But where DO WHILE evaluates an expression at the start of each iteration, DO UNTIL evaluates an expression at the END. Consequently, DO UNTIL always executes a loop at least once, even if the expression is initially not true. The following DO UNTIL loop calculates the sum of digits from 1 through 10 (1 + 2 + 3 + ... + 10):

```
DCL   (J, K)     BIN FIXED (15) INIT (0) ;

DO J = 1 BY 1 UNTIL (J = 10) ;
      K = K + J ;
END ;
```

The loop adds J to K repetitively until J becomes 10. At that point, the loop terminates with K equal to 55. The logic for the loop appears as follows. Note that the test for J = 10, although at the END, precedes the statement that increments J.

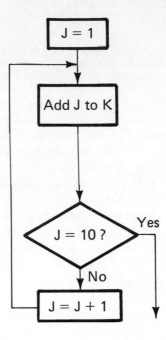

DO UNTIL (EOF) could substitute for DO WHILE (¬ EOF). Be sure you understand the differences between DO WHILE and DO UNTIL before using DO UNTIL (if your compiler supports it).

The REPEAT Clause

The BY and TO options of a DO-loop allow only increments that are arithmetic progressions. REPEAT, however, enables you to vary the control variable of a DO-loop nonlinearly. The following DO-loop initializes K to 1 and then increments K to 2, 4, 8, 16, and 32 before terminating:

```
DO K = 1 REPEAT 2*K UNTIL (K = 32) ;
     PUT LIST (K) ;
END ;
```

PROGRAM TERMINATION

The programs to this point terminate processing when the flow of execution reaches the END statement. More complex programs often require termination at points other than the END. You can use any of the following three statements to cause end of execution in any logical place in the program:

1. SIGNAL FINISH ;
2. RETURN ;
3. STOP ;

Although many programmers use the STOP statement, technically it indicates an "abnormal termination." SIGNAL FINISH perhaps most clearly indicates what the program is doing. Positive indication of end of execution provides better program clarity; consequently, the use of one of these statements is recommended even if the program terminates at the END statement.

DEBUGGING TIPS

Programming logic provides the greatest scope for errors. Because the compiler does not normally deteot logic errors, a program may execute through to its END, but produce incorrect results. Consequently, you may have to scan the logic thoroughly, checking the flow of execution with imaginary data.

* An IF Statement uses incorrect comparison operators, for example, $>$ instead of $\neg >$, or $>$ instead of $> =$.
* A nested IF does not match an ELSE with the correct IF.
* A THEN or ELSE has omitted DO . . . END for multiple action statements.
* A THEN DO or ELSE DO omits its END.
* A DO WHILE or DO-loop fails to initialize properly (so it does not execute) or fails to ensure termination (so it executes indefinitely).
* A compound expression contains incorrect logic. For example, an expression may be always true or never true.
* Although a DO UNTIL expression is often easier to understand than a DO WHILE expression, use DO WHILE if there is any possibility that the expression may be true on initialization. One case is a control loop that tests for end-of-file:

```
DCL   EOF         BIT (1)    INIT ('0'B) ;

ON ENDFILE(SYSIN) EOF = '1'B ;
GET LIST ( ... ) ;
DO UNTIL (EOF) ;
     .
     .
     GET LIST ( ... ) ;
END ;
```

If there are no input records, the first GET causes the ENDFILE condition. But since DO UNTIL tests EOF at the END, the GET in the DO-loop will attempt to GET a record, causing an input error.

• The IF statement references an *element-expression* and consequently may reference an element of a structure or array but not a structure name (major or minor level) or an unsubscripted array name.

• A BIT logic indicator such as EOF used in this chapter is defined as BIT (1). Any other length will cause unpredictable results. Be sure also to initialize the declarative to zero.

• Watch for reversing logic, especially between the use of DO WHILE and DO UNTIL. Assume the following declarative statement:

DCL (EOF, FULL) BIT (1) INIT ('0'B);

DO WHILE (¬ EOF) has the same effect as DO UNTIL (EOF), and DO WHILE (¬ FULL & ¬ EOF) has the same effect as DO UNTIL (FULL | EOF). The double negatives in the DO WHILE make it more difficult to understand.

PROBLEMS

7–1. Use the declaratives given to code the PL/I statements for the following questions:
(a) If the contents of NAME is blank, print a message "MISSING NAME."
(b) If the contents of AMOUNT is zero, print a message "ZERO AMOUNT."
(c) If either NAME is blank or AMOUNT is zero, print a message "INCOM-PLETE DATA."

7–2. Code the complete IF statements for the following flowcharts using proper indentation. Assume that variables are defined as Decimal Fixed. There are a number of valid solutions.

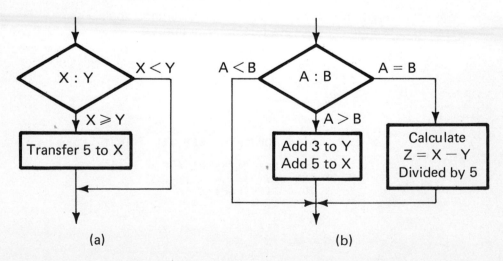

(a)   (b)

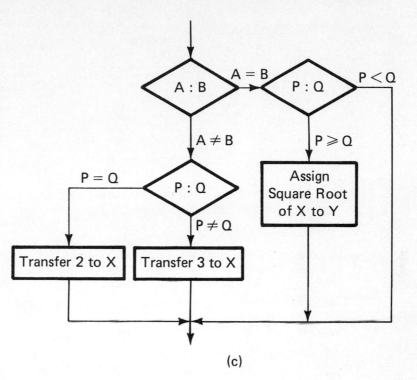

(c)

7–3. Code the necessary PL/I logic for the following problem. If a customer (CUSTNO) has a balance owed (BALANCE) that exceeds the credit limit (CREDLIM), then calculate the difference (DIFF) and set CUSTSWITCH to '10'. For other customers who have a negative balance and their customer number is between 2500 and 5000 inclusive, set CUSTSWITCH to '01'. For all other customers, set CUSTSWITCH to '00'.

```
DCL   CUSTNO          CHAR (5),
      BALANCE         DEC FIXED (7,2),
      CREDLIM         DEC FIXED (5,0),
      DIFF            DEC FIXED (7,2),
      CUSTSWITCH      BIT (2) ;
```

7–4. Recode the following statements so that the logic is the same but the THEN/ELSE actions are reversed:
(a) IF FACTOR > 0 & PRODUCT = 4307 THEN
    RESULT = FACTOR * RATE1;
    ELSE RESULT = 0;
(b) IF FACTOR < 25 | PRODUCT ¬ = 4307 THEN
    RESULT = FACTOR * RATE2;
    ELSE RESULT = 0;

7–5. Set PAY–RATE according to SHIFT–CODE:

SHIFT	SHIFT_CODE	PAY_RATE
Day	'D'	10.50
Afternoon	'A'	11.25
Night	'N'	12.10

If SHIFT–CODE is invalid, store zero in PAY–RATE. Code the logic using (a) IF (b) SELECT.

7–6. Code a PL/I program to convert Fahrenheit temperatures to Celsius (Centigrade). Using C for Celsius and F for Fahrenheit, the formula is

$$C = 5 \times (F - 32) / 9$$

Generate all Celsius values from 30°F through 70°F to two decimal places. Manually check a number of your output values including the first and last ones.

7–7. Code a PL/I program to print a loan repayment schedule. Input is customer name, old balance of loan, regular monthly payment, and annual rate of interest (xx.xx%).

Interest = previous balance × rate-of-interest × 30 /365, and
New balance = previous balance + interest − payment.

Calculate interest and new balance for each month (30 days) until the loan expires (new balance is less than or equal to zero). For example, if the old balance is $200, the payment is $50, and the rate is 20.00%, then the repayment schedule could appear as follows:

MONTH	OLD BALANCE	INTEREST	PAYMENT	NEW BALANCE
1	200.00	3.29	50.00	153.29
2	153.29	2.52	50.00	105.81
3	105.81	1.74	50.00	57.55 etc...

Print a heading and a line for each month of the loan repayment.

Note 1:   Unless the payment is large enough to reduce the balance, the repayment schedule will run endlessly. What action should the program take if this occurs?

Note 2:   The last payment may reduce the new balance to less than zero. What action should the program take if this occurs?

Note on precision: An interest calculation should be accurate to the nearest cent. If a principal amount is $1,316.17 and the annual rate is 18.5% (0.185), then monthly interest is

$1,316.17 × .185 ÷ 12 = $20.290954, rounded to $20.29.

Since both the rate and the divisor 12 are constant values for each loan schedule, you may want to calculate the monthly interest rate at the start of the loop. Accuracy of the calculation depends on the precision of the stored monthly rate. For example, assume three decimal places:

$$.185 \div 12 = 0.015$$

With this rate, interest is calculated as $1,316.17 \times 0.015 = 19.74, an inaccurate result. The monthly rate should be accurate for the largest principal and rate that could ever occur. In this example, a precision of seven decimal places yields a monthly rate of 0.0154166 and interest of $20.290953, rounded to $20.29, the correct result.

CHAPTER 8

ARRAYS

OBJECTIVE:
To define arrays and introduce the simple
processing of arrays.

INTRODUCTION

Any types of data items may be grouped together to form data collections of two types: structures and arrays. An *array,* or *table,* is by definition an n-dimensional collection of elements, all of which have identical attributes. An array can be used to define data by categories so that program routines can locate the data (for example, an income tax table) or used to accumulate data by categories (for example, temperature or pressure readings). The format for de-claring an array is

DCL name (dimension) attributes ;

The dimension attribute is of the form $(x_1, x_2, x_3, \ldots, x_n)$, which denotes the number of dimensions. A one-dimensional array has a dimension attribute (x_1), coded, for example, as

DCL TABLE (6) DECIMAL FIXED (5,2) ;

For TABLE, the dimension attribute (6) indicates a one-dimensional array containing six arithmetic elements, each with identical attributes. The *bounds* of the array are its beginning and ending elements, namely 1 and 6. (PL/I bounds need not begin with 1, as shown later). The *extent* is the number of integers inclusively between the upper and lower bounds; in this case, the extent is 6.

You may code an array with or without the initializing INIT attribute. Initialization follows the normal rules of Declares: arithmetic constants in arithmetic arrays and alphanumeric literals in character arrays. You may initialize all or some of the elements.

ARITHMETIC ARRAYS

An arithmetic array may contain only the digits 0 through 9 with an optional sign and decimal point. You may code as many constants in the INIT as there are elements in the array; the compiler stores the first constant in element-1, the second constant in element-2, and so on. Consider the following declaration of arithmetic arrays:

```
DCL   TABLEA (5) DEC FIXED (5,2) INIT (0),            0 ? ? ? ?
      TABLEB (5) DEC FIXED (5,2) INIT (0, 0, 0, 0, 0),  0 0 0 0 0
      TABLEC (5) DEC FIXED (5,2) INIT ( (5) 0 ),        0 0 0 0 0
      TABLED (5) DEC FIXED (5,2) INIT (0, 0, *, 5, 5),  0 0 ? 5 5
      TABLEE (5) DEC FIXED (5,2) INIT ( (3) 0, (2) 5) ; 0 0 0 5 5
```

1. TABLEA defines an arithmetic array of five elements, of which only the *first* element is initialized. The contents of an uninitialized element is unknown.
2. TABLEB defines a similar array, with each element initialized to zero—note the five constants separated by commas.
3. TABLEC illustrates the *iteration factor* (5); the compiler generates five identical constants, one for each element.
4. TABLED initializes the first two elements with zero. The asterisk (*) tells the compiler not to initialize the third element. The fourth and fifth elements are initialized with 5.
5. TABLEE uses two iteration factors. The first iteration factor (3) initializes the first three elements, and the second (2) initializes the last two elements.

CHARACTER ARRAYS

A character array contains alphanumeric values. You may code as many literals in the INIT as there are elements in the array; the compiler stores the first literal in element-1, the second literal in element-2, and so on. Consider the following declaration of Character arrays:

```
DCL   CHARRAYA (4)        CHAR(15)   INIT('DATATECH CORP.',
                                          'ACE ELECTRONICS',
                                          'BYTE SHOP',
                                          'SYSTEMS DESIGN');
DCL   CHARRAYB (4)        CHAR(15)   INIT('DATATECH CORP.');
DCL   CHARRAYC (4)        CHAR(15)   INIT( (4) ' ' );
                                                   Repetition factor
                          Iteration factor

DCL   CHARRAYD (4)        CHAR(15)   INIT(4)(5) ' ' ),
      CHARRAYE (4)        CHAR(5)    INIT( (4)(1) 'SPACE' );
```

1. CHARRAYA defines a 4-element array, with the four literals initializing the elements in the sequence in which they are coded.

2. CHARRAYB defines a similar array, with the literal initializing only the first element. The contents of the other elements is unknown.

3. CHARRAYC attempts to initialize each element to blank using a *repetition factor*. In the case of character arrays, however, the repetition factor causes the compiler to generate a single 4-character blank field, assigned to the first element only. The other three elements are uninitialized—a common error!

4. CHARRAYD uses both a *string repetition factor* and an *iteration factor:* the repetition factor generates one 5-byte blank constant, and the iteration factor assigns the constant to each of the four elements. Coding of only one factor causes the compiler to assume that it is the repetition factor. Consequently, you should normally code an iteration factor and a repetition factor. (PL/C does not support the string repetition factor.)

5. CHARRAYE assigns the constant 'SPACE' to each element. The repetition factor tells the compiler to generate one copy of the constant, and the iteration factor assigns the constant to each of the four elements.

BIT ARRAYS

The next two examples define Bit arrays:

```
DCL   BITD (3)    BIT (8)     INIT ( (3)(8)'0'B ),
      BITE (8)    BIT (1) ;
```

1. BITD defines an array of three elements, each eight bits long. The repetition factor (8) tells the compiler to generate a constant of eight 0-bits. The iteration factor (3) causes the compiler to load the generated constant into each of the three elements. (Not available in PL/C.)

2. BITE is an array of eight elements, each one byte long. The compiler aligns

each bit element on a byte boundary, thereby requiring a full byte of storage for each byte, but using only the leftmost bit of each byte. It is an easy mistake to think that this declarative defines an array of eight bits in a single byte.

SUBSCRIPTS

Assume the following arithmetic array:

DCL TABLE(5) DEC FIXED(7,2) INIT((5) 0) ;

A reference to the name TABLE is to the entire array, that is, to all five elements. A reference to a specific element is according to a *subscript,* coded as

TABLE (subscript)

The subscript is an expression in parentheses following the array name that references one of the elements. A subscript may contain an absolute decimal value, a variable name, or an expression that combines both. A subscript must reference an element within the bounds of the array. Consequently, if the bounds of an array are 1 and 10, then a subscript referencing the array may be only 1 through 10. Values outside the bounds cause a SUBSCRIPTRANGE error, covered in a later chapter.

A subscript variable is most efficiently defined as Binary Fixed. The reason?—since IBM computers perform addressing in Binary format, the PL/I compiler must generate code to convert any other arithmetic format to Binary. Clearly, then, the use of a Character or Bit subscript will generate some very inefficient code and would be invalid on small PL/I versions.

Consider the following uses of subscripts:

```
DCL (J,K) BINARY FIXED (15) ;
1. TABLE (3) = 25 ;
2. TABLE (K + J) = 0 ;
```

Statement-1 assigns the value 25 to the third element of TABLE. In statement-2, K and J are Binary Fixed variables. If K contains 2 and J contains 3, then the statement causes zeros to store in the 5th element of TABLE.

ARITHMETIC ARRAY ASSIGNMENTS

You may perform character assignments on character arrays, and arithmetic assignments on arithmetic arrays, according to the normal rules for PL/I processing. You may assign arithmetic constants and variables to array elements and assign array elements to variables according to the normal rules of arithmetic assignments. PL/I also permits arithmetic processing on entire arrays. An array expression, however, is not an expression of conventional matrix algebra. Assume the following declaratives:

```
DCL   TABLEA (5)   DEC FIXED (7,2),
      TABLEB (5)   DEC FIXED (5,2)   INIT ( (5) 25 ),
      TABLEC (5)   DEC FIXED (5,2)   INIT ( (5) 50 ),
      SAVEVAL      DEC FIXED (5,2) ;
```

1.   Assign an arithmetic constant to every array element:

TABLEA = 0 ;   0 0 0 0 0

The effect of the assignment statement is to assign zero to each element of TABLEA as if the coding were

TABLEA(1) = 0 ;
TABLEA (2) = 0 ; etc. . .

2.   Assign an arithmetic constant to a single element:

Result in Receiving Array:
TABLEA (3) = 0 ;   ? ? 0 ? ?

or $\begin{cases} K = 3 ; \\ TABLEA (K) = 0 ; \end{cases}$

3.   Assign an array element to a variable:

SAVEVAL = TABLEB (3) ;

The statement assigns the contents of the third element of TABLEB to the variable SAVEVAL.

4.   Assign an array to an array. In such statements, both arrays must have the same number of dimensions, of identical bounds. The following statement assigns element-1 of TABLEB to element-1 of TABLEA, element-2 to element-2, and so on:

TABLEA = TABLEB ;   25 25 25 25 25

5.   Add the contents of two arrays to another array (with the same number of dimensions, and identical bounds) element-for-element:

TABLEA = TABLEB + TABLEC ;   75 75 75 75 75

6.   Perform special operations on arrays. In the following, the first statement

uses a minus prefix to reverse the sign in TABLEB, and the second statement divides each element of TABLEC by 5:

```
TABLEB = −TABLEB ;       −25 −25 −25 −25 −25 ·
TABLEC = TABLEC / 5 ;      10  10  10  10  10
```

CHARACTER ARRAY ASSIGNMENTS

You may assign Character values to array elements, and assign array elements to Character variables according to the normal rules of string assignments. Consider the following examples:

```
DCL   CHARTABA (4)    CHAR(15),
      CHARTABB (4)    CHAR(15),
      SAVEFIELD       CHAR(15);
```

1. Assign a character constant to every element:

    CHARTABA = ' ' ;

    The effect is to assign blanks to each element as if the coding were

    CHARTABA(1) = ' ' ;
    CHARTABA(2) = ' ' ; etc . . .

2. Assign a character literal to a single element:

    CHARTABA(3) = 'SYSTEMS CORP' ;

    The statement assigns the literal to the third element of the array.

3. Assign an array element to a variable:

    SAVEFIELD = CHARTABA(3) ;

    The statement assigns the contents of the third element to the variable SAVEFIELD.

4. Assign an array to another array.

    CHARTABB = CHARTABA ;

    Both arrays must have the same number of dimensions, of identical bounds. If element lengths differ, the operation truncates or pads blanks on the right according to usual string assignments.

BIT ARRAY ASSIGNMENTS

You may assign Bit string values to array elements, and assign array elements to Bit variables according to the normal rules of Bit string assignments and array processing. Rules are similar to those for Character strings, except that a Bit constant is coded with a trailing letter B, as '10110'B.

THE ITERATIVE DO-LOOP

The three types of DO-groups were introduced in Chapter 7. Of these, the third type, the iterative DO-loop, is of particular value in the processing of arrays. The DO-loop terminates with an END statement. Its general format is

DO variable = expression1 TO expression 2 [BY expression3] [WHILE (expression4)] ;

     1   2   3   4   5

1. *Control variable.* Initialized and incremented by the DO.
2. *Initial value.* Assigned initially to the control variable.
3. *Limit value.* A limit that the DO-loop checks. When the control variable exceeds this limit, the operation exits past the END to the next statement.
4. *Increment value.* The value that the operation uses to increment the control variable each time it repeats the loop. If you omit the increment, the compiler assumes 1. The value may also be negative, to facilitate a *countdown*.
5. *WHILE.* An optional WHILE condition, covered later.

For example, assume that you want to add the contents of the ten elements of an array TABLE to a variable called TOTAL. The following example uses the Binary Fixed variable K as a counter and subscript to add each element of TABLE successively.

```
DCL   TABLE(10) DEC FIXED(5,2),
      TOTAL     DEC FIXED(7,2) INIT (0),
      K         BIN FIXED(15) ;

DO K = 1 TO 10 BY 1 ;
     TOTAL = TOTAL + TABLE(K) ;
END ;
```

The DO operation performs the following, as illustrated by the accompanying flowchart:

1. Initializes the control variable K to 1.
2. Tests the control variable: If K > 10, processing exits to the statement following the END. If K is not greater than 10, the program processes the statements up to the END (it adds the contents of the Kth element of TABLE to TOTAL).
3. At END, adds the increment value 1 to the control variable K and returns to the compare statement (point 2).

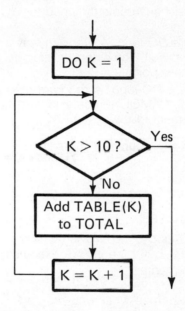

Rules and Features of DO-Loops

- *The loop.* The program executes the loop a specified number of times. On each iteration, the control variable is incremented at the END. In the previous example, at the termination of the loop, the contents of the control variable K is 11, not 10. If the limit value already exists at initialization, instead of executing the iterative DO-loop, the program drops through past the END.
- *The increment.* An increment may be negative, causing iterations that step "backward." In such a case, the operation decrements the control variable until it is lower than the limit value. BY expression-3 is optional; if omitted, the compiler assumes an increment of 1.
- *The control variable.* You may modify a control variable at any point within the loop, although this practice is not normally recommended.
- *Linking to the END statement.* An END statement may have a label, and an

IF statement may validly GO TO the label (whereupon the control variable is incremented and control returns to check the control variable to the limit):

```
        DO K = 1 TO 10 ;
            IF TABLE(K) = 0 THEN GO TO D2OEND ;
                •
                •
                •
D2OEND:   END ;
```

This use of GO TO is one of its few acceptable uses: program control goes *forward* directly to the END of a logical module. Normally, however, a nested DO-group can easily overcome the need for GO TO.

- *Entering a DO-loop.* A program may *enter* a DO-loop only through the DO statement itself. The compiler attempts to prevent statements from entering at any other point.
- *Exit from a DO-loop.* A program may *exit* from a loop at any time. In the following, if AMOUNT contains zero the LEAVE statement links directly to the statement following the END:

```
        DO K = 1 TO 10 ;
            IF TABLE(K) = 0 THEN LEAVE ;
                •
                •
                •
        END ;
```

If the DO-loop continues through to normal completion, at the end, K will contain 11, but if the LEAVE executes, K will contain the value to which it was incremented.

There are times when you may want to exit from a loop, perform some operation, and return to the point of exit. The following example uses a CALL statement to exit, print a heading, and return if LINE-COUNTER exceeds 50:

```
        DO K = 1 TO 100;
            PUT SKIP LIST (TABLE(K));
            LINE_COUNT = LINE_COUNT + 1;
            IF LINE_COUNT > 50 THEN CALL P100_HEADING;
        END;
            •
            •
            •
P100_HEADING: PROCEDURE;
        PUT PAGE ('LIST OF TABLE ELEMENTS');
        LINE_COUNT = 0;
        PAGE_COUNT = PAGE_COUNT + 1;
            •
            •
        END P100_HEADING;
```

The example defines P10PRINT as a "Procedure" (Chapter 10). CALL P10PRINT causes execution of the Procedure through to its END, where there is an automatic return to the statement following the CALL.

The WHILE Option

The WHILE option in the optimizing compiler introduces another limit value. Its format is

WHILE (expression)

Assume the following DO-loop:

DO I = J TO K WHILE (M > 25) ;

.
.
.

END ;

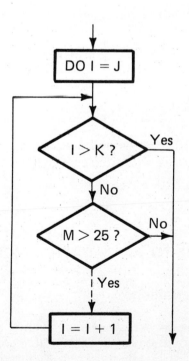

The WHILE option is enclosed in parentheses and is tested after the limit value, as shown in the flowchart. If *either* the limit value is exceeded or the WHILE condition is false, the program drops through past the END.

More Than One Specification

It is possible to code several specifications in one DO-statement, as follows:

DO J = 2 TO 6 BY 2, 8 TO 12, 16 TO 24

.

.

END ;

A use for this format occurs in plotting graphs. The operation performs the following:

1.   Initializes J to 2, executes 3 times, incrementing J by 2.
2.   Initializes J to 8, executes 5 times, incrementing J by 1.
3.   Initializes J to 16, executes 9 times, incrementing J by 1.

Another form of the DO statement involving more than one specification is the following:

DO K = L, M, N ;

.

.

END ;

The operation initializes and performs the loop three separate times. The first iteration initializes K to L, the second iteration sets K to M, and the third iteration sets K to N.

PROGRAM: ADDING TO AN ARRAY OF MONTHS

Problem Definition

Sales records contain a numeric month of sale and an amount sold. There are any number of sales for a month, in random sequence. A program has to store each amount sold in an array of twelve elements according to month: month 01 adds to element-1, month 02 adds to element-2, and so on. The program should ensure that each month is valid and should print the contents of the sales array and a total of all sales at the end.

Solution

An array of 12 months is required, defined as Decimal Fixed and initialized to zeros. The program should read the value for month into a binary declarative since it is to be used as a subscript. The program should check that the month is not lower than 01 or higher than 12 since these subscript values are outside the bounds of the array. The subscript is used to add the amount sold to the correct array element. When all input has been processed, the program can use a DO-loop to print the contents of the array. Figure 8–1 provides the program coding, with example output results. Note the following points:

STATEMENT	EXPLANATION
2	Defines MONTH as Binary because it is used as a subscript, and defines SALES_TAB(12) as a 12-month array initialized to zero.
5	Gets the first month and amount sold.
6 and 10	Control repetitive processing of DO WHILE . . . END.
7	If month is invalid, prints an error message.
8	If month is valid, adds amount sold to sales array according to month.
9	Gets next month and amount sold (if any).
11 and 14	Control DO-loop for printing 12 months' totals.
12	Prints sales by month, from 01 through 12.
13	Adds months' sales to total sales.
16	Prints total sales for all months.

Input data is as follows:

10	37.50	03	25.95	09	59.27	12	58.55
07	25.00	06	50.25	03	142.35	07	33.00
12	23.95	10	35.25	04	95.23	08	52.28
11	65.85	05	87.25	09	44.73	08	75.00

NESTED DO-LOOPS

A DO-loop may be nested within another DO-loop provided that the inner (nested) loop is completely nested. Each DO-loop should have its own END statement. The maximum number of nested DO-loops is 49 (the Subset allows only three). The program executes the innermost nested loop the required number of times,

```
1       0   PROG8A:   PROCEDURE OPTIONS(MAIN) ;

2   1   0   DCL       MONTH                  BIN FIXED (15) ,
                      AMT_SOLD               DEC FIXED (5,2),
                      SALES_TOT              DEC FIXED (7,2) INIT (0) ,
                      SALES_TAB(12)          DEC FIXED (7,2) INIT ( (12) 0 );
3   1   0   DCL       EOF                    BIT (1)         INIT ('0'B);

4   1   0             ON ENDFILE(SYSIN) EOF = '1'B ;
5   1   0             GET LIST (MONTH, AMT_SOLD) ;

        /*        ADD SALES TO ARRAY BY MONTH    */

6   1   0             DO WHILE (¬EOF) ;
7   1   1               IF MONTH < 01 | MONTH > 12 THEN
                           PUT SKIP LIST ('INVALID MONTH', MONTH) ;
8   1   1               ELSE
                           SALES_TAB(MONTH) = SALES_TAB(MONTH) + AMT_SOLD;
9   1   1               GET LIST (MONTH, AMT_SOLD) ;
10  1   1             END ;

        /*        PRINT STORED MONTH'S TOTALS        */

11  1   0             DO MONTH = 1 TO 12 ;
12  1   1               PUT SKIP LIST ( MONTH, SALES_TAB(MONTH) ) ;
13  1   1               SALES_TOT = SALES_TOT + SALES_TAB(MONTH) ;
14  1   1             END ;

15  1   0             PUT SKIP(2) LIST ('TOTAL SALES', SALES_TOT) ;
16  1   0             SIGNAL FINISH ;
17  1   0         END PROG8A ;
```

```
Output:-
                1            0.00
                2            0.00
                3          168.30
                4           95.23
                5           87.25
                6           50.25
                7           58.00
                8          127.28
                9          104.00
               10           72.75
               11           65.85
               12           82.50

        TOTAL SALES       911.41
```

FIGURE 8-1 Adding to an Array.

then the outer loop(s). An example should make the processing clear. Assume two arrays named TABLEA and TABLEB:

```
DCL   TABLEA(4) DEC FIXED (3) INIT (4, 3, 6, 2),
      TABLEB(5) DEC FIXED (3) INIT (5, 1, 3, 0, 4);
```

A program has to add the contents of all elements of TABLEA to each element of TABLEB. For example, it adds 4 + 3 + 6 + 2 to element 1 of TABLEB, giving

20, and adds 4 + 3 + 6 + 2 to element 2 of TABLEB, giving 16, and so forth. Nested DO loops are required. In the following statements, the inner loop controls TABLEA, using a subscript J to add each element from the table. The outer loop controls TABLEB, using a subscript K to add the elements to TABLEB:

```
DO K = 1 TO 5 ;
  DO J = 1 TO 4 ;
    TABLEB(K) = TABLEB(K) + TABLEA(J) ;
  END ;
END ;
```

The routine initializes K to 1, J to 1, and executes the inner loop four times. It then performs an iteration of the outer loop: increments K to 2, initializes J to 1, and executes the inner loop four more times. It continues in this manner until K equals 6.

The example is illustrative only. It is more efficient simply to add the elements of TABLEA once and then add the sum to each element of TABLEB—two separate DO-loops.

MULTIDIMENSIONAL ARRAYS

You may define an array with more than one dimension, as

$$\text{DCL ARRAY } (x_1, x_2, x_3, \ldots, x_n) \text{ attributes ;}$$

The maximum number of dimensions is 15 (the Subset is 3). Any subscripted name must have as many subscripts as there are dimensions in the array. The simplest case is a 2-dimensional array. Assume the following:

DCL TABLEA (4,3) DECIMAL FIXED (5,2) ;
       ↑ ↑
    ROW COLUMN

The dimension attribute (4,3) designates an array with two dimensions, as shown in the chart, with four rows and three columns. The chart shows a representation of how you can think of the rows and columns. In fact, the compiler stores the elements one after another, in row-major sequence, as (1,1), (1,2), (1,3), . . . , (4,3).

	Column: 1	2	3
Row: 1	1,1	1,2	1,3
2	2,1	2,2	2,3
3	3,1	3,2	3,3
4	4,1	4,2	4,3

It is important to remember this sequence because you initialize such an array like a one-dimensional array, with constants defined in row-major sequence as INIT((12) 0) or INIT (25, 10, 15, 20, 18, 7, 9, 3, 14, 12, 21, 8). The latter example would be stored as follows:

25	10	15
20	18	7
9	3	14
12	21	8

Two-dimensional Array Example: Transposing a Matrix

Figure 8–2 defines a two-dimensional array called MATRIX. The coding transposes the contents of the rows and the columns into another array called TRANMAT.

```
PROG8B:    PROCEDURE OPTIONS(MAIN);
    DCL    MATRIX (3,3) DEC FIXED (3) INIT (1, 2, 3,
                                            4, 5, 6,
                                            7, 8, 9) ;

    DCL    TRANMAT(3,3) DEC FIXED (3) ;

    DO K = 1 TO 3 ;
      DO L = 1 TO 3 ;
          TRANMAT(L,K) = MATRIX(K,L) ;
      END ;
    END ;
    PUT SKIP LIST (TRANMAT);
END PROG8B;
```

FIGURE 8–2 Transposing a Matrix.

On completion of the processing, TRANMAT will contain

```
(1, 4, 7
 2, 5, 8
 3, 6, 9)
```

A useful application of this example is for reversing an axis; for example, you may want to print a histogram vertically instead of horizontally.

Cross Sections of Arrays

An asterisk (*) in a subscript represents a "cross section of an array," indicating a use of the entire extent (not in the Subset). For example, in the previous array,

MATRIX, an expression MATRIX(*,2) would reference *every* element in column 2; that is, MATRIX(1,2), MATRIX(2,2), MATRIX(3,2), and MATRIX(4,2). For example

MATRIX(*,2) = 0 ;

sets each of these elements to zero.

The previous example transposed a matrix. The next example recodes it using a cross section of the array:

```
DO K = 1 TO 3;
        TRANMAT(*, K) = MATRIX(K, *);
END;
```

Some compilers permit a reference to a cross section of an *array of structures* (but not the Subset or the DOS optimizer).

Bounds

Normally the specification in a dimension attribute designates the upper bounds, as

DCL TABLE (3,4) DEC FIXED (5,2) ;

The compiler assumes that the lower bound is always 1; consequently, for the row, the bounds are 1 and 3, and for the column, the bounds are 1 and 4. You could also declare TABLE explicitly stating the two bounds, as

DCL TABLE (1:3, 1:4) DEC FIXED (5,2) ;

Although in this case the coding of lower bounds is redundant (and unavailable in the Subset), there are times when you may want to express the lower bound as a value other than 1. For example, assume a 2-dimensional graph, with an axis of zero. A declaration for an array to store data in such a form could be

DCL GRAPH (– 3:3, – 3:3) DEC FIXED (3) ;

Because the lower bound for both row and column is minus, there is now a valid zero position. The extent for both dimensions is 7.

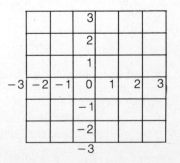

ARRAY HANDLING BUILT-IN FUNCTIONS

PL/I has a number of built-in functions that process arrays:

- ALL and ANY determine respectively if all or any bits in specified positions in an array are '1' bits (see Chapter 19).
- SUM and PROD perform arithmetic on arrays declared as floating-point (see Chapter 13). Under the DOS and OS Optimizing compilers, SUM and PROD also process arrays declared as fixed-point.
- DIM, HBOUND, and LBOUND return respectively the extent, the high bound, and the low bound of an array (not in the Subset). They are most likely used in a Procedure where they are not declared but where the array is passed as a "parameter" from another Procedure.
- POLY calculates the floating-point value of a polynominal (see Chapter 13).

DEBUGGING TIPS

- One of the most common errors involving arrays is failure to initialize or incomplete initialization. If you intend to add values to array elements, the array must be fully initialized using an iteration factor, as

      DCL ARRAY1(20) DEC FIXED (5) INIT ((20) 0);

  An attempt to add to an uninitialized DEC FIXED array will cause a Data Exception and termination of program execution.
      A CHAR or a BIT array must be initialized using both an iteration factor and a repetition factor, as

      DCL ARRAY2(20) CHAR (10) INIT ((20)(10) '');

- As a debugging aid, if you want to print the contents of an array, code a PUT statement such as

      PUT SKIP LIST (ARRAY1);

  Be sure that an arithmetic array contains valid data (that it has been initialized). An attempt to print an invalid arithmetic value will cause the program to terminate.

- Subscripts also cause error possibilities: a subscript reference must be within the bounds of an array. If a program assigns data to an array, for example, as

ARRAY(K) = VALUE;

and K references a storage area outside the array, the results are unpredictable. The assignment may erase part of another storage area in the program or even an input/output module, which the system stores at the end of programs. In the latter case, a succeeding GET or PUT may fail—with no clue as to the statement that caused the error. You can force a program to check for invalid subscripts using a *condition prefix* for SUBSCRIPTRANGE (abbreviated as SUBRG) coded before the PROCEDURE OPTIONS(MAIN) statement, as

(SUBRG):
PROGO8: PROCEDURE OPTIONS(MAIN);

The compiler will generate code to check all subscript values. Any statement that contains an invalid subscript will cause the program to terminate immediately and to print an error diagnostic.

Chapter 21 covers condition prefixes In detail.

PROBLEMS

8–1. What is the most efficient base/scale attribute for subscripts? Explain why.

8–2. Given the following array named TABLE, determine (a) its dimension, (b) the number of elements, and (c) the number of columns.

DCL TABLE(8,5) DEC FIXED (5,2);

8–3. Complete the initialization for the following arrays:
(a) DCL ARRAYA(5) DEC FIXED(5,2)   INIT . . . ; (all elements zero)
(b) DCL ARRAYB(5) CHAR(20)   INIT . . . ; (all elements blank)
(c) DCL ARRAYC(5) BIT(8)   INIT . . . ; (all elements zero)

8–4. Given the following declaratives, code a DO-loop to add the contents of each element of the array ARRVALUES to ACCUM:

DCL ACCUM   DEC FIXED(9,2) INIT (0);
DCL ARRVALUES(25) DEC FIXED(5,2);

8–5. Using TABLE defined in Problem 8–2, code a statement that adds the contents of the element in row-4, column-2 to the element in row-5, column-3.

8–6. Given K = 2 and J = 3, to which element does TABLE(K*2, J+K) refer?

8–7. Using TABLE defined in Problem 8–2, code a routine using DO statement(s) to add the value 5 to each element in columns 2 and 4.

8–8. Using TABLE defined in Problem 8–2, code routines that print the contents of each element (a) according to rows and then columns, as (1,1), (1,2), (1,3), . . ., (2,1), (2,2), (2,3), etc., and then (b) according to columns and then rows, as (1,1), (2,1), (3,1), . . ., (1,2), (2,2), (3,2) etc.

8–9. Determine the contents of GARRAY after completion of the loop.

```
DCL GARRY(6)DEC FIXED(5,2) INIT (1, 2, 3, 4, 5, 6);
DO M = 1 TO 6 BY 2;
   GARRY(M) = GARRAY(M) + 1;
END;
```

8–10. Given the following arrays:

```
DCL TABLA(5,5) DEC FIXED(5,2),
TABLB(5,5) DEC FIXED(7,2);
```

write a routine that adds respectively each element of *columns* 2, 3, anu 4 of TABLA to each element of *rows* 3, 4, and 5 of TABLB. ((1,2) adds to (3,1), (2,2) adds to (3,2), and so on.)

8–11. Determine at the end of the following DO-loop the contents of each of the variables J, K, M, P, Q, and X. Show step-by-step results for each iteration.

```
J = 11;
K = 2;
P = 14;
Q = -2;
X = 0;
DO M = 1 TO J BY K WHILE (P > Q);
   X = X + M;
   Q = Q + (X - K);
END;
```

CHAPTER 9

STRUCTURES

OBJECTIVE:

To cover the requirements for defining and handling data collections as structures and arrays of structures.

INTRODUCTION

Chapter 8 introduced one type of data collection, arrays for defining related element variables. Another type, structures, is used primarily to define fields in input records and output records and is useful for combining with arrays as arrays of structures.

DEFINING A STRUCTURE

You indicate a structure with the DCL keyword followed by the digit 1 and the name of the structure. (Blanks precede and follow the 1.) The 1 means "level 1" and designates "major level." Within the major level are defined lower levels (elements) that contain the attributes and in effect *redefine* the major level. A simple example of a structure containing related data is the following customer record:

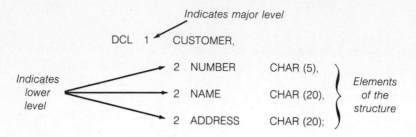

In this example, the elements NUMBER, NAME, and ADDRESS are contained in and redefine CUSTOMER. The following are points concerning the structure:

- The entire customer record, CUSTOMER, consists of NUMBER, NAME, and ADDRESS, all contained within CUSTOMER, and totaling 45 characters.

- It is possible to reference each element separately by name. A reference to NUMBER is to the 5-byte customer number field, and a reference to CUSTOMER is to the entire 45-byte record.

- The number 1 (in DCL 1 CUSTOMER) tells the compiler that this statement defines a structure and that lower-level identifiers follow. Level 1 is the major structure level. The major level may not contain a data definition (such as CHAR) or the INITIAL attribute. The major level, however, may have such attributes as DEFINED, ALIGNED or UNALIGNED, and INTERNAL or EXTERNAL.

- A comma separates each identifier in the structure.

- The number 2 in this example indicates a lower level, in this case the *elementary level*. Each identifier is coded on a separate line with the lower level indented only for ease of reading. It is possible to code more than one identifier on a line—a practice that is not recommended because of difficulty in reading.

An ordinary assignment statement can assign a value to an element in the elementary level, as

```
NUMBER = '12345' ;
NAME = 'S. HOLMES' ;
ADDRESS = '221-B BAKER ST.' ;
```

Similarly, you can initialize constants in elements of the structure just as you initialize ordinary variables:

```
DCL 1 CUSTOMER,
      2 NUMBER  CHAR (5)   INIT ('12345'),
      2 NAME    CHAR(20)   INIT ('S. HOLMES'),
      2 ADDRESS CHAR(20)   INIT ('221-B BAKER ST.') ;
```

A more complex example following illustrates other rules. This structure depicts a payroll record called PAYROLL, with three levels:

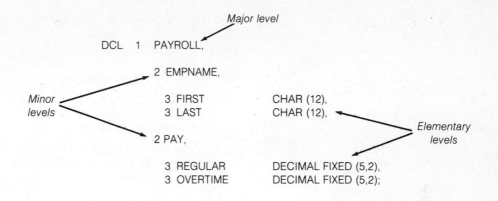

```
                              Major level

        DCL   1   PAYROLL,

                  2 EMPNAME,

Minor                 3 FIRST          CHAR (12),
levels                3 LAST           CHAR (12),
                                                          Elementary
                  2 PAY,                                  levels

                      3 REGULAR        DECIMAL FIXED (5,2),
                      3 OVERTIME       DECIMAL FIXED (5,2);
```

The structure could appear graphically as follows:

PAYROLL			
EMPNAME		PAY	
FIRST	LAST	REGULAR	OVERTIME

Note the following features of this structure:

1. DCL 1 PAYROLL denotes the major level.
2. Within PAYROLL, the number 2 signifies minor levels: EMPNAME (Employee Name) and PAY. These minor levels, which are contained within PAYROLL, are divided into lower, elementary levels.
3. The minor level EMPNAME contains two elements: FIRST and LAST (for first Name and last Name). The minor level PAY consists of two elements: REGULAR and OVERTIME. Only this lowest elementary level may have the data definition attribute.

Given the preceding structure PAYROLL, statements to calculate total pay (regular plus overtime) are as follows:

```
        DCL TOTALPAY DECIMAL FIXED (7,2) ;
        TOTALPAY = REGULAR + OVERTIME ;
```

The maximum number of levels under OS and the DOS Optimizer compiler is 15, and under the Subset, 8.

ARRAYS OF STRUCTURES

You can apply a dimension attribute to a structureat the major level or at minor levels (not in the Subset). The following declarative establishes twelve repetitions of the structure PROFIT, one structure for each month of the year:

```
              ┌─Dimension attribute generates 12 structures
    DCL 1 PROFIT(12),
          2 REVENUE,
            3 SALES          DEC FIXED (7,2),
            3 INVESTINC      DEC FIXED (7,2),
          2 EXPENSES,
            3 COSTSALES      DEC FIXED (7,2),
            3 SALARIES       DEC FIXED (7,2),
            3 OFFICEXP       DEC FIXED (7,2);
```

You may now reference the entire structure for a month as PROFIT(K), and if K contains 7, the reference is to July's profit. REVENUE(K) refers to the revenue elements for one month, and SALES(K) refers to the sales for one month.

You may also use the INIT option to initialize values. For example, to initialize each element to zero, use a repetition factor, as

3 SALES DEC FIXED (7,2) INIT ((12) 0), etc.

STRUCTURE OF ARRAYS

A structure may contain one or more arrays as elements. For example, you could recode the preceding array of structures with the dimension attribute at the elementary levels:

```
    DCL 1 PROFIT,
          2 REVENUE,
            3 SALES(12)        DEC FIXED (7,2),
            3 INVESTINC(12)    DEC FIXED (7,2),
          2 EXPENSES,
            3 COSTSALES(12)    DEC FIXED (7,2),
            3 SALARIES (12)    DEC FIXED (7,2),
            3 OFFICEXP (12)    DEC FIXED (7,2);
```

You can reference an array of structures or a structure of arrays the same way, although internally the elements are not in the same sequence. For either method of defining, a program references elementary items by means of a subscript, for example, as

SALES(K) = SALES(K) + CURRENTSALES;

You may also combine arrays of structures with a structure of arrays. Assume that a company has 10 departments and that each department has 12 expenses.

An array for this situation could be as follows:

```
DCL 1 DEPTEXPS(10),
      3 DEPTS              CHAR(3) INIT('005','063','096'...),
      3 EXPENSES(12)       DEC FIXED(7,2) INIT ( (120) 0 );
```

You can reference DEPTS as a one-dimensional array, DEPTS(K). EXPENSES, however, is a two-dimensional array, in effect 10 by 12, referenced as EXPENSES(K, L) where K refers to the department level and L to a specific expense within a department. For example, EXPENSES(2, 5) refers to the fifth expense for department '063' (see the INIT for DEPTS).

Another way to reference EXPENSES is by means of a subscripted qualified name, as follows:

DEPTEXPS(K).EXPENSES(L)

The reference is to the Kth occurrence of DEPTEXPS, and within it, the Lth element of EXPENSES. A period between the two variable names implies a qualified name.

PROGRAM: ANNUAL WEATHER

The program in Figure 9–1 defines an array of structures named WEATHER containing the average temperature and average humidity by month for one year. The program contains a DO-loop to print the contents of temperature and humidity by month (01 through 12). Assuming that the array of structures, WEATHER, contains valid data, output from the program could appear as follows:

MONTH	AVE TEMP	AVE HUMIDITY
01	42.35	25.67
02	51.63	28.75

```
1     0  PROG9A:   PROCEDURE OPTIONS(MAIN);
2   1 0  DCL 1     WEATHER(12),
                   3 TEMPERATURE        DEC FIXED (5,2),
                   3 HUMIDITY           DEC FIXED (5,2);
3   1 0  DCL       K                    BIN FIXED (15);

4   1 0            PUT SKIP LIST ('MONTH', 'AVE TEMP.', 'AVE HUMIDITY');
5   1 0            PUT SKIP;
6   1 0            DO K = 1 TO 12;
7   1 1                PUT SKIP LIST (K, TEMPERATURE(K), HUMIDITY(K));
8   1 1            END;

9   1 0        END PROG9A;
```

Figure 9-1 Annual weather.

PROBLEMS

9–1. Locate the six errors in the following structure:

```
DCL     STRUCT

        3  A        CHAR (2),
        3  B        CHAR (2),
           5  C     CHAR (4),
           5  D     CHAR (2),
        4  B        CHAR (50),
```

9–2. Define a structure named EMPLOYEE_RECORD that contains the following related data:

Employee number	(5 characters)
Employee name	(25 characters)
Date of birth	(month, day, year, each 2 characters)
Date hired	(month, day, year, each 2 characters)
Job title	(20 characters)
Salary	(maximum xxxxx.xx)

9–3. (a) Define the following as an array of structures:

Four part numbers:	0263, 0542, 2254, 2397.
Four part descriptions:	CABLES, MOLDERS, ASSEMBLERS, PATTERNS.
Four part prices:	732.25, 6033.50, 232.70, 83.95.

(b) Perform a DO-loop that prints the contents of the initialized elements as one line per part.

CHAPTER 10

PROGRAMMING STRATEGY AND STYLE

OBJECTIVE:

To examine programming style and techniques
for more maintainable and efficient programs.

INTRODUCTION

In a computer installation, programs are often revised because of errors and changes in specifications. Both the original programmer and other programmers spend considerable time rereading programs to make these changes. Installations have thrown out many sloppy programs that were easier to rewrite than to correct. Consequently, one objective of writing a program should be ease of maintenance.

Important features of improving readability and maintainability are style and technique. As programs become more complex, it is even more necessary to adopt recognizable conventions and to use the clearest, most readable programming style. There are generally accepted techniques that apply to all programming languages, and those that apply to a particular one. In this regard, this chapter covers the *structured programming* approach, program objectives, specific good PL/I practices, and programming efficiency.

STRUCTURED PROGRAMMING

Structured programming originated as a response to the need for readable programs. In established installations, 60 to 80 percent of programming effort has been devoted to maintenance—correcting and revising existing programs. In many cases, programs were found to be incomprehensible, with peculiar names, little apparent organization, and GO TO statements directing control from page to page. To remedy the situation, a more systematic approach to programming was required, and what materialized was structured programming.

Structured programming involves an approach that results in well-organized and easily maintained code. Those who have adopted it have claimed a dramatic improvement in programming performance. This section covers the basic ideas of structured programming. Because a number of textbooks are devoted exclusively to this topic, this one will not attempt to belabor the subject nor give it the pretence of scientific method.

Any reader who has followed the material to this point will have no trouble with the topic. The previous program examples were all structured in style: organized into logical modules, containing indented subsidiary statements, and lacking GO TO statements. A true structured program has the following features:

Three Basic Control Structures

A structured program consists of three basic control structures that can perform any function:

1. *Simple Sequence.* One operation directly follows another, with no logic tests to change the sequence. A simple example is "Move data to the print area" followed by "Print a line."

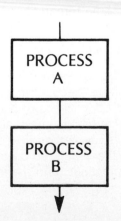

2. *Selection.* The program branches conditionally to one of two processes and returns. PL/I expresses this logic as

IF . . . THEN . . . ELSE . . .

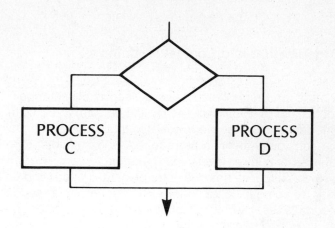

3. *Repetition.* The program repeats an operation (or series of operations) a specified number of times. There are two variations on the test. PL/I expresses the logic as

DO WHILE and DO UNTIL.

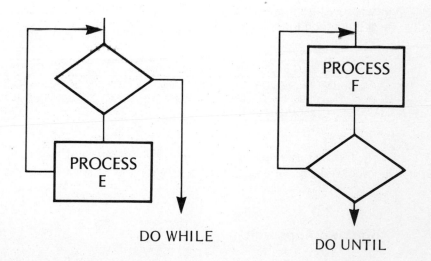

DO WHILE   DO UNTIL

Elimination of GO TO Statements

The GO TO (or unconditional Branch operation) is said to be the greatest cause of adding to program complexity. PL/I has the powerful DO statement to permit looping without use of GO TOs and to eliminate jumping forward and backward between routines. Basically, the flow of logic should be *forward*. The mind can more easily follow code that moves forward in a linear fashion rather than code that jumps back and forth between pages.

Organization into Logical Modules

A large program should have a section of main logic and various subsidiary sections of related logic. The routines are *localized* so that each routine performs only operations that are relevant to that routine. The main logic routine performs the subsidiary routines as required, and subsidiary routines can perform other routines at a lower level.

Each routine has one entry-point (at the top) and one exit (at the end). There may be some exceptions for exits, especially on serious error conditions. Each routine is restricted to 50–60 lines that may appear on a printed page, or fewer on a visual display terminal.

Indentation

To clarify the program logic, statements that are subsidiary to others should be indented. The following are two examples of an IF statement, the first not indented and the second indented:

NOT INDENTED	INDENTED
IF STOCK_QTY < RE_ORDER_POINT THEN	IF STOCK_QTY < RE_ORDER_POINT THEN
IF QTY_ON_ORDER = 0 THEN	IF QTY_ON_ORDER = 0 THEN
MESSAGE = 'RE-ORDER STOCK';	MESSAGE = 'RE-ORDER STOCK';

The first example does not clearly indicate that the three statements are uniquely related, whereas the second example makes the relationship quite clear.

Top-down Approach

The small programs to this point have required little special organization. But large programs are generally complex and are often organized, coded, and tested in segments. The program is designed around a main logic routine with various subsidiary routines that are at any low level:

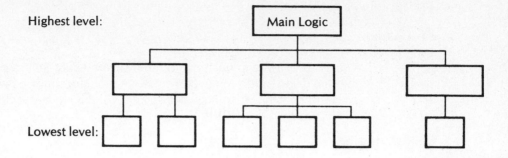

Highest level:

Lowest level:

The main logic, the highest level, provides the skeleton of the program and should be coded and tested first. Even if there is little output, the test will help to validate the overall logic. As the routines of the next lower level are coded, they are attached to the main logic for testing. Since the main logic is known to work, any error is quickly located in its subsidiary routine. Routines of lower levels are coded and tested until in time there is a fully working program.

Structured programming may require more initial added coding effort, but users who have seriously adopted it claim that their programs are more readable, have fewer errors, and are easier to maintain. The net result is a shorter time period in which programs become operational. Fortunately, PL/I lends itself very well to the structured programming style.

PROGRAMMING OBJECTIVES

The objectives of a computer program are accuracy, relevance, efficiency, and maintainability:

Accuracy

Obviously, a program should produce correct answers. This objective is first and foremost because a program that is inaccurate is useless.

Relevance

A program should produce the information that is required. Many programmers have coded 100 percent accurate programs that did not give the client the required information.

Efficiency

Subject to the deadline allowed to get the program working accurately, a program should be efficient. A good programmer can code the problem using less storage and less execution time, even without spending much (if any) more coding time.

Maintainability

A program must be revised constantly to meet new conditions and new technological releases. As a result, a program should be written with the knowledge that it will eventually have to be rewritten.

Accuracy and efficiency result from a thorough working knowledge of the computer and its language and from painstaking care in coding and testing. Maintainability results from a good approach and attitude to programming and may be accomplished by the following:

Clarity.   Use program comments wherever necessary to explain what a routine is supposed to accomplish, especially calculations and logic. Use meaningful, descriptive names for data areas. Adopt standards regarding the names of data areas, instructions, documentation, and programming style. Ensure that the coding matches the flow and logic in the flowchart. Keep in mind that a simple solution is almost always the best one.

Organization.   A good program is one that is well organized. Organize the coding into logical sections, so that related operations are together. Limit each routine if possible to one page of computer listing (about 60 lines). What is best understood is what the eye can see all at once and held in the mind. Organize Routines into a logical sequence so that the commonly performed important routines are first and the seldom-performed routines are last. Avoid instructions that jump from one routine to another and back.

Coding Techniques.   Whereas organization is concerned with the approach to programming, coding techniques involve the use of the instructions. Every language has its peculiarities and its pitfalls of redundancy. Always, the best program is simple and clear and avoids using complicated, tricky routines to solve relatively simple problems. For example, a programmer could code an extremely sophisticated PL/I routine consisting of loops within loops to scan a table of data for some specified code; PL/I, however, provides DO statements that could accomplish the same results in a few statements.

Flexibility and Expandability.   Programs should be written with the fact in mind that over time requirements change. For example, file sizes grow and price levels increase. Defined field lengths should provide for future larger values. Up to a point, main storage is cheaper than programming time, and defining a few extra bytes for larger field lengths is low-cost insurance against program revisions.

STATEMENT LABELS

Any PL/I statement may have a *label* (or *name,* or technically *label prefix*), followed by a colon. For example, a label for the name of a program precedes the Main Procedure, as

    label: PROCEDURE OPTIONS (MAIN);

In this case, the label is an external identifier, limited to six or seven characters depending on the compiler. Other labels within a program preceding statements such as

    A20READ: GET LIST (CODE, ITEM);

are internal identifiers, limited to 31 characters. By means of a label, a program can reference the statement from any other part of the program. An acceptable use of labels is to help associate an END with its DO, especially where DO statements are nested:

    label: DO WHILE (. . .);
                .
                .
                .
    END label;

GO TO STATEMENT

The normal flow of program execution is sequential, one statement after another. Certain *control statements* permit the program to "branch" to other statements in the program. These include

    GO TO (unconditional branch), IF (conditional branch), CALL, DO, RETURN, END

The GO TO statement enables you to branch unconditionally to any statement label. The general format is

GO TO label ; or GOTO label ;

Because extensive use of GO TO statements can make a program confusing, a standard in many installations is to avoid them completely.

LEAVE STATEMENT (PL/I OPTIMIZER)

LEAVE is a relatively new and useful statement that is available in the PL/I Optimizer compilers. LEAVE permits program control to exit from a DO-group or DO-loop directly to the statement following the corresponding END. Because its format permits an optional label operand, LEAVE can specify an exit-point:

LEAVE [label] ;

Assume the following nested DO statements, each with a label:

```
P100:       DO ... ;
P200:          DO ... ;
P300:             DO ... ;
                     IF CODE = '35' THEN LEAVE ;
                     ...
                  END P300 ;
               END P200 ;
            END P100 ;
```

The IF statement with a conditional LEAVE is in the innermost nested DO labeled P300. As coded, LEAVE would exit only from the P300 loop past END P300, but would continue in P200. You can specify exiting from outer levels by use of a label on LEAVE. For example, LEAVE P200 would designate an exit from the DO-group labeled P200; program control, however, would still be in the DO-group labeled P100. LEAVE P100 would designate an exit from all three levels past P100. The use of such labels not only facilitates the use of LEAVE but also clearly associates an END with its originating DO.

PROCEDURES AND CALL

Larger programs generally consist of logical sections of code. For example, a payroll program involves calculation of wage, income tax, FICA, and other deductions. Each of these calculations is logically independent of the others. You can then organize them into separate *internal procedures,* as in Figure 10–1.

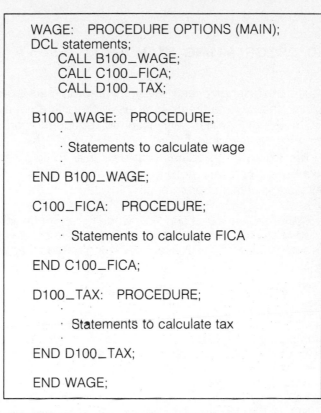

```
WAGE:   PROCEDURE OPTIONS (MAIN);
DCL statements;
    CALL B100_WAGE;
    CALL C100_FICA;
    CALL D100_TAX;

B100_WAGE:   PROCEDURE;
        ·
        · Statements to calculate wage
        ·
END B100_WAGE;

C100_FICA:   PROCEDURE;
        ·
        · Statements to calculate FICA
        ·
END C100_FICA;

D100_TAX:   PROCEDURE;
        ·
        · Statements to calculate tax
        ·
END D100_TAX;

END WAGE;
```

FIGURE 10–1 Organization of Procedures.

Only a CALL statement can execute a Procedure. Consequently, the statement

```
CALL B100_WAGE;
```

would cause program control to begin execution of B100_WAGE at its first executable statement. When the Procedure executes its END statement, program control returns to the statement following the CALL.

Normal processing of a Procedure is therefore entry at the top and exit at the bottom. Procedures have much more to them than just the above description. For now, assume that all Procedures are fully defined within the MAIN Procedure, and that the MAIN Procedure contains all DCL statements.

The use of Procedures is an important element of structured programming. Later chapters use Procedures extensively and fully describe their use.

STRUCTURED PROGRAMMING STANDARDS

Because of debugging and revising, programmers spend more time reading programs than writing them. As a result, there is a need for readability—simple code, meaningful names, elimination of redundant words and statements, and clear, straightforward flow of logic.

The following guidelines provide some common structured programming conventions. There are no universal standards, and actual practices vary by installation or personal preference.

1. *Declare all variables and files.* Code full attributes for variables. Allowing the compiler to default various attributes can be a source of confusion and potential errors. Also, avoid declaring names that are PL/I keywords, such as

   DCL DECIMAL FIXED DECIMAL(5,2);

2. *Use descriptive names to make the program self-documenting.* Avoid meaningless names like A, B, and X, or even AMOUNT_1 and SWITCH. There is a trade-off between meaningful names (often long) and a natural reluctance to repeatedly spell out long names. It is advisable to use clear abbreviations to reduce verbiage and spelling errors. Thus, the name PREVIOUS_CUSTOMER_NUMBER is still clear when coded as PREV_CUST_NO. But be careful of ambiguities: TEMP could mean "temporary" or "temperature," and INV could mean "inventory," "invoice," or "inverse."

3. *Use comments where necessary.* If variables have meaningful names, you can reduce the need for comments. It is always desirable to code a comment before each Procedure to explain its purpose and wherever necessary to clarify logic or an algorithm.

4. *Align and indent consistently.* Adopt the installation standards for aligning, beginning in columns, such as

   ```
   COLUMN

       2   DCL and labels
       8   Executable statements and comments if a full line
      31   Attribute lists
      41   Comments if on the same line as a statement
   ```

5. *Minimize use of abbreviations.* Use abbreviations only for common keywords such as CHAR, PIC, DEC, and BIN. For clarity, fully code less common

keywords such as SUBSCRIPTRANGE (instead of SUBRG) and FIXEDOV-
ERFLOW (instead of FOFL).

6. *Code only one statement on a line.* PL/I "free format" is a mixed blessing
   that encourages sloppy coding practices. Statements normally should align
   directly one under the other, with any comments similarly aligned:

```
INTEREST  =  PRINCIPAL * RATE ;                    /* CALCULATE  INTEREST*/
NEW_BALANCE = PRINCIPAL + INTEREST ;               /* UPDATE NEW BALANCE*/
```

7. *Indent clauses of IF statements.* One common practice matches the ELSE
   directly under the IF:

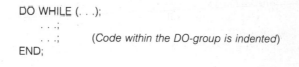

8. *Indent statements within DO-groups.* Also, align each END with its matching
   DO.

```
DO WHILE (. . .);
    . . .;
    . . .;       (Code within the DO-group is indented)
END;
```

9. *Insert blank lines between logical sections of code.* Spaces between declaratives and executable statements, for example, help make a program
   more readable.

10. *Number and indent structure levels consistently.* The structure name must
    be numbered 1, but other levels may be any higher number. Some instal-
    lations use a standard of numbering, such as 1, 3, 5, for each level so that
    space is left if another level must be inserted. In any event, each minor level
    and elementary level should be indented consistently.

11. *Minimize the use of GO TO statements.* Extravagant use of GO TO state-
    ments can result in a confusing program that jumps about from page to
    page. The use of indentation coupled with intelligent use of IF..THEN DO,
    DO WHILE, and SELECT tend to provide clearer logic.

12. *Use blanks around arithmetic and comparison operations.* For example:

```
PAY = ROUND (HOURS * RATE, 2) ;
```

is clearer than

```
PAY=ROUND(HOURS*RATE,2);
```

13. *Explicitly code program termination.* Instead of letting program execution

"drop off" the program end, code SIGNAL FINISH or RETURN to clearly indicate end of execution.

14. *Restrict internal procedures to one printed page.* It is easier for the mind to entertain logic that is contained on one page. Also, every such routine should have one entry-point (at the top) and one exit (at the bottom). Procedure labels should be in alphabetic sequence to aid in locating them:

```
A100MAIN: PROCEDURE;
  .
  .
B100CALC: PROCEDURE;
  .
  .
C100END: PROCEDURE:
  .
  .
etc.
```

PROGRAM CONTROL

Earlier programs introduced a structured programming technique to handle input logic by using an initial GET and a DO WHILE that processed the record and read the next one. The approach merits further explanation. Assume the following code, with no initial GET, but with the GET at the beginning of the DO WHILE:

```
ON ENDFILE (SYSIN) EOF = '1'B;
DO WHILE ( ¬ EOF);
  GET LIST (. . .);
    .
    .
  PUT SKIP LIST (. . .);
END;
```

In this case, the program would read and process correctly until reaching the end-of-file. At this point, however, ON ENDFILE moves '1' to EOF and *continues processing statements following the GET.* Because no new record was read, the program reprocesses items from the last input record (that were already processed prior to reaching end-of-file) before reaching the END and returning to the main logic. The solution is to code an initial GET and another GET in the DO WHILE group immediately before the END.

PROGRAM LOGIC

A solution to difficult programming logic may require some ingenuity. Assume that a customer record contains aged balances owed: current due, 31–60 days, 61–90 days, and over 90 days due. Any payment that the customer makes applies to the oldest amount—first to over 90, then to 61–90, then to 31–60, then to current due. For example, a customer's balance is

CURRENT	31–60	61–90	OVER 90 DAYS
$200	$250	$150	$210

A payment of $500 erases the over 90 days balance ($210), then the 61–90 balance ($150), and finally part of the 31–60 ($140). The account is now

CURRENT	31–60	61–90	OVER 90 DAYS
$200	$110	$0	$0

Let's try a programming approach to solve the logic:

	curr	31–60	61–90	over 90	payment
If payment ≤ over90, subtract payment from over90, exit;	200	250	150	210	500
Else subtract over90 from payment,	200	250	150	210	290
clear over90 to zero	200	250	150	0	210

The program would have to repeat for 61–90, 31–60, and current. *There must be a simpler way.* Let's start again:

	200	250	150	210	500
Subtract payment from over 90	200	250	150	− 290	
If over 90 < 0, add over 90 to over 60, clear over 90 to zero;	200	250	− 140	0	
If over 60 < 0, add over 60 to over 30, clear over 60 to zero;	200	110	0	0	
If over 30 < 0, add over 30 to current, clear over 30 to zero.	200	110	0	0	

The second solution involves only three IF statements. Since they are nested, a balance >0 causes the logic to bypass remaining statements.

PROGRAM EFFICIENCY

Today, the major concern of most computer installations is *user* efficiency rather than computer efficiency. Because programming costs are increasing and computer costs are declining, the former has become the largest share of the installation budget. It is justifiable, therefore, to place an emphasis on programmer efficiency. However, if two programmers were each to write a program to solve the same problem, one program may be very efficient in its use of storage and execution time, whereas the other could be extravagant in space and execution time. If both programs require the same time to code and are equally clear and maintainable, then why not adopt the practices that produce an efficient program?

Some practices that generate efficient code include the following:

- *Initialization.* Initialize variables with blanks or zeros rather than assign such values at the start of program execution. If you do not intend to use dynamic allocation, then the use of the STATIC attribute will reduce storage space. You can code

    DEFAULT RANGE(*) STATIC;

    which will cause declaratives to default to the STATIC attribute.

- *Field length.* Define as the same length fields that are to be moved or compared one to the other.
- *Comparison.* Compare fields of the same data format: numeric to numeric and character to character.
- *Data alignment.* In the following structure, both BINFIELD and FLTFIELD align on fullword (4-byte) boundaries:

```
DCL 1 SAVERECORD,
      3 CHFIELD      CHAR (5),
      3 BINFIELD     BIN FIXED (31),
      3 DECFIELD     DEC FIXED (09),
      3 FLTFIELD     DEC FLOAT (16);
```

Consequently, there could be three unused bytes following CHFIELD and three unused bytes following DECFIELD. Not many at all, but if SAVE-RECORD is an array of a structure,

    DCL 1 SAVERECORD(200),

then the wasted space is 6 × 200 = 1200 bytes. The structure can be recoded with no wasted space if the Binary Fixed and Decimal Float variables are defined first.

- *Use of DEFINED.* Use the DEFINED attribute wherever possible instead of String-handling operations such as SUBSTR and STRING.
- *Arithmetic fields.* For 370-type computers, Fixed Decimal fields should be defined as an odd number of digits. The IBM 360/370 stores Fixed Decimal fields in packed format, two digits per byte, plus a half-byte for the sign. The following depicts 2-, 3-, and 4-byte fields respectively containing 3, 5, and 7 digits:

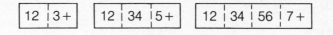

The compiler generates the most efficient code if fields being added or compared have the same attributes and precision.

• *Choice of base and scale.* Use Binary Fixed for all subscripting and DO-loop control variables—the most efficient attributes. Use Decimal Fixed for all ordinary arithmetic used on data that is entered from cards or terminals and that is to be printed or displayed. Use Decimal Float only where another arithmetic format cannot handle the calculations.

• *Arithmetic expressions.* In an arithmetic expression, perform division last if possible. For example, in an expression such as

$$10 * (3 / 6)$$

the divide executes first. You can generally gain better precision if you perform the multiplication before division, as

$$(10 * 3) / 6.$$

Become familiar with the computer's Assembler (low-level) language to gain an insight into the machine's operation, storage handling of data, and generated machine code. It is difficult to state specifically the most efficient coding techniques in all cases because different PL/I compilers may generate different Assembler code. Consequently, an efficient practice for one version may not be so efficient for another. The manufacturers' manuals provide suggestions for efficient practices for compiler versions.

The Optimizing compilers will print the Assembler code if you stipulate LIST in the PROCESS statement; a reader familiar with Assembler language will be amazed at some of the clumsy generated code.

CONTROL OVER ARITHMETIC PROCESSING: BUILT-IN FUNCTIONS

It is sometimes necessary to control the precision of arithmetic values generated by expressions. Such control is often required for a Decimal Fixed expression because of its limited precision (15 decimal digits).

Arithmetic built-in functions enable you to control the conversion of base, scale, mode, and precision during arithmetic operations. Maximum precisions are Decimal Fixed = 15, Binary Fixed = 31, Decimal Float = 16 (or 33 with extended precision), and Binary Float = 53. In this section, p means the total length of the variable in digits, and q is the number of digits after the decimal or binary point.

ABS

This function returns the absolute value of an expression. In the following example, the absolute value of -25 is 25, delivered to MAG:

```
DCL   MAG      DECIMAL FIXED (5) ,
      NEGAT    DECIMAL FIXED (5) INIT (−25) ;

MAG = ABS(NEGAT) ;
```

ADD, MULTIPLY, and DIVIDE

These functions are useful in controlling precision during fixed-point arithmetic operations, especially where there is danger of raising the FIXEDOVERFLOW condition.

The ADD format is

$$sum = ADD(a, b, p, q) ;$$

For ADD, a and b are the two fields to be added, and p is the number of decimal or binary digits the operation is to maintain. For fixed-point arithmetic, q gives the number of decimal or binary places of precision, and for floating-point, q is omitted. In the following, Example I exceeds the maximum number of digits generated for Decimal Fixed, 15, and raises the FIXEDOVERFLOW condition. Example II uses ADD to control precision and avoid the error.

```
DCL SUMA      DEC FIXED (15,6) INIT (123456789) ,
    SUMB      DEC FIXED (15,6) INIT (880000000) ,
    TOTAL     DEC FIXED (13, 3) ;
```

I − TOTAL = SUMA + SUMB ;   II − TOTAL = ADD (SUMA, SUMB, 15, 3) ;

METHOD I—INVALID	METHOD II USING ADD—VALID
123456789.000000	123456789.000
880000000.000000	880000000.000
(1) 003456789.000000	001003456789.000
↑	
Overflow 15 digits	15 digits

The MULTIPLY format is

$$product = MULTIPLY(a, b, p, q);$$

The multiplicand and multiplier are a and b. The precision p and q works the same as for ADD.

The DIVIDE format is

$$quotient = DIVIDE(a, b, p, q) ;$$

The dividend is a, and the divisor is b. The precision p and q work the same as for ADD and MULTIPLY.

BINARY and DECIMAL

These functions are used to convert bases according to specified precision. Especially for very small values, converting from one base to another can yield inaccurate results; these functions can help reduce the error. BINARY converts a decimal value to binary, and DECIMAL converts a binary value to decimal. The BINARY and DECIMAL formats are

binary-value = BINARY(decimal-value, p, q) ;
decimal-value = DECIMAL(binary-value, p, q) ;

- p gives the constant specifying the number of digits to be maintained.
- q for fixed-point values only is a constant specifying the scale factor.

CEIL and FLOOR

CEIL returns the smallest integer greater than or equal to a given value, and FLOOR returns the highest integer less than or equal to a given value. For example:

```
DCL   RATEA       DEC FIXED (3,2) INIT (5.74),
      RATEB       DEC FIXED (3,2) ;

      RATEB = CEIL(RATEA) ;    /* ANSWER = 6.00 */
      RATEB = FLOOR(RATEA) ;   /* ANSWER = 5.00 */
```

MAX and MIN

MAX returns the largest value from a set of two or more arguments, and MIN returns the smallest value. There may be up to 64 arguments, but these may not include array names. For example:

```
DCL   SCOREA      DEC FIXED (5,2) INIT (3.50),
      SCOREB      DEC FIXED (5,2) INIT (7.20),
      SCOREC      DEC FIXED (5,2) ;

      SCOREC = MAX(SCOREA, SCOREB) ; /* ANSWER = 7.20 */
      SCOREC = MIN(SCOREA, SCOREB) ; /* ANSWER = 3.50 */
```

MOD

In effect, MOD extracts the *remainder* of a specified division (by definition, the smallest positive value that must be subtracted from the dividend to make it precisely divisible by the divisor). The MOD format is

remainder = MOD(dividend, divisor) ;

For example, if the dividend is 62 and the divisor is 12, then the remainder is 2. For negative dividends, the operation returns the *modular equivalent* of the remainder. For example, if the remainder in the preceding were −2, then the modular equivalent that would be returned is 12 minus 2, or 10.

PRECISION

This function enables you to specify the precision and rightmost truncation of an arithmetic value. The PRECISION format is

result = PRECISION(expression, p, q) ;

* p is the number of digits of required precision,
* q (for fixed-point only) is an integer designating the scale factor.

In the following, Example I causes a FIXEDOVERFLOW. Dividing 1 by 3 causes the program to generate extensive precision—it assumes that the result will not exceed 1.0 and can safely generate 14 digits to the right of the decimal point. But adding this value to 125.0 causes truncation of the leftmost 12. Example II uses PRECISION to avoid the overflow:

DCL CTR DEC FIXED (5) INIT (125) ;

I: ANS = CTR + 1/3 ;   II: ANS = CTR + PRECISION (1/3, 11, 6) ;

EXAMPLE I—INVALID	EXAMPLE II USING PRECISION—VALID
0.33333333333333	00000.333333
125.00000000000000	00125.000000
125.33333333333333	00125.333333
FOFL 15 digits	

SIGN

This function delivers a Binary Fixed integer signifying whether a value is positive (+1), zero (0), or negative (−1). Assume the following example:

```
DCL   K        BIN FIXED (15),
      TOTAL    DEC FIXED (5,2) INIT (-25.00) ;

      K = SIGN(TOTAL) ;        /* K NOW CONTAINS -1 */
```

TRUNC

This function truncates the fractional part of a specified value and delivers the integer portion. For example:

```
DCL  AMOUNT   DEC FIXED (5,2) INIT (123.45) ;

     AMOUNT = TRUNC(AMOUNT) ; /* AMOUNT IS NOW 123.00 */
```

DEBUGGING TIPS

You may define Procedures that are internal to the MAIN Procedure. Each internal Procedure should be defined as separate from other Procedures, with no overlapping. Technically, you may define a Procedure *within* another Procedure provided that the contained Procedure is fully contained.

Any declarative defined within an internal Procedure is unique to that Procedure. For now, define all declaratives in the MAIN Procedure so that all internal Procedures recognize them. Chapter 20 covers Procedures in detail.

PROBLEMS

10–1. What are the features of a structured program?

10–2. What are the objectives of a computer program?

10–3. What practices can make programs more easily maintained? Explain.

10–4. What are the advantages (if any) of organizing a program into a main logic section and various separate routines?

10–5. Why does current thinking consider the use of GO TO statements undesirable?

10–6. Code the following program that calculates annual depreciation on company assets. Records are in sequence of Asset number.

COLUMN	
1–2	Record code (84)
4–7	Asset number
9–28	Description
30–31	Year purchased
33–34	Life expectancy in years
36–41	Original cost (no cents)
43–48	Salvage value (no cents)

There is only one record per asset number. Each record requires calculation of a depreciation rate. Show all details on the print line, including description and calculated rate.

The company uses the "sum of years' digits" depreciation method. Assume that an asset purchased in 1984 for $1,000 has a life expectancy of five years and an estimated salvage value at the end of five years of $200. The calculation of depreciation for each year based on $800 ($1,000 − 200) is as follows:

YEAR		ANNUAL RATE	DEPRECIATION
1984	1	5/15	$266.67 (5/15 × $800)
1985	2	4/15	213.33
1986	3	3/15	160.00
1987	4	2/15	106.67
1988	5	1/15	53.33
Totals		15/15	$800.00

The sum of digits formula, where n = life expectancy, is

$$\frac{n(n + 1)}{2} = \frac{5(5 + 1)}{2} = \frac{30}{2} = 15$$

The formula for the depreciation rate is

$$r = \frac{\text{number of remaining years}}{\text{sum of digits of life in years}}$$

In the example, if the current year is 1986, there are three years remaining. Current year's depreciation is

$$\frac{3}{15} \times \$800 = \$160.00$$

For each asset, calculate depreciation only for the current year. Provide test data with various years of purchase, life expectancy, original cost, and salvage value.   For assets that are already fully depreciated (for example,   purchased 12 years ago   with a life expectancy of ten years), calculate zero depreciation.

At end-of-file, print total depreciation for all records. You will need the date as first record to provide the current year.

PART III

PL/I PROGRAMMING IN MATHEMATICS AND SCIENCE

CHAPTER 11

FUNDAMENTAL SCIENCE PROGRAMMING

OBJECTIVE:

To examine fundamental features of science programming, including binary data and the mathematical built-in functions.

INTRODUCTION

Business programming is concerned chiefly with processing of *files.* The files consist, for example, of all the records for customers, for inventory stock, and for employees. Maintaining the files, sorting files, and producing reports is a large part of the computing effort. Science programming, on the other hand, is more concerned with *algorithms.* There are generally fewer records and fewer exceptions, but computations are more complex.

There is no definite distinction between business and science programming. Many installations have already programmed the conventional business applications and are applying scientific analysis to business problems such as inventory control, marketing strategies, transportation/distribution, and production control.

ARITHMETIC FORMATS

PL/I provides four arithmetic formats using a base of DECIMAL or BINARY and a scale of FIXED or FLOAT. The business programmer uses Decimal Fixed extensively for normal arithmetic programming of values such as prices, quantities, rates, and hours and uses Binary Fixed for subscripting arrays and DO-loop control variables. The scientific programmer has a different emphasis for arithmetic formats:

1. *Decimal Fixed.* Use for values that enter from a terminal or cards and that involve conventional computations that do not exceed 15-digit precision.
2. *Binary Fixed.* Use for subscripts, for DO-loop control variables, and for computations that do not exceed 31 binary digits of precision.
3. *Floating-point.* Use for values that are extremely large or small and for computations in which the precision of the answer is unknown.

Keep in mind that floating-point is often an inefficient way to process. A data item enters main storage from terminal or cards as a *character* value. The code that the compiler generates converts the character value to Decimal Fixed (technically, "packs" it into *packed* format). The program then converts the packed value into *binary* in a general-purpose register and then converts the binary value into *floating-point* in a floating-point register. This latter conversion involves quite a few steps because it generates an exponent for the floating-point value.

SIMPLIFYING A FORMULA

You can often reduce computation time considerably (and perhaps improve precision) by simplifying an algorithm. For example, the distance (d) that an object falls in time (t) in general terms is

$$d = \tfrac{1}{2}at^2$$

Since acceleration (a) is a fixed value 32 feet/sec^2, then the formula is simplified to

$$d = 16t^2$$

Similarly, the calculation of time taken to fall a given distance,

$$t = \sqrt{\frac{2d}{32}}$$

can be simplified to

$$t = \sqrt{\frac{d}{16}}$$

and further to

$$t = \frac{\sqrt{d}}{4}$$

In PL/I, the coding could be

T = SQRT (DIST) /4 ; or T = SQRT (DIST) *.25 ;

Since the computer can multiply faster than divide, the second example that multiplies by .25 (the reciprocal of 4) will execute faster, especially if there are many repeated computations.

EXPONENTIATION

Many formulas involve the use of exponentiation. The following provides the various algebraic rules concerning use of exponents:

EXPRESSION	EQUIVALENT EXPRESSION	EXAMPLE
x^0	1, if $x \neq 0$	$4^0 = 1$
x^n	$x \cdot x \cdot x \cdots \cdot x$	$4^3 = 4 \cdot 4 \cdot 4 = 64$
x^{-n}	$\frac{1}{x^n}$	$4^{-3} = \frac{1}{4^3} = \frac{1}{64}$
$x^{1/n}$	$\sqrt[n]{x}$	$4^{1/2} = \sqrt[2]{4} = 2$
$x^{-1/n}$	$\frac{1}{\sqrt[n]{x}}$	$4^{-1/2} = \frac{1}{\sqrt[2]{4}} = \frac{1}{2}$
$x^{m/n}$	$\left(\sqrt[n]{x}\right)^m$	$64^{2/3} = \left(\sqrt[3]{64}\right)^2$
$x^{-m/n}$	$\frac{1}{(\sqrt[n]{x})^m}$	$64^{-2/3} = \frac{1}{\left(\sqrt[3]{64}\right)^2} = \frac{1}{4^2} = \frac{1}{16}$

BINARY DATA FORMAT

Binary format is the basic means by which a computer processes data and is the most efficient format for repetitive processing.

Internal Representation

The internal representation of Binary Fixed data is either 15 or 31 digits:

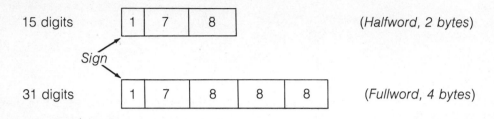

The sign is the leftmost bit: a 0-bit means positive and a 1-bit means negative. The compiler converts a literal coded as decimal value 25 into 15-digit binary precision as

0	0000000	00011001

Binary Arithmetic

The rules of simple binary arithmetic are

$$
\begin{array}{ccccc}
0 & 0 & 1 & 1 & 1 \\
+0 & +1 & +0 & +1 & +1 \\
\hline
0 & 1 & 1 & 10(2) & +1 \\
& & & & \overline{11(3)}
\end{array}
$$

For simplicity, the following examples of decimal and binary addition assume five-bit values, with the leftmost bit the sign:

Dec	Binary	Dec	Binary	Dec	Binary
4	0 0100	7	0 0111	7	0 0111
+2 =	0 0010	+2 =	0 0010	+7 =	0 0111
6	0 0110	9	0 1001	14	0 1110

Negative numbers are expressed in what is called *two's complement* form. To obtain a negative binary number, reverse all the bits of its positive value (a 0-bit becomes 1, and a 1-bit becomes 0), then add 1. (The same procedure converts negative values to positive values.) For example, assuming a five-bit field, what is the binary representation of -7?:

Decimal value 7 = 0 0111
Reverse bits = 1 1000
Add 1 = 1 1001 (two's complement representation of −7)

$\uparrow$
Sign bit

For subtraction, the field being subtracted is converted to its two's complement and then added:

Decimal value   7   0 0111   0 0111
Subtract   −5 = −0 0101 = 1 1011 (add two's complement of 5)
Result   2   0 0010 (binary value 2)

Note that there is a *carry into and out of the sign position.* Where there is both a carry into and out of the sign bit, the result is correct, not an overflow. *Invalid overflows* occur on the following conditions:

1. *Overflow caused by carry into the sign position:*

Decimal value   9   0 1001
Add   +9 = 0 1001
Result   18   1 0010 (negative value, minus 14)

There is a carry into the sign position, and none out of it. The sum is an incorrect negative value. To determine the value of 1 0010, reverse the bits (0 1101), then add '1' (0 1110). Since this value is +14, then 1 0010 has a value of −14, but was supposed to be +18.

2. *Overflow caused by carry out of the sign position:*

Decimal value   −9   1 0111
Add   +(−9)= 1 0111
Result   −18   0 1110 (positive value, plus 14)

There is no carry into the sign position but one out of it. The sum is an incorrect positive value, +14 instead of −18.

Binary Point

It is also possible to express a binary (binal) point. The following converts a binary number to its decimal equivalent:

$$101.111 = 2^2 + 0^1 + 2^0 + 2^{-1} + 2^{-2} + 2^{-4}$$
$$= 4 \ + 0 + 1 + \frac{1}{2} + \frac{1}{4} + \frac{1}{8} = 5.875$$

Warning: Mixing decimal and binary values in an arithmetic statement can cause unexpected results. The following is supposed to add the binary value .01B (¼):

DCL INT BINARY FIXED (15, 3) INIT (1B) ;

Incorrect: INT = INT + .01 ;   /* Result = 1 + 1/100 */
Correct: INT = INT + .01B ;   /* Result = 1 + 1/4   */

Decimal value
Binary value

The first example that adds .01 (or 1/100) is incorrect, whereas the second example that adds .01B (or 1/4) is correct.

Defining Binary Values

There are only two lengths for Binary—defined lengths up to 15 become 15, and lengths from 16 through 31 become 31. You will see the significance of this rule later in this chapter.

You can initialize a binary declarative with either a binary or a decimal constant. The following both generate the identical binary value:

DCL J BIN FIXED (15) INIT (25) ,
K BIN FIXED (15) INIT (11001B) ;

Remember, however, that a binary constant contains only 0 and 1 digits and is followed by the letter B. Omission of the B causes the compiler to assume a decimal value. Watch out for confusing the two bases. For example, let's define a value for pi as binary with maximum precision in the fraction:

DCL PI BIN FIXED (31,30) INIT (3.14159) ;

There is a *serious error* in this definition: the compiler will store the constant as a binary value that is equivalent to 1.14159. Can you see why? Examine the *binary* representation of the constant and the defined (p,q) precision. The binary representation of 3.0 is 11.0, but the precision of PI (31,30) provides for only one integer digit. Consequently, the leftmost digit is truncated (technically, a SIZE error). A correct definition would be

DCL PI BIN FIXED (31,29) INIT (3.14159) ;

Each decimal digit is represented by $\log_2 10$ (about 3.32) bits, and you can easily lose precision on either side of the decimal point.

You can define an array of binary values in the usual way. The following statement defines an array of 25 binary elements, all initialized to zero:

DCL BINARR1 (25) BIN FIXED (15) INIT ((25) 0) ;

Do not, however, suppose that the following array saves any storage space:

DCL BINARR2 (25) BIN FIXED (06) INIT ((25) 0) ;

The compiler automatically applies 15-bit precision for each element, so that BINARR2 is the same size as BINARR1.

Limitations of Binary Arithmetic

Binary format is efficient for counting and subscripting. If you define a binary value with digits to the right of the binary point, be careful of its use in an arithmetic expression. Assume the following example:

```
DCL SCORE BINARY FIXED(31,10) INIT (50);
SUM = SCORE**2;
```

A PL/I program generates as much precision as possible for an expression. In this case, the exponent times the binary precision is $2 \times 10 = 20$, resulting in 20 positions to the right of the binary point. The exponentiation in the expression will therefore generate a value of $50^2 = 2500$, or, in binary

100111000100.0—(20)—0

In order to contain the value in the 31-bit maximum length, the operation truncates the leftmost 1-bit, causing a FIXEDOVERFLOW error (see Chapter 21 for details). In PL/I, you should normally perform extended computations, especially those that involve exponentiation, in floating-point.

PROGRAM: CALCULATE THE VALUE OF PI

Problem Definition

A program is to calculate the value of pi. The following geometric progression (in simple terms) is known to converge on the value of pi:

$$\pi = \frac{4}{1} - \frac{4}{3} + \frac{4}{5} - \frac{4}{7} + \frac{4}{9} - \frac{4}{11} \ldots \pm \frac{4}{n}$$

Unfortunately, even after 1000 computations, the result of 3.14259158 reaches only two decimal places of accuracy. Admittedly, this exercise is not very practical but does illustrate some useful points.

Solution

Figure 11–1 gives the program solution. A DO-loop controls the repetitive calculations and the divisor K (DO K = 1 TO 2001 BY 2). The loop has to alternate the sign of each result, starting with positive. A Bit logic operation resolves this problem, and a positive sign is changed to negative by the use of a minus prefix operator:

$$FACTOR = -FACTOR;$$

```
1      0  PROG11A:
                  PROCEDURE OPTIONS(MAIN) ;

2    1  0  DCL      (PI,
                    FACTOR)      BIN FIXED (31,28) INIT (0B);
3    1  0  DCL      (K, TEST)    BIN FIXED (15),
                    KTRUNC       BIN FIXED (15,8) ;
4    1  0  DCL      MINUS        BIT (1)           INIT ('0'B);

5    1  0          DO K = 1 TO 2001 BY 2 ;
6    1  1              FACTOR = 4.0 / K ;
7    1  1              IF MINUS THEN
                          DO;
8    1  2                  FACTOR = -FACTOR ;
9    1  2                  MINUS  = '0'B ;
10   1  2              END;
11   1  1              ELSE
                          MINUS  = '1'B ;
12   1  1              PI = PI + FACTOR ;
13   1  1              KTRUNC = K ;
14   1  1              TEST = KTRUNC ;
15   1  1              IF TEST = 01 THEN PUT SKIP LIST (PI) ;
16   1  1          END;

17   1  0          PUT SKIP LIST (PI) ;
18   1  0          SIGNAL FINISH ;
19   1  0      END PROG11A;
```

Output:-

```
        4.000000000
        3.149344481
        3.145483672
        3.144190035
        3.143541939
        3.143152646
        3.142892986
        3.142707407
        3.142591580
```

FIGURE 11-1 Calculate Value of pi.

The precision for PI is binary (31, 28) to provide three digits in the integer portion for the first computation, 4 ÷ 1 = 4 or 100B, and to allow the maximum possible precision.

To help check the progress of the results, the program prints each 64th iteration (since K is incremented by 2) by checking the seven rightmost digits of the counter K; whenever these digits contain 0000001, then K equals 1, 129, 257, 385, 513, 641, and so on. If you were to assign K to a binary field with precision (7,0), you could check if the contents equals 01. But because the compiler automatically converts binary precision (7) to (15), the attempt does not work. How about assigning K to a Decimal Fixed variable with precision (2, 0) and testing it for 01 to print iterations 01, 101, 201, and so on? The compiler stores Decimal Fixed variables as *odd* numbers, so the true precision would be (3, 0), and the program would print only when K equals 1, 1001, and 2001. In this example, the program truncates the leftmost digits by assigning K to another variable KTRUNC with precision (15, 8)—technically a SIZE condition—and by assigning KTRUNC to a variable TEST with precision (15, 0). Now, if TEST contains 0000001, the value of pi is printed. The program also prints pi at the end, when K = 2001.

PROGRAM: MULTIPLICATION OF MATRICES

In linear algebra, addition of two matrices is possible if both are the same size (the same number of rows and the same number of columns). Addition is directly element-for-element, so that matrix A plus matrix B in PL/I is simply C = A + B ;.

Multiplication of matrices can occur only when the number of *columns* of the first matrix equals the number of *rows* of the second matrix. Consequently, if A is an m × n matrix and B is an n × p matrix, then their product C is an m × p matrix with elements Cij given by

$$C_{ij} = \sum_{k=1}^{n} a_{ik}b_{kj}, i = 1, 2, \ldots, m; j = 1, 2, \ldots, p$$

Problem Definition

Assume matrices A, B, and their product C:

$$A = \begin{bmatrix} 2 & -1 & 3 \\ 1 & -2 & -1 \end{bmatrix} \quad B = \begin{bmatrix} 3 & -1 \\ 1 & 2 \\ -1 & 1 \end{bmatrix} \quad C = \begin{bmatrix} 2 & -1 \\ 2 & -6 \end{bmatrix}$$

For example, row-1, column-1 of C is calculated by multiplying each element in row-1 of A by the corresponding element in column-1 of B and summing the products:

$$(2 \times 3) + (-1 \times 1) + (3 \times -1) = 6 - 1 - 3 = 2.$$

Solution

Assume matrices MATA (2,4), MATB (4,3), and their product MATC (2,3). To start, multiply each element in row 1 of MATA by each element in column 1 of MATB

$$\text{MATA } (1,K) * \text{MATB } (K,1)$$

and add each product to MATC (1,1). This calculation is done for four columns of MATA and four rows of MATB, as follows:

```
DO K = 1 TO 4 ;
     MATC(1,1) = MATC(1,1) + MATA(1,K) * MATB(K,1);
END ;
```

Expand the calculation to multiply next (1) row-1 of MATA by column-2 of MATB and add the results in column-2 of MATC, and (2) row-1 of MATA by column-3 of MATB and add the results to column-3 of MATC:

```
DO J = 1 TO 3 ;
  DO K = 1 TO 4 ;
       MATC(I,J) = MATC(I,J) +  MATA(I,K) * MATB(K,J);
   END ;
END ;
```

These DO-loops take care of row-1 of MATA. Now repeat the entire process for row-2, achieving this by nesting the above in another DO-loop

$$\text{DO I} = 1 \text{ TO } 2 ; \ldots$$

as shown in the completed program in Figure 11–2.

MATHEMATICAL BUILT-IN FUNCTIONS

The mathematical built-in functions operate in floating-point and convert all arguments to that format.

```
1        0    PROG11B:
                  PROCEDURE OPTIONS(MAIN) ;

2    1   0   DCL      MATA(2,4)      DEC FIXED (3) INIT (1,0,3,4,
                                                         2,4,5,0) ;
3    1   0   DCL      MATB(4,3)      DEC FIXED (3) INIT (4,2,7,
                                                         6,1,3,
                                                         2,5,5,
                                                         0,2,1) ;
4    1   0   DCL      MATC(2,3)      DEC FIXED (3) INIT ( (6) 0) ;

             /*       MULTPLY MATA X MATB        */

5    1   0            DO I = 1 TO 2 ;
6    1   1              DO J = 1 TO 3 ;
7    1   2                DO K = 1 TO 4 ;
8    1   3                  MATC(I,J) = MATC(I,J) + MATA(I,K) * MATB(K,J);
9    1   3                END;
10   1   2              END ;
11   1   1            END;

             /*       PRINT PRODUCT: MATC        */

12   1   0            DO I = 1 TO 2 ;
13   1   1              PUT SKIP LIST (MATC(I,1), MATC(I,2), MATC(I,3)) ;
14   1   1            END ;

15   1   0            SIGNAL FINISH ;
16   1   0        END PROG11B ;


             10                        25                     26
             42                        33                     51
```

FIGURE 11–2 Multiplication of Matrices.

SQRT

The SQRT function returns the square root of a given expression:

```
DCL   ANS         DEC FIXED (5,2),
      VALUE       DEC FIXED (5,2) INIT (36) ;

      ANS = SQRT(VALUE) ;  /* ANS NOW CONTAINS 6.00 */
```

The calculation is performed in floating-point. If the argument is negative, the operation raises an error condition and terminates the program. It is also possible to code with an exponent, as

$$ANS = VALUE**.5 ;$$

but this method involves a generalized, less efficient routine.

The following lists the various mathematical built-in functions:

FUNCTION	CALCULATION	LIMITATION
ACOS (x)	arcos (x) in radians	$-1 <= x <= +1$
ASIN (x)	arcsine (x) in radians	$-1 <= x <= +1$
ATAN (x), ATAN (x,y)	arctan (x) or arctan (x/y) in radians	x and $y \neq 0$
ATAND (x) or	arctan (x) or	
ATAND (x,y)	arctan (x/y) in degrees	
ATANH (x)	$\tanh^{-1}(x)$	$-1 <= x <= +1$
COS (x)	cosine (x) in radians	
COSD (x)	cosine (x) in degrees	
COSH (x)	hyperbolic cosine: cosh (x)	
ERF (x)	error function of x: $$ERF\ (x) = \frac{2}{\sqrt{pi}} \int_{o}^{x} e - t^2 {}_{dt}$$	
ERFC (x)	complement of error function = 1-ERF (x)	
EXP (x)	base of natural logarithm e to power x	
LOG (x)	natural logarithm (base e) of x	$x > 0$
LOG2 (x)	binary logarithm (base 2) of x	$x > 0$
LOG10 (x)	common logarithm (base 10) of x	$x > 0$
SIN (x)	sine (x) in radians	
SIND (x)	sine (x) in degrees	
SINH (x)	hyperbolic sine: sinh (x)	
TAN (x)	tangent (x) in radians	
TAND (x)	tangent (x) in degrees	TAND (90) invalid
TANH (x)	hyperbolic tangent: tanh (x) in radians	

PROGRAM: CONVERSION OF COORDINATES

Problem Definition

Given the rectangular coordinates (x,y), what are the corresponding polar co-ordinates (r, Θ) ?

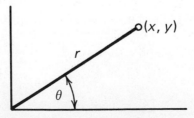

The value for r, based on $r^2 = x^2 + y^2$, is

$$r = \pm\sqrt{x^2 + y^2}$$

The value for θ, based on $\tan\theta = \dfrac{y}{x}$, is

$$\theta = \tan^{-1}\left(\frac{y}{x}\right) = \arctan\frac{y}{x}$$

```
1     0   PROG11C:
                PROCEDURE OPTIONS(MAIN) ;

2   1 0   DCL      (X, Y, R, TH,
                    XCAL, YCAL,
                    RCAL, TCAL)          DEC FIXED (15,10);
3   1 0   DCL      EOF                   BIT(1)   INIT ('0'B);
4   1 0   DCL   (SQRT, ATAND, COSD, SIND) BUILTIN ;

5   1 0            ON ENDFILE(SYSIN) EOF = '1'B;
6   1 0            PUT SKIP LIST ('     X =',
                                  '     Y =',
                                  '     R =',
                                  '       THETA =');
7   1 0            PUT SKIP ;
8   1 0            GET LIST (X, Y, R, TH) ;

9   1 0            DO WHILE (¬EOF) ;

                   /*    CALCULATE POLAR COORDINATES    */
                   /*    **************************     */

10  1 1              RCAL = SQRT(X**2 + Y**2) ;
11  1 1              TCAL = ATAND(Y, X) ;
12  1 1              PUT SKIP LIST (X, Y, RCAL, TCAL) ;

                   /*    CALCULATE RECTANGULAR COORDINATES */
                   /*    **************************     */

13  1 1              XCAL = R * COSD(TH) ;
14  1 1              YCAL = R * SIND(TH) ;
15  1 1              PUT SKIP LIST (XCAL, YCAL, R, TH) ;
16  1 1              PUT SKIP ;
17  1 1              GET LIST (X, Y, R, TH) ;
18  1 1            END;

19  1 0            SIGNAL FINISH ;
20  1 0   END PROG11C ;
```

Output:-

X =	Y =	R =	THETA =
3.0000000000	5.0000000000	5.8309518948	59.0362434679
2.5711504387	3.0641777724	4.0000000000	50.0000000000
2.0000000000	2.0000000000	2.8284271247	45.0000000000
2.5980762113	1.4999999999	3.0000000000	30.0000000000
1.0000000000	4.0000000000	4.1231056256	75.9637565320
2.5000000000	4.3301270189	5.0000000000	60.0000000000

FIGURE 11–3 Conversion of Coordinates.

A program can safely calculate r because the function is always positive. In calculating θ, however, you should ensure that x is not zero. You can also convert polar coordinates to rectangular coordinates as:

$$x = r\text{Cos } \theta$$
$$y = r\text{Sin } \theta$$

Solution

The PL/I statements to convert coordinates could be coded as follows:

1.   Convert rectangular to polar:

```
R = SQRT (X**2 + Y**2) ;
THETA = ATAND (Y,X) ;
```

2.   Convert polar to rectangular:

```
X = R * COSD(THETA) ;
Y = R * SIND(THETA) ;
```

Figure 11–3 gives the program solution that reads values for x, y, r, and θ. The conversion of (x,y) to the corresponding polar coordinates prints on the first line, and the conversion of (r,θ) to the corresponding rectangular coordinates prints on the second line. You can determine the original input values from the printed output.

PROGRAM: PLOTTING A GRAPH

A program is to plot the path of a projectile. Basically, there are two problems to solve. The first is determining the *algorithm(s)* for the path itself, and the second is determining the *scale* of the graph as an array.

The Algorithm

Assume that the initial velocity v_i and the angle θ to the ground are known. It is also known that the projectile descends with the same velocity and angle. Because of the force of gravity, the initial velocity has two components (ignoring air resistance): vertical velocity v_v and horizontal velocity v_h. Let's assume that v_i is 1000 feet/second and angle θ is 30°. Consequently,

$$v_v = v_i\text{sin}\theta = 1000\text{sin}30° = 1000(.5) = 500 \text{ feet/second, and}$$
$$v_h = v_i\text{cos}\theta = 1000(.866) = 866 \text{ feet/second.}$$

The two values can be used to compute the altitude a and distance d of the projectile after each second using the formulas

$$a = v_v t + \tfrac{1}{2}gt^2 \ (g = -32) \text{ and}$$
$$d = v_h t$$

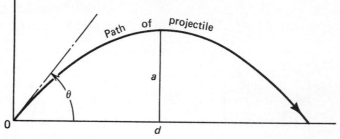

Scale of the Graph

Before programming the problem, you should have some idea of the scale of the graph. If the results are totally unknown, you can print computed values for stated intervals, such as distance and altitude after each second. You may also want to use floating-point format for this purpose (Chapter 13). For this particular problem, the scale of the graph can be calculated using the formulas

$$d = \frac{v_i^2 \ sin2\theta}{g} = \frac{1000^2 \left(\frac{\sqrt{3}}{2}\right)}{32} = 27{,}019.2 \text{ feet}$$

$$t = \frac{2v_i sin\theta}{g} = \frac{2(1000)\,(.5)}{32} = 31.2 \text{ seconds}$$

The maximum altitude occurs at the halfway point along the path, at 15.6 seconds:

$$a = \frac{v_v t}{2} = \frac{500\,(15.6)}{2} = 3900 \text{ feet.}$$

Given these values, you can get a good idea of the dimensions of the graph. A two-dimensional array of altitude and distance will have to be reduced in scale to print on a page. Dividing a and d each by 100 would give a relative altitude of 39 and distance of 270. The distance exceeds the page width unless it is printed *sideways*. However, let's print the graph right way up and reduce the scale to 1/300th so that the dimensions are 13 for altitude and 90 for distance. Let's also plot points with asterisks for (a, d) after each second from 0 through 31. The array for the graph can start its bounds at zero:

DCL GRAPH (0:13, 0:90) CHAR(1) INIT ((1274)(1) ' ');

Note the initialization of the array to blanks (remember iteration factor and string repetition factor?). The altitude is the row and the distance is the column.

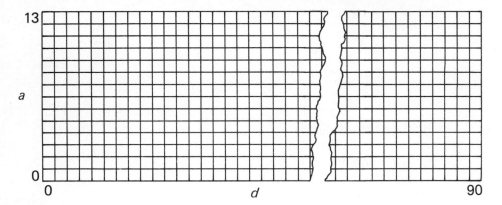

The program is to insert an asterisk into GRAPH after each second of flight according to altitude and distance. The formulas for altitude (a) and distance (d) by seconds (t) involves vertical velocity (V_v) and horizontal velocity (v_h) calculated earlier:

$$a = v_v t + \tfrac{1}{2} g\, t^2 \quad (g = -32)$$
$$d = v_h t$$

At zero seconds, a and d are (0, 0). After one second,

$$a = 500(1) - .5(32)(1^2) = 484 \text{ feet, and}$$
$$d = 866(1) = 866 \text{ feet.}$$

The program can divide these values by 300 (rounding is suggested) and use the results J and K as subscripts to insert an asterisk into GRAPH as follows

GRAPH (J, K) = '*';

and can continue up to 31 seconds.

Note: There is a strong possibility of errors in the formulas, the estimates of the array bounds, the reversal of axes, or the coding. You are advised to *print and check the results* in an early run of the program before storing values based on calculated subscripts.

Printing the Array

This array can be printed exactly as it is represented in storage. If you start printing from the bottom of the array up (row 0 through 13), the array will print upside down. Consequently, the program should start printing from the top of the array, as

DO J = 13 TO 0 BY − 1;

In Figure 11–4, the program prints each row of the array GRAPH as follows:

PUT SKIP LIST (J, STRING(GRAPH(J, *)));

The cross section of GRAPH(J, *) tells the program to process all (*) of the columns for the Jth row. The STRING built-in function gathers the entire referenced row of elements into one character string (91 characters in this case). (Without STRING, each element of the row would print in positions 25, 49, 73, and so on.) STRING and SUBSTR are useful for such processing and are covered in detail in Chapter 19. Output could also be on a video display terminal. Note that the plotted curve is *not smooth* because of the reduction of scale to 1/300th.

If your compiler does not support cross sections of arrays, you can define a one-dimensional array and transfer each row of GRAPH successively to this array for printing, as

```
DCL  LINE_ARRAY(0:90)    CHAR(1);

DO J = 13 TO 0 BY −1;
    DO K = 0 TO 90;
        LINE_ARRAY(K) = GRAPH(J, K);
    END;
    PUT SKIP LIST (J, STRING(LINE_ARRAY));
END;
```

COMPLEX MODE

The mode of an arithmetic variable may be REAL or COMPLEX (not in the Subset). A complex number in PL/I is followed by the letter I to represent $\sqrt{-1}$ as follows:

Decimal fixed:	53I
Decimal float:	2.734E3I
Binary fixed:	1011.01BI

Each of these constants is considered to have a real part of zero. Representation of a complex value with a nonzero real part requires a pair of numbers: first a real part, and second an imaginary part, as

real constant ± imaginary constant

```
1   PROG11D:
         PROCEDURE OPTIONS(MAIN) ;

2   DCL       ANGLE             BIN FIXED (15) INIT (30),
              VINIT             BIN FIXED (31) INIT (1000),
              (VVERT,
              VHORZ,
              ALTD,
              DIST)             BIN FIXED (31,15) ,
              (T, J, K)         BIN FIXED (15) ;
3   DCL       GRAPH(0:13,0:90)
                                CHAR (1)   INIT ( (1274)(1)' ');
4   DCL       TENS_LINE         CHAR (91) INIT ('          1          2
    3         4         5         6         7         8         9'),
              UNITS_LINE        CHAR (91) INIT ('012345678901234567890123456789
    012345678901234567890123456789012345678901234567890') ;

5   DCL       (SIND, COSD,
              STRING)           BUILTIN;


6             PUT SKIP LIST ('ANGLE = 30 DEGREES',
                             'INITIAL VELOCITY = 1000 FT/SEC');

    /*        CALCULATE VERTICAL & HORIZONTAL VELOCITY  */
    /*        **************************************** */

7             VVERT = VINIT * SIND(ANGLE);
8             VHORZ = VINIT * COSD(ANGLE);
9             PUT SKIP LIST ('VERTICAL VELOCITY =', VVERT,
                             'HORIZONTAL VELOCITY =', VHORZ) ;
10            PUT SKIP ;

    /*        CALCULATE DISTANCES & ALTITUDES      */
    /*        ****************************** */

11            PUT SKIP LIST ('TIME IN SECONDS',
                             '     DISTANCE',
                             '     ALTITUDE',
                             ' DIST/300', '  ALT/300') ;
12            PUT SKIP ;
13  A100:     DO T = 0 TO 31;
14                DIST = VHORZ * T ;
15                ALTD =(VVERT * T) - (16 * T**2) ;
16                K = DIST / 300 + .5 ;
17                J = ALTD / 300 + .5 ;
18                GRAPH(J, K) = '*' ;
19                PUT SKIP LIST (T, DIST, ALTD, K, J);
20            END A100;

    /*        PRINT PLOTTED GRAPH                  */
    /*        ****************** */

21            PUT SKIP(2) LIST ('     ALT') ;
22  B100:     DO J = 13 TO 0 BY -1;
23                PUT SKIP LIST (J, STRING(GRAPH(J, *)));
24            END B100;

25            PUT SKIP LIST (' ', TENS_LINE) ;
26            PUT SKIP LIST ('         DIST', UNITS_LINE) ;
27            SIGNAL FINISH ;
28        END PROG11D ;
```

FIGURE 11–4 Plotted Graph of a Projectile.

FIGURE 11–4 (cont.)

ANGLE = 30 DEGREES
VERTICAL VELOCITY =   INITIAL VELOCITY = 1000 FT/SEC
499.99993   HORIZONTAL VELOCITY =   866.02536

TIME IN SECONDS	DISTANCE	ALTITUDE	DIST/300	ALT/300
0	0.00000	0.00000	0	0
1	866.02536	483.99993	3	2
2	1732.05072	935.99987	6	3
3	2598.07608	1355.99981	9	5
4	3464.10144	1743.99975	12	6
5	4330.12680	2099.99969	14	7
6	5196.15216	2423.99963	17	8
7	6062.17752	2715.99957	20	9
8	6928.20288	2975.99951	23	10
9	7794.22824	3203.99945	26	11
10	8660.25360	3399.99938	29	11
11	9526.27896	3563.99932	32	12
12	10392.30432	3695.99926	35	12
13	11258.32968	3795.99920	38	13
14	12124.35504	3863.99914	40	13
15	12990.38040	3899.99908	43	13
16	13856.40576	3903.99902	46	13
17	14722.43112	3875.99896	49	13
18	15588.45648	3815.99890	52	13
19	16454.48184	3723.99884	55	12
20	17320.50720	3599.99877	58	12
21	18186.53256	3443.99871	61	11
22	19052.55792	3255.99865	64	11
23	19918.58328	3035.99859	66	10
24	20784.60864	2783.99853	69	9
25	21650.63400	2499.99847	72	8
26	22516.65936	2183.99841	75	7
27	23382.68472	1835.99835	78	6
28	24248.71008	1455.99829	81	5
29	25114.73544	1043.99822	84	3
30	25980.76080	599.99816	87	2
31	26846.78616	123.99810	89	0

You could write a complex value as 25 + 32I.

A complex variable must have the COMPLEX attribute, as

DCL COMPVAL DEC FLOAT(16) COMPLEX ;

Built-in Functions

There are four arithmetic built-in functions that process complex numbers: COMPLEX, CONJG, IMAG, and REAL.

COMPLEX.   The COMPLEX built-in function returns a complex value formed from two given values x and y (expressions or variables):

result = COMPLEX (x,y) ;

where x is a real value to represent the real part of the result, y is a real value to represent the imaginary part of the result. For example, form a complex value using a real part from a REAL constant stored in REALA and an imaginary part from a constant 25:

```
DCL   COMPY      DEC FLOAT (16) COMPLEX,
      REALA      DEC FLOAT (16) REAL;

COMPY = COMPLEX(REALA, 25) ;
```

CONJG.   The CONJG built-in function, coded as

result = CONJG (x) ;

returns the conjugate of a given complex value x (the sign of the imaginary part is reversed). If x is real, the operation converts it to complex.

IMAG.   The IMAG built-in function returns the imaginary part of a complex value and converts it to real mode. For example, using the above declaratives for COMPY and REALA:

REALA = IMAG (COMPY) ;

REAL.   The REAL built-in function returns the real part of a complex value, as

REALA = REAL (COMPY) ;

Pseudovariables

COMPLEX, IMAG, and REAL can also act as pseudovariables, coded on the left of an assignment statement. Assume the following declaratives:

```
DCL (REALA, REALB) DEC FLOAT (16) REAL,
    COMPY          DEC FLOAT (16) COMPLEX ;
```

1.   Assign the real part of COMPY to REALA and the imaginary part of COMPY to REALB (and convert to real mode) :

```
COMPLEX (REALA, REALB) = COMPY ;
```

2.   Assign 25 to the real part of COMPY (the imaginary part is unchanged) :

```
REAL (COMPY) = 25 ;
```

3.   Assign 25 to the imaginary part of COMPY (the real part is unchanged) ;

```
IMAG (COMPY) = 25 ;
```

DEBUGGING TIPS

- Avoid binary format for extended arithmetic expressions.
- Remember that Binary Fixed assumes a precision of 15 or 31 regardless of what other precision you may code.
- Watch for specific limitations on mathematical built-in functions. For example, the SIN argument is in radians, whereas the SIND argument is in degrees.
- Double-check that the size of a graph can accommodate extreme values. You may be wise in early tests to check if subscripts are outside the bounds of arrays using a condition prefix for SUBSCRIPTRANGE, as (SUBRG): before the PROCEDURE OPTIONS(MAIN) statement.

Problems

11–1. Use a 6-bit field to represent the binary values for the following. Watch for overflow results.
   (a) 11 + 5 = 16   (b) 25 − 10 = 15
   (c) 12 − 19 = −7   (d) 23 + 12 = 35

11-2. Represent the decimal values for the following binary values:
(a) 0101100
(b) 011100101
(c) 11011000 (negative)

11-3. What is the length in *bytes* of the following variable? Explain.

DCL BINFLD BIN FIXED(10);

11-4. Determine the value that each of the following mathematical built-in functions returns:
(a) SQRT(36) (b) COS(0) (c) COS(1.047) (d) COSD(1) (e) COSD(60)
(f) SIN(0.524) (g) SIND(45) (h) EXP(2.5) (i) TAND(45)

11-5. Write a program that plots graphs for the following:
(a) A parabola: $y^2 = 8x$. Vary y from -20 to $+20$.

(b) An ellipse: $\dfrac{x^2}{225} + \dfrac{y^2}{100} = 1$. Vary y from -10 to $+10$.

(c) A hyperbola: $\dfrac{x^2}{16} - \dfrac{y^2}{9} = 1$. Vary x from -27 to -4 and from $+4$ to $+27$.

11-6. Logarithms to the base e are called natural logarithms, and exp $x = e^x$ for all x. The actual numeric value of e is $2.71828+$. Write a program that computes the value of e using the formula

$$e = 1 + \frac{1}{1!} + \frac{1}{2!} + \frac{1}{3!} + \ldots$$

Note that for each iteration, you can use the product from the previous iteration. Thus,

$$\frac{1}{4!} = \frac{1}{4 \times 3 \times 2 \times 1} = \frac{1}{24} \quad \text{and}$$

$$\frac{1}{5!} = \frac{1}{5 \times 4 \times 3 \times 2 \times 1} = \frac{1}{5 \times 24}, \text{ etc.}$$

Try about 30 iterations.

11-7. For the quadratic equation $ax^2 + bx + c = 0$, the roots are given by the formula

$$x = \frac{-b \pm \sqrt{b^2 - 4ac}}{2a}$$

If $a = 0$, the equation is "linear" instead of quadratic. If the discriminant $b^2 - 4ac \geq 0$, the roots are real, and if < 0, the roots are complex. Code a program to solve for x using the following input values for a, b, and c:

a	b	c
2	5	3
4	8	0
4	8	4

Note that there are two values for x. Print a, b, c, x_1, and x_2.

CHAPTER 12

FULL STREAM INPUT/OUTPUT

OBJECTIVE:

To cover the specifications for Data-Directed and Edit-Directed stream I/O.

INTRODUCTION

PL/I provides two types of data input/output transmission:

1. Stream I/O. The main use of Stream I/O is in mathematical and scientific programming and as a convenient aid in debugging. Data transmits in the form of a continuous stream—the system does not automatically recognize the physical boundaries of a record. Stream I/O uses GET for input and PUT for output. One GET statement may, for example, read data from part of a record, a full record, or more than one record.

2. Record I/O. The main use of Record I/O is in business programming. Each record is unique and distinct under this type. Record I/O uses READ and WRITE for input and output operations. Although there is more coding for Declare and assignment statements, Record I/O generates less machine code and executes faster.

Earlier chapters used the simple List-Directed feature of Stream I/O. The two other types that this chapter covers are Data-directed and Edit-directed Stream

I/O. The latter feature provides much better control over formatting of input and output records.

STREAM I/O FILE DECLARE STATEMENTS

Except for the Subset, PL/I compilers do not require a definition of a stream I/O file. For a GET statement, the default is the system input device SYSIN, and for a PUT statement, the default is the system printer SYSPRINT. Some reasons, however, for defining files are as follows:

1. As an ongoing practice, an explicit declaration provides better program control and documentation.
2. Since more compilers require an explicit declaration, defining a file makes a program more "portable" from system to system.
3. Record I/O, used for tape and disk processing, requires file declarations.

INPUT FILES

IBM OS

The following defines an input file for the OS PL/I Optimizer:

```
DCL filename FILE STREAM INPUT ENV (F BLKSIZE (80)) ;
```

*   filename is an external identifier, a maximum of seven characters (six under the Subset).
*   FILE specifies definition of a file.
*   STREAM indicates Stream I/O (instead of RECORD).
*   INPUT indicates an input file to be used with GET.
*   ENV (or ENVIRONMENT) provides the format for input records, in this case F (for fixed length) and a "block size" of 80 characters long. (This is PL/I Optimizer coding; other versions use F(80).) OS permits omission of the ENV entry. A common definition using the name SYSIN is

```
DCL SYSIN FILE STREAM INPUT ;
```

IBM DOS

The following defines an input file for the DOS PL/I Optimizer:

```
DCL name FILE STREAM INPUT ENV( F BLKSIZE(80) MEDIUM (SYSIPT,2501) BUFFERS(2) );
```

DOS requires a MEDIUM entry designating the type of input device. This example specifies that the system input device, SYSIPT, is an IBM 2501 reader. You may use SYSIN for the name of the file and let the compiler assume 80-character, fixed-length, as

```
DCL SYSIN FILE STREAM INPUT ENV( MEDIUM (SYSIPT) BUFFERS(2) );
```

Buffers

A *buffer* is an area in main storage reserved for an input/output record. The compiler reserves at least one buffer for each file. Additional buffers enable a program to execute more efficiently because the system can overlap input/output with processing. OS users usually specify the number of buffers with a DD (Data Definition) job entry. DOS allows a maximum of only two buffers; omission of the BUFFERS option causes the compiler to default to one buffer.

PRINTER FILES

IBM OS

The following defines a printer file for the OS PL/I Optimizer:

```
DCL name FILE STREAM PRINT ENV (F BLKSIZE (121) ) ;
```

PRINT, which indicates a printer output file, causes the compiler to reserve the first position of the print area for a special *forms control character* that Stream output handles entirely. If the print width is 120 or 132 characters, you code (121) or (133) respectively.

A common OS definition omitting the ENV option and using the name SYS-PRINT is

```
DCL SYSPRINT FILE PRINT ;
```

IBM DOS

The following defines a DOS PL/I Optimizer print file:

```
DCL filename FILE STREAM PRINT ENV( F BLKSIZE(121) MEDIUM (SYSLST,3230) BUFFERS(2) );
```

DOS requires a MEDIUM entry designating the type of printer device; in this case, the system listing device, SYSLST, is an IBM 3230 printer. You may also use

SYSPRINT for the name of the file and let the compiler assume 121-character fixed-length, as

```
DCL SYSPRINT FILE PRINT ENV (BUFFERS(2) ) ;
```

SYSPRINT assumes that the number of print positions is 120 and that the number of lines on a page is 60. In the event of no other programmer action, the system automatically ejects to the top of the next page after printing the 60th line, at line one.

　　Warning: File declares vary by PL/I version and operating system, and the precise coding for your installation may differ from the examples given.

OPENING AND CLOSING FILES

Before a program attempts to read or write the first record, the files must be "opened." Opening a file causes the system to check that the device is ready (the power is on) and available (no other program is using it). When a program has completed processing of a file, the file should be "closed." Closing a file causes the system to make the device available to other programs. There are special PL/I OPEN and CLOSE statements. However, under Stream I/O (OS and the DOS Optimizer) you need not explicitly code the OPEN and CLOSE for SYSIN and SYSPRINT. Some programmers feel that *all* files should be explicitly declared, opened, and closed.

The OPEN Statement

OPEN, if coded, appears before any GET or PUT statement. You may OPEN files in one statement as

```
OPEN FILE (SYSIN), FILE (SYSPRINT) ;
```

or in two statements as

```
OPEN FILE (SYSIN) ;
OPEN FILE (SYSPRINT) ;
```

The CLOSE Statement

CLOSE, if coded, appears after all GET and PUT processing is completed. You may CLOSE files in one statement as

```
CLOSE FILE (SYSIN), FILE (SYSPRINT) ;
```

or in two statements as:

CLOSE FILE (SYSIN) ;
CLOSE FILE (SYSPRINT) ;

Once a file is closed, any attempt to GET or PUT it will cause an I/O error on smaller systems.

OPEN and CLOSE Illustration

A program coded with file declares, OPEN, and CLOSE would look like the skeleton example in Figure 12–1.

```
PROGRAM: PROCEDURE OPTIONS(MAIN) ;
    DCL  SYSIN    FILE STREAM INPUT   ;
    DCL  SYSPRINT FILE STREAM PRINT   ;

         OPEN FILE(SYSIN), FILE(SYSPRINT) ;
         ON ENDFILE(SYSIN) EOF = '1'B ;
         GET LIST (QTY, PRICE) ;

         DO WHILE (¬EOF) ;
             VALUE = QTY * PRICE ;
             PUT LIST (QTY, PRICE, VALUE) ;
             GET LIST (QTY, PRICE) ;
         END ;

         CLOSE FILE(SYSIN), FILE(SYSPRINT) ;
    END PROGRAM ;
```

FIGURE 12–1 Skeleton Program Depicting Input/Output.

OPEN Options

A Stream OPEN statement can alter the standard number of lines on a page (up to 255) with the PAGESIZE option and the number of print positions on a line with the LINESIZE option. The following establishes PAGESIZE at 50 and LINESIZE at 100:

OPEN FILE(SYSIN), FILE(SYSPRINT) PAGESIZE(50) LINESIZE(100) ;

ON ENDPAGE

You can use the ON ENDPAGE statement to check for the end of a page, for example, to print a heading at the top of a page. After the 60th line is printed (the standard line count), the following statement will direct the program to a page heading routine:

ON ENDPAGE(SYSPRINT) action ;

Actions for the ON statement include CALL, SIGNAL, unlabeled BEGIN blocks, and GO TO. However, it is not always necessary or desirable to use the PAGESIZE and ON ENDPAGE features. You can control the page overflow situation better by writing the program to count the lines spaced.

CONTROL FORMAT OPTIONS

Under Stream I/O, you use the control format options SKIP and LINE to space lines (provided you coded PRINT instead of OUTPUT in the DCL statement) and PAGE to eject the forms to a new page.

SKIP Option

SKIP controls the number of lines to space the printer form. SKIP(0) causes no spacing, and SKIP is the same as SKIP(1) (under the Subset, the maximum is 3). The following example spaces three lines without printing:

PUT SKIP (3) ;

LINE Option

For Stream output, PL/I maintains a *current line counter* that it increments for each line printed or skipped. The following example causes the printer to move directly to line 4 of the page:

PUT LINE (4) ;

If the print form is already past line 4, the printer will eject to the next page.

PAGE Option

PAGE causes the printer to eject the forms to line 1 of the next page, as

PUT PAGE ;

If you do not provide special coding to eject to a new page, at the end of a page (line 60), the system automatically ejects the forms. You may code PAGE and

LINE in the same statement (PAGE always executes first), but SKIP may not occur with either PAGE or LINE.

DATA-DIRECTED STREAM I/O

Data-directed Stream I/O (not in the Subset version) is a simple method to enter and print data. Although it has significant disadvantages as an input method for large volumes of data, it is convenient to enter mathematical data and to print the contents of variables during program execution to aid in debugging.

Data-directed Input

The standard format for Data-Directed input is

GET [FILE (filename)] DATA [(data-list)] ;

Omission of FILE(filename) causes the compiler to assume that SYSIN is to be the input file. The data-list specifies the names of items, structure names, and array names. For this type of processing, you record data on input "records" as assignment statements separated by a comma or any number of blanks. The end of the data for a given GET DATA statement is signified by a semicolon. Negative arithmetic values have the minus sign to the left, and string data elements are enclosed in apostrophes. The following illustrates some typical data:

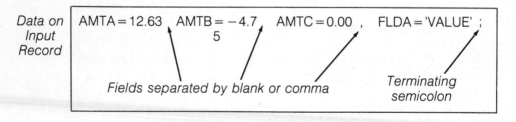

Assuming that data input is on SYSIN, the coding to read the data is

```
DCL  (AMTA,
      AMTB,
      AMTC)      DEC FIXED (5,2),
      FLDA       CHAR (6) ;

GET DATA (AMTA, AMTB, AMTC, FLDA) ;
```

The GET operation causes the values 12.63, −4.75, and 0.00 to be translated to Decimal Fixed and assigned respectively to AMTA, AMTB, and AMTC, *aligning on the decimal points,* and assigns the character string 'VALUE' to FLDA. It is also possible to enter the data items on more than one record:

3	FLDA = 'VALUE' ;	
2	AMTB = − 4.75	AMTC = 0.00 ,
1	AMTA = 12.63	

The same GET operation would read the three records and assign the four items into their respective fields. In any case, the semicolon following the fourth data item terminates the operation. Note: The data list in the input stream need not be in the same sequence as that on the GET statement.

Mismatching Data Lists.   It is possible that the data-list in the GET statement does not agree with the data on the input record(s).

1.   *More items in the GET statement data-list than on the record.* Assume the same Declares and input data as the previous example, and the following Declare and GET statements:

```
DCL AMTD DEC FIXED (5,2) ;
GET DATA (AMTA, AMTB, AMTC, FLDA, AMTD) ;
```

In this case, the operation assigns the values for AMTA, AMTB, AMTC, and FLDA as before, but since there is no input data for AMTD, it is left unassigned. The coding is not necessarily an error.

2.   *Fewer items in the GET data-list than on the input record.* Assume the same input data as before and the following GET statement:

```
GET DATA (AMTA, AMTC, FLDA) ;
```

The input stream contains data for AMTA, AMTB, AMTC, and FLDA. But since the GET does not specify receiving data for AMTB, the result is an execution error. (The system "raises the NAME condition" as described in Chapter 21, prints an error message, and resumes processing.)

Input Data Lists

FLDA = 'ONE', AMTC = 6.34 AMTB = 22 ; AMTC = 5.2 ; FLDA = 'TWO', AMTB = 27.3 ; AMTB = 19.5 FLDX = '14' ;

Figure 12–2 illustrates most of the features of the preceding discussion. In the input data list shown, items follow one another without regard for input record boundaries. A semicolon in the input stream terminates each GET. During program execution, the following occurs on each GET as terminated by the semicolon in the input stream:

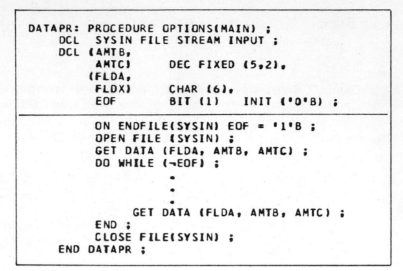

```
DATAPR: PROCEDURE OPTIONS(MAIN) ;
    DCL  SYSIN FILE STREAM INPUT ;
    DCL (AMTB,
         AMTC)      DEC FIXED (5,2),
        (FLDA,
         FLDX)      CHAR (6),
         EOF        BIT (1)   INIT ('0'B) ;

         ON ENDFILE(SYSIN) EOF = '1'B ;
         OPEN FILE (SYSIN) ;
         GET DATA (FLDA, AMTB, AMTC) ;
         DO WHILE (¬EOF) ;
                  •
                  •
                  •
              GET DATA (FLDA, AMTB, AMTC) ;
         END ;
         CLOSE FILE(SYSIN) ;
    END DATAPR ;
```

FIGURE 12–2 Data-Directed Input.

| EXECUTION OF | CONTENTS OF VARIABLE AFTER GET | | |
GET	FLDA	AMTB	AMTC
1	'ONE	22.00	6.34
2	unchanged	unchanged	5.20
3	'TWO '	27.30	unchanged
4	unchanged	19.50	unchanged

At this point, however, an entry in FLDX appears in the input stream, and although FLDX is defined in the program, it is not an entry in the GET data-list. The system raises the NAME error condition, prints a message, and resumes processing. Since there is no more data in the input stream, the program executes the ENDFILE condition and terminates processing.

Omission of Data Lists.   It is possible to omit the data-list using GET DATA ; The program will automatically read and assign each item in the input stream up to each semicolon. The same general rules as discussed still apply.

Data-directed Output

Data-directed output provides convenient identification of output as assignment statements and is a useful debugging aid. The standard format is

PUT [FILE (filename)] DATA [(data-list)] ;

Omission of FILE (filename) causes the compiler to assume SYSPRINT, the standard system output device (usually the printer). SYSPRINT assumes 120 print positions and 60 lines per page. The data-list may consist of variables, array names, array elements, structure names, and structure elements. The printed output is in the form of assignment statements, with each item aligned on preset print positions, typically positions 1, 25, 49, 73, and 97 (and 121 if the line width exceeds 120). The last item printed on the list terminates with a semicolon. The following illustrates this:

```
DCL   HOUR    DEC FIXED (5,2)   INIT (25.00) ,
      RATE    DEC FIXED (4,2)   INIT (12.50) ,
      MONTH   CHAR (6)          INIT ('JAN 28')  ;
```

PUT DATA (HOUR, RATE, MONTH) ;

Output:

```
HOUR = 25.00     RATE = 12.50     MONTH = 'JAN 28'  ;
  ↑                ↑                ↑                 ↑
```

Position: 1   25   49   *Terminating semicolon*

Other formats: A Bit-string value prints, for example, as '10110011'B, but a Binary Fixed value converts to ordinary decimal notation for ease of reading.

The following illustrates line spacing with the control format options SKIP, LINE, and PAGE; each occurs before printing.

```
PUT SKIP(3) DATA ( . . . ) ; /* SKIP THREE LINES BEFORE PRINTING */
PUT LINE(4) DATA ( . . . ) ; /* SKIP TO LINE 4 BEFORE PRINTING */
PUT PAGE   DATA ( . . . ) ; /* SKIP TO A NEW PAGE BEFORE PRINTING */
```

Omission of the SKIP option, as in earlier examples, causes the next item to print immediately after the last one printed, possibly on the same line. The statement PUT DATA; will cause every item in the program (technically, in the "block" in which the PUT occurs) to be listed. You can also print every element of an array or structure as

```
DCL TABLE(25) DECIMAL FIXED (7,2) ;
        PUT DATA (TABLE) ;
```

The program lists the contents of each element of TABLE as

```
TABLE(1) = . . . TABLE(2) = . . . TABLE(3) = . . . etc.
```

EDIT-DIRECTED STREAM I/O

Edit-directed I/O provides better control over input/output data and has considerably more features and complexity than Data-directed I/O and List-directed I/O.

EDIT-DIRECTED INPUT

The standard format for Edit-Directed input is

GET [FILE (filename)] EDIT (data-list) (format-list) ;

Omission of FILE (filename) causes the compiler to assume SYSIN. The data-list is identical to that for List-directed and designates the identifiers to which the operation is to assign input data. Each data-list item has (or should have) a corresponding format-list entry. The GET operation terminates when it has processed all the items in the data-list. The format-list entries describe the external appearance of the input data. In the following explanation of format-list entries, the w indicates the "width" of the input field:

A(w)	Specifies that the input field is alphabetic (character format) and gives its length in bytes (w).
B(w)	Designates a field to be assigned to a Bit-string (the input field contains only character 0's and 1's).
F(w,d)	Means that the input field is to be assigned to a Fixed-point variable. The length of the input field is w bytes, with d decimal places. If the implicit decimal place is to the right of the field, you may omit the d and code F(w). It is not necessary or normally desirable to enter the decimal point in the input field. A negative value has a minus sign to the left that counts as part of the length (w), so that the format item for an input field such as -12345 could be F(6,2).
E(w,d)	Designates an input field entered in floating-point format.
X(m)	Specifies the number (m) of unused contiguous record positions that the operation is to skip.
COLUMN(n)	Establishes a specific record column (n) as the leftmost position of the next input field. Abbreviation (not in the Subset) is COL(n).

The input data requires no separators between fields, since the format-list specifies field lengths. (You may therefore record data the same way as for Record

I/O.) A String data field is not enclosed in apostrophes, and decimal points for arithmetic fields are optional. The following example illustrates this:

Columns: 1 2   3   7 8 9   10   15 16   80

Record:

A A	A A A A A	b b	± F F F F F	b ⌇⎯⎯⎯⎯⌇ b
CODE	CTLNO		VALUE	

```
DCL  CODE  CHAR (2) ,
     CTLNO CHAR (5) ,
     VALUE  DEC FIXED (5,2) ;

     GET FILE (SYSIN) EDIT ( CODE, CTLNO, VALUE ) ⟵⎯⎯⎯⎯ Data-list

                          ( A(2), A(5), X(2), F(6,2), X(65) ) ; ⟵⎯⎯⎯⎯ Format-list
```

The GET operation executes by stepping through the format-list, input record, and data-list from left to right. The format-list controls the operation, as follows:

A(2)	The first two input positions are alphabetic. The operation associates the A(2) with the first data-list item, CODE, and assigns the contents of the input positions into the 2-byte Character field CODE.
A(5)	The next five input positions are also alphabetic. The operation selects the next data-list item, CTLNO, and assigns columns 3–7 into it.
X(2)	The operation ignores the next two positions (8 and 9).
F(6,2)	The next six positions are arithmetic, with two decimal places. The operation assigns these positions to VALUE, as coded in the data-list.
X(65)	The remaining 65 input positions are unused.

At this point, the data-list is exhausted, and the operation terminates. The following figure gives the pictorial representation of the assignment of the input data to the program variables:

Format-list: A(2)   A(5)   X(2)   F(6,2)   X(65)

Record:

A A	A A A A A	b b	F F F F F F	b⌇⎯⎯⌇ b
CODE	CTLNO		VALUE	

Program variables: CODE   CTLNO   VALUE

Note: since the data-list terminates the operation, some compiler versions will ignore the X(65) in the format-list. The next GET, if coded identically, will begin processing the input stream beginning at record column 16. A better approach uses the COLUMN control format as follows:

GET FILE (SYSIN) EDIT (CODE, CTLNO, VALUE) (COL(1), A(2), A(5), X(2), F(6,2)) ;

In this case, the format-list designates COLUMN(1) or COL(1) in order to initialize each input record at column 1. The operation processes CODE, CTLNO, and VALUE as before. The format-list does not need X(65) to define the rest of the record. The next time the program executes the GET, it initializes at column 1 of the next record, thereby avoiding the possible error in the preceding example.

Mis-matching Data-List and Format-List.   Desirably, the items in the format-list should *match* those in the data-list, both in number of items and in attributes. Failure to match can cause unusual and unpredictable results. In the next statement, the data-list has three items, and the format-list has two:

GET EDIT (LENGTH, WIDTH, HEIGHT) (F(5), F(6)) ;

Here, F(5) applies to LENGTH and F(6) to WIDTH. Then because the format-list is exhausted but not the data-list, the operation *repeats* the format-list and applies the first item, F(5), to HEIGHT. In the following statement, the data-list has two entries and the format-list has three. The compiler *ignores* the extra format item F(4):

GET EDIT (LENGTH, WIDTH) (F(5), F(6), F(4)) ;

Iteration Factor.   The following format-list contains three successive identical specifications coded as F(5):

GET EDIT (LENGTH, WIDTH, HEIGHT) (COL(1), F(5), F(5), F(5)) ;

You can use an "iteration factor" for the three F(5) entries:

GET EDIT (LENGTH, WIDTH, HEIGHT) (COL(1), 3 F(5)) ;

Iteration factor (followed by blank)

A blank follows the iteration factor. Full PL/I allows the iteration factor in parentheses, as (3)F(5) with no required space.

Coded Decimal Point.   For some applications, the decimal point is actually entered on the record. (This practice is not generally recommended because of the extra keying and error possibilities.)

Column 1	The format specification for this field is F(7,2) because the decimal point occupies one record column and the field length is seven characters. You can assign the input field to an identifier with a precision of F(6,2) because PL/I does not store the decimal point.
↓	
0312.65	

If the decimal point in the input field does not match the decimal point in the format-list, the punched decimal point overrides. For example, if the record in the previous example were entered as 031.265 and the format-list item were F(7,2), the field would be treated as having three decimal places. However, if the field were then assigned to a variable declared as DECIMAL FIXED (6,2), the stored value would become 0031.26.

Input to Structures. A GET statement may assign an input record directly to a structure. The following GET statement reads an 80-position record directly into an 80-character area named INPUT that redefines a structure CUSTOMER:

```
DCL 1 CUSTOMER,
      2 NAME        CHAR(20),
      2 STREET      CHAR(30),
      2 CITY        CHAR(30);
DCL   INPUT         CHAR(80) DEFINED CUSTOMER ;

    GET EDIT (INPUT) ( A(80) ) ;
```

Input to Arrays.   There are various ways that the program can GET data directly from the input stream into an array. Assume an array of 50 elements and that the input stream contains 50 items to be assigned to the elements of the array. The following DO-loop performs iterations to store the data:

```
DCL   TABLE(50)       DEC FIXED (5,2) ;

    DO I = 1 TO 50 ;
        GET EDIT ( TABLE(I) ) ( F(5,2) ) ;
    END ;
```

Each GET reads one item from the input stream and assigns it to an element of TABLE. Alternatively, you can code the DO loop (with no END) in the data-list itself, as shown in the following:

```
GET EDIT ( (TABLE(I) DO I = 1 TO 50) ) ( F(5,2) ) ;
```

The data-list contains two sets of parentheses: The inner set encloses the repetitive specification and the outer set encloses the data-list. A data-list that contains two repetitive specifications would require three sets of parentheses.

EDIT-DIRECTED OUTPUT

Although Data-directed and List-directed output both limit print fields to preset positions, Edit-directed output enables you to place the output field in any print position. The standard format for Edit-directed output is

PUT [FILE (filename)] EDIT (data-list) (format-list) ;

Omission of FILE (filename) causes the compiler to assume SYSPRINT. The data-list for Edit-directed is coded the same as for List-directed output and permits constants, expressions, and variables that are to be printed. Each data-list item normally has a corresponding format-list entry. The PUT operation terminates when it has processed all items in the data-list. The format-list entries describe the external appearance of the output data. In the following explanation of format-list entries, the w indicates the "width" of the print field:

A(w)	Specifies that the output field is alphabetic (character format). For A items on output only, you may omit the (w) and let the compiler calculate the length from the data-list item.
B(w)	Designates output of a Bit-string of 0's and 1's.
F(w,d)	Means that output is an arithmetic field. The width of the print field is w bytes including minus sign to the left and decimal point, if any. An item such as
	DCL TOTAL DEC FIXED(5,3) ;
	could have a format-list entry F(7,3). If this format entry were F(6,2), the operation would round and truncate the third decimal place before printing. The operation also suppresses leading zeros and inserts a decimal point (unless you code F(w)).
E(w,d)	Designates an output field as a floating-point value. The operation rounds before printing.
X(m) and	
COLUMN (n)	Work the same for output as for input.

The control format options PAGE, SKIP, and LINE are the same for Edit-directed output as for Data- and List-directed output. Although you can enter them in the format-list, they are more commonly coded preceding the data-list. Regardless of where they appear, the operation acts on the control option *before* printing. The following examples illustrate this:

```
DCL   ITEM           CHAR(05),
      DESCRIPTION    CHAR(20),
      VALUE          DEC FIXED(5,2),
      PAGECTR        DEC FIXED(3) ;
```

1.   PUT PAGE EDIT ('SYSTEMS COMPANY') (COL(60), A) ; Eject the forms
     to a new page before printing the title.
2.   PUT LINE(3) EDIT ('ITEM VALUES', 'PAGE', PAGECTR)
                    (COL(20), A, COL(75), A, COL(80), F(5)) ;
     Skip to line 3 and print the two character literals and the variable PAGECTR.
3.   PUT SKIP(2) EDIT (ITEM, DESCRIPTION, VALUE)
                    (COL(20), A(5), X(3), A(20), X(3), F(7,2)) ;
     Space 2 lines and print the three variables.

An EDIT statement can contain more than one data/format list. The next
recodes Example 3 with each data-item immediately followed by its format. This
practice greatly improves clarity of the statement:

```
PUT SKIP(2) EDIT (ITEM       ) ( COL(20), A(5)    )
                 (DESCRIPTION) ( X(3),    A(20)   )
                 (VALUE       ) ( X(3),    F(7,2) );
```

Iteration Factor.   A number of consecutive items in a format-list may be identical,
as follows:

```
PUT SKIP EDIT (NAME, AMT1, AMT2, AMT3)
              (A(20), F(7,2), F(7,2), F(7,2)) ;
```

You can use an iteration factor in the format-list, as follows:

```
PUT SKIP EDIT (NAME, AMT1, AMT2, AMT3)
              (A(20), 3 F(7,2)) ;
```

The iteration factor for this use is followed by a blank. Full PL/I allows the iteration
factor in parentheses, as (3)F(7,2) with no required space, or even coded as an
expression, as (J)F(7,2).
     In order to space the amounts across the page, you can place parentheses
around more than one item in the format-list. In the following format-list, three
spaces, X(3), immediately follow each amount:

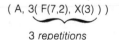

(A, 3(F(7,2), X(3)))

3 repetitions

PROGRAM: CALCULATION OF MEAN AND STANDARD DEVIATION

Problem Definition

A program is to calculate the mean average and the standard deviation of scores.
Each input record contains ten scores. The calculation of mean and standard
deviation are as follows:

$$\text{Mean} = \Sigma scores \div N,$$
$$\text{and Standard deviation} = \sqrt{\frac{(N \times \Sigma scores^2) - (\Sigma scores)^2}{N(N-1)}}$$

where

  N = Number of scores,
  Σscores = Sum of the value of the scores,
  Σscores^2 = Sum of the squared scores.

Solution

The program is to read the ten scores from each input record into an array, SCORESIN; add the total value of the scores; add the total of the square of the scores; and add the number of scores. Figure 12–3 provides the program solution.

  After reading all input scores, the program performs the calculation of standard deviation in three steps because an extended arithmetic expression in fixed-point scale can cause a FIXEDOVERFLOW error. If the computation were in floating-point, you could code the calculation of standard deviation in one statement, as

```
STDEV = SQRT( (NO * SUMSQ − SUMSCOR**2) / (NO * (NO − 1) ) );
```

Handling the ENDPAGE Condition

In Stream output, you can easily handle page overflow by counting the lines skipped and testing if the count exceeds some maximum. For illustrative purposes, this program introduces the use of an "internal procedure," the CALL statement, and the SIGNAL statement.

  P10PAGE is the routine that skips to a new page to print the heading. It is coded as a PROCEDURE that is internal to (within) the main procedure PROGS10. Only a CALL statement can cause a Procedure to execute, as in the statement

```
ON ENDPAGE(SYSPRINT) CALL P10PAGE ; .
```

Since the OPEN statement specifies 30 lines per page, when the system passes line 30, it performs the ENDPAGE condition and executes the P10PAGE procedure through to its END statement.

  One problem remains: At the start of a program it may be necessary to print a heading on the first page. The statement

```
SIGNAL ENDPAGE(SYSPRINT) ;
```

forces the ENDPAGE condition, causing the program to execute the P10PAGE procedure. The program resumes processing from the point where it was interrupted.

```
1   PROG12B:
         PROCEDURE OPTIONS(MAIN) ;

2   DCL     SYSIN     FILE STREAM INPUT ENV( MEDIUM(SYSIPT)
                                              BUFFERS(2) ) ;
3   DCL     SYSPRINT FILE PRINT ENV(BUFFERS(2) ) ;

4   DCL     ( I, NO )          BIN FIXED (15) INIT(0B) ;
5   DCL     SCORESIN(10)       DEC FIXED (5,1) ,
            SCORE              DEC FIXED (5,1) ;

6   DCL     (SUMSCOR,
            SUMSQ,
            STDEV,
            MEAN)              DEC FLOAT (16) INIT (0) ;

7   DCL     EOF                BIT (1)        INIT ('0'B) ;

    /*          INITIALIZATION & MAIN PROCESSING      */

8           OPEN FILE(SYSIN), FILE(SYSPRINT) ;
9           ON ENDFILE(SYSIN) EOF = '1'B ;
10          ON ENDPAGE(SYSPRINT) CALL P100PAGE;
11          SIGNAL ENDPAGE(SYSPRINT);

12          GET EDIT (SCORESIN) (COL(1), 10 F(4,1));
13          DO WHILE (¬EOF) ;
14              DO I = 1 TO 10 WHILE (SCORESIN(I) ¬= 999.9) ;
15                  SCORE = SCORESIN(I);
16                  SUMSCOR = SUMSCOR + SCORE ;
17                  SUMSQ = SUMSQ + SCORE**2 ;
18                  NO = NO + 1 ;
19                  PUT SKIP EDIT (NO, SCORE)
                        (COLUMN(9), F(2), X(3), F(5,1) ) ;
20              END ;
21              GET EDIT (SCORESIN) (COL(1), 10 F(4,1));
22          END ;

    /*    END OF INPUT: CALCULATE MEAN & STD DEVIATION */

23          PUT SKIP(2) EDIT ( SUMSCOR ) ( COLUMN(12), F(7,1) ) ;
24          MEAN = SUMSCOR / NO;
25          STDEV = SQRT( (NO * SUMSQ - SUMSCOR**2) /
                            (NO * (NO - 1) ) ) ;
26          PUT SKIP(2) EDIT ( 'MEAN = ', MEAN, 'STD DEVN = ', STDEV )
                    ( COLUMN(10), A, F(5,2), X(3), A, F(5,2) ) ;

27          CLOSE FILE(SYSIN), FILE(SYSPRINT) ;
28          SIGNAL FINISH ;

29  P100PAGE:
        PROCEDURE ;
30          PUT PAGE EDIT (' N')     (COL(09), A)
                            ('SCORE') (COL(14), A);
31          PUT SKIP(2);
32      END P100PAGE ;

33      END PROG12B ;
```

FIGURE 12–3 Calculate Mean and Standard Deviation.

Output:-   N   SCORE

1	36.5
2	40.0
3	30.9
4	41.2
5	44.1
6	40.5
7	43.3
8	23.0
9	40.5
10	35.8
11	21.9
12	34.6
13	34.2
14	39.6
15	46.1
16	28.7
17	39.8
18	59.1
19	34.4
20	46.3
21	36.4
22	44.0

840.9

MEAN = 38.22   STD DEVN =   8.11

FIGURE 12–3 (cont.)

PICTURE FORMAT FOR EDIT INPUT/OUTPUT

Picture format (not in the Subset) may be used in place of F(w,d) to *describe* the data in an input or output field, with a description enclosed in apostrophes, as

P'description'

The advantage of P-format is that it facilitates *editing* of printed arithmetic values, such as suppression of leftmost zeros and insertion of commas, decimal point, and minus sign or CR symbol to the right.

Some commonly used Picture characters follow. Except for V, each character represents a full storage position.

CHARACTER	PURPOSE	INPUT OR OUTPUT
9	Digit specifier, representing an arithmetic diglt (0–9)	Both
Z	Zero suppress character, representing a leftmost digit, that if zero, converts to blank. (Z may be used for input if arithmetic positions are blank.) For example, the value 00025 edited by P'ZZZZZ' prints as 25.	Usually output

CHARACTER	PURPOSE	INPUT OR OUTPUT
V	Decimal-point specifier, *indicating* the position where the decimal point is to be aligned. V uses no storage position.	Both
R	Digit specifier for a digit (usually the rightmost) that could have an 11-zone overpunch. Such a punch means that the value is negative. Coding the position with a '9' would cause the 11-zone to be automatically stripped on input.	Input
CR or −	Credit sign or minus to indicate a negative output value.	Output
,	Comma insert character for output.	Output
.	Decimal point insert character to cause a decimal point to print.	Usually output

Examples of P-format

Input.   Assume an input record containing a temperature reading in record positions 5–9. There is no decimal point in the record—the Picture V indicates that the field has two digits to the right of the (assumed) decimal point. A negative reading would contain an '11' zone over the rightmost digit. For example, 12.36° below zero is

$$0123\bar{6}$$

The Declarative for TEMPERATURE and the GET statement would be

```
DCL TEMPERATURE DEC FIXED (5,2) ;
GET FILE(SYSIN) EDIT (TEMPERATURE) ( COL(5), P'999V9R' ) ;
```

Output.   Assume that the program is to print TEMPERATURE with suppression of leftmost zeros and insertion of a decimal point. The PUT statement is

```
PUT SKIP EDIT (TEMPERATURE) ( COL(25), P'ZZZV.99 − ' ) ;
```

In the Picture, the V indicates that the decimal position in TEMPERATURE is to align at this location. The V uses no print position nor would it alone cause a decimal point to print. The period (.) in the Picture stipulates *printing* a decimal point in this position. The use of both characters is not redundant because at times you may want to print a decimal point other than where the V indicates. For example, you would print a fraction 1.2345 as a *percentage* (123.45%) as follows:

```
P'9V99.99'
```

Remote Format

If the same format-list, or part of one, is used in several GET or PUT statements, it may be more convenient to use the Remote R-format. For example, you could code a GET statement as

```
FORMA:      FORMAT (COLUMN(5), A(20), P'99VR', P'99V99' ) ; /* DEFINE R=FORMAT */
            GET FILE (SYSIN) EDIT ( NAME, HOURS, RATE ) ( R(FORMA) ) ;
  Any valid name
```

More than one GET statement may now reference R(FORMA) for a format-list.

STREAM BUILT-IN FUNCTIONS

The two built-in functions associated with Stream I/O are COUNT and LINENO. (LINENO is not in the Subset.)

1.   COUNT(filename) returns a Binary Fixed integer specifying the number of data items that the last GET or PUT transmitted. The following would store in K the number of data items that the last GET received from SYSIN:

```
K = COUNT( SYSIN ) ;
```

2.   LINENO(filename) returns a Binary Fixed integer specifying the current line number of the printer, a convenience if you want to handle page overflow without using ON ENDPAGE. The file must have the PRINT attribute. The following would store in K the current line number from SYSPRINT:

```
DCL SYSPRINT FILE PRINT . . . ;
K = LINENO( SYSPRINT ) ;
```

DEBUGGING TIPS

- Data-directed output is convenient for self-defining printed output, but data-directed input is clumsy and prone to errors.
- Edit-directed I/O is the most powerful of the three Stream I/O features but is also the most complicated. Carefully coordinate the data-list, the format-list, and the actual input/output record.
- When using Edit I/O, be especially careful of defining fixed-point formats. An input field need not contain a decimal point, so that a value such as

−23527 must contain a format-list entry F(6,2), assuming two decimal places. A format-list entry for output must provide for leading minus sign (if any) and decimal point (if any). The previous arithmetic value would therefore be defined for output as F(7,2) to print as −235.27.

PROBLEMS

12–1. Input records contain date (as FEB 06 19xx), temperature, and barometer reading. Declaratives for these fields are

```
DCL RDGDATE    CHAR(11),
    TEMP       DEC FIXED(5,2),
    BAROM      DEC FIXED(5,2);
```

Depict the input record format, the GET DATA statement, and the PUT DATA statement.

12–2. An input record contains the following data:

```
SCORE1 = 125, SCORE3 = 106, SCORE2 = 97 ;
```

Explain the effect of the following GET DATA statements assuming that the scores are defined as DEC FIXED(3):

(a) GET DATA (SCORE1, SCORE2, SCORE3);
(b) GET DATA (SCORE1, SCORE2);
(c) GET DATA (SCORE1, SCORE2, VALUE3);

12–3. Assume that an input record is defined as follows:

COLUMN	
1–5	Candidate number
6–25	Candidate name
26–29	
30–33	Exam scores
34–37	

Based on the following declaratives, provide the GET EDIT statement.

```
DCL CANDIDNO        CHAR(5),
    CANDNAME        CHAR(20),
    (SCORE1, SCORE2, SCORE3) DEC FIXED(4,1);
```

12–4. Code the PUT EDIT statement based on the declaratives in Problem 12–3 and the following print positions:

COLUMN	
12	Candidate number
20	Candidate name
43	Score 1
51	Score 2
59	Score 3

12–5. Three scores are defined as DEC FIXED(3). Explain the effect of the following GET EDIT statements:

(a) GET EDIT (SCOREA, SCOREB) (F(3), F(3), F(3));
(b) GET EDIT (SCOREA, SCOREB, SCOREC) (F(3), F(3));
(c) GET EDIT (SCOREA, SCOREB, SCOREC) (3 F(3));

12–6. Input records contain up to 40 scores in total and are to be stored in ARRAY defined as

```
DCL ARRAY(40) DEC FIXED(3);
```

Read the data items into the array

(a) Using a conventional DO-loop, GET EDIT, and END.
(b) Using a DO-loop within the EDIT data-list.

CHAPTER 13

FLOATING-POINT DATA

OBJECTIVE:

To cover the defining and use of floating-point data.

INTRODUCTION

Floating-point format is particularly useful to the scientific and statistical programmer. It gives the facility to process extremely small and large values, ranging from 10^{-78} to 10^{75}, for applications that require generally only up to 16 digits of accuracy. A floating-point expression may contain many variables and constants and unlike fixed-point format will not cause a FIXEDOVERFLOW error condition. Floating-point, therefore, lends itself well to statistical calculations, such as the example program at the end of this chapter. For conventional applications, floating-point has two main disadvantages:

1. Floating-point precision is generally not adequate for dollar and cents calculations.
2. Floating-point operations involve large PL/I routines to handle conversions between bases and other features, resulting in a program that may require considerably more storage than one using fixed-point.

IBM computers have floating-point registers for performing computations but have no hardware to convert into and out of floating-point format. Consider the steps involved. A numeric amount from a card or terminal enters main storage as a *character* value. The compiler generates code to convert it into *decimal* (packed) format, maintaining the position of the decimal point. It then converts into a *binary* value, maintaining the binary point. Finally, the compiler generates a complex module for converting the binary value into floating-point format. In order for a program to print or display a float value, the compiler generates code to unwind through binary, decimal, and then into character format. Despite these steps, coding floating-point in PL/I is quite simple.

FLOATING-POINT FORMATS

There are two float formats in PL/I: Decimal Float and Binary Float. The system stores and processes both formats in the same way, but the reason for two formats is for programming convenience. In some instances, you may need Binary Float to control the precision of data by specifying the number of bits instead of digits required. Figure 13–1 lists the features of the two formats.

FORMAT	DECIMAL FLOAT	BINARY FLOAT
Default precision	6 decimal digits	21 binary digits
DOS maximum	16 decimal digits	53 binary digits
OS maximum	33 decimal digits	109 binary digits
Range of values	10^{-78} to 10^{75}	2^{-260} to 2^{252}

FIGURE 13–1 Floating-point Formats.

FLOATING-POINT CONSTANTS

You may specify floating-point constants in assignment statements, declaratives, and even as input or output data. A typical floating-point constant follows:

means 2.5×10^3

1. The decimal value may contain a decimal point and a plus or minus sign to the left.
2. The letter E indicates exponential format.
3. The integer exponent may contain a leading plus or minus sign. Omission of the sign implies a plus. For example, E0 means $10^0 = 1$, E1 means $10^1 = 10$, E3 means $10^3 = 1000$, and E-2 means $10^{-2} = .01$.

Examples of floating-point constants follow:

Floating-point Constant	Fixed-point Representation		
.314159E1	.314159 $\times 10^1$ $= .314159$	$\times 10$	$= 3.14159$
314.159E-2	314.159 $\times 10^{-2} = 314.159$	$\times .01$	$= 3.14159$
.0314159E2	.0314159 $\times 10^2$ $= .0314159$	$\times 100$	$= 3.14159$
-2.5E$+3$	-2.5 $\times 10^3$ $= -2.5$	$\times 1000$	$= -2500$
-2.5E-3	-2.5 $\times 10^{-3} = -2.5$	$\times .001$	$= -.0025$

Declaring Floating-Point Constants

Decimal Float format permits initializing constants in any valid numeric format, so that you may code a constant as either Fixed-point or Floating-point. The compiler converts the constant·according to your declared precision: floating point single-precision (6) or double-precision (16). Double-precision provides more digits for accuracy. Assume the following examples:

```
DCL   FLOATA    DEC FLOAT (6)   INIT (3.14159),
      FLOATB    DEC FLOAT (6)   INIT (.314159E1),
      FLOATC    DEC FLOAT (16)  INIT (123.45),
      FLOATD    DEC FLOAT (16)  INIT (-1234.5E-1) ;
```

FLOATA and FLOATB are single-precision, and FLOATC and FLOATD are double-precision. FLOATA and FLOATC are initialized with fixed-point constants, and FLOATB and FLOATD with floating-point constants; the compiler stores them as float. Examples of BINARY FLOAT are

```
DCL   FLOATE    BIN FLOAT (05) INIT (10101E3B),
      FLOATF    BIN FLOAT (25) INIT (10111E-5B) ;
```

PROGRAM: FREQUENCY OF A CIRCUIT

Problem Definition

A program is to compute the frequency of *LRC* circuits using the formula

$$F = \sqrt{\frac{1}{LC} - \left(\frac{R}{2L}\right)^2}$$

where *L* is inductance,
R is resistance,
C is capacitance.

```
1   0   PROG13A:
        PROCEDURE OPTIONS(MAIN) ;

2   1   0   DCL   (L, R, C, F, A, B)   DEC FLOAT (16),
                  EOF                  BIT (1)  INIT ('0'B) ;

3   1   0       PUT SKIP LIST ('L', 'R', 'C', 'F') ;
4   1   0       PUT SKIP ;
5   1   0       ON ENDFILE(SYSIN) EOF = '1'B ;
6   1   3       GET LIST (L, R, C) ;

7   1   0       DO WHILE (¬EOF);
8   1   1          DO;
9   1   2             F = 0;
10  1   2             IF L = 0 | C = 0 THEN LEAVE ;
11  1   2             A = 1.0 / (L * C) ;
12  1   2             B = ( R / (2*L) ) ** 2 ;
13  1   2             IF B > A THEN LEAVE ;
14  1   2             F = SQRT (A - B) ;
15  1   2          END;
16  1   1          PUT SKIP LIST (L, R, C, F) ;
17  1   1          GET LIST (L, R, C) ;
18  1   1       END;

19  1   0       SIGNAL FINISH ;
20  1   0   END PROG13A ;
```

Output:-

L	R	C	F
5.0000000000000000E-01	1.0000000000000000E+00	5.0000000000000000E-01	1.9999999999999999E-01	3.0000000000000000E+00
2.9999999999999999E-01	5.0000000000000000E-01	3.9999999999999999E-01	2.76385391962833E+00

FIGURE 13-2 Frequency of LRC Circuits.

Solution

The program is to accept various input values for *L, R,* and *C.* Before calculating *F,* the program must check for two possible error conditions:

1.   Either *L* or *C* could be zero, causing a zero divisor;
2.   The computed value under the square root symbol could be negative.

Figure 13–2 provides the program solution using floating-point values.

EDIT-DIRECTED I/O—THE E-FORMAT

For Edit-directed Stream I/O, you may express a float value in the format-list by means of E-format, coded for input as E(w,d) or for output as E(w,d,s):

w	The length in characters of the entire input or output field, including + or − sign, decimal point, and letter E. For output, the operation rounds the value. If w exceeds the number of characters to be printed, the operation pads blanks; and if it is shorter, the operation truncates.
d	The number of decimal places in the value.
s	An optional scaling factor to specify the number of digits to print left of the decimal point (the default is 1).

INPUT OF FLOATING-POINT DATA

An arithmetic value on the input record may be entered in any valid arithmetic format, generally either as a decimal fixed-point value (which the program converts to float) or as a floating-point value. The following illustrates various input formats:

```
DCL   VALUEFLT   DECIMAL FLOAT (6) ,
      VALUEFXD   DECIMAL FIXED (5,2) ;
```

1. Use of GET LIST to read as Floating-Point: Typical Input Data:

```
GET LIST ( VALUEFLT ) ;
```
          −123.45 or −1.2345E2

2. Use of GET LIST to read as Decimal Fixed:

```
GET LIST ( VALUEFXD ) ;
VALUEFLT = VALUEFXD ;
```
          −123.45

3. Use of GET EDIT with E-Format:

GET EDIT (VALUEFLT) (COLUMN(1), E(9,4)) ;   − 1.2345E2

4. Use of GET EDIT with F-Format:

GET EDIT (VALUEFLT) (COLUMN(1), F(7,2)) ;   − 123.45

or

GET EDIT (VALUEFXD) (COLUMN(1), F(7,2)) ;
VALUEFLT = VALUEFXD ;

5. Use of GET EDIT with P-Format:

GET EDIT (VALUEFLT) (COLUMN(1), P'999V9R') ;   1234$\overline{5}$

OUTPUT OF FLOATING-POINT DATA

PL/I allows you to read or write an arithmetic value in any valid format— fixed or floating point, decimal or binary, and Picture. The following examples assume that VALUEFLT, initialized to − 123.45, contains − 123.449.

DCL   VALUEFLT DEC FLOAT (6) INIT(− 123.45),(contains − 123.449)
          VALUEFXD DEC FIXED (5,2) ;

1. Use of PUT LIST to write a Floating-Point value: Output:

PUT LIST (VALUEFLT) ;   − 1.23449E + 02 *

2. Use of PUT LIST to write a Decimal-Fixed value:

VALUEFXD = VALUEFLT ;
PUT LIST (VALUEFXD) ;   − 123.44 *

3. Use of PUT EDIT with E-Format:

PUT EDIT (VALUEFLT) (COLUMN(9), E(12,4)) ;   − 1.2345E + 02 **

4. Use of PUT EDIT with F-Format:

PUT EDIT (VALUEFLT) (COLUMN(9), F(7,2)) ;   − 123.45 **

or

```
VALUEFXD = VALUEFLT ;
PUT EDIT ( VALUEFXD ) ( COLUMN(9), F(7,2) ) ;              – 123.44 *
```

5. Use of PUT EDIT with P-Format:

```
PUT EDIT ( VALUEFLT ) ( COLUMN(9), P'ZZ9V.99 – ') ;        123.44 – *
```

The advantage of E-format is that it enables you to express extremely large or small values. If you do not know the magnitude of a value, use E(23,16).

---

* Note the loss of precision because floating-point internal representation is in hexadecimal (base-16). Round before printing for more accurate results:

```
VALUEFXD = VALUEFLT – .005 ;
PUT EDIT (VALUEFXD) (COL(9), F(7,2)) ; /* –123.45 */
```

**PUT EDIT rounds floating-point values before printing. E and F formats also round fixed-point if there is rightmost truncation:

```
DCL   VALUEFXD        DEC FIXED (6,3) ;
      VALUEFXD = VALUEFLT ;
      PUT EDIT (VALUEFXD) (COL(9), F(7,2)) ; /* –123.45 */
```

PROGRAM: CORRELATION ANALYSIS

Problem Definition

A survey has been conducted to assess the relationship between educational level and income. An investigator has taken a random survey of 14 cities in a 10-state geographical region and has determined the percentage of the city population that is college graduates (x) and the city's median income in dollars (y). A program has to use the method of least squares to fit a line to the data and calculate the coefficient of correlation and the standard error of estimate. The least squares line is based on the formula for a line:

$$y = a + bx$$

where y is the vertical axis, a is the intercept on the y-axis, b is the slope of the line, and x is the horizontal axis. The formulas for a and b based on the values of percentage of population (x) and median income are

$$a = \frac{(\Sigma y)(\Sigma x^2) - (\Sigma x)(\Sigma xy)}{n(\Sigma x^2) - (\Sigma x)^2}$$

$$b = \frac{n(\Sigma xy) - (\Sigma x)(\Sigma y)}{n(\Sigma x^2) - (\Sigma x)^2}$$

The formulas for the coefficient of correlation (r) and for the standard error of estimate (s_e) are

$$r = \frac{n(\Sigma xy) - (\Sigma x)(\Sigma y)}{\sqrt{n(\Sigma x^2) - (\Sigma x)^2} \sqrt{n(\Sigma y^2) - (\Sigma y)^2}}$$

$$S_e = \sqrt{\frac{\Sigma y^2 - a(\Sigma y) - b(\Sigma xy)}{n-2}}$$

Solution

The formulas are sufficiently complex that calculations using fixed-point format would require a number of separate steps to avoid FIXEDOVERFLOW. Also, for a programmer who is not experienced in statistics, the precision of output is initially difficult to assess. Consequently, floating-point format would be a good choice. Some factors in the formulas are common. For example, the denominator for a is also the denominator for b and occurs in the denominator for r; the numerator for b is the same for r. Rather than repeatedly calculate these values, the program should calculate them once and store them.

The program has to accumulate the sum of x (Σx), the sum of y (Σy), the sum of x times y (Σxy), and the sums of x^2 (Σx^2) and y^2 (Σy^2). The last score for x is 999.9 to signify end-of-data.

FLOATING-POINT BUILT-IN FUNCTIONS

The built-in functions that process floating-point data include the arithmetic functions FIXED and FLOAT and the array functions SUM, PROD, and POLY.

FIXED and FLOAT

The FIXED and FLOAT functions are used to convert scales according to a specified precision. FIXED converts a floating-point value to fixed-point, and FLOAT converts a fixed-point value to floating-point. Their formats are

```
fixed-value  = FIXED( float-value, p, q );
float-value  = FLOAT( fixed-value, p );
```

where p is a decimal integer specifying the number of digits in the result, q is the FIXED scale factor for the result.

```
 1      0   PROG13B:
                PROCEDURE OPTIONS(MAIN) ;
 2   1  0   DCL      SYSIN    FILE STREAM INPUT ENV( MEDIUM(SYSIPT)
                                             BUFFERS(2) ) ;
 3   1  0   DCL      SYSPRINT FILE STREAM OUTPUT ENV(MEDIUM(SYSLST) F
                                             BUFFERS(2) ) ;
 4   1  0            DEFAULT RANGE(*) STATIC ;
 5   1  0   DCL      TABSCRIN(8)           DEC FIXED (4,1) ;
 6   1  0   DCL      (I, N)                BIN FIXED (15) INIT (0);
 7   1  0   DCL      (X, Y,
                     XSUM, YSUM, XYSUM,
                     XSQSUM, YSQSUM)       DEC FLOAT (16) INIT (0);
 8   1  0   DCL      (A, B, R,
                     ADEN, BNUM,
                     RDEN, RNUM,
                     SE, XY,
                     XSQR, YSQR )          DEC FLOAT (16) ;
 9   1  0   DCL      EOF                   BIT (01)  INIT ('0'B) ;

            /*          M A I N   L O G I C                          */
            /*         *************************************************/
10   1  0            OPEN FILE(SYSIN), FILE(SYSPRINT);
11   1  0            ON ENDFILE(SYSIN) EOF = '1'B;
12   1  0            PUT PAGE EDIT ('CORRELATION BETWEEN EDUCATIONAL')
                                              (COL(30), A) ;
13   1  0            PUT EDIT ('LEVEL AND INCOME')
                                              (COL(62), A) ;
14   1  0            PUT SKIP EDIT ('X'   ) (COL(29), A)
                                   ('Y'   ) (COL(49), A)
                                   ('X(X)') (COL(68), A)
                                   ('X(Y)') (COL(88), A)
                                   ('Y(Y)') (COL(108),A) ;
15   1  0            PUT SKIP ;
16   1  0            GET EDIT (TABSCRIN) (COL(1), 8 F(4,1)) ;
17   1  0            DO WHILE (¬EOF) ;
18   1  1                CALL C10STORE ;
19   1  1                GET EDIT (TABSCRIN) (COL(1),8 F(4,1)) ;
20   1  1            END ;
21   1  0            CALL E10CALC ;
22   1  0            CLOSE FILE(SYSIN), FILE(SYSPRINT);
23   1  0            SIGNAL FINISH ;

            /*          PROCESSING OF X, Y PAIRS                      */
            /*         *************************************************/
24   1  0   C10STORE:
                PROCEDURE ;
25   2  0   C20:     DO I = 1 TO 7 BY 2 WHILE (TABSCRIN(I) ¬= 999.9) ;
26   2  1                N = N + 1 ;
27   2  1                X = TABSCRIN(I) ;
28   2  1                Y = TABSCRIN(I+1) ;
29   2  1                XSUM = XSUM + X;
30   2  1                YSUM = YSUM + Y;
31   2  1                XY = X * Y ;
32   2  1                XYSUM = XYSUM + XY;
33   2  1                XSQR = X**2 ;
34   2  1                YSQR = Y**2 ;
35   2  1                XSQSUM = XSQSUM + XSQR;
36   2  1                YSQSUM = YSQSUM + YSQR;
37   2  1                PUT SKIP EDIT ( N   ) ( COL(15), F(3,0) )
                                       ( X   ) ( COL(24), F(6,1) )
                                       ( Y   ) ( COL(44), F(6,1) )
                                       ( XSQR) ( COL(63), F(9,2) )
                                       ( XY  ) ( COL(83), F(9,2) )
                                       ( YSQR) ( COL(102),F(10,2));
38   2  1            END C20 ;
39   2  0        END C10STORE ;
```

FIGURE 13–3 Correlation Analysis.

```
          /*             CALCULATION OF VALUES                          */
          /*    ********************************************************/
40  1  0  E10CALC:
              PROCEDURE ;
41  2  0          PUT SKIP(2) EDIT
                               ('SUM'      )  ( COL(17), A )
                               ( XSUM      )  ( COL(23), F(7,1) )
                               ( YSUM      )  ( COL(43), F(7,1) )
                               ( XSQSUM    )  ( COL(61), F(11,2))
                               ( XYSUM     )  ( COL(81), F(11,2))
                               ( YSQSUM    )  ( COL(99), F(13,2)) ;
42  2  0          PUT SKIP ;

          /*         CALCULATION OF SLOPE & Y-INTERCEPT                 */
          /*    ********************************************************/
43  2  0      ADEN = (N * XSQSUM) - (XSUM**2) ;
44  2  0      A    = ( (YSUM * XSQSUM) - (XSUM * XYSUM) ) / ADEN;
45  2  0      BNUM = (N * XYSUM) - (XSUM * YSUM) ;
46  2  0      B = BNUM / ADEN;

          /*        CALCULATION OF STANDARD ERROR OF ESTIMATE           */
          /*    ********************************************************/
47  2  0      SE   = SQRT((YSQSUM - (A * YSUM) - (B * XYSUM) )
                               / (N - 2) );

          /*        CALCULATION OF COEFFICIENT OF CORRELATION           */
          /*    ********************************************************/
48  2  0      RDEN = SQRT(ADEN) * SQRT( (N * YSQSUM) - YSUM**2 );
49  2  0      R    = BNUM / RDEN ;

50  2  0      PUT SKIP EDIT ('Y = A + BX')         ( COL(17), A )
                            ('COEFF. OF CORR. =')  ( COL(56), A )
                            ( R )                  ( COL(75), F(9,3));
51  2  0      PUT SKIP EDIT ('A =')               ( COL(17), A    )
                            ( A    )              ( COL(21), F(9,3));
52  2  0      PUT SKIP(2) EDIT ('B =')            ( COL(17), A    )
                            ( B   )               ( COL(21), F(9,3))
                            ('STD ERR OF EST. =') ( COL(56), A    )
                            ( SE  )               ( COL(75), F(9,3));
53  2  0  END E10CALC ;
54  1  0  END PROG13B ;
```

Output:-

```
             CORRELATION BETWEEN EDUCATIONAL LEVEL AND INCOME
               X          Y          X(X)        X(Y)        Y(Y)

       1      7.2       12.7        51.84        91.44       161.29
       2      6.7       14.7        44.89        98.49       216.09
       3     17.0       21.1       289.00       358.70       445.21
       4     12.5       18.6       156.25       232.50       345.96
       5      6.3       11.4        39.69        71.82       129.96
       6     23.9       22.7       571.21       542.53       515.29
       7      6.0       13.3        36.00        79.80       176.89
       8     10.2       16.2       104.04       165.24       262.44
       9     11.5       17.6       132.25       202.40       309.76
      10     19.6       20.8       384.16       407.68       432.64
      11     14.3       18.9       204.49       270.27       357.21
      12     16.5       20.0       272.25       330.00       400.00
      13      9.8       15.5        96.04       151.90       240.25
      14     11.8       17.4       139.24       205.32       302.76

     SUM    173.3      240.9      2521.35      3208.09      4295.75

   Y = A + BX                        COEFF. OF CORR. =      0.950
   A =     9.767

   B =     0.601                     STD ERR OF EST. =      1.105
```

FIGURE 13-3 (cont.)

SUM and PROD

The SUM and PROD functions calculate the sum and the product of all the elements in an array. Their general formats are

```
result  =  SUM ( array );
result  =  PROD ( array);
```

The PL/I-D and PL/I-F compilers perform the operation in floating-point; if the array is not declared as float, the functions convert each element to float, with a possible loss of precision. The Optimizing compilers process either floating-point or fixed-point arrays. The following example sums the contents of the three elements of ARRAY:

```
DCL    ANS         DEC FLOAT(16),
       ARRAY(3)  DEC FLOAT(16)   INIT (10, 5, 25) ;

       ANS = SUM(ARRAY) ;   /* ANS NOW CONTAINS 40 */
```

POLY (not in PL/C)

The general format of the POLY built-in function is

```
result = POLY (a, x);
```

POLY calculates the floating-point value representing the polynomial formed by the one-dimensional array (a) and the variable or one-dimensional array (x). The following example illustrates the use of POLY:

```
DCL    ANS2         DEC FLOAT(16),
       X            DEC FLOAT(16),
       ARRAY2(3) DEC FLOAT(16)   INIT (10, 5, 25) ;

       ANS2 = POLY(ARRAY2, X) ;
```

The result of the statement is $10 + 5x + 25x^2$.

INTERNAL REPRESENTATION

The PL/I compiler converts a float constant to hexadecimal digits (base-16) and stores it as 6 or 14 hex digits, plus two digits for the exponent. (14 hex digits is equivalent to storing 16 decimal digits.) Larger computer systems also provide for "extended double-precision." The conversion between bases sometimes causes a loss of precision.

Conversion of Decimal to Hexadecimal

A decimal value 123.45 would convert to a six-digit hexadecimal value as follows:

1. Integer portion (123). Divide 16 into 123 and collect the remainders in reverse sequence:
2. 1st divide: 16 $\underline{|123}$
   7 = quotient, 11 (X'B') = remainder
3. 2nd divide: 16 $\underline{|7}$
   0 = quotient, 7 = remainder
4. Remainders in reverse sequence are 7 and B, or X'7B' (equals 123_{10}).
5. Fraction portion (.45). Multiply successively by 16:

	0.45		
	× 16	Multiply by 16	
=	7.20	Extract the 7	= .7000
	0.20		
	× 16	Multiply by 16	
=	3.20	Extract the 3	= .0300
	0.20		
	× 16	Multiply by 16	
=	3.20	Extract the 3	= .0030
	0.20		
	× 16	Multiply by 16	
=	3.20	Extract the 3	= .0003

Hexadecimal value   .7333

The hex representation or 123.45 is therefore 7B.7333. Float numbers are stored as 6 digits in single-precision or 14 digits in double-precision. The value is represented in single-precision as 7B.7333 but is expressed more accurately with double-precision as 7B.733333333333—there is no exact hex representation for 123.45. Floating-point is stored as a *normalized* value with the radix point to the left, in effect $16^2 \times .7B7333$, stored without the base (16) as:

02	7B7333

       Exponent   *Fraction*

Conversion of Hexadecimal to Decimal

The following shows the conversion of the hex value 7B.7333 into its decimal equivalent. Note that hex 'B' = decimal value 11.

$$7B.7333 = 7 \times 16^1 + 11 \times 16^0 + 7 \times 16^{-1} + 3 \times 16^{-2} + 3 \times 16^{-3} + 3 \times 16^{-4}$$

$$
\begin{aligned}
&= 112.000000000 \\
&11.000000000 \\
&.437500000 \\
&.011718750 \\
&.000732421 \\
&\underline{.000045776} \\
&123.449996947
\end{aligned}
$$

Assigning the float value to a Decimal Fixed variable with precision (5,2) would cause truncation of the rightmost seven digits and would yield 123.44. This loss of precision is not really serious, however, because you can *round* to maintain accuracy.

DEBUGGING TIPS

Floating-point computations are more likely to result in fewer execution-time errors because of the extreme range of permitted values (about 10^{-78} to 10^{75}). However, floating-point can be an inefficient way to process. It should be selected, for example, if arithmetic values are extremely high or low, if the precision of the calculated result is unknown, or if an arithmetic expression involves many steps. You may be wise in initial runs of a program to print results in floating-point notation in order to determine the precision.

Errors in floating-point are likely to arise from rounding or lack of rounding, from dividing by zero (floating-point overflow), and from coding a computation that loops endlessly (floating-point overflow or underflow).

PROBLEMS

13–1. Under what circumstances would you select floating-point format to process arithmetic data?

13–2. An input record contains two arithmetic values. The value +632.74E2 begins in column 1, and −2.534E-2 begins in column 12. An input statement is to assign the values to two variables declared respectively as FLOAT1 and FLOAT2. Define the two variables as single-precision and code a GET statement as (a) GET LIST and (b) GET EDIT using E-format.

13–3. Assume an input record contains two arithmetic values. The value 632.74 begins in column 1, and −2.534 begins in column 12. Use the same two floating-point declaratives as in Problem 13–2 and code GET statements as (a) GET LIST and (b) GET EDIT using F-format.

13–4. Assume that a GET statement is to use P-format. Based on Problem 13–3, how would the input and the GET EDIT statement appear?

13–5. Assume the same values and declaratives as in Problem 13–2. Determine the PUT statements and the appearance of the output for the following. Where possible, begin FLOAT1 in column 20 and FLOAT2 in column 35. (a) PUT LIST as floating-point, (b) PUT LIST as Decimal Fixed, (c) PUT EDIT using F-format, (d) PUT EDIT using E-format, (e) PUT EDIT using P-format.

13–6. Express the following decimal values as floating-point. Make the exponent base-10 and normalize the fraction with the decimal point to the left. For example, $47.563 = 10^2 \times .47563$. (a) 6254.78 (b) 59246524.96 (c) 0.00000648

13–7. Convert the decimal value 325.546 to normalized single-precision floating-point in hexadecimal notation. Show step-by-step calculations.

13–8. Convert the floating-point value 02 8C8000 to a decimal value. The 02 is the exponent, and the 8C8000 is the fraction as hex digits normalized with a leading radix point.

PART IV

PL/I PROGRAMMING IN BUSINESS

CHAPTER 14

FUNDAMENTALS OF BUSINESS PROGRAMMING

OBJECTIVE:
To cover the basic principles of business data processing and systems.

INTRODUCTION

Business computer systems are almost entirely involved with the entry of data, verifying the data, sorting records, updating files, and producing reports. The enormous volume of data records requires a great amount of effort devoted to systems analysis, record design, report design, and file organization techniques.

This chapter takes an overview of business data processing activities, including data entry of source documents, batch systems, and on-line systems.

BUSINESS APPLICATIONS

Among the standard data processing applications that most business installations perform are the following:

Accounts Receivable and Billing.

A company sells items on credit and must maintain records of customers. Data maintained includes customer number, customer name and address, and current amount owed. Accounting for sales, payments, N.S.F. checks, overdue payments, and calculation of interest can be a large part of the installation's programming effort.

Inventory

Many companies maintain a large stock of inventory items that are sold to customers or issued to manufacturing departments within the company. Data maintained includes stock number, stock description, current quantity on hand, unit cost of items, and selling price. Accounting for stock issues, receipts, returned goods, out-of-stock items, and reordering stock can be a major application.

Accounts Payable

Most companies purchase goods from other companies, either finished goods for resale or unfinished for manufacturing. They order the goods and set up an "account payable" for the supplier, who eventually sends an invoice requesting payment. The system must provide for paying the supplier and take advantage of discounts.

Payroll

For a company with thousands of employees, the accounting for wages earned, labor distribution, tax deductions, and pension deductions can be burdensome. Because payroll is complex and subject to regular changes, it is difficult to program, and an economic evaluation may suggest that it should not be given high priority among other applications that have a better economic justification.

Sales Analysis and Forecasting

Sales departments require information on sales by category, such as sales area, salesman, and product. A well-planned system can provide useful forecasting of expected sales for future periods.

INPUT DATA

The function of a data processing system is to accept data, to process it, and to produce information. Some estimates show that preparation of data entry involves up to one-third of data processing costs. The input data originates from various source documents and enters the system by means of data entry devices.

The processing stage involves the computer, input/output devices, and various processing programs. To be of any use, the information must have the qualities of accuracy, completeness, and timeliness.

The well-known expression "garbage-in, garbage-out" (GIGO) implies that if the input data is inaccurate, then the resulting information is invalid. But not only must the data be accurate; the processing programs must be thoroughly reliable. Only 100% accurate data and 100% accurate processing will yield 100% accurate information. The programs can be tested and retested for all conceivable conditions, but in a complex system, many conditions are completely unforeseen. Many programmers have expressed dismay that their program has run error-free for six months—and then a "bug" turned up.

The computer processing stage is concerned with verifying the data, combining different types of data, summarizing, and performing calculations. The first step, verifying the data, attempts to ensure that the input data is reasonably valid. Note that most accounting systems provide for correcting and reversing entries; consequently, entries for fields such as hours worked and quantity issued may be validly negative.

Data-entry of a Source Document

The initial input data is normally on a *source document.* For example, a vendor fills out a Sales Invoice when making a sale to a customer. The computer system requires the entry of certain data fields from the invoice, such as invoice number, date, customer number, item number, quantity sold, and unit price. An operator keys these fields into a punched card, magnetic tape, or disk, depending on the data-entry device. When the operators have completed the day's data, or a specified portion of it, the records are usually entered as a "batch" into the computer system.

Data Records

A file contains all the records associated with a particular application, such as inventory. A *record* contains the data associated with one particular item, such as an inventory stock item. The record contains whatever *fields* the analysts have decided necessary so that the system can produce the required information regarding each record and the entire file. Unlike the fixed length of punched cards, disk and tape support records may be any practical length, such as 25 or 2500 characters.

A group of records (card, tape, or disk) that contains related information is called a *file,* or *data set.* There are two main types of files: *master files* and *transaction* (or *detail*) *files.*

A *master file* contains permanent or semipermanent information. For example, an inventory master file may consist of one master record for each inventory item. Each master record contains the inventory stock number, description, unit cost, quantity on hand, and current date. A *transaction file* contains temporary data that applies only to the current period. Inventory receipts for the current period may be keyed as one transaction record for each receipt for each stock number. The record contains stock number, unit cost, quantity, and date. The transaction records are used to update the data on the master file. A computer program reads the two files; for each stock number, the program adds the quantity received from the transaction record to the quantity on hand in the master record and produces new updated master records.

BATCH SYSTEMS

There are three basic phases in a typical business computer system, as shown in Figure 14–1. The example illustrates a "batch" system in which the source documents are gathered in a "batch," keyed, and then entered into the computer system for processing. The three phases are as follows:

1. Creation of a transaction file.
2. Updating of master files with transactions.
3. File reporting.

A program when run on the computer typically prints some information about what has been accomplished. Programs should use the system printer to leave an indication at least that the job was done and when. This printout constitutes a form of "audit trail."

A *file creation run* requires input data from punched cards, a terminal, or diskette into a format that the system can accept for subsequent updating of the master file. Assume that the transaction records are payments made by customers and are to be used to update customer master records. The payments are in no particular sequence. Before the master file is updated, the program that creates the transaction file must ensure that the total of the payments is "in balance." Control clerks would already have added the total dollar value of payments on the source documents and the total number of payments made. The file creation program can add the total payments and number of records and print these at the end of the run. Control clerks can then check that the totals printed at the end of the run agree with the totals from the source documents, thus helping to ensure that the records were keyed correctly.

If there are missing records, the control clerks can then determine how many and what is the dollar value. They can use a program to list the transaction records; since the file is still in the same sequence as the source documents, the clerks can easily compare the listing against the source documents to locate missing or incorrect records.

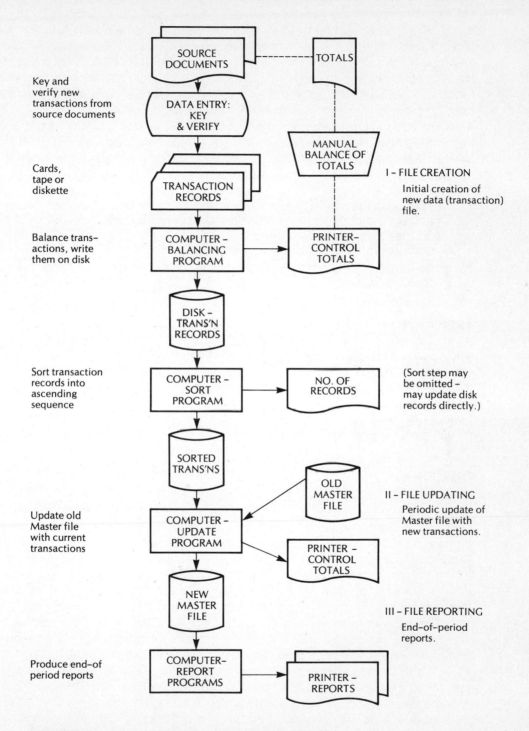

FIGURE 14–1 Typical Business Processing System.

Once the transaction file is found to be correct, the next step is to sort the records into ascending sequence by customer. This step is necessary for card and tape master files and optional for certain disk files. (Many disk systems apply transactions "directly" to the disk master file.) The sort could be considered the "second phase" in the system. However, a sort is not always done, and sort programs are almost always supplied by the manufacturer.

The second phase, the *file update run,* involves applying one or more trans-action files against a master file. In the file creation example, assume that the transactions are customer payment records. The exact update depends on the system and type of devices. However, most file updates have a common pattern:

1.   Each master record has a unique control field, such as customer account number. There is only one customer master record for an account number, and the master records are stored in ascending sequence. (The customer numbers are not necessarily consecutive.)
2.   There may be any number of transaction payments for a customer master record, or none.

Tape Files

A typical tape-oriented system has three or more tape drives, each of which can act as either input or output. The master tape file is "loaded" onto one tape drive, and the transactions, in the same sequence, on another tape drive. The program writes a new updated master tape file on a third drive. The old master file is temporarily preserved so that there is a "backup" master file in case the job must be rerun because of error or breakdowns.

Disk Files

A disk system may have, for example, 2, 3, or 4 disk drives. A disk file may be updated sequentially like a tape file, or updated directly. For example, when processing a disk directly, a program may enter the unsorted transactions in any sequence and may update the disk master records "in place." The program locates the master record for the transaction and rewrites the new changed record directly over the original master disk record. Direct processing must be done accurately because there is no automatic "back-up" if the job must be rerun.

The biggest problem in a file update is the existence of a transaction for which there is no corresponding master record. The program logic can be quite complex, especially if a programmer does not adopt some rational strategy.

The third phase, *file reporting,* comprises a large part of the programming effort. You may produce reports based on transaction files, master files, or both. In some cases a program in the system may produce a summarized "report file" on tape or disk as a by-product of some other processing. Other programs may selectively use the data in the report file to produce various reports.

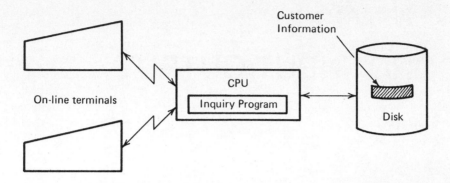

FIGURE 14–2 On-line System: Customer Inquiry.

ON-LINE SYSTEMS

In an on-line system, remote terminals are attached to a central processor, and the processor has access to required disk files. Figure 14–2 illustrates a customer inquiry system. When customers make a purchase, a sales clerk keys in their number (or enters their credit card). Customer numbers are transmitted to the central processor, which contains a program that accesses a disk file containing the customers' credit rating. The program then returns the credit ratings to the sales clerk.

Typically, an on-line system operates in a *multiprogramming* environment. The customer inquiry program is only one of several programs active in main storage at the same time. Also, the customer information file is only one of a number of files on disk. The system can therefore process not only customer inquiries but also, for example, inventory and personnel records. An on-line system typically accesses disk files directly.

PROBLEMS

14–1. Distinguish between a master file and a transaction file.

14–2. What is a major processing difference between updating a magnetic tape file and updating a disk file?

14–3. Distinguish between the features of a batch system and an on-line system.

CHAPTER 15

RECORD INPUT/OUTPUT

OBJECTIVE:

To cover the specifications for Record input/output and the use of Picture format to describe arithmetic input fields and to edit printed values.

INTRODUCTION

Record input/output is the common format for processing files in business programming and is more efficient than Stream input/output. Record I/O reads records into a main storage area and writes records out of main storage character-for-character with no conversion of arithmetic data. The closest parallel to Record I/O is Edit-directed Stream I/O using structures for input/output areas.

Under Record I/O, the standard practice is to explicitly declare a file, OPEN the file prior to processing, and CLOSE the file when finished. The READ and WRITE statements handle input and output. In earlier chapters, arithmetic fields were defined with DECIMAL or BINARY base and FIXED or FLOAT scale. But Record I/O does not permit these formats as input from cards or terminals. These arithmetic formats are valid only as input from tape or disk, provided they were initially written that way. This chapter covers the use of Picture format to facilitate input of arithmetic values and output of edited values.

RECORD I/O FILE DECLARE STATEMENTS

Under Record I/O, every file requires a file Declare statement to inform the compiler of the type of device and other characteristics. A file name is an external identifier, limited to seven characters (six under PL/C).

INPUT FILES

This section describes defining of input devices—specifically the system input reader—for both IBM OS and DOS Optimizer compilers.

IBM OS

The following defines an input file for the OS PL/I Optimizer:

```
DCL filename FILE RECORD INPUT ENV (F BLKSIZE(80)) ;
```

- FILE means that the Declarative defines a file.
- RECORD tells the compiler that the data is to be read as "records" using the READ statement.
- INPUT means that this is an input, not an output, file.
- ENV (or ENVIRONMENT) provides the format for input records, in this case F (for fixed length) and a "block size" of 80-character records. (This is PL/I Optimizer coding; other versions may use F(80).) OS permits omission of the ENV entry because it provides specifications on a DD (Data Definition) job entry.

IBM DOS

The following defines an input file for the DOS PL/I Optimizer:

```
DCL filename FILE RECORD INPUT ENV( MEDIUM (SYSIPT) F RECSIZE(80) BUFFERS(2) );
```

- MEDIUM tells the compiler that the records are to be read on SYSIPT, the system input device.
- F specifies fixed length records, all the same length.
- RECSIZE defines each record block as 80 bytes long.

- BUFFERS(2) Specifies two "buffers," which facilitate overlapping reading and processing for more efficient operation. Omission of BUFFERS(2) causes the compiler to default to (1).

PRINTER FILES

The first byte of a print record is reserved for a special "forms control character"; under Record I/O, your program must assign the character to cause the printer to space or eject to a new page. If the print width is 120 or 132 characters, you code (121) or (133) respectively.

IBM OS

The following defines a printer file for the OS PL/I Optimizer:

```
DCL filename FILE RECORD OUTPUT ENV (F BLKSIZE(133)) ;
```

IBM DOS

The following defines a printer file for the DOS PL/I Optimizer:

```
DCL filename FILE RECORD OUTPUT ENV( MEDIUM (SYSLST) F RECSIZE(121)
                    BUFFERS(2) CTLASA );
```

- MEDIUM denotes SYSLST, the standard system output device.
- RECSIZE gives the length of the print area as 121 bytes. The first position, reserved for a special forms control character, does not print. For REC-SIZE(133), you have to code a printer device number (such as 1403, 3203, etc.) in the MEDIUM entry, as MEDIUM(SYSLST,3203).
- BUFFERS defines two buffers to improve print speed.
- CTLASA tells the compiler that the program will use the ASA forms control characters, instead of the alternative, CTL360.

Warning: File declares vary by PL/I version and operating system, and the precise coding for your installation may differ from the examples given.

THE OPEN STATEMENT

Prior to reading or writing the first record, a program should OPEN the files. A statement may OPEN one file at a time, as

OPEN FILE (filename-1) ;
OPEN FILE (filename-2) ;

or may OPEN several files, as

OPEN FILE (filename-1), FILE (filename-2), . . . ;

The OPEN statement performs the following functions:

- Checks that the files specified actually *exist* (this check is especially important for tape and disk processing).
- Checks if the file is *available*. Under a multiprogramming system where the computer executes a number of programs concurrently, another program may already be processing the required files. If the file is available, the system allocates the file for the program.
- Performs special checks for tape and disk files (for example, is it permissible to write over a tape that contains records?).

THE CLOSE STATEMENT

Once the program has finished reading and writing all records, it should CLOSE the files. A statement may CLOSE one file at a time, as

CLOSE FILE (fIlename-1) ;
CLOSE FILE (filename-2) ;

or may CLOSE several files, as

CLOSE FILE (filename-1), FILE (filename-2), . . . ;

The CLOSE statement performs the following functions:

- Writes out any records still in main storage (in a "buffer") and not yet written.
- Makes the file available to other programs in the system.
- Under tape and disk, the system performs other functions.

SYSPRINT

Some systems direct diagnostic messages for execution errors onto the printer only if the program explicitly or implicitly declares a special file called SYSPRINT (a STREAM file). Messages are otherwise recorded on disk. An *explicit* declaration involves a DCL statement, as

DCL SYSPRINT FILE PRINT ;

An *implicit* declaration simply involves opening (and closing) the file, as

OPEN FILE (SYSPRINT) ;

THE READ STATEMENT

The basic format for reading input data under Record I/O is

READ FILE (filename) INTO (inputarea) ;

- *filename* is the name of the input file declarative.
- *inputarea* is the name of an element variable or structure reserved for input records. The area has the same length as the RECSIZE or BLKSIZE option in the file declarative.
- READ copies an input record character-for-character directly into an input area, erasing any previous contents. There is no conversion of arithmetic data types. Consequently, a blank or decimal point in an input record becomes a blank or decimal point in the input area. Even if a record contains unused blank positions, the input area must be defined as the full length of the record. As a result, a READ statement (unlike GET) always reads one record, no more and no less.

THE WRITE STATEMENT

The basic format for writing data under Record I/O is

WRITE FILE (filename) FROM (outputarea) ;

- *filename* is the name of the output file declarative.
- *outputarea* is the name of an element variable or structure reserved for a print record. The area has the same length as the RECSIZE or BLKSIZE option in the file declarative. Typical lengths are 121 and 133, which provide for a forms control character in the leftmost position of the area.
- WRITE copies the print record character-for-character directly onto the print file. Any blank, decimal point, or other special character appears on the printer in exactly the position specified in the print record. WRITE does not automatically clear the print area to blank.

CTLASA FORMS CONTROL

When printing a record, you must tell the system whether to space one, two, or three lines before printing, or skip to a new page. The first character of the print area is reserved for a special forms control character that tells the system what action to perform. The following lists the most commonly used ASA options. (ASA stands for American Standards Association; the control characters are common on various computer systems.)

ASA CHAR:	ACTION:
+ (Plus)	No space before printing (useful for underlining)
b (Blank)	Space one line and print
0 (Zero)	Space two lines and print
− (Minus)	Space three lines and print
1 (One)	Skip to a new page and print

The system treats any invalid control character as a blank, causing a single space before printing. To space without printing, the practice is to "print" a blank record. To indicate use of ASA forms control, code CTLASA in the ENV option of the file declarative. Another option, CTL360, is for use with IBM machine codes.

You can either *initialize* a control character, as

```
DCL 1 PRINT,
       2 CTLCHR      CHAR (1) INIT ('1'),
```

or *assign* a control character, as

```
CTLCHR = '1' ;
```

PROGRAM: PRINTING CUSTOMER RECORDS

Problem Definition

A program is to print customer records that contain names and addresses using Record I/O.

Solution

The input and print formats are as follows:

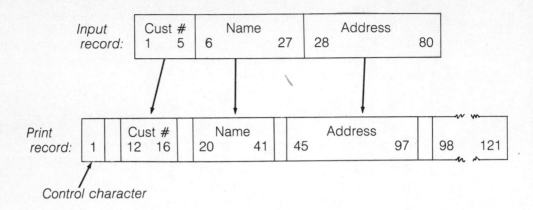

Control character

The program simply assigns each element of the input structure to the respective element of the print structure.

Note the following points in the program in Figure 15–1:

STATEMENT	EXPLANATION
2	Defines FILEIN as a RECORD input file with record size of 80.
3	Defines PRTR as a RECORD output file with record size of 121 and CTLASA forms control.
5	Defines the input record, named RECORDIN, as a structure that accounts for the entire size of the record. Matches RECSIZE(80) in statement 2.
6	Defines HEADING as a heading line for the customer name and address. The control character in position 1 contains '1' to direct WRITE to skip to a new page for printing. The heading is designed to print exactly over the columns for customer number, name, and address. All elements of the structure contain initialized character values to ensure that no "garbage" prints in the heading. Total length is 121 to match the printer file definition in statement 3.
7	Defines CUST_LINE as a detail line for printing each customer name and address record. The control character in position 1 contains blank to direct the WRITE to space one line before printing. For readability, the printed fields are separated by spaces. Customer number, name, and address need not be initialized because the program assigns input fields to them. Unreferenced fields are initialized to blank because they may otherwise contain garbage.

```
1    PROG15:
         PROCEDURE OPTIONS(MAIN) ;

2    DCL     FILEIN FILE RECORD  INPUT ENV ( MEDIUM (SYSIPT)
                            F RECSIZE(80) BUFFERS(2) ) ;
3    DCL     PRTR    FILE RECORD OUTPUT ENV ( MEDIUM (SYSLST)
                            F RECSIZE(121)BUFFERS(2) CTLASA ) ;
4    DCL     SYSPRINT FILE PRINT ENV ( BUFFERS(2) ) ;

5    DCL     1 RECORDIN,
               3 CUSTNOIN      CHAR (05),
               3 NAMEIN        CHAR (22),
               3 ADDRIN        CHAR (53);

6    DCL     1 HEADING,
               3 CTLCHAR       CHAR (01) INIT ('1'),
               3 SPACE0        CHAR (10) INIT (' '),
               3 TITLE1        CHAR (05) INIT ('CUST#'),
               3 SPACE1        CHAR (03) INIT (' '),
               3 TITLE2        CHAR (22) INIT ('NAME'),
               3 SPACE2        CHAR (03) INIT (' '),
               3 TITLE3        CHAR (53) INIT ('ADDRESS'),
               3 SPACE3        CHAR (24) INIT (' ');

7    DCL     1 CUST_LINE,
               3 SPACE0        CHAR (10) INIT (' '),
               3 CTLCHAR       CHAR (01) INIT (' '),
               3 CUSTNOUT      CHAR (05),
               3 SPACE1        CHAR (03) INIT (' '),
               3 NAMEOUT       CHAR (22),
               3 SPACE2        CHAR (03) INIT (' '),
               3 ADDROUT       CHAR (53),
               3 SPACE3        CHAR (24) INIT (' ');

8    DCL     EOF               BIT  (01) INIT ('0'B) ;

9            OPEN FILE(FILEIN), FILE(PRTR) ;
10           ON ENDFILE(FILEIN) EOF = '1'B;
11           WRITE FILE(PRTR) FROM (HEADING); /* PRINT HEADING */
12           READ FILE(FILEIN) INTO (RECORDIN) ;

13           DO WHILE (¬EOF);
14               CUSTNOUT = CUSTNOIN ;
15               NAMEOUT  = NAMEIN ;
16               ADDROUT  = ADDRIN ;
17               WRITE FILE(PRTR) FROM (CUST_LINE);
18               READ FILE(FILEIN) INTO (RECORDIN) ;
19           END ;

20           CLOSE FILE(FILEIN), FILE(PRTR) ;
21           SIGNAL FINISH ;
22       END PROG15 ;
```

Output:-

```
CUST#   NAME                    ADDRESS
10225   J SMITH                 222 WEST 43RD AVENUE
25443   AP BROWN                4327 CHESTNUT DRIVE
30668   JA RICHARDSON           4157 LAKE BOULEVARD
```

FIGURE 15–1 Record Input/Output.

Within a structure, each element name is unique. Note, however, that HEAD-ING and CUST_LINE contain some identical names such as SPACE1 and SPACE2. This practice is valid as long as no other statement references them. The control character on the left that directs the WRITE operation does not print. The remaining 120 characters are printed. If the structure length does not agree with the RECSIZE entry in the associated DCL statement for the file, an error (the RECORD condition) will occur during execution.

THE PICTURE ATTRIBUTE

Basically, an arithmetic field is entered on cards the same as a character field, and the computer reads it as "characters." But in order to perform arithmetic on such an input field, the program should define the field with the attribute PICTURE (abbreviation PIC). (Except for the Subset, it is possible to define arithmetic input fields as Character, but such a practice causes the compiler to generate inefficient conversion routines from character format into arithmetic format.) Picture format is

PICTURE 'description' or PIC 'description'

PICTURE tells the compiler

- That the field is to be used for arithmetic.
- The location of the implicit decimal point.
- The location of the minus sign (if any).

Input Pictures

Examples of typical Picture declaratives used for input are

		PRECISION	POSITIONS
QTYIN	PIC '99999'	(5,0)	5
AMTIN	PIC '999V99'	(5, 2)	5
VALUEIN	PIC '99999V9R'	(7, 2)	7

- QTYIN provides for a positive input value of five digits (5,0), with no fractional part. The decimal point is understood to the right.
- AMTIN defines a positive input field with precision (5,2). The decimal point is not punched, and the V indicates where the point aligns for arithmetic.
- In both QTYIN and AMTIN, a negative value punched as 12345̄ would have the minus overpunch stripped, causing the value to become positive. VAL-UEIN uses the R character to permit input of a possible negative value, with

precision (7,2). Note: always use R if there is any possibility of a negative value in an input field.

Output Pictures

Examples of typical Picture declaratives used for printing are

		PRECISION	PRINT POSITIONS
QTYOUT	PIC '99999'	(5, 0)	5
AMTOUT	PIC 'ZZZV.99'	(5, 2)	6
VALUEOUT	PIC 'ZZ,ZZZV.99CR'	(7, 2)	11

- QTYOUT provides for printing a 5-digit arithmetic value with precision (5,0). A negative value will print with no minus indication. A value such as 00123 will print with leading zeros, as 00123.
- AMTOUT allows for precision (5,2) and leftmost zero suppression. The V indicates where the decimal point aligns, and the decimal point (.) specifies printing the point in that position. The Z acts like a digit position '9,' but with an additional characteristic: leading (leftmost) zeros are replaced with blanks. A value such as 001.25 prints as 1.25. A negative amount prints with no minus indication.
- VALUEOUT will accommodate an arithmetic value with precision (7,2). An amount such as −01234 56 prints as 1,234.56CR, and −0001.25 prints as 1.25CR. A positive value prints with the CR suppressed.

It is a common error to confuse the V and the decimal point. Later examples should make the difference clear.

PROCESSING PICTURE FORMAT

The main purpose of Picture format is to *describe* arithmetic fields used in input and output records. An input field defined as Picture is actually in character format as far as machine representation is concerned. You can perform arithmetic on a Picture value because the PL/I compiler generates code to convert it to Decimal Fixed (packed) format. Generally, processing is more efficient if you convert input Picture fields to Decimal Fixed and then convert them to Picture for printing:

Arithmetic processing:

| INPUT: PICTURE | → | CALCULATIONS: DECIMAL FIXED | → | OUTPUT: PICTURE |

Assume that an inventory record consists of record code, stock number, description, quantity, and unit cost:

```
DCL 1 STOCKIN,
      2 CODEIN          CHAR(02),
      2 STOCKNOIN       CHAR(05),
      2 DESCRIPIN       CHAR(20),
      2 QUANTIN         PIC '9999',
      2 UNITCOSTIN      PIC '999V99',
      2 FILL            CHAR(44) ;
```

QUANTIN (quantity) is a 4-digit arithmetic field, with a '9' to indicate each digit. The implied decimal point is to the right. An alternate definition is PIC '9999V', where V indicates the implicit decimal point. UNITCOSTIN is a 5-digit arithmetic field, with two decimal places. The V indicator takes no storage space, and the Character and Picture fields add up to 80 positions.

Note: Coding UNITCOSTIN as PIC '999.99' would mean the unlikely event that the field has a decimal point entered in that position in the input record.

Assume that the program has to multiply quantity by unit cost to obtain VALUE. It is permissible to perform arithmetic in Picture format as follows:

```
DCL   VALUE       DEC FIXED(9,2) ;

READ FILE(FILEIN) INTO (STOCKIN) ;
VALUE = QUANTIN * UNITCOSTIN ;
```

To perform such arithmetic, the PL/I program has to generate code to convert the Picture fields to Decimal Fixed format. Therefore, if the same Picture field is used more than once for arithmetic, it is often more efficient to assign the Picture fields directly to Decimal Fixed and to perform arithmetic on the Decimal Fixed fields, as follows:

```
DCL   QUANT      DEC FIXED(4),
      UNITCOST   DEC FIXED(5,2),
      VALUE      DEC FIXED(9,2);

READ FILE(FILEIN) INTO (STOCKIN) ;
QUANT    = QUANTIN ;      /* ASSIGN PIC TO */
UNITCOST = UNITCOSTIN ;   /* DECIMAL FORMAT*/
VALUE    = QUANT * UNITCOST ;
```

The previous example assumed that the arithmetic fields would always be positive. In business programming, the minus sign is usually punched as an 11-zone over the units (rightmost) position of the amount field: $1234\bar{5}$ (minus sign). For example, a 5-digit amount field with two decimal places, and which could be negative, is coded as follows:

```
DCL AMOUNTIN PIC '999V9R' ;
```

The 'R' acts just like a '9' in PIC, but the R tells the compiler that this position could have a minus punch. The program will now accept both positive and negative values in AMOUNTIN. (Coding AMOUNTIN as PIC '999V99' would cause the program to treat all input amounts, positive or negative, as positive.) Note: an input field designated for arithmetic is defined as PIC; all other fields should normally be CHARACTER.

EDIT CHARACTERS

The Picture attribute is designed also to "edit" amount fields on output for dollar sign ($), commas (,), decimal point (.), and sign (− or CR). The programmer defines the Picture format in the required print positions and assigns the arithmetic field to this Picture field. The arithmetic field being edited may contain only the digits 0 through 9 and optionally a decimal point and sign.

The Picture Edit Characters are as follows:

9	Digit Specifier—Represents a digit (0–9) from the arithmetic field for formatting (see Examples 1 and 2 in Figure15–2).
V	Decimal-Point Specifier—Specifies the position in the Picture format where the decimal Is to be aligned. If the V is omitted, the compiler assumes it to be to the right of the Picture (see Examples 6 through 11).
Z	Zero Suppress Character—Replaces leftmost zeros with blanks. The Z may also cause blanks to replace commas and other characters, as shown later. Z must always be coded to the *left* of all Picture 9's (see Examples 3 and 4). Z coded to the right of the V means that *all* characters to the right must be Z (see Example 8).
*	Asterisk Suppress Character—Used in place of Z to insert leading asterisks (see Example 14).
,	Comma Insert Character—Unless zero-suppressed, causes a comma to print at the position specified (Example 9). Other available insertion characters are slash (/) and blank (B), both used the same way as comma.
.	Decimal Insert Character—Unless zero-suppressed, causes a decimal point to print at the position specified. The '.' does not signify decimal point alignment—the 'V' does that (whether coded, or omitted and assumed to the right). 'V' and '.' can be coded in either sequence:

- V. prints the '.' if there is an unsuppressed digit anywhere in the field. This is the common requirement (see Example 10).
- .V prints the '.' only if there is an unsuppressed digit to the left of the V (see Example 11).

DCL P1 PIC '99999' ,	P2 PIC 'ZZZZZ' ,
P3 PIC 'ZZZV99' ,	P4 PIC 'ZZZV.ZZ' ,
P5 PIC 'ZZ,ZZZV.99' ,	P6 PIC 'ZZ,ZZZ.V99' ;

Example	Assignment Statement:	Result in receiving field Picture:
1	P1 = 12345 ;	12345
2	P1 = 1 ;	00001
3	P2 = 12345 ;	12345
4	P2 = 1 ;	1
5	P2 = 123.45 ;	123
6	P3 = 1 ;	100
7	P3 = 1234 ;	23400
8	P4 = 0 ;	blank
9	P5 = 12345.67 ;	12,345.67
10	P5 = 0 ;	.00
11	P6 = 0 ;	00

FIGURE 15–2 Examples of Editing Statements.

Examples 5 and 6 align the decimal point in the constant according to the V in the Picture format. Example 7 does this as well, but in addition its truncation of the leftmost significant digit could cause a processing error (SIZE condition).
The following are the currency symbols and signs:

$	Currency Symbol—May be coded to the left of all digit positions (the usual case—see Examples 17 and 18), or to the right.
–	Minus Sign—If the arithmetic field could be negative, then it is possible to code a minus sign to print either to the left of all digit positions (common in scientific programs) or to the right (common in business). If the field is positive, the program replaces the minus with a blank (see Examples 12, 13, and 14).
+	Plus Sign—Acts like the minus, except the program prints + if positive and replaces the plus sign with blank if negative.
S	Sign—Acts like the + and the –, except that it prints + if positive and – if negative. A minus sign acts as a *hyphen* if embedded in a Picture, as PIC '999-99-9999' (not in the Subset).
CR	Credit Symbol—Acts like the ' – ' in that it prints CR if the amount field is negative (see Examples 17, 18, and 19), but must be coded to the right of all digit positions. There is also a DB for debit, used like CR.

Note: It is a common error to confuse the Digit specifier 'R' with CR. 'R' normally represents the units position of an input amount that may contain a minus overpunch. CR, on the other hand, denotes an output amount that may be negative. For example, a 5-digit field used for input could be PIC '999V9R', and for output could be PIC '999V.99CR'.

DCL	P7	PIC '9,999V.99 – ',	P8	PIC '*,***V.99 – ',
	P9	PIC '99/99/99' ,	P10	PIC '99B99B99' ,
	P11	PIC '$Z,ZZ9V.99CR ,	P12	PIC '$,$$9V.99CR' ,
	P13	PIC '– – –9V.99' ;		

Example	Assignment Statement	Result in Receiving Field
12	P7 = – 1000.00 ;	1,000.00 –
13	P7 = 100 ;	0,100.00
14	P8 = – 1.00 ;	****1.00 –
15	P9 = 123456 ;	12/34/56
16	P10 = 123456 ;	12 34 56
17	P11 = – 1000.00 ;	$1,000.00CR
18	P11 = 0 ;	$ 0.00
19	P12 = 0 ;	$0.00
20	P13 = – 1 ;	– 1.00

FIGURE 15–3 Examples of Editing Statements.

The symbols $, –, +, and S have two uses—*static* and *drifting:*

1. *Static:* The Picture contains only one of the symbols coded such as PIC '$999V.99' which the compiler processes normally.
2. *Drifting:* The Picture contains a string of multiple characters, such as PIC '$$$V.99'. This feature not only suppresses leftmost zeros, but also causes the drift character (in this case $) to float to the right (see Example 19 and compare it to 18). The drifting string may contain commas, dollar signs, periods, or B for blanks. The Picture may contain only one drifting string, and it must be to the left of all digit positions.

Figure 15–3 illustrates the various Picture characters. Other Picture symbols that are less important are Y, T, I, and floating-point specifiers.

Note: Sometimes you may want to print a decimal value as a percent. For example, the decimal value 0.146 is expressed as a percent as 14.6%. The following illustrates printing the decimal point in a position other than where the V is placed:

```
DCL   VALUE      DEC FIXED(5,2) INIT (12.55),
      TOTAL      DEC FIXED(5,2) INIT (85.75),
      PCT        DEC FIXED(4,3),
      PCTOUT     PIC 'ZV99.9' ;

      PCT    = VALUE / TOTAL ; /* PCT IS 0.146    */
      PCTOUT = PCT ;           /* PCTOUT IS 014.6 */
```

The example calculates PCT as 0.146 . When PCT is assigned to PCTOUT, the program automatically aligns the decimal point in PCT on the V in PCTOUT. PCTOUT will now therefore print as 014.6 , as a correct percentage.

The PICTURE Repetition Factor

Often a Picture definition contains a series of identical characters, such as the 9's in PIC '99999V999'. Such cases permit the use of the Picture repetition factor, contained in brackets, indicating the number of characters. For example

PIC '(5)9V(3)9' is the same as PIC '99999V999'.

The INITIAL Attribute

It is valid to define Picture data with the INITIAL attribute, as PIC '999V99' INIT (123.45). But since Picture is normally used for defining input and output fields, there is seldom any purpose in initializing Picture data. Arithmetic constants and accumulators are always more efficient in PL/I if defined as DECIMAL or BINARY.

PROGRAM: CALCULATION OF STOCK VALUES

Problem Definition

A file of inventory records contains stock number, stock description, quantity, and unit cost. A program is to calculate stock value (quantity times unit cost) and is to print all input fields and the computed value. Arithmetic output fields are to be edited.

Solution

Figure 15–4 provides the program solution. The input structure is RECORDIN, the heading structure is HEADING, and the print structure for stock items is STOCK_LINE. The program multiplies the Picture fields UNCOSTIN and QTYIN to calculate VALUEOUT. Although Picture format for arithmetic is valid, it is sometimes inefficient. If a Picture variable is used in more than one arithmetic expression, it is usually more efficient to convert it to a DECIMAL FIXED variable that is then used in the arithmetic expressions.

Other useful programming features that Figure 15–4 could include are provision for checking the sequence of the input file by stock number and printing a final total of stock value.

```
1    PROG15B:
         PROCEDURE OPTIONS(MAIN) ;

2    DCL      FILEIN FILE RECORD  INPUT ENV ( MEDIUM (SYSIPT)
                                    F RECSIZE(80) BUFFERS(2) ) ;
3    DCL      PRTR    FILE RECORD OUTPUT ENV ( MEDIUM (SYSLST)
                                    F RECSIZE(121)BUFFERS(2) CTLASA ) ;
4    DCL      SYSPRINT FILE PRINT ENV ( BUFFERS(2) ) ;

5    DCL      1 RECORDIN ,
               3 STOCKIN          CHAR (05) ,
               3 DESCRIN          CHAR (20) ,
               3 QTYIN            PIC '999R' ,
               3 UNCOSIN          PIC '999V99',
               3 UNUSED           CHAR (46) ;

6    DCL      1 HEADING_LINE,
               3 CTLCHR           CHAR (01) INIT ('1'),
               3 BLANK1           CHAR (10) INIT (' '),
               3 TITLE1           CHAR (08) INIT ('STOCK'),
               3 TITLE2           CHAR (24) INIT ('DESCRIPTION'),
               3 TITLE3           CHAR (06) INIT ('QTY'),
               3 TITLE4           CHAR (14) INIT ('UN COST'),
               3 TITLE5           CHAR (58) INIT ('VALUE');

7    DCL      1 STOCK_LINE,
               3 CTLCHR           CHAR (01) INIT (' '),
               3 BLANK1           CHAR (10) INIT (' '),
               3 STOCKOUT         CHAR (05) ,
               3 BLANK2           CHAR (03) INIT (' '),
               3 DESCROUT         CHAR (23) ,
               3 QTYOUT           PIC 'ZZZ9-',
               3 BLANK3           CHAR (03) INIT (' '),
               3 UNCOSOUT         PIC 'ZZ9V.99',
               3 BLANK4           CHAR (1)  INIT (' '),
               3 VALUEOUT         PIC 'ZZZZ,ZZ9V.99-' ,
               3 BLANK5           CHAR (52) INIT (' ') ;

8    DCL      SPACE_LINE          CHAR (121) INIT (' ');
9    DCL      EOF                 BIT (1)    INIT ('0'B);

10            ON ENDFILE(FILEIN) EOF = '1'B ;
11            OPEN FILE (FILEIN), FILE (PRTR) ;
12            WRITE FILE(PRTR) FROM (HEADING_LINE);
13            WRITE FILE(PRTR) FROM (SPACE_LINE);
14            READ FILE (FILEIN) INTO (RECORDIN) ;

15            DO WHILE (¬EOF) ;
16                STOCKOUT = STOCKIN ;
17                DESCROUT = DESCRIN ;
18                QTYOUT   = QTYIN   ;
19                UNCOSOUT = UNCOSIN ;
20                VALUEOUT = UNCOSIN * QTYIN ;
21                WRITE FILE(PRTR) FROM (STOCK_LINE);
22                READ FILE (FILEIN) INTO (RECORDIN) ;
23            END;

24            CLOSE FILE(FILEIN), FILE(PRTR) ;
25            SIGNAL FINISH ;
26       END PROG15B;
```

Output:-

STOCK	DESCRIPTION	QTY	UN COST	VALUE
13265	DRILL PRESS	25-	32.65	816.25-
25447	ASSEMBLERS	1225	452.36	554,141.00
26359	REGULATORS	73	43.86	3,201.78
32166	ANALYZERS	152	125.67	19,101.84

FIGURE 15–4. Calculation of Stock Values.

CTL360 FORMS CONTROL

PL/I supports both the CTLASA printer forms control character for Record I/O and CTL360, which is more versatile and somewhat more efficient. For CTLASA, the ASA stands for American Standards Association and is a universal code for various computers. CTL360 is a specific code for IBM 360 and 370 computers. The main difference is that CTLASA spaces first and then prints, whereas CTL360 can print first and then space. CTL360 has more control possibilities and requires the use of Bit strings. The most commonly used CTL360 bit codes are as follows:

Action	After Printing	No Printing
Print, no space	00000001	–
Space one line	00001001	00001011
Space two lines	00010001	00010011
Space three lines	00011001	00011011
Eject to new page	10001001	10001011

The following illustrates print and space one line, and space one line without printing. Under DOS, the MEDIUM entry must contain the device number.

```
DCL   PRTR FILE RECORD OUTPUT ENV(MEDIUM(SYSLST,3203) F
                       RECSIZE(133) BUFFERS(2) CTL360) ;
DCL 1 PRINT,
      2 CTLCHR       BIT(8),
      2 PRAREA       CHAR(132) ;

      CTLCHR = '00001001'B ;         /* PRINT & SPACE   */
      WRITE FILE(PRTR) FROM (PRINT); /*  ONE LINE       */
        .
        .
      CTLCHR = '00001011'B ;         /* SPACE ONE LINE  */
      WRITE FILE(PRTR) FROM (PRINT) ; /* NO PRINTING    */
```

Note that BIT(8) means one byte, so that the total PRINT record is 133 bytes, of which the first is the control byte, which does not print. It is also valid to use INIT to define a Bit string for forms control. The following initializes the control character for spacing one line after printing:

```
DCL 1PRINT ,
    3 CTLCHR BIT(8) INIT ('00001001'B),
    . . . ;
```

.BUFFERS

The use of buffers makes input/output more efficient. A buffer is simply an area in main storage that the compiler reserves for an input or output record. Unless you specify otherwise, most compilers assume one buffer for each file.

Input Buffers

Assume, for example, an input area called RECORDIN and two buffers. When the program reads the first input record, the system delivers it from the input device into main storage, in buffer-1. It then transfers the record from buffer-1 into the program's input area, RECORDIN. Then, while the program is processing the record, the system reads ahead, delivering the second record into buffer-2:

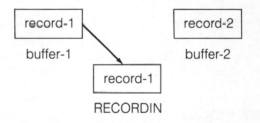

Now, when the program attempts to read a second record, it is (possibly) already in main storage, and the system need only transfer it to RECORDIN. Once again, while the program is processing record-2, the system reads ahead, delivering record-3 from the input device into buffer-1:

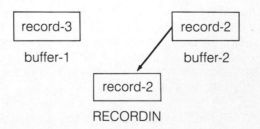

In this way, buffers facilitate overlapping of reading and processing.

Output Buffers

In a parallel fashion, writing can also overlap with processing. The system moves the output record to one of the output buffers, and the program can continue processing without waiting for the actual writing to occur. The CLOSE statement writes the contents of the last record stored in a buffer.

DEBUGGING TIPS

- Use Picture format for input fields that are to be used for arithmetic. Other input fields such as a code or a customer number should be CHAR format for efficiency.
- Use the letter R to represent a possible negative input value such as PIC '999R' (a four-digit input field) and CR or minus sign for printed output such as PIC '9999CR'.
- The defined length of a record being read or written must be the same length as in the file DCL statement (or in the DD entry for OS). Otherwise, the system terminates processing with a RECORD condition. Under DOS, for CTLASA where RECSIZE is (133) and for CTL360, the MEDIUM entry must contain a printer device number, such as (SYSLST,1403) or (SYSLST,3203).
- The use of CTLASA results in less efficient processing than CTL360, but also results in fewer errors and recompiles, especially in a student environment. An invalid CTLASA character defaults to space and print.

  An invalid CTL360 control character causes a program to "bomb." For example, a control character is not initialized or not assigned, or instead of BIT(8), the BIT format is declared as CHAR or as BIT(1).
- For efficiency, specify BUFFERS(2) under DOS or two or more buffers with OS job control.
- Although a PUT and a WRITE may reference the same printer device, they use different buffers. As a result, if you use WRITE to print detail lines and PUT to print total lines, the totals will not print on the correct line. In a program in which the main printing is WRITE, PUT may be useful for printing error diagnostics; do not expect, however, that the WRITE and PUT lines will be clearly coordinated.

A WRITE that uses CTL360 causes a print and space, whereas PUT acts as space and print. The use of these two methods in the same program may result in information overprinting on the same line.

PROBLEMS

15–1. Correct the following file declarative statements:

        (a) DCL DEVIN RECORD FILE OUTPUT ENV(MEDIUM(SYSIPT));
        (b) DCL PRTR INPUT RECORD FILE ENV(MEDIUM(SYSPRINT) CTLUSA);

15–2. What are three functions of an OPEN statement?

15–3. Provide the CTLASA control characters for the following:
        (a) Skip to a page and print.
        (b) Space one line and print.
        (c) Space two lines and print.
        (d) Space three lines and print.
        (e) Print without spacing.

15–4. Provide the CTL360 BIT control characters for the following:
        (a) Skip to a new page without printing.
        (b) Print and space one line.
        (c) Print and space two lines.
        (d) Space one line without printing.
        (e) Space three lines without printing.

15–5. What would be the contents of AMTIN defined below after a program has read a value containing 0123$\bar{4}$ (negative value)?

        DCL AMTIN PIC '999V99';

15–6. Code the structure for the following input record:

COLUMN	
2–8	Customer ID
9–28	Customer name
30–35	Balance owed (XXXX‸XX) (may be negative)
36–39	Credit limit (XXXX)
75–80	Date (mmddyy) Define the 6-character date *and* each subfield.

15–7. Code the structure for the following 121-character print record that is to space two lines and print. Fields are based on Problem 15–6 and begin in the following columns:

COLUMN	
3	Customer ID
13	Customer name
34	Balance owed (provide for zero suppression, comma, decimal point, and CR)
46	Credit limit
53	Overlimit (for balances that exceed credit limit, the difference)

15–8. Code the program that reads the input records defined in Problem 15–6 and writes the records defined in Problem 15–7. Print the overlimit amount for any balance owed that exceeds the credit limit. Provide suitable page headings.

15–9. Depict the results of the following assignment statements:

```
DCL FLDA PIC '999V9R',
    FLDB PIC 'ZZZVZZ',
    FLDC PIC 'Z,ZZZV.99CR';
```

(a) FLDA = 20.25;
(b) FLDA = −150;
(c) FLDB = 0;
(d) FLDB = 25;
(e) FLDC = −1000;
(f) FLDC = 0;
(g) FLDC = 12345.678;

15–10. Code the declaratives for the following print fields (a structure is not required).
   (a) An amount field xxxx.xx to print with $, comma, decimal point, and CR if negative. Suppress leading zeros up to the decimal point.
   (b) An amount field xxxx.xx to print as blank if an assigned value contains all zeros.
   (c) A date field mmddyy that inserts slashes so that the date prints as mm/dd/yy.

15–11. Depict the result of the following editing:

```
DCL AMTPR1 PIC 'Z,ZZZV.99CR',
    AMTPR2 PIC 'Z,ZZZ.V99CR',
    AMTPR3 PIC '$,$$$V.99CR';
```

   (a) AMTPR1 = 0;
   (b) AMTPR2 = 0;
   (c) AMTPR3   0;

15–12. A variable called AMOUNT contains 000.67. Show the edited difference between printing AMOUNT using

(a) ZZZV.99 and ZZZ.V99

(b) ZZZV.99 and ZZ9V.99.

15–13. A variable called VALUE with attributes DEC FIXED (7,2) contains 2356.27 − . Show the result of editing VALUE using the following edit words:

(a) PIC '99,999V.99CR'

(b) PIC '$ZZ,ZZ9V.99CR'

(c) PIC '$$,$$$V.99CR'

(d) PIC '−−,−−−V.99'

15–14. What is the purpose of buffers?

CHAPTER 16

PROCESSING STRUCTURES

OBJECTIVE:

To cover the requirements for assigning data between structures and variables, between different structures, handling of structure arithmetic, and other special features.

INTRODUCTION

This chapter discusses the techniques and limitations regarding structure assignment statements: assigning variables to structures, transfer of data between elements and ordinary variables, between structures, and between structures and variables.

Some programs require more than one type of input record; for this purpose there is the DEFINED attribute to redefine an area with different names and formats.

STRUCTURE ASSIGNMENT STATEMENTS

It is possible to assign data into structures at the elementary, minor, or major levels, and to assign data from structures. This section gives examples of the various possibilities, and requires the following structure definition:

```
DCL 1    PAYROLL,
         2 EMPNAME,
           3 FIRST           CHAR (12),
           3 LAST            CHAR (12),
         2 PAY,
           3 REGULAR         DEC FIXED (5,2),
           3 OVERTIME        DEC FIXED (5,2);
```

Assigning Data to Structures

The normal practice is to assign data to the elementary level of a structure. The following example assigns character literals to FIRST and to LAST of the PAYROLL structure defined earlier:

> FIRST = 'ELECTRONICS';
> LAST = 'INDUSTRIES';

However, a statement that assigns data to a major or minor level of a structure may generate invalid results, as shown next:

> EMPNAME = 'ELECTRONICS INDUSTRIES';

Because this statement assigns to a minor level rather than an elementary level, the compiler generates two statements that assign the same literal to both elements, as follows:

> FIRST = 'ELECTRONICS INDUSTRIES';
> LAST = 'ELECTRONICS INDUSTRIES';

Because FIRST and LAST are each 12 characters long, when the program executes it assigns only the first 12 characters of each literal, and FIRST and LAST will both contain 'ELECTRONICS'.

Sometimes this feature can be used to advantage, for example to clear the contents of a structure:

1. The statement EMPNAME = ' '; causes the compiler to generate two statements that validly clear both character elements to blank, as follows:

> FIRST = ' ';
> LAST = ' ';

2. The statement PAY = 0; causes the compiler to generate two statements that clear both arithmetic elements to zero, as follows:

> REGULAR = 0;
> OVERTIME = 0;

3. The statement PAYROLL = ' '; is invalid. The compiler generates statements to assign blanks to each element of PAYROLL, but it is invalid to assign a character string (blanks) to arithmetic fields (REGULAR and OVERTIME).

4. The statement PAYROLL = 0; assigns arithmetic zeros to each element of PAYROLL. But it is not normally a desirable practice to assign an arithmetic value to character fields such as FIRST and LAST.

5. The statement PAYROLL = ''; assigns a "null string" (apostrophes with no contents), and validly clears each element of the structure, character fields to blank and arithmetic fields to zeros.

Assigning between Elements and Variables

Elementary level identifiers act just like ordinary variables. Subject to the usual rules of conversion (compatible data attributes and lengths), it is permissible to assign a structure element to a variable, and a variable to a structure element. The next example illustrates both types of assignments:

```
DCL    PLACE              CHAR (8) ;    (variable)

DCL 1 INVENTORY,
      2 STOCKNUMBER       CHAR (5),
      2 DESCRIPTION       CHAR(12),     (elements)
      2 LOCATION          CHAR (8);
```

1. LOCATION = PLACE ; /* ASSIGN VARIABLE TO ELEMENT */
2. PLACE = LOCATION ; /* ASSIGN ELEMENT TO VARIABLE */

Statement-1 assigns the variable PLACE to the element LOCATION. Statement-2 assigns the element LOCATION to the variable PLACE.

Assigning Structure to Structure

It is also permissible to assign the contents of a major or a minor structure to another major or minor structure provided that both are *identically declared*. This requirement means the same relative structure—the same minor structuring with the same number of elements for each minor level. Attributes of corresponding elements may differ, but as long as they are compatible, the compiler assigns them according to the normal rules of conversion.

Assume the following structures and assignment statement:

```
DCL 1 INVENTORY,
        2 STOCKNUMBER       CHAR (5),
        2 DESCRIPTION        CHAR(12),
        2 LOCATION          CHAR (8);

DCL 1 STOCK,
        2 NUMBER            CHAR (5),
        2 DESCRIP           CHAR(12),
        2 LOCATN            CHAR (8);

     STOCK = INVENTORY ; /* ASSIGN STRUCTURE TO STRUCTURE */
```

The statement STOCK = INVENTORY; works correctly because the two structures are identically declared. It generates the following three valid statements:

```
NUMBER = STOCKNUMBER ;
DESCRIP = DESCRIPTION ;
LOCATN  = LOCATION ;
```

Assigning between Structures and Variables and the Defined Attribute

There are times when it is necessary to assign a structure to a variable, and a variable to a structure. (This need frequently arises when you are processing input and output areas.) Assume the following additional statements:

```
DCL AREA      CHAR (25) ;
AREA = STOCK ;
```

The assignment statement AREA = STOCK; is invalid—assigning a structure (STOCK) to a variable (AREA) will not execute. This obstacle is best overcome by means of the DEFINED attribute (not in PL/C). *DEFINED permits the redefining (and thereby renaming) of any variable, structure, or array, in almost any way.* For example:

```
DCL    STOCKDEF          CHAR (25) DEFINED STOCK ;
        AREA = STOCKDEF ;    /* ASSIGN DEFINED VARIABLE TO VARIABLE */
```

This example simply redefines the structure STOCK as a variable STOCKDEF. STOCKDEF is defined exactly on top of STOCK, but whereas it is invalid to assign the *structure* STOCK to the variable AREA, it is valid to assign the *variable* STOCK-DEF to AREA. The redefining merely informs the compiler of an additional way to define the same storage locations, and generates only a little more program overhead.

It is also possible to redefine AREA as a structure and to assign structure to structure, as long as they are identically declared:

```
DCL 1 AREADEF          DEFINED AREA,
      2 NUM            CHAR (5),
      2 DESCRIP        CHAR(12),
      2 LOCATN         CHAR (8);

      AREADEF = STOCK ;    /* ASSIGN STRUCTURE TO STRUCTURE */
```

Note the following points:

- In the preceding example, STOCKDEF and AREADEF are the *defined variables,* and the area on which they are defined, STOCK and AREA, are the *base variables.* A base variable cannot have the DEFINED attribute.
- The defined variable may not contain the INITIAL attribute. The reason: The compiler cannot define a constant on top of another. Only one constant is permitted—in the base variable. If a defined variable is a structure, it may be only level-1.
- The defined variable may be shorter than the base variable. In such a case, the compiler aligns the defined variable on the first (leftmost) position of the base variable.
- It is permissible to define Character on Picture format and vice versa, although some compilers print a spurious warning message. But there are restrictions regarding redefining on arithmetic fields because of field length and alignment problems. The section on Data Alignment at the end of this chapter provides more detail.

DEFINED STRUCTURES FOR INPUT/OUTPUT

The input to programs in earlier chapters was relatively simple. This section introduces more complex programs that accept more than one type of input record and output record format.

Redefining Input

Assume that an input record is defined with the following fields:

COLUMN	
1–2	Record code (a number that uniquely identifies the record)
3–4	Plant number
5–9	Employee number
10–29	Employee name
30–80	Unused

The following structure defines the input record:

```
DCL 1 EMPLOYEE,
      2 CODE21        CHAR(02),
      2 PLANT         CHAR(02),      ⎫
      2 EMPNUMBER     CHAR(05),      ⎬  80 bytes
      2 EMPNAME       CHAR(20),      ⎭
      2 UNUSED        CHAR(51);
```

Assume that the record code must always be the number '21'. The following statements read a record and test the validity of the code:

```
DCL   FILEIN FILE RECORD INPUT ;

      READ FILE(FILEIN) INTO (EMPLOYEE) ;
      IF CODE21 ⌐= '21' THEN
          DO ;
          /* IF INVALID CODE
              PERFORM ERROR ROUTINE */
          END ;
```

Assume that the program could expect more than one type of record format as input. The next structure depicts a second type of record (code 22) that is input to the same program:

```
DCL 1 STAFF DEFINED EMPLOYEE,
      2 CODE22        CHAR(02),      ⎫
      2 DEPARTMENT    CHAR(03),      ⎬  31 bytes
      2 STAFFNO       CHAR(06),      ⎭
      2 STAFFNAME     CHAR(20);
```

All input records read into the same storage area. In order that the program may know which type of record is being read, the input record EMPLOYEE is redefined as STAFF. (Notice that a DEFINED structure does not have to redefine the entire base structure.) After reading a record, the program now has to test for record type and can move the Name field (a different position in each record) to a variable called NAME:

```
DCL   NAME        CHAR(20) ;

      READ FILE(FILEIN) INTO (EMPLOYEE) ;
      IF CODE21 = '21' THEN NAME = EMPNAME ;
      ELSE IF CODE22 = '22' THEN NAME = STAFFNAME ;
          ELSE DO ;
                  /* CODE ERROR ROUTINE */
                  END ;
```

Although the READ statement references EMPLOYEE, both structures refer to the same input data because STAFF redefines EMPLOYEE. In the program, a reference to CODE21 in EMPLOYEE is to exactly the same two positions as CODE22 in STAFF. The following statements would achieve the same results as the previous example:

```
IF CODE22 = '21' THEN NAME = EMPNAME ;
    ELSE IF CODE21 = '22' THEN . . . ;
```

Redefining Output

It is also possible to redefine output areas. Assume that a program prints different record formats and uses one print area with the different formats redefined as follows. Note: only the based variable, PRINT, is initialized.

```
DCL    PRINT            CHAR(121) INIT (' ') ;

DCL 1 PR1  DEFINED      PRINT,          /* REDEFINES PRINT */
      2 CTLCHR          CHAR(01),
      2 NAME            CHAR(20),
      2 UNUSED          CHAR(04),
      2 ADDRESS         CHAR(20) ;

DCL 1 PR2  DEFINED      PRINT,          /* REDEFINES PRINT */
      2 CTLCHR          CHAR(01),
      2 NUMBER          CHAR(05),
      2 UNUSED          CHAR(03),
      2 TITLE           CHAR(25);

WRITE FILE(PRTR) FROM (PRINT) ;
```

The program can assign values to either redefined structure PR1 or PR2, depending on which format is to print. The WRITE statement writes the contents of PRINT, which now contains the assigned data. (The PL/I Subset permits reading into and writing from only the base structure, not the defined structure.)

PROGRAM: CALCULATION OF EMPLOYEE WAGES

Problem Definition

A program is required to produce employee wages. Input records contain employee number, employee name, hours worked, and rate-of-pay. Employee numbers may be in equal or higher sequence, but lower sequence is invalid. The program is to print page headings, the detail of each record including calculated wage (hours times rate), and a total of wages at the end.

Solution

Figure 16–1 provides the program solution.

Organization

Because of its large size, the program is organized into a separate main logic routine, a Procedure for processing each employee record, a Procedure for printing the final total, and a Procedure for the page heading.

Sequence Checking

The program performs sequence checking by initially storing the employee number from the first input record in a variable named PREVEMP (statement 18), and subsequently testing that each input employee number is not lower than the previously processed one (statement 28). If low sequence, the program stores an error message in the print area and bypasses calculation of wage.

Clearing the Print Area

After printing each employee detail line, the program clears the print area to blanks. For example, the print record could contain the wage from the previous employee when the program is printing a line for an employee record out-of-sequence, and the last employee name could be in the print area when the program is printing the final total. To clear the print are, a statement

```
PRDETAIL = ' ';
```

would cause a compiler error because of an attempt to assign character blanks to arithmetic Picture fields. You could assign a "null string" (PR DETAIL = '';) but it would cause zeros in the Picture fields instead of blanks. The program therefore *redefines* PRDETAIL as

```
DCL 1 PRDETAIL DEFINED PRINT,
```

and can now assign blanks to the character field PRINT using the statement

```
PRINT = ' ';
```

```
1   PROG16B:
        PROCEDURE OPTIONS(MAIN) ;
2   DCL FILEIN FILE INPUT RECORD ENV( MEDIUM(SYSIPT) F
                              RECSIZE(80) BUFFERS(2) ) ;
3   DCL PRTR   FILE OUTPUT RECORD ENV( MEDIUM(SYSLST,3203) F
                RECSIZE(121) BUFFERS(2) CTL360 ) ;
4   DCL       SYSPRINT FILE PRINT ENV( BUFFERS(2) ) ;
5             DEFAULT RANGE(*) STATIC ;

6   DCL 1     RECORDIN ,
        2     FILL1         CHAR (02) ,
        2     EMPIN         CHAR (05) ,
        2     NAMIN         CHAR (20) ,
        2     HRSIN         PIC '99V9R',
        2     RATEIN        PIC '9V99' ,
        2     FILL2         CHAR (46) ;

7   DCL 1     PRHEAD ,                      /* STRUCTURE FOR HEADING */
        2     CTLCHDPR      BIT  (08) ,
        2     FILL1         CHAR (05) INIT(' ') ,
        2     HEAD1         CHAR (08) INIT('EMPLOYEE') ,
        2     FILL2         CHAR (20) INIT (' ') ,
        2     HEAD2         CHAR (23) INIT('HOURS     RATE     WAGE'),
        2     FILL3         CHAR (10) INIT (' ') ,
        2     PAGETITLE     CHAR (06) INIT ('PAGE' ) ,
        2     PAGEOT        PIC 'ZZ9' ,
        2     FILL4         CHAR (45) INIT (' ') ;

8   DCL       PRINT         CHAR (121)INIT(' ') ;
9   DCL 1     PRDETAIL  DEFINED PRINT ,     /* STRUCTURE FOR DETAIL LINE */
        2     CTLCHDET      BIT  (08) ,
        2     FILL1         CHAR (05) ,
        2     EMPOT         CHAR (05) ,
        2     FILL2         CHAR (01) ,
        2     NAMOT         CHAR (20) ,
        2     FILL3         CHAR (01) ,
        2     HRSOT         PIC 'ZZZV.99CR' ,
        2     FILL4         CHAR (03) ,
        2     RATEOT        PIC 'ZV.99' ,
        2     FILL5         CHAR (03) ,
        2     WAGEOT        PIC 'ZZ9V.99CR' ,
        2     MESSAGOT      CHAR (19) ,
        2     FILL6         CHAR (43) ;

10  DCL 1     PRTOTAL ,
        2     CTLCHTOT      BIT  (08) INIT ('00010001'B) ,
        2     FILL1         CHAR (16) INIT (' ') ,
        2     TITLEOT       CHAR (13) INIT ('TOTALS') ,
        2     TOTALHOUROT   PIC 'ZZ,ZZ9V.99CR' ,
        2     FILL2         CHAR (07) INIT (' ') ,
        2     TOTALWAGEOT   PIC 'ZZ,ZZ9V.99CR' ,
        2     FILL3         CHAR (62) INIT (' ') ;

11  DCL       LINECT        DEC FIXED (3) INIT (0) ,
              PAGECT        DEC FIXED (3) INIT (1) ,
              RATE          DEC FIXED (3,2) ,
              (HOURS,
              WAGE)         DEC FIXED (5,2) ,
              (WAGETOTAL,
              HOURTOTAL)    DEC FIXED (7,2) INIT(0) ;
12  DCL       EOF           BIT  (01) INIT ('0'B) ,
              PREVEMP       CHAR (05) INIT (' ') ;
13  DCL       ROUND         BUILTIN ;
```

FIGURE 16–1 Calculation of Employee Wages.

```
     /*          M A I N   L O G I C       */

14            OPEN FILE(FILEIN), FILE(PRTR);
15            ON ENDFILE(FILEIN) EOF = '1'B;
16            CALL P100_PAGE ;
17            READ FILE(FILEIN) INTO(RECORDIN);
18            PREVEMP = EMPIN ;
19            DO WHILE (¬EOF) ;
20               IF LINECT > 50 THEN CALL P100_PAGE ;
21               CALL B100_EMP ;
22               READ FILE(FILEIN) INTO (RECORDIN) ;
23            END ;
24            CALL F100_FINAL ;
25            CLOSE FILE(FILEIN), FILE(PRTR);
26            SIGNAL FINISH ;


     /*        E M P L O Y E E   P R O C E S S I N G     */
27   B100_EMP:
         PROCEDURE ;
28            IF EMPIN < PREVEMP THEN
                 MESSAGOT = 'OUT OF SEQUENCE' ;
29            ELSE DO ;
30               HOURS = HRSIN ;
31               RATE  = RATEIN ;
32               WAGE  = ROUND(HOURS * RATE, 2) ;
33               WAGETOTAL = WAGETOTAL + WAGE ;
34               HOURTOTAL = HOURTOTAL + HOURS;
35               WAGEOT = WAGE ;
36               RATEOT = RATE ;
37               PREVEMP = EMPIN ;
38               HRSOT  = HOURS;
39            END ;
                                          /* WRITE EMPLOYEE RECORD */
40            NAMOT = NAMIN ;
41            EMPOT = EMPIN ;
42            CTLCHDET = '00001001'B ;
43            WRITE FILE(PRTR) FROM (PRINT) ;
44            PRINT = ' ' ;                /* CLEAR PRINT AREA */
45            LINECT = LINECT + 1 ;
46         END B100_EMP ;


     /*        E N D   O F   F I L E   P R O C E S S I N G     */
47   F100_FINAL:
         PROCEDURE ;
48            CTLCHDET = '00001011'B ;
49            WRITE FILE(PRTR) FROM (PRINT) ;
50            TOTALWAGEOT = WAGETOTAL ;
51            TOTALHOUROT = HOURTOTAL ;
52            WRITE FILE(PRTR) FROM (PRTOTAL) ;
53         END F100_FINAL ;


     /*        P A G E   H E A D I N G     */
54   P100_PAGE:
         PROCEDURE ;
55            CTLCHDPR = '10001011'B ;        /* EJECT TO NEXT PAGE   */
56            WRITE FILE(PRTR) FROM (PRHEAD) ;
57            PAGEOT = PAGECT ;
58            CTLCHDPR = '00010001'B ;        /* PRINT & SPACE 2      */
59            WRITE FILE(PRTR) FROM (PRHEAD) ;
60            LINECT = 0 ;                    /* CLEAR LINE COUNTER   */
61            PAGECT = PAGECT + 1 ;           /* INCREMENT PAGE COUNT */
62         END P100_PAGE ;

63      END PROG16B ;
```

FIGURE 16-1 (con't.)

Output:-

```
  EMPLOYEE                    HOURS    RATE    WAGE            PAGE     1

  00125 SJ ADAMS              2.00     4.25     8.50
  01247 JL BROWN              2.00     5.50    11.00
  01227                                                 OUT OF SEQUENCE
  02345 AK CHOW               2.00     8.55    17.10
  31644 MN DAVISON            2.00     5.04    10.08
  33229 P  EDDINGTON         99.99     9.99   998.90
  40415 JB FERRARI          10.00CR    6.50    65.00CR

            TOTALS          97.99             980.58
```

FIGURE 16–1 (con't.)

Page Overflow

The printer uses *continuous forms,* generally paper about 14 or 15 inches wide, with perforations every 11 inches down the page. Each page can accommodate about 66 lines, at six lines per inch. A statement in the program counts the number of lines printed; when the count exceeds 50, the program CALLs the page heading Procedure, which ejects to the top of the next page, prints the report heading, and resets the line count.

ADDITIONAL STRUCTURE FEATURES

Other features concerned with structures include qualified names, the LIKE attribute, structure arithmetic, and the BY NAME assignment.

Qualified Names

Within a program and within a structure, minor levels and elementary levels may have the same names. Assume the following structure:

```
DCL  1  INVENTORY,
        2  STOCKNO        CHAR(05),
        2  DESCRIPTION    CHAR(10),
        2  QUANTITY       DEC FIXED(4),
        2  PRICE,
           3  SALES       DEC FIXED(5,2),
           3  COST        DEC FIXED(5,2),
        2  VALUE,
           3  SALES       DEC FIXED(9,2),
           3  COST        DEC FIXED(9,2);
```

In the structure INVENTORY, the names SALES and COST appear twice. A statement such as SALES = 1.00; is an *ambiguous reference* because the compiler does not know which identifier to reference. (Some PL/I versions arbitrarily select one of them and issue a warning.) There are two ways to avoid such ambiguities:

1. Avoid the use of duplicate names wherever possible.
2. Use a *qualified name*—an elementary name or minor structure name that is made unique by qualifying it with one or more names at a higher level. A qualified name uses a period (.) between names as follows:

```
PRICE.SALES = 1.00 ;                      /* VALID QUALIFIED NAME       */
INVENTORY.PRICE.SALES = 1.00 ;            /* VALID QUALIFIED NAME       */
INVENTORY.SALES = 1.00 ;                  /* AMBIGUOUS QUALIFIED NAME */
```

The first two statements are valid, and both uniquely qualify the identifier SALES defined in the minor structure PRICE. The third statement, although qualified, is still ambiguous because it could reference either element called SALES.

The LIKE Attribute (not in PL/C or the Subset)

Assume the following structure:

```
DCL 1 ACTUALEXPENSE,
      2 PLANT,
        3 LABOR           DEC FIXED(7,2),
        3 HEATLIGHT       DEC FIXED(7,2),
        3 REPAIRS         DEC FIXED(7,2),
      2 HEADOFFICE,
        3 SALARIES        DEC FIXED(7,2),
        3 RENT            DEC FIXED(7,2),
        3 ADVERTISING     DEC FIXED(7,2);
```

Assume that the program requires another structure called BUDGET, declared identically to ACTUALEXPENSE. It is possible to declare BUDGET line-for-line exactly like ACTUALEXPENSE. An easier solution is to declare BUDGET with a one-line statement using the LIKE attribute:

```
DCL 1 BUDGET LIKE ACTUALEXPENSE ;
```

The LIKE attribute causes generation of the same minor and elementary names and attributes.

Structure Arithmetic

Two structures may be identically declared—the same minor structuring with the same number of elements for each minor level. In such a case, it is possible to assign one structure to the other, or to perform arithmetic from one to the other. In the previous structure examples ACTUALEXPENSE and BUDGET, you could code six subtract statements in order to subtract each element respectively in ACTUALEXPENSE from each element in BUDGET:

BUDGET.PLANT.LABOR = BUDGET.PLANT.LABOR − ACTUALEXPENSE.PLANT.LABOR ; etc. . .

Structure arithmetic permits subtraction at major or minor levels provided the structures are identically declared. This example requires only one statement to subtract each of the respective elements:

BUDGET = BUDGET − ACTUALEXPENSE ;

It is also possible to multiply or divide each element in a structure by an expression:

```
BUDGET = BUDGET * 2 ;                    /* MULTIPLY ALL ELEMENTS   */
BUDGET.PLANT = BUDGET. PLANT * 2 ;       /*MULTIPLY PLANT ELEMENTS */
```

BY NAME Assignment

Assume the following input structures:

```
DCL 1 RECORDIN,                     DCL 1 PRINTAREA,
      2 CODE       CHAR(02),              2 CTLCHAR    CHAR(01),
      2 STOCKNO    CHAR(05),              2 BLANK1     CHAR(03),
      2 STOCKNAME  CHAR(15),              2 STOCKNO    CHAR(05),
      2 QUANTITY   PIC '99R',             2 BLANK2     CHAR(03),
      2 PRICE      PIC '999V99',          2 STOCKNAME  CHAR(15),
      2 FILLIN     CHAR(50);              2 BLANK3     CHAR(03),
                                          2 QUANTITY   PIC 'ZZ9-',
                                          2 BLANK4     CHAR(03),
                                          2 PRICE      PIC 'ZZ9V.99',
                                          2 BLANK5     CHAR(78);
```

The assignment statement

PRINTAREA = RECORDIN, BY NAME;

causes the program to assign those elements of RECORDIN to those of PRIN-TAREA that have the same unique name. The elements assigned are STOCKNO,

STOCKNAME, QUANTITY, and PRICE. In effect, from the one coded statement the compiler generates four assignment statements. The phrase BY NAME is coded in the assignment statement, preceded by a comma.

The NAME assignment is the only exception to the rule that both structures must have the same relative structuring to permit an assignment statement. This feature is not available under the Subset.

DATA ALIGNMENT

In PL/I, data may be declared as ALIGNED or UNALIGNED. The default where the attribute is not specified is

Unaligned:	BIT, CHARACTER, and PICTURE.
Aligned:	All other formats including arithmetic.

The reason for alignment is a characteristic of the IBM 360/370 storage design. For some data formats, the computer executes faster if the data is aligned on an integral storage boundary. For example, the normal starting position for BINARY FIXED (15) is alignment on a storage location evenly divisible by two, and BINARY FIXED (31) on a location evenly divisible by four. There may be times when a programmer wants this automatic alignment in order to gain faster execution speed. But, if structures or arrays contain many elements that automatically align, there may be considerable storage space lost because of the compiler adjusting data onto boundaries. In such cases, if the saving in space is more urgent than the saving in execute-time, the use of the UNALIGNED attribute may help reduce storage. The following defaults to the ALIGNED attribute:

```
DCL 1 STRUCTA,
      2 FLDA    BIN FIXED (31),
      2 FLDB    BIN FIXED (15),
      2 FLDC    BIN FIXED (31);
```

FLDA and FLDC are each four bytes long, aligned on an address evenly divisible by four, and FLDB is two bytes, on an even address. If FLDA happened to align on location 10,000, then FLDB would be aligned next, then two unused bytes, and then FLDC on 10,008, as shown:

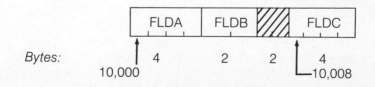

Bytes:

To avoid such a loss of storage space, STRUCTA may be given the UNA-LIGNED attribute, as

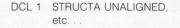

DCL 1   STRUCTA UNALIGNED,
            etc. . . .

The compiler will store the three elements with no alignment and no loss of storage space, as follows:

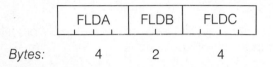

The compiler will store the three elements with no alignment and no loss of storage space, as follows:

FLDA	FLDB	FLDC

Bytes: 4   2   4

Alignment requirements for the various formats are listed in Figure 16–2.

A problem may arise from the use of DEFINED where data is defined on unaligned data, or vice versa. For example:

```
DCL 1 STRUCTB,
      2 A        CHAR (1),
      2 B        BIN FIXED (15),
      2 C        DEC FIXED (5) ,
      2 D        BIN FIXED (31);

DCL   FIELD CHAR(10) DEFINED STRUCTB ;
```

Assuming that element B aligns on an even location 10,000, then STRUCTB would align in storage as

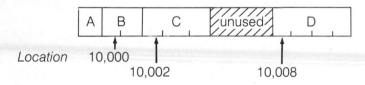

The compiler aligns B on an address divisible by two and D on one divisible by four, leaving three unused bytes in the structure. For the declarative FIELD defined on STRUCTB, the compiler will issue a warning message because the contents of FIELD may not contain the data that the programmer expects. Defining STRUCTB as UNALIGNED will avoid the alignment problem.

The normal practice is to redefine like data formats, such as Character on Character. An allowable safe exception is Character defined on Picture, and vice versa. The same basic rules apply to redefining arrays. The PL/I manual has a more complete coverage for the appropriate version of the compiler.

FORMAT		REQUIRED STORAGE	ALIGNMENT
1. BIT (n)	ALIGNED	CEIL (n/8 bytes)*	On next byte boundary.
	UNALIGNED	n bits	On next bit boundary.
2. BIT (n) VARYING			
	ALIGNED	CEIL (n/8 bytes)* + 2-byte prefix	On halfword boundary.
	UNALIGNED	n bits + 2-byte prefix	On byte boundary.
3. CHAR (n)	ALIGNED	n bytes	On byte boundary.
	UNALIGNED	n bytes	On byte boundary.
4. CHAR (n)VARYING			
	ALIGNED	n + 2-byte prefix	On halfword boundary.
	UNALIGNED	n + 2-byte prefix	On byte boundary.
5. PICTURE	ALIGNED	Number of PIC characters except V & K.	On byte boundary.
	UNALIGNED	Same.	Same.
6. DECIMAL FIXED (p,q)			
	ALIGNED	CEIL((p + 1)/2)*	On byte boundary.
	UNALIGNED	Same.	Same.
7. BINARY FIXED (p,q)			
p<=15	ALIGNED	2 bytes	Halfword.
p> 15	ALIGNED	4 bytes	Fullword.
p<=15	UNALIGNED	2 bytes	On byte boundary.
p> 15	UNALIGNED	4 bytes	On byte boundary.
8. DECIMAL FLOAT (p)			
p<7	ALIGNED	4 bytes	Fullword.
p>=7	ALIGNED	8 bytes	Doubleword.
p<7	UNALIGNED	4 bytes	On byte boundary.
p>=7	UNALIGNED	8 bytes	On byte boundary.
9. Other formats: POINTER, OFFSET, FILE, ENTRY, LABEL			
	ALIGNED	4 bytes	Fullword.
	UNALIGNED	4 bytes	On byte boundary.

Halfword   : 2 bytes, on boundary evenly divisible by 2.

Fullword   : 4 bytes, on boundary evenly divisible by 4.

Doubleword: 8 bytes, on boundary evenly divisible by 8.

DECIMAL FIXED data requires $\frac{1}{2}$-byte per digit + $\frac{1}{2}$-byte for the sign.

*CEIL means the next highest integer if not evenly divisible.

FIGURE 16–2 Alignment for Data Formats.

Note: UNALIGNED is especially useful for tape and disk input/output records that contain fields in Binary format. In the structure for the I/O record, it is necessary to prevent the compiler from aligning the Binary fields erroneously.

DEBUGGING TIPS

- Watch for possible alignment problems when coding BINARY or FLOAT in a structure.
- You may assign the contents of one structure to another only if they are "identically declared."
- A common error occurs when an arithmetic input field is blank. When a program attempts to process a blank PIC field, the system generates a "data exception" and terminates processing. One solution is to redefine the PIC field as CHAR, and if the CHAR variable contains blanks, store zeros in the PIC format, as follows:

```
DCL 1 RECORDIN,
      3 ... ;
      3 AMTIN          PIC '999V9R',
      3 ... ;
DCL   AMTCHIN          CHAR(5) DEFINED AMTIN ;
      .
      .
      .
IF AMTCHIN = ' ' THEN AMTIN = 0.00 ;
```

- If a print structure contains Picture items, you cannot directly clear the structure to blanks. Either assign a null string or use DEFINED to redefine the structure as CHAR (133) and clear the redefined structure to blanks.

- When using Picture format, you may have to redefine Character and Picture variables. The use of DEFINED to redefine Character over Picture and vice versa causes the compiler (depending on compiler version) to generate an E-level message:

INVALID USE OF 'DEFINED' IN DECLARATION OF 'variable-name'.

Ignore the "error" message; the compiler still generates the correct executable code. Both PIC and CHAR occupy one byte of storage per character and are basically similar. However, actual errors may occur if you redefine DECIMAL/BINARY and FIXED/FLOAT variables.

- The IF statement permits comparison only of element-expressions. Consequently, you cannot directly compare major or minor structures. Assume that you want to check if DEPTPRODIN in the following structure contains '23057':

```
DCL 1    RECORDIN,
         2  DEPTPRODIN,
            3 DEPTIN        CHAR(2),
            3 PRODIN        CHAR(3),
         2  etc. . . ;
```

The statement IF DEPTPRODIN = '23057' is invalid because DEPTPRODIN is not at the elementary level. Possible solutions include the following:

1.   DEFINED:

```
DCL DEPRODEF CHAR (5) DEFINED DEPTPRODIN;
IF DEPRODEF = '23057' THEN . . . ;
```

2.   Compound Expression:

```
IF DEPTIN = '23' & PRODIN = '057' THEN . . . ;
```

3.   STRING:

```
IF STRING(DEPTPRODIN) = '23057' THEN . . . ;
```

4.   Concatenation:

```
IF DEPTIN || PRODIN = '23057' THEN . . . ;
```

Chapter 19 covers the STRING built-in function and concatenation.

PROBLEMS

16–1. Assign the contents of STRUCTA to STRUCTB defined below. Be careful—the structures are not "identically declared," and you may have to make additional definitions.

```
DCL 1    STRUCTA,
         2  A        CHAR (5),
         2  B        CHAR (4),
         2  C        CHAR (3);
```

```
DCL 1      STRUCTB,
           2 D,
           3 D1          CHAR (3),
           3 D2          CHAR (4),
           2 E           CHAR (5);
```

16–2. Locate and correct the three errors in the following related declaratives:

```
DCL        FLD1         CHAR(45);
DCL 1      STRUCA       DEFINED FLD1,
           2 NAME1      CHAR(20) INIT (' '),
           2 ADDR1      CHAR(25) INIT (' ');
DCL 1      STRUCB       DEFINED STRUCA,
           2 NAME2      CHAR(20),
           2 ADDR2      CHAR(30);
```

16–3. In the following, assume that RATE now contains '073081012025.' What is the effect of the assignment statement? Explain.

```
DCL 1      WEATHER,
           2 TEMP       CHAR(3),
           2 HUMIDITY   CHAR(3),
           2 WIND       CHAR(3),
           2 RAINFALL   CHAR(3);


DCL        RATE         CHAR(12);
           WEATHER = RATE;
```

Show how else you may correctly assign the contents of RATE to the elements of WEATHER.

16–4. The following is an array of structures called EMPTABLE that contains employee name (NAMETAB), hours worked (HOURTAB), and rate-of-pay (RATETAB). Assume that an earlier routine has already loaded the arrays from input records. The routine has also counted the number of records stored in a variable called KOUNT. Code the routine only for the following:

- For each employee in the table, calculate wage = hours × rate-of-pay.
- For each employee, print employee name, hours, rate, and wage, By-pass any employee with zero hours worked. Some hours may validly be negative because of reversing and correcting entries.
- Define a print structure with about three spaces between each item.

```
DCL        PRTR FILE RECORD OUTPUT;
DCL 1      EMPTABLE(100),
           2 NAMETAB    CHAR(25),
           2 HOURTAB    DEC FIXED (3,1),
           2 RATETAB    DEC FIXED(4,2);
DCL        KOUNT        BIN FIXED(15);
```

16–5. In the following structure, determine the length of each element, its alignment, and the length of the structure.

```
DCL 1      STRUCTYOUR,
           2 B          BINARY FIXED (31),
           2 C          CHAR (1),
           2 D          BINARY FIXED (31),
           2 E          DECIMAL FIXED (5,2),
           2 F          BINARY FIXED (15) UNALIGNED;
```

CHAPTER 17

CONTROL BREAKS

OBJECTIVE:
To cover the input logic to handle sequence-
checking and control breaks.

INTRODUCTION

To produce a report, a file usually must be in a predetermined sequence, and programs must be coded to process the file accordingly. Each record may contain one or more control fields such as department number or inventory stock number that a program checks to determine the action to take. For example, it is often necessary to perform a "control break" in which totals are printed according to a specified control field.

Also, a program should not assume that records are in the correct sequence. A simple test can check the file sequence in order to terminate the program before it produces pages of garbage. This chapter is concerned with the strategy of testing control fields and determining the action to take.

SEQUENCE CHECKING

In a typical file processing program, the basic decision around which the program logic pivots is the sequence check. Because most files contain records in ascending sequence by a control word, the control word of an input record is higher than, equal to, or lower than the control word of the previously processed record. A sequence test is therefore a major determinant in the direction of program logic. As a general rule in data processing, every program that processes a file sequentially tests its sequence. For a file in ascending sequence, two special conditions may exist:

1.   *The control number for each input record is unique.* In an Inventory master file, no two Stock numbers may be the same. As shown, each succeeding record that the program reads may be only high—an equal control number means a duplicate record, and low means that the record is out of sequence:

```
Read First Stock record;
DO WHILE not end-of-file ;
    New Stock number : previous Stock number ,
        If low — error, out-of-sequence ,
        If equal — error, duplicate record ,
        Else high — process record, store new Stock
                        number in previous ;
    Read next stock record ;
End of DO WHILE ;
```

2.   *The control number for each input record is not unique.* There may be more than one record for each control word, such as Stock issues and receipts that are current transactions for the same Stock item. As shown, a succeeding record may be validly high or equal, but low is still an error:

```
Read First Stock record ;
DO WHILE not end-of-file ;
    New Stock number : previous Stock number ,
        If low — error, out-of-sequence ,
        If equal — same Stock number, process ,
        Else high — new Stock number, process, store
                        new Stock number in previous ;
    Read next Stock record ;
END of DO WHILE ;
```

When embarking upon a new programming problem, concern your initial strategy with the sequence of the input file(s). You can design the associated logic around this fundamental test. In all the examples in this chapter, the sequence check occurs as the central instruction.

SIMPLE CONTROL BREAKS

A *control break* occurs when a program encounters a high sequence on the control word and has to produce totals to that point. For example, assume that there may be any number of payments per customer for a file of customer payment transactions. The program requires the total amount paid by each customer. The basic program logic checks the sequence of customer for each input record by comparing the new customer number to the previously read (and stored) customer number:

```
ON ENDFILE (set end-of-file) ;
Read first customer record;
DO WHILE ( not end-of-file) ;
    New customer # : previous customer # ;
      If low — error, out-of-sequence ;
      If high (control break)
         Print stored customer total ,
         Add customer total to final total ,
         Clear customer total ,
         Store new customer # in previous customer # ;
      Else equal (same customer as previous) ;
    Add payments to customer total ;
    Read next customer record ;
END of DO WHILE ;
```

For each newly read customer number that is equal to the one previously read, the program adds the payment to the customer's total. On a high sequence there is a control break; the program must print the total payments for the *previously stored* customer. It then adds those total payments to a final total and clears to zero the customer payment total. But avoid two common programming errors. *First, it is necessary now to initialize the sequence check for the next input record:* store the new customer number in a field designated as "previous" Customer number. *Second, the record that caused the control break is still in the input area and has not yet been processed.* The program executes the instructions that process the new customer (add the payment to the customer total).

The coding is incomplete for two reasons. First, the first input record will cause a *false control break.* Assuming that "previous customer" is initialized to blanks, the first record will always be higher than "previous," and the program will break control and print zero totals for the first "stored" customer. Second, the end-of-file condition is not complete. On end-of-file, if you simply print final totals, you will fail to print the stored totals for the last customer. Both first record and end-of-file conditions are the cause of many programming errors and require special treatment.

First Record Condition

On a sequence check, the first input record may cause a "false control break." If the Main Logic initialization has a READ operation, you can avert this situation by storing the new input control word in the previous control word:

```
OPEN FILE(FILEIN) ... ;
ON ENDFILE(FILEIN) EOF = '1'B ;
READ FILE (FILEIN) INTO (RECORDIN) ;
PREV_CUST = CUST_IN ;
DO WHILE (¬EOF) ;
    IF ...
        .
        .
        .
END ;
```

With the new Customer number assigned to PREV_CUST, the first sequence test will always generate an equal condition, thus preventing a false control break.

End-of-file Condition

Although the program has processed all input records when the end-of-file occurs, it may not have completed all processing to that point. The program still has to print the stored total for the last customer in the file. It may help to think of the end-of-file condition as a special control break requiring the printing of all stored totals to that point.

There are several ways to handle the end-of-file. The simplest solution on encountering the end would print the last stored customer total and then print the final total. This solution may be adequate if there is little processing on the control break. But programs often have many instructions involved in the printing of total lines. Recoding instructions causes additional coding time, more debugging, and larger program size.

The solution is to organize the program into a main logic routine and various related subroutines (procedures). The printing of customer totals would be one of the subroutines that the program performs on both a high control break and on end-of-file.

PROGRAM: SIMPLE CONTROL BREAK

Figure 17–1 provides the flowchart for a program that handles a control break on Customer number. In this and following examples, the flowchart depicts the general logic and does not indicate every operation that the program executes, such as clearing the print line and adding to the line count (simple operations that almost every program performs). Many instructions, although important to the program's execution, are logically trivial. Many experienced programmers (if they draw a flowchart at all) are inclined to design only the logical pattern from which they code the detailed instructions.

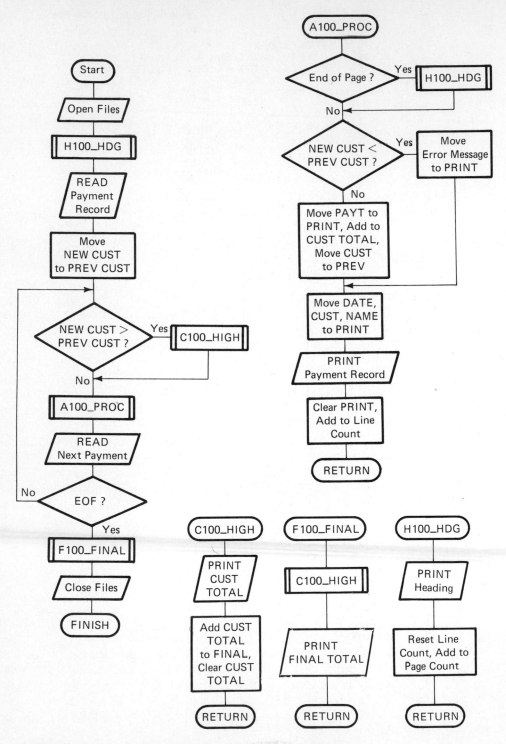

FIGURE 17-1 Flowchart for One-level Control Break.

Figure 17–2 shows the program listing. Note that after the initial READ, there is an assignment statement that stores CUST_IN in PREV_CUST. As a result, on the first sequence-check, the first record tests as equal and consequently there is no false control break.

```
1      0   PROG17A:
               PROCEDURE OPTIONS(MAIN) ;

2    1 0   DCL FILEIN FILE INPUT RECORD ENV( MEDIUM(SYSIPT) F
                                       RECSIZE(080) BUFFERS(2) ) ;
3    1 0   DCL PRTR   FILE OUTPUT RECORD ENV( MEDIUM(SYSLST,3203) F
                                       CTL360 RECSIZE(133)BUFFERS(2) ) ;
4    1 0   DCL SYSPRINT FILE PRINT ENV(BUFFERS(2));

5    1 0       DEFAULT RANGE(*) STATIC ;
6    1 0   DCL     CUSTOTAL            DEC FIXED (7,2) INIT (0) ,
                   FINALTOTAL          DEC FIXED (9,2) INIT (0) ,
                   LINECTR             DEC FIXED (3)   INIT (0) ,
                   PAGECTR             DEC FIXED (3)   INIT (1) ,
                   ENDPAGE             DEC FIXED (3)   INIT (25) ;

7    1 0   DCL     EOF                 BIT (01) INIT ('0'B) ,
                   PREV_CUST           CHAR (05) ;

8    1 0   DCL 1   RECORDIN ,
                   3 FILL1             CHAR (05) ,
                   3 CUST_IN           CHAR (05) ,
                   3 NAME_IN           CHAR (20) ,
                   3 PAYT_IN           PIC '9999V9R' ,
                   3 DATE_IN           PIC '(6)9',
                   3 FILL2             CHAR (38) ;

9    1 0   DCL 1   CUST_LINE ,
                   3 CTLPR1            BIT (08) ,
                   3 FILL              CHAR (20) INIT (' ') ,
                   3 CUST_PR           CHAR (07) ,
                   3 NAME_PR           CHAR (21) ,
                   3 PAYT_PR           PIC 'ZZ,ZZ9V.99CR' ,
                   3 FILLC             CHAR (02) INIT (' ') ,
                   3 DATE_PR           PIC '99/99/99',
                   3 ERR_MESS_PR       CHAR (63) INIT (' ') ;

10   1 0   DCL 1   TOTAL_LINE ,
                   3 FILLA             BIT (08) INIT ('00010001'B) ,
                   3 FILLB             CHAR (46) INIT (' ') ,
                   3 CUSTOTAL_PR       PIC 'ZZZZ,ZZ9V.99CR' ,
                   3 ASTERISK_PR       CHAR (02) INIT ('*') ,
                   3 FILLC             CHAR (71) INIT (' ') ;

11   1 0   DCL 1   HDG_LINE ,
                   3 CTLHDG            BIT (08) ,
                   3 FILLB             CHAR (20) INIT (' ') ,
                   3 FILLC             CHAR (07) INIT ('CUSTR') ,
                   3 FILLD             CHAR (23) INIT ('NAME') ,
                   3 FILLE             CHAR (13) INIT ('PAYMENT') ,
                   3 FILLF             CHAR (14) INIT ('DATE    PAGE') ,
                   3 PAGE_PR           PIC 'ZZ9' ,
                   3 FILLG             CHAR (52) INIT (' ') ;
```

FIGURE 17–2 One-Level Control Break.

```
               /*        M A I N   L O G I C     */
  12    1   0       ON ENDFILE(FILEIN) EOF = '1'B;
  13    1   0       OPEN FILE(FILEIN), FILE(PRTR);
  14    1   0       CALL H100_HDG;
  15    1   0       READ FILE(FILEIN) INTO (RECORDIN);
  16    1   0       PREV_CUST = CUST_IN;
  17    1   0       DO WHILE (¬EOF);
  18    1   1           IF CUST_IN > PREV_CUST THEN CALL C100_HIGH_CUST;
  19    1   1           CALL A100_PROC_CUST ;
  20    1   1           READ FILE(FILEIN) INTO (RECORDIN) ;
  21    1   1       END;
  22    1   0       CALL F100_FINAL ;
  23    1   0       CLOSE FILE(FILEIN), FILE(PRTR) ;
  24    1   0       SIGNAL FINISH ;

               /*      C U S T O M E R   P R O C E S S I N G    */
  25    1   0   A100_PROC_CUST: PROCEDURE ;
  26    2   0       IF LINECTR > ENDPAGE THEN CALL H100_HDG ;
  27    2   0       IF CUST_IN < PREV_CUST THEN
                       ERR_MESS_PR = 'OUT OF SEQUENCE';
  28    2   0       ELSE DO ;
  29    2   1           PAYT_PR   = PAYT_IN ;
  30    2   1           CUSTOTAL  = CUSTOTAL+ PAYT_IN ;
  31    2   1           PREV_CUST = CUST_IN ;
  32    2   1           END ;
  33    2   0       DATE_PR = DATE_IN ;
  34    2   0       CUST_PR = CUST_IN ;
  35    2   0       NAME_PR = NAME_IN ;
  36    2   0       CTLPR1 = '00001001'B ;
  37    2   0       WRITE FILE(PRTR) FROM (CUST_LINE) ;
  38    2   0       CUST_LINE = '' ;
  39    2   0       LINECTR = LINECTR + 1 ;
  40    2   0   END A100_PROC_CUST ;

               /*      C U S T O M E R   C O N T R O L   B R E A K */
  41    1   0   C100_HIGH_CUST: PROCEDURE ;
  42    2   0       CUSTOTAL_PR = CUSTOTAL ;
  43    2   0       WRITE FILE(PRTR) FROM (TOTAL_LINE) ;
  44    2   0       FINALTOTAL = FINALTOTAL + CUSTOTAL ;
  45    2   0       CUSTOTAL = 0 ;
  46    2   0       LINECTR = LINECTR + 2 ;
  47    2   0   END C100_HIGH_CUST ;

               /*        F I N A L   T O T A L S         */
  48    1   0   F100_FINAL: PROCEDURE ;
  49    2   0       CALL C100_HIGH_CUST ;
  50    2   0       CUSTOTAL_PR = FINALTOTAL ;
  51    2   0       ASTERISK_PR = '**' ;
  52    2   0       WRITE FILE(PRTR) FROM (TOTAL_LINE) ;
  53    2   0   END F100_FINAL ;

               /*        P A G E   H E A D I N G         */
  54    1   0   H100_HDG: PROCEDURE ;
  55    2   0       CTLHDG = '10001011'B ;
  56    2   0       WRITE FILE(PRTR) FROM (HDG_LINE) ;
  57    2   0       CTLHDG = '00010001'B ;
  58    2   0       PAGE_PR = PAGECTR ;
  59    2   0       WRITE FILE(PRTR) FROM (HDG_LINE) ;
  60    2   0       LINECTR = 3 ;
  61    2   0       PAGECTR = PAGECTR + 1 ;
  62    2   0   END H100_HDG ;

  63    1   0   END PROG17A ;
```

FIGURE 17–2 (con't.)

Input data:-

```
        12554RL ANDERSON      002575090389
        12554RL ANDERSON      002575090389
        12554RL ANDERSON      002575090389
        23856JL BROWN         012438100489
        23856JL BROWN         012438100489
```

Output:-

```
  CUSTR  NAME                  PAYMENT    DATE     PAGE    1

  12554  RL ANDERSON            25.75    09/03/89
  12554  RL ANDERSON            25.75    09/03/89
  12554  RL ANDERSON            25.75    09/03/89
                                77.25  *

  23856  JL BROWN              124.38    10/04/89
  23856  JL BROWN              124.38    10/04/89
                               248.76  *

                               326.01  **
```

FIGURE 17-2   (con't)

The program is organized with a main logic routine that OPENs the files, CALLs the page heading procedure, and reads the initial input record. It then executes a DO WHILE loop that performs the customer control break, CALLs the procedure that processes the customer record, and reads the next input record. All input logic pivots around this DO WHILE. At end-of-file, the program CALLs the final processing routine and CLOSEes the files. Internal procedures contain related logic: process a customer record, perform control break, perform final totals, and print the page heading.

Following the program listing is a printout of the input data and the printed output from the program's execution.

ERROR TESTING

The only error test that Figure 17-1 makes is for low sequence. Another common test is for valid record code. A good programming practice is to check these items soon after reading the record, before doing any significant processing of the record. In a production environment, often on locating a serious error (especially out-of-sequence), the practice is to cancel the run. For card input, be sure to run out the input file before the CLOSE, as

```
                IF CUST_IN < PREV_CUST THEN CALL R100_SEQ_ERROR;
                    •
                    •
                    •
        R100_SEQ_ERROR:
            PROCEDURE ;
                PUT SKIP LIST (CUST_IN, 'OUT OF SEQUENCE') ;
                DO WHILE (¬EOF) ;
                    READ FILE(FILEIN) INTO (RECORDIN) ;
                END ;
                CLOSE FILE(FILEIN), FILE(PRTR) ;
            END R100_SEQ_ERROR ;
```

TWO-LEVEL CONTROL BREAKS

The previous example had only Customer number for the control word. A control word, however, could consist of more than one field. Consider a Sales file containing records in sequence of Department (major) and Product number (minor). The input record appears as

Control Fields

There may be any number of Sales for a Product within a Department. Since Product numbers are in ascending sequence within Department, the first Product of a Department may be validly lower than the last one of the preceding Department. The program has to produce a report that lists each Sale for the Product, and control totals of Sales by Product and by Department, as in Figure 17–3.

```
                        SALES REPORT

        DEPT    PROD    DESCRIPTION     QTY     SALES($)

        025     2430    TURNTABLES      1          243.00
                2430    TURNTABLES      3          645.25
                2430    TURNTABLES      1          119.00
                                                 1,007.25 *

                2628    RECEIVERS       1          226.00
                2628    RECEIVERS       2          314.00
                2628    RECEIVERS       1          140.50
                                                   680.50 *
                                                 1,687.75 **

        040     0320    PROCESSORS      1        2,164.00
                                                        ETC...
```

Figure 17-3 Report With Two-Level Totals.

A logical approach is to compare the new and previous Department numbers first:

NEW DEPT	ACTION
High	Print Product totals, then Department totals
Equal	Same Department, but could be a new Product
Low	Department is out of sequence

On a high Department sequence, the program prints the total of the last stored Product, and then the total for the stored Department. It can then continue with normal processing of the input record. If the comparison of Department is equal, the program should check for a change of Product. If high, Product totals should be printed. The program continues with processing the input record.

PROGRAM: TWO-LEVEL CONTROL BREAK

Figure 17–4 provides the new program listing, which is similar in approach to the simple control break. Note how A100-SALES tests the Department/Product jointly for low sequence:

```
IF STRING(DEPT_PROD_IN) < STRING(DEPT_PROD_PREV) THEN
     ERRMESS_PR = 'OUT OF SEQUENCE' ;
```

Both DEPT_PROD_IN and DEPT_PROD_PREV are structure names that cannot be referenced in an IF statement. The program uses the STRING built-in function (see Chapter 19) that makes a valid string of the adjacent structure elements.

A change of Department always automatically causes a change of Product as well. When the program detects a high Department, it CALLs the Department total routine, D100_DEPT. But Product total must print before Department total, so the first statement within D100_DEPT is one that CALLs Product total,B100_ PROD. After printing the Product total, the program "unwinds," and returns to print the Department total. On end-of-file, the program CALLs F100_FINAL, which CALLs D100_DEPT, which in turn CALLs the last Product total and then prints the final total.

Group Indication

A simple program prints the Department number repetitively down the page, as shown below to the left. A more elegant approach called *group indication* prints

```
1      0   PROG17B:
                PROCEDURE OPTIONS(MAIN) ;

2   1  0   DCL FILEIN FILE INPUT RECORD ENV( MEDIUM(SYSIPT) F
                                            RECSIZE(080) BUFFERS(2) ) ;
3   1  0   DCL PRTR   FILE OUTPUT RECORD ENV( MEDIUM(SYSLST,3203) F
                                            CTL360 RECSIZE(133)BUFFERS(2) ) ;
4   1  0   DCL SYSPRINT FILE PRINT ENV(BUFFERS(2));
5   1  0   DEFAULT  RANGE(*)  STATIC ;

6   1  0   DCL 1   SALES_RECORD,
                    3 FILLA             CHAR (04),
                    3 DEPT_PROD_IN,
                      5 DEPT_IN         CHAR (03),
                      5 PROD_IN         CHAR (04),
                    3 DESCRIP_IN        CHAR (20),
                    3 QTY_IN            PIC '99R',
                    3 SALES_IN          PIC '(5)9V9R',
                    3 FILLB             CHAR (39) ;

7   1  0   DCL 1   HEADING_LINE,
                    3 CTLHDG            BIT (08),
                    3 FILLA             CHAR (24) INIT (' '),
                    3 FILLB             CHAR (13) INIT ('DPT   PROD'),
                    3 FILLC             CHAR (23) INIT ('DESCRIPTION'),
                    3 FILLD             CHAR (72) INIT ('QTY      SALES($)');

8   1  0   DCL     PRINT               CHAR (133) INIT (' ');
9   1  0   DCL 1   SALES_LINE          DEFINED PRINT,
                    3 CTLSALES          BIT (08),
                    3 FILLA             CHAR (24),
                    3 DEPT_PR           CHAR (06),
                    3 PROD_PR           CHAR (07),
                    3 DESCRIP_PR        CHAR (23),
                    3 QTY_PR            PIC 'ZZ9-',
                    3 FILLB             CHAR (03),
                    3 SALES_PR          PIC 'ZZ,ZZ9V.99CR',
                    3 ERRMESS_PR        CHAR (20) ;

10  1  0   DCL 1   TOTAL_LINE,
                    3 CTLTOT            BIT (08) INIT ('00010001'B),
                    3 FILLA             CHAR (65) INIT (' '),
                    3 TOTALSALES_PR     PIC 'ZZZZ,ZZ9V.99CR',
                    3 ASTERISK_PR       CHAR (54) INIT ('*') ;

11  1  0   DCL 1   DEPT_PROD_PREV,
                    3 PREV_DEPT         CHAR (03),
                    3 PREV_PROD         CHAR (04) ;

12  1  0   DCL     EOF                 BIT (01)  INIT ('0'B) ;
13  1  0   DCL     STRING              BUILTIN ;

14  1  0   DCL     (SALES_AMT,
                    DEPT_SALES ,
                    FINAL_SALES,
                    PROD_SALES)         DEC FIXED (7,2) INIT (0),
                    LINE_CTR            DEC FIXED (3,0) INIT (0) ;
```

FIGURE 17-4 Two-Level Control Break.

```
            /*        M A I N   L O G I C            */
15    1  0          ON ENDFILE(FILEIN) EOF = '1'B ;
16    1  0          OPEN  FILE(FILEIN), FILE(PRTR) ;
17    1  0          CALL H100_HDG ;
18    1  0          READ FILE(FILEIN) INTO (SALES_RECORD) ;
19    1  0          DEPT_PROD_PREV = DEPT_PROD_IN ;
20    1  0          DO WHILE (¬EOF) ;
21    1  1              IF DEPT_IN > PREV_DEPT THEN CALL D100_DEPT ;
22    1  1              ELSE
                       IF PROD_IN > PREV_PROD THEN CALL B100_PROD ;
23    1  1              CALL A100_SALES ;
24    1  1              READ FILE(FILEIN) INTO (SALES_RECORD) ;
25    1  1          END ;
26    1  0          CALL F100_FINAL ;
27    1  0          CLOSE FILE(FILEIN), FILE(PRTR) ;
28    1  0          SIGNAL FINISH ;

            /*        P R O C E S S   S A L E S        */
29    1  0   A100_SALES: PROCEDURE ;
30    2  0          IF LINE_CTR > 55 THEN CALL H100_HDG ;
31    2  0          IF STRING(DEPT_PROD_IN) < STRING(DEPT_PROD_PREV) THEN
                       ERRMESS_PR = 'OUT OF SEQUENCE' ;
32    2  0          ELSE DO ;
33    2  1              SALES_AMT  = SALES_IN ;
34    2  1              QTY_PR     = QTY_IN ;
35    2  1              SALES_PR   = SALES_AMT ;
36    2  1              PROD_SALES = PROD_SALES + SALES_AMT ;
37    2  1          END ;

38    2  0          IF STRING(DEPT_PROD_IN) ¬= STRING(DEPT_PROD_PREV)
                       | LINE_CTR = 3 THEN
                       DO ;
39    2  1              DESCRIP_PR = DESCRIP_IN ;
40    2  1              PROD_PR    = PROD_IN ;
41    2  1              DEPT_PR    = DEPT_IN ;
42    2  1          END ;

43    2  0          CTLSALES = '00001001'B ;
44    2  0          WRITE FILE(PRTR) FROM (PRINT) ;
45    2  0          PRINT = ' ' ;
46    2  0          LINE_CTR = LINE_CTR + 1 ;
47    2  0          DEPT_PROD_PREV = DEPT_PROD_IN ;
48    2  0      END A100_SALES ;

            /*        P R O D U C T   T O T A L        */
49    1  0   B100_PROD: PROCEDURE ;
50    2  0          TOTALSALES_PR = PROD_SALES ;
51    2  0          ASTERISK_PR = '*' ;
52    2  0          WRITE FILE(PRTR) FROM (TOTAL_LINE) ;
53    2  0          DEPT_SALES = DEPT_SALES + PROD_SALES ;
54    2  0          PROD_SALES = 0 ;
55    2  0      END B100_PROD ;

            /*        D E P A R T M E N T   T O T A L   */
56    1  0   D100_DEPT: PROCEDURE ;
57    2  0          CALL B100_PROD ;
58    2  0          TOTALSALES_PR = DEPT_SALES ;
59    2  0          ASTERISK_PR = '**' ;
60    2  0          WRITE FILE(PRTR) FROM (TOTAL_LINE) ;
61    2  0          FINAL_SALES = FINAL_SALES + DEPT_SALES ;
62    2  0          DEPT_SALES  = 0 ;
63    2  0      END D100_DEPT ;
```

FIGURE 17–4 (con't.)

```
                 /*        F I N A L   T O T A L          */
64    1   0    F100_FINAL: PROCEDURE ;
65    2   0            CALL D100_DEPT ;
66    2   0            TOTALSALES_PR = FINAL_SALES ;
67    2   0            ASTERISK_PR = '***' ;
68    2   0            WRITE FILE(PRTR) FROM (TOTAL_LINE) ;
69    2   0        END F100_FINAL ;
```

```
                 /*        P A G E   H E A D I N G        */
70    1   0    H100_HDG: PROCEDURE ;
71    2   0            CTLHDG = '10001011'B ;
72    2   0            WRITE FILE(PRTR) FROM (HEADING_LINE) ;
73    2   0            CTLHDG = '00010001'B ;
74    2   0            WRITE FILE(PRTR) FROM (HEADING_LINE) ;
75    2   0            LINE_CTR = 3 ;
76    2   0        END H100_HDG ;

77    1   0        END PROG17B ;
```

Output:-

DPT	PROD	DESCRIPTION	QTY	SALES($)	
025	2430	TURNTABLES	1	243.00	
			3	645.35	
			1	119.00	
				1,007.35	*
025	2628	RECEIVERS	1	226.00	
			2	140.50	
			1	680.50	
				1,047.00	*
				2,054.35	**
030	0320	PROCESSORS	1	2,164.00	
				2,164.00	*
				2,164.00	**
040	0440	DISK STORAGE	4	1,847.50	
			6	3,242.90	
				5,090.40	*
040	1623	TERMINALS	15	6,627.35	
			3	1,225.30	
				7,852.65	*
				12,943.05	**
125	0347	RECORDS	20	85.60	
				85.60	*
125	0392	CASSETTE TAPE	12	49.12	
				49.12	*
125	0395	8-TRACK TAPE	7	25.20	
				25.20	*
				159.92	**
				17,321.32	***

FIGURE 17–4 (con't.)

the Department number only for the first Product of each set, as shown to the right:

DEPT	PROD	DEPT	PROD
001	2430	001	2430
001	2430		2430
001	2430		2430

The program in Figure 17–4 handles the suppression of control words by printing them only when at the top of a page and when printing the first Product of a Department:

```
IF STRING(DEPT_PROD_IN) ¬= STRING(DEPT_PROD_PREV)
   | LINE_CTR = 3   THEN
   DO ;
      DESCRIP_PR = DESCRIPTION ;
      PROD_PR = PROD_IN ;
      DEPT_PR = DEPT_IN ;
   END ;
```

PAGE OVERFLOW

An earlier chapter covered page overflows for simple processing with no control breaks. In a more complex program, placement of the page overflow test is critical. Many installations prefer to avoid printing total lines immediately at the top of a page. In the following example, the page begins with two total lines for Plant and Department, but the totals do not clearly indicate the set of data to which they belong:

PLANT DEPARTMENT NAME	HOURS	RATE	WAGE
			52,325.38 *
			265,547.97 **

Many prefer to print totals at the bottom of the previous page, or with at least one detail line (in this case Employee) at the top of the page. On most reports, the strategy for handling page overflows, regardless of the number of control break levels, is relatively simple:

1.   Set the line count maximum to several lines fewer than the page can accommodate, usually about 60. This practice allows space at the bottom of a page for possible totals.
2.   Count every line printed and spaced.

3.   Although there may be two or three control break levels, it is not necessary to test for page overflow everywhere the program prints totals. *Insert the test for page overflow in one place only—before printing a detail line* (a *detail line* is the lowest level of printing in the program).

4.   Do not test if the line count *equals* some maximum value. If the program increments the line count by one, two, or three depending on spacing, it is possible to bypass the maximum value and to continue through the perforation without ejecting to a new page. Instead, test if the line count *exceeds* the maximum value.

Most programs should require only two CALLs of the page heading routine: one at the time of initialization and the other prior to printing the detail line. Adherence to this procedure will ensure that the program will never print totals on the first line of a page—at least one detail line will immediately precede the total line.

In the case of Figure 17–4, the page overflow test belongs in A100_SALES Procedure, prior to processing a detail line.

THREE-LEVEL CONTROL BREAKS

Figure 17–4 illustrated records with two control fields: Department and Product. Extending the program logic to handle three or more control fields is relatively simple, provided you adhere to a sound consistent strategy: test the control fields jointly to determine the high/low/equal condition. If the comparison is high, there is a control break at least of the lowest level. If equal, process the record (add or print, as required). If low, the record is out-of-sequence. There is little difficulty if the program is organized to handle the control levels properly, such as a major total always forcing a minor total level first.

Figure 17–5 depicts a Sales report with three total levels: Branch (major), Department (intermediate), and Product (minor). Sales are accumulated (not listed) to show total Sales by Product, then by Department, then by Branch, with a final total at the end of the run.

A program to handle this problem would test for control breaks as follows:

A CHANGE OF	CAUSES THE PROGRAM TO PRODUCE
Branch	Product, then Department, then Branch totals.
Department	Product, then Department totals.
Product	Product totals only.

Consequently, a control break at any level (including end-of-file) automatically triggers control breaks at all lower levels.

```
BRANCH  DEPT   PROD   DESCRIPTION          SALES($)

  01    001    2430   TURNTABLES           1,500.00
               2628   RECEIVERS              125.00
               2635   SPEAKERS               205.00
                                          1,830.00 *

  01    004    2365   RECORDS                750.00
               2386   8-TRACK TAPE           550.00
                                          1,300.00 *

                                          3,130.00 **

  02    001    2430   TURNTABLES             860.00
               2628   RECEIVERS            1,000.00
               2635   SPEAKERS               500.00
                                          2,360.00 *  ETC...
```

FIGURE 17–5 Report with Three-level Totals.

PROGRAMMING STRATEGY

When attempting to organize and write a program, you may find it difficult to know where to begin. Usually there are many special conditions and exceptions that complicate the solution to the extent that they confuse the relatively simple strategy in approaching the problem. It is important to detect the essential problem that is to be solved. You can do this by ignoring all the exceptions, error conditions, and complex calculations. *It is necessary to isolate the main logic first and to build the program around this skeleton.* The main logic is the main loop of the program, which almost always centers upon the input logic. Once you have determined the input logic, you may realize that the program is a typical "multiple control break" or a "file update" problem with a standard solution.

Typically, the rest of the program arranges itself into logical sections. These should be coded so that they appear in approximately the sequence in which the program will execute them. The exceptions to this sequence are the page heading routine (generally similar from program to program) and error routines (which occur infrequently). These less important routines should be separated toward the end where they do not clutter the main business of the program.

As an example, consider Figure 17–4 with the two-level control break. The program is concerned with accumulating Sales by Product and Department. The program is basically quite simple, indeed far simpler than a typical business problem. There are a number of subroutines, all subsidiary to the main logic. Although there are many ways to organize a program, especially the main processing routines, in this approach the program begins with an overall main logic that can more or less apply to most programs:

Open files.
Read the first record.
Perform sequencing and reading until end-of-file.
Perform final processing.
Close files.

Similar strategy could apply to many business programs, especially those producing reports. Although there are many other possible approaches, the best ones organize the program into logical routines. A program should be organized ideally into main logic and subroutines. For example, assume a program that performs calculations on each input record and prints totals by minor level and major level. A sound, consistent strategy would organize the program into relatively independent subroutines, with the more important and more commonly used ones first:

- The main logic is first and includes initialization, an initial READ, a DO WHILE for looping, and CLOSE.
- The subroutine for processing each input record is the next in importance. It performs calculations and writes the detail lines.
- The minor total subroutine is executed the next most often.
- The major total subroutine would be next.
- The final total subroutine is next.
- The Page heading subroutine occurs only periodically. Although it executes more often than final totals, the sequence of minor/major/final is sequentially logical.
- Error routines and other occasionally used subroutines could be last.

By this organization, each routine is placed logically and is easy to locate. A variation that has much merit is to place the minor/major/final subroutines in reverse sequence, so that the final CALLs major total (which is further *forward* in the program) and major total CALLs minor total (which is further forward).

DEBUGGING TIPS

The material in this chapter introduces the concepts of input logic: sequence-checking and control breaks. Adherence to sound programming strategy will cause few errors in this critical area. The following are some areas where careful coding can prevent serious errors:

1. Ensure that the first input record does not cause a false control break.
2. Ensure that the end-of-file situation properly handles the last stored data.
3. Program a high control break so that it automatically triggers breaks on lower levels.

4. After a control break, ensure that the program returns to process the input record that caused the control break.
5. Arrange the page overflow test so that it does not print totals at the top of a page.

This chapter concludes the basic material on logic and control breaks. The next part introduces many advanced programming techniques. The only other material on input logic is in Chapter 25, which covers handling more than one input file.

PROBLEMS

17–1. A first record may cause a "false control break." What is this condition and how can it be avoided?

17–2. In a program that prints detail lines and a control total level, where should the test(s) for page overflow be placed?

17–3. Draw the flowchart logic for a program that performs control breaks. Input records contain stock number, quantity sold, and value sold. There are any number of records for a stock number. The program is to print each record, total value by stock number, and at the end a total of all stock value. Provide for page overflow.

17–4. Code and test the program in Problem 17–3. Supply enough input data to force a page overflow.

17–5. Expand Problem 17–3 and 17–4 to handle a second control break level: records are in sequence by stock number within department. Do not print each detail input record; instead, print totals by stock number, totals by department, and final total. Use group indication for department number.

PART V

SPECIAL TOPICS

CHAPTER 18

SEARCHING AND SORTING

OBJECTIVE:
To cover array handling techniques for table searching and sorting.

INTRODUCTION

A large portion of computer processing involves searching through arrays for required values and sorting arrays into another specified sequence. This chapter covers such practical techniques as table searching, loading of tables, sorting of table entries, and binary search.

SEQUENTIAL TABLES

Consider a situation in which a firm sells five inventory stock items with the following prices:

STOCK ITEM	SELLING PRICE
203	$2.25
206	5.27
240	0.25
244	10.37
265	3.25

The company sells various quantities of each item and keys in a computer record for each sale of stock number and quantity sold. Instead of an operator keying in the selling price and calculated value (quantity times price), a program is to check the stock number, determine its selling price, and calculate value sold. The following illustrates the program logic:

```
IF STOCKIN = '203' THEN PRICE = 2.25 ;
ELSE IF STOCKIN = '206' THEN PRICE = 5.27 ;
   ELSE IF STOCKIN = '240' THEN PRICE = 0.25 ;
      ELSE IF STOCKIN = '244' THEN PRICE = 10.37 ;
         ELSE IF STOCKIN = '265' THEN PRICE = 3.25 ;
```

Although the programming is straightforward, most tables are much larger, and coding a program to test for many items separately is inefficient. The solution is to define the stock items and selling prices as arrays and to use a DO-loop for repetitive processing and a subscript to locate the required item. The table in the preceding example consists of two parts: an array of stock items called the *table argument* and an array of prices called the *function*. Arguments and functions may be declared as *separate arrays,* as

```
DCL   STOCKTAB(5) CHAR(3) INIT('203','206','240','244','265');
DCL   PRICETAB(5) DEC FIXED(5,2)
                          INIT( 2.25, 5.27, 0.25,10.37, 3.25);
```

The table could also be defined as an *array of structures,* as follows:

```
DCL 1 INVTABLE(5),
      3 STOCKTAB CHAR(3) INIT('...') ,
      3 PRICETAB DEC FIXED(5,2)
                          INIT( ... ) ;
```

Another valid possibility is to define the table as a *structure of arrays,* as

```
DCL 1 INVTABLE2,
      3 STOCKTAB(5)  CHAR(3) INIT ('...') ,
      3 PRICETAB(5)  DEC FIXED(5,2)
                          INIT ( ... ) ;
```

Although an array of structures and a structure of arrays do not reduce the space for storing the table, they more clearly indicate the relation between arguments and their related functions.

The table arguments must be defined with identical attributes, with the same length and data type (arithmetic or character). In the preceding example, each table argument must have a corresponding function. The functions can have any suitable definition, but must all be defined alike. To perform a table search, input records would contain a stock number and quantity sold. A program would use the input stock number, the "search argument," to locate the same item in the table of arguments and the corresponding price from the table of functions, using the same subscript. The program would then calculate the value sold by multiplying quantity sold from the input record by the located price in the table. Note that the search argument has the same attributes as the table arguments.

Within a table, the arguments are typically arranged either as *unique entries* or as *steps.*

TABLES WITH UNIQUE ENTRIES

A table with unique entries includes such arguments as stock numbers, employee numbers, and customer numbers. Table arguments need not be consecutive (one argument immediately following another argument, as 7, 8, 9) nor sequential (each argument higher than the preceding one), although a sequential arrangement is more common. Each argument value, however, should appear only once in a table.

Assume the same stock table as before, with the stock items as table arguments in ascending sequence. The program reads an input record and compares successively the input stock number against each table argument, a *table lookup,* or *table search,* as follows:

```
DCL     STOCKIN    CHAR(3),
        K          BIN FIXED(15) ;

        DO K = 1 TO 5 ;
          IF STOCKIN = STOCKTAB(K) THEN          /* FOUND */ ;
          ELSE IF STOCKIN < STOCKTAB(K) THEN /* ERROR */ ;
        END ;
```

The key instruction in the DO-loop is the IF statement. The result of comparing the search argument against the table argument is as follows:

Equal:	Argument is found, extract the function.
Low:	Because the arguments are in ascending sequence, a low compare indicates that the argument is not in the table.
High:	The required argument may be a higher entry in the table—increment the subscript to compare the next entry.

A low compare merits further examination. Consider the table argument entries 203, 206, 240, 244, and 265. If a search argument is 165, then the result of the first compare is low, and because all table arguments are higher, by definition the required argument is not in the table. If a search argument is 204, then the first compare is high but the second compare is low, and so that argument is also not in the table.

The problem now is for the program to know how it exited from the DO-loop—either by means of a equal (found) or low (error). Let's use a Bit indicator called FOUND that can be set in the loop and tested after exiting. Let's also omit the test for low; if an item is not in the table, the DO-loop will automatically terminate when K equals 6.

```
DCL   FOUND       BIT(1) INIT ('0'B) ;

      FOUND = '0'B ;
      DO K = 1 TO 5 WHILE (¬FOUND) ;
         IF STOCKIN = STOCKTAB(K) THEN FOUND = '1'B ;
      END ;
      IF FOUND THEN VALUE = QTYIN * PRICETAB(K) ;
      ELSE PUT SKIP LIST (STOCKIN, 'NOT IN TABLE') ;
```

There is still a problem remaining: after a stock item is found equal, the DO-loop automatically increments K by 1 before testing if K > 5 and FOUND = '1'B. Consequently, if STOCKIN were 206, the search would stop at the second table argument, but the subscript would be incremented to 3. In this example, the program should therefore deduct 1 from K as

IF FOUND THEN VALUE = QTYIN * PRICETAB(K-1) ;

This problem may be clearer if you understand the sequence in which a DO-loop processes. Basically, it generates code that would resemble the following (although not recommended to use as such):

```
           FOUND = '0'B ;
           K = 1 ;
LOOP:      IF K > 5 THEN GO TO OUT ;
           IF FOUND = '1'B THEN GO TO OUT ;
           IF STOCKIN = STOCKTAB(5) THEN FOUND = '1'B ;
           K = K + 1 ;
           GO TO LOOP ;
OUT:       ... ;
```

If your compiler supports the LEAVE statement, you could code the DO-loop as

```
           FOUND = '0'B ;
P100:      DO K = 1 TO 5 ;
              IF STOCKIN = STOCKTAB(K)  THEN
P200:            DO ;
                    FOUND = '1'B ;
                    LEAVE P100 ;
                 END P200 ;
           END P100 ;
```

The LEAVE statement exits out of the inner DO-loop labelled D200 and out of the loop labeled P100, past END P100. K contains the correct subscript value on exiting because LEAVE exits before the DO-loop increments the subscript.

The preceding examples could also calculate VALUE *inside* the DO-loop, as

```
FOUND = '0'B ;
DO K = 1 TO 5 WHILE (¬FOUND) ;
   IF STOCKIN = STOCKTAB(K) THEN
       DO ;
          VALUE = QTYIN * PRICETAB(K) ;
          FOUND = '1'B ;
       END ;
END ;
IF ¬FOUND THEN PUT SKIP LIST (STOCKIN, 'NOT IN TABLE');
```

Yet another table search example that may look strange at first is the following:

```
DO K = 1 TO 5 WHILE(STOCKIN ¬= STOCKTAB(K)) ;
END ;
IF K < 6 THEN VALUE = QTYIN * PRICETAB(K) ;
ELSE PUT SKIP LIST (STOCKIN, 'NOT IN TABLE ') ;
```

Pareto's Law

In many applications, 15–20 percent of the items involve 80–85 percent of the activity. If a table is large, it may be more efficient to insert the most commonly used items at the start of the table. Because the table is no longer in ascending sequence, a compare should test only for equal or unequal. To determine if an item is not in the table involves a search through all the table arguments.

TABLES WITH ARGUMENTS IN STEPS

In the first type of table, each argument was unique. In the second type of table, arguments represented a range of values. Consider the following income tax table:

ANNUAL TAXABLE INCOME	TAX FORMULA
up to $ 2,500	10% of Taxable Income
2,501 to 5,000	12% of Taxable Income less $ 50
5,001 to 8,000	15% of Taxable Income less 200
8,001 to 12,000	19% of Taxable Income less 520
12,001 to 20,000	24% of Taxable Income less 1,120
20,001 and over	30% of Taxable Income less 2,320

The "annual taxable income" is the argument, and the "tax formula," consisting of two parts, is the function. The first part of the function is the tax rate, and the second part is a *correction factor.* The simplest way to arrange the arguments is to use the high value of each step with the corresponding functions in an array of structures:

```
DCL 1 TAXTABLE(6),
       3 INCTABLE     DEC FIXED(7,2) INIT (2500.00,
                                           5000.00,
                                           8000.00,
                                          12000.00,
                                          20000.00,
                                          99999.99),
       3 PCTTABLE     DEC FIXED(3,3) INIT (0.10,
                                           0.12,
                                           0.15,
                                           0.19,
                                           0.24,
                                           0.30),
       3 ADJTABLE     DEC FIXED(7,2) INIT (0000.00,
                                           0050.00,
                                           0200.00,
                                           0520.00,
                                           1120.00,
                                           2320.00) ;
```

Assume a routine to compare successively an employee's annual taxable income against each table argument. If the employee's income is $2,500 or less, then tax is 10% of income. For an income of $3,000, the table search stops on the second step where $3,000 is lower than $5,000. The calculation is accordingly

$$Tax = \$3,000 \times 0.12 - \$50$$
$$= \$360 - \$50 = \$310$$

In this table, either an equal or low compare means that the required argument is found. And as long as arguments are in ascending sequence (they should be) and the last argument contains the highest possible value (in this case arithmetic 9's), then by definition, any possible taxable income is *always* equal to or lower than at least one of the table arguments.

A DO-loop for the table search follows:

```
DO K = 1 BY 1 ;
       IF  INCOME ¬> INCTABLE(K) THEN LEAVE ;
END ;
TAX = INCOME * PCTTABLE(K) - ADJTABLE(K) ;
```

In this case, because LEAVE causes an immediate exit, the subscript K contains the correct value. If your compiler does not support the LEAVE statement, you could use a logical operator, called FOUND, in the following:

```
DCL   FOUND       BIT(1) ;

FOUND = '0'B ;
DO K = 1 BY 1 WHILE (¬FOUND) ;
      IF INCOME ¬> INCTABLE(K) THEN FOUND = '1'B ;
END ;
K = K - 1 ;
TAX = INCOME * PCTTABLE(K) - ADJTABLE(K) ;
```

Note that is necessary to decrement K on exiting from the loop (although you could perform the computation inside the DO-loop). You could also perform the DO-loop in the following way:

```
DO K = 1 BY 1 WHILE (INCOMEIN > INCTABLE(K)) ;
END ;
TAX = INCOME * PCTTABLE(K) - ADJTABLE(K) ;
```

SUBSCRIPTS

The value in a subscript indicates the relative element in an array. Each reference to a subscripted element causes the program to calculate an actual storage address. If more than one statement references the same subscripted array element, it is usually more efficient to assign the element to an ordinary variable, as follows:

```
DCL   PCT         DEC FIXED(3,3),
      ADJ         DEC FIXED(7,2);

PCT = PCTTABLE (K) ;
ADJ = ADJTABLE(K) ;
TAX = INCOME * PCT - ADJ ;
```

When a program uses a subscript, its value must be within the bounds of the array that it references. For example, if an array is defined as STOCKTAB(5), a subscript may contain only 1, 2, 3, 4, or 5. A subscript that references an address outside an array causes a serious SUBSCRIPTRANGE error (PL/C intercepts the error and recovers).

Although technically you may define a subscript with any arithmetic value, BINARY FIXED is the most efficient attribute.

LOADING TABLES

There are two common ways to provide entry values to tables. The simplest way shown earlier is to define the items and compile them into the final machine language program. The second method is to maintain the entries on an external file, such as cards or disk. You define this type of table with no initial values. During execution, the program reads the table entries from the external file into the table. Both initializing values and loading them into a table provide the same effect, but have different advantages:

1. *Initializing Table Contents.* Simplest to program, and a useful approach if the table entries seldom change. But changing, adding, or deleting an entry means that the program must be recompiled.
2. *Loading Table Contents.* More complex to program but more versatile. Changing, adding, or deleting a table entry does not require recompiling the program, and the same table is available for use by all other programs in the system.

If the table is stored on cards, each card may contain one or more entries. However, storing one entry per card facilitates deleting and adding entries. Typically, the table cards will precede the regular input data. For identification, card formats should contain unique record codes, all in the same position. Often, the last table entry contains a high value such as all 9's to indicate end of the table.

If the table is stored on disk, a program must define the disk table as a unique file, OPEN it, READ and store each entry, and CLOSE it on end-of-file. Otherwise, storing of disk table entries is similar to card processing.

If table entries are supposed to be in ascending sequence (such as job number), the program should check the sequence before storing each entry in the table. If a table search expects entries to be sequential, an out-of-sequence entry is a serious error. A program, however, may accept entries in random sequence; there are two possibilities:

1. The most commonly referenced entries are at the start of the table to facilitate efficient processing. (A useful practice to check the activity is to keep a count for each table entry.)
2. The program will *sort* the random entries into ascending sequence to facilitate a sequential search.

If the table is on cards, you must ensure that the program does not treat the following data cards as table entries. The program can check the record codes or test for a high value in the last table entry (assuming that such a record is always present). For disk, an attempt to read the end-of-file causes the program to execute the ON ENDFILE statement for the disk table file.

If the table is sequential, the program can insert a high value in the table following the last stored table argument to act as a table stopper. For example, if table arguments are Character format, store HIGH(n), and if arguments are arithmetic format, store 9's.

When a program reads and stores table entries, it should increment a subscript for each entry stored. The subscript acts as both the address pointer for storing the entries and a count of the number of entries actually stored. But a serious error can occur if the number of table entries exceeds the dimensions of the table. An attempt to store an entry past the upper bound of a table causes a SUBSCRIPTRANGE error in PL/I and may cause a disaster. (PL/C intercepts the error.)

To prevent a table from overloading, a program should define a reserved area large enough to allow for normal expected expansion. The program should count the entries, and if table capacity is reached, print an error message and possibly cancel the job.

PROGRAM: LOADING A TABLE, SORTING, AND BINARY SEARCH

Problem Definition

A program is to produce a payroll report. Input records contain employee number, employee name, job number, and hours worked. Each job number has an associated rate-of-pay, and the program is to calculate wage (hours times rate-of-pay) for each employee. Job numbers and rates-of-pay are subject to frequent change.

Solution

The job numbers and rates-of-pay can be arranged into a table stored on cards or disk. The program should define two related arrays that are large enough for all current jobs plus an allowance for expansion. Figure 18–1 provides the complete solution with two other features:

1.   The job table entries are assumed to be in random (unsorted) sequence. After storing them in the array, the program *sorts* the array into ascending sequence.
2.   After sorting the job table entries, the program reads employee time records and uses the input job number to locate the associated rate-of-pay in the table. Instead of a conventional sequential search, the program performs a *binary search.*

Later sections explain table sorting and binary search in detail.

Organization

The program is clearly organized into a main logic routine, a Procedure for processing each employee time record, a Procedure for loading the table, a Procedure for sorting the table, and a Procedure for performing binary search. Other features (omitted because of space limitations) could include a control break by employee number (to print total hours and wage by employee) and a final total of hours and wages.

Loading the Table

The main logic routine CALLs L100_LOAD to load the job table entries. The Procedure executes repetitively until either end-of-file (in case there are no employee time records following) or the table is loaded (all the table entries have been stored). If there are too many entries for the defined table, the Procedure prints an error message and runs out the remaining input records causing an end-of-file condition. The Procedure keeps a count of the number of records stored in a variable named KOUNT, to be used later for the sort and the binary search.

Debugging Tip

When testing a larger program, you may want to see the contents of variables at different stages of execution. In its early stages, this program contained statements to print the contents of the arrays after loading and after sorting. In this way, you can check that the coding actually works to that point and can more clearly isolate errors.

SORTING TABLE ENTRIES

Sometimes table entries are in a random sequence that is not suitable for subsequent processing. A program may have loaded the table from an external source, such as cards or disk, in a random sequence or in a sequence that was suitable for another program. The program must then sort the table entries into some other required sequence. Sort programs that manufacturers supply sort *records* on tape and disk and are extremely complex. Sorting *table entries* into a predetermined sequence is relatively simple. The technique involves successive comparisons and interchange of entries. The following table lists scores made by candidates on a college entrance test; the maximum score is 150:

ENTRY NUMBER	SCORE
1	120
2	135
3	087
4	106
5	095
6	142
7	116

```
1   PROG18A:
        PROCEDURE OPTIONS(MAIN) ;

2   DCL FILEIN FILE INPUT RECORD ENV( MEDIUM(SYSIPT) F
                                      RECSIZE(080) BUFFERS(2) ) ;
3   DCL PRTR  FILE OUTPUT RECORD ENV( MEDIUM(SYSLST,3203) F
                                CTL360 RECSIZE(133)BUFFERS(2) ) ;
4   DCL SYSPRINT FILE PRINT ENV(BUFFERS(2));
5   DEFAULT RANGE(*)  STATIC ;

6   DCL       RECORDIN             CHAR (80) ;

7   DCL 1     TIME_RECORD DEFINED RECORDIN ,
              3    TIMECODEIN      CHAR (02)
              3    EMPNIN          CHAR (05),
              3    NAMEIN          CHAR (15),
              3    JOBNIN          CHAR (02),
              3    HOURIN          PIC '99VR',
              3    FILL            CHAR (53) ;

8   DCL 1     TABLE_RECORD DEFINED RECORDIN,
              3    TABLECODEIN     CHAR (02),
              3    JOBTABIN        CHAR (02),
              3    RATETABIN       PIC '99V99',
              3    FILL            CHAR (72) ;

9   DCL       (EOF, FOUND,
              TABLE_LOADED)        BIT (01)     INIT ('0'B),
              SWITCHED             BIT (01)     INIT ('1'B);
10  DCL       HOURS                DEC FIXED (3,1),
              RATE                 DEC FIXED (5,2),
              WAGE                 DEC FIXED (7,2) ;

11  DCL       (SUB,
              HI, LO, MID,
              PREVMID, KOUNT)      BIN FIXED (15) ;
12  DCL       (HIGH, ROUND)        BUILTIN ;

13  DCL 1     JOB_RATE_TABLE(50) ,
              3 JOBN_TAB           CHAR (02) INIT ((50)(2)' '),
              3 RATE_TAB           DEC FIXED(5,2)
                                             INIT ((50) 0) ;
14  DCL 1     ENTRY_SAVE,
              3 JOB_SAVE           CHAR (2),
              3 RATE_SAVE          DEC FIXED (5,2) ;

15  DCL 1     HEADING_LINE ,
              3    CTLHDG          BIT (08) INIT ('10001011'B),
              3    FILL1           CHAR (12) INIT (' '),
              3    FILL2           CHAR (10) INIT ('EMPLOYEE'),
              3    FILL3           CHAR (16) INIT ('NAME'),
              3    FILL4           CHAR (12) INIT ('JOB    RATE'),
              3    FILL5           CHAR (15) INIT ('HOURS'),
              3    FILL6           CHAR (67) INIT ('WAGE') ;
```

FIGURE 18–1 Load Table, Sort, and Binary Search.

```
16   DCL 1       DETAIL_LINE ,
             3    CTLDET           BIT  (08),
             3    FILL1            CHAR (14),
             3    EMPNPR           CHAR (08),
             3    NAMEPR           CHAR (17),
             3    JOBNPR           CHAR (02),
             3    RATEPR           PIC  'ZZZ9V.99',
             3    FILL2            CHAR (03),
             3    HOURPR           PIC  'Z9V.9-',
             3    FILL3            CHAR (04),
             3    WAGEPR           PIC  'ZZ,ZZ9V.99CR',
             3    ERRMESSPR        CHAR (61) ;

     /*       M A I N   L O G I C     */
17            OPEN FILE(FILEIN), FILE(PRTR) ;
18            ON ENDFILE(FILEIN) EOF = '1'B ;
19            WRITE FILE(PRTR) FROM (HEADING_LINE) ;
20            CTLHDG = '00010001'B ;
21            WRITE FILE(PRTR) FROM (HEADING_LINE) ;
22            READ FILE(FILEIN) INTO (RECORDIN) ;
23            CALL L100_LOAD ;
24            CALL S100_SORT ;
25            DO WHILE (¬EOF) ;
26                CALL B100_PROC ;
27                READ FILE(FILEIN) INTO (RECORDIN) ;
28            END ;
29            CLOSE FILE(FILEIN), FILE(PRTR) ;
30            SIGNAL FINISH ;

     /*       E M P L O Y E E    P R O C E S S I N G   */
31   B100_PROC: PROCEDURE ;
32            HOURS = HOURIN ;
33            DETAIL_LINE = '' ;
34            CALL C100_SEARCH ;
35            IF FOUND THEN
                DO ;
36                RATE = RATE_TAB(MID) ;
37                WAGE = ROUND(HOURS * RATE, 2) ;
38                WAGEPR = WAGE ;
39                HOURPR = HOURS ;
40                RATEPR = RATE ;
41              END ;
42            ELSE ERRMESSPR = 'JOB NOT IN TABLE' ;
43            JOBNPR = JOBNIN ;
44            NAMEPR = NAMEIN ;
45            EMPNPR = EMPNIN ;
46            CTLDET = '00001001'B ;
47            WRITE FILE(PRTR) FROM (DETAIL_LINE) ;
48         END B100_PROC ;
```

FIGURE 18-1 (con't.)

```
       /*        B I N A R Y   S E A R C H              */
49   C100_SEARCH: PROCEDURE ;
50           FOUND = '0'B ;
51           HI, MID = KOUNT+1 ;
52           LO, PREVMID = 1 ;
53   C200:    DO WHILE (¬FOUND & MID ¬= PREVMID) ;
54               PREVMID = MID ;
55               MID = (LO + HI) / 2 ;

56               IF JOBNIN < JOBN_TAB(MID) THEN
                    HI = MID ;
57               ELSE IF JOBNIN > JOBN_TAB(MID)
                    THEN LO = MID ;
58               ELSE FOUND = '1'B ;
59           END C200 ;
60       END C100_SEARCH ;

       /*        T A B L E   L O A D   R O U T I N E     */
61   L100_LOAD: PROCEDURE ;
62   L200:    DO SUB = 1 BY 1 UNTIL (EOF | TABLE_LOADED) ;
63               KOUNT = SUB ;
64               IF TABLECODEIN ¬= '01' THEN
                    DO ;
65                     TABLE_LOADED = '1'B ;
66                     JOBN_TAB(SUB) = HIGH(2) ;
67                     LEAVE L200 ;
68                  END ;
69               IF SUB > 50 THEN
                    DO ;
70                     PUT SKIP LIST ('TABLE IS TOO SMALL');
71                     DO WHILE (¬EOF) ;
72                        READ FILE(FILEIN) INTO (RECORDIN);
73                     END ;
74                     LEAVE L200 ;
75                  END ;
76               JOBN_TAB(SUB) = JOBTABIN ;
77               RATE_TAB(SUB) = RATETABIN ;
78               READ FILE(FILEIN) INTO (RECORDIN) ;
79           END L200 ;
80       END L100_LOAD ;

       /*        T A B L E   S O R T   R O U T I N E     */
81   S100_SORT: PROCEDURE ;
82   S200:    DO WHILE (SWITCHED);
83               SWITCHED = '0'B;
84   S300:       DO SUB = 1 TO KOUNT - 1;
85                  IF JOBN_TAB(SUB) > JOBN_TAB(SUB+1) THEN
                       DO ;
86                        ENTRY_SAVE = JOB_RATE_TABLE(SUB+1);
87                        JOB_RATE_TABLE(SUB+1) = JOB_RATE_TABLE(SUB);
88                        JOB_RATE_TABLE(SUB) = ENTRY_SAVE ;
89                        SWITCHED = '1'B;
90                     END ;
91               END S300;
92           END S200 ;
93       END S100_SORT ;

94       END PROG18A ;
```

FIGURE 18–1 (con't.)

EMPLOYEE	NAME	JOB	RATE	HOURS	WAGE	
22222	BROWN	02	6.15	40.0	246.00	
22222	BROWN	02	6.15	50.0	307.50	
22233	CARPENTER	01	7.25	99.9	724.28	
22233	CARPENTER	04	7.45	1.0-	7.45CR	
22233	CARPENTER	02	6.15	25.0	153.75	
22235	DIXON	02	6.15	40.0	246.00	
22240	EMMETT	01	7.25	15.0	108.75	
22240	EMMETT	01	7.25	15.0	108.75	
22240	EMMETT	04	7.45	5.0	37.25	
22301	FLANDERS	01	7.25	25.5	184.88	
22301	FLANDERS	01	7.25	25.5	184.88	
22301	FLANDERS	03	0.00	0.0	0.00	JOB NOT IN TABLE
22301	FLANDERS	01	7.25	5.0	36.25	
22355	GARFIELD	04	7.45	1.5	11.18	
22355	GARFIELD	02	6.15	10.5	64.58	
22355	GARFIELD	04	7.45	1.5	11.18	
22360	HENDERSON	02	6.15	8.0	49.20	
22360	HENDERSON	02	6.15	8.0	49.20	
22360	HENDERSON	04	7.45	7.5	55.88	
22360	HENDERSON	01	7.25	7.5	54.38	
22360	HENDERSON	02	6.15	8.0	49.20	

FIGURE 18–1 (con't.)

The following routine illustrates a simple table sort. The basic programming steps to sort the scores into ascending sequence are:

1. Compare entry-1 in the table against entry-2 and exchange them if entry-1 is a higher value.
2. Compare entry-2 against entry-3 and exchange them if entry-2 is higher.
3. Continue in this fashion comparing entry-3 to entry-4, entry-4 to entry-5, entry-5 to entry-6, and entry-6 to entry-7.
4. Repeat the preceding steps until no more exchanges are made.

Let's follow this procedure using the table of scores defined above. Compare entry-1 (score 120) with entry-2 (score 135); since 120 is lower, there is no exchange. Compare entry-2 (135) with entry-3 (087); since 135 is higher, exchange them in the table. Now compare entry-3 (now 135) with entry-4 (106) and exchange, compare entry-4 (135) with entry-5 (095) and exchange, compare entry-5 (135) with entry-6 (142) and do no exchange, and finally compare entry-6 (142) with entry-7 (116) and exchange them. After one iteration, the table appears as follows:

ENTRY NUMBER	SCORE
1	120
2	087
3	106
4	095
5	135
6	116
7	142

Repeat the procedure exactly as before comparing entry-1 to entry-2, 2 to 3, and so forth until a complete pass through the table occurs with no exchanges. At this point, the table is fully sorted.

The flowchart for the sort routine in Fig. 18–2 is suitable for a table containing any number of entries. Little extra programming effort is required if the table contains functions as well as arguments.

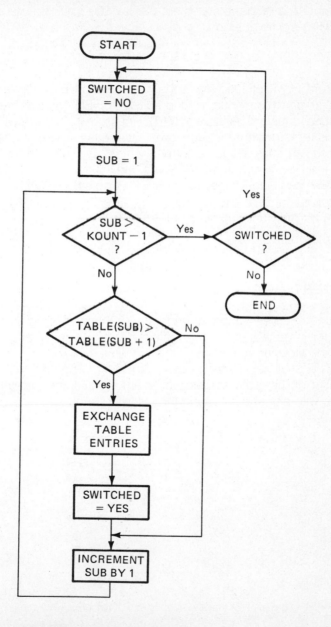

FIGURE 18–2 Simple Sort.

Example Sort

The program in Figure 18–1 loads a table with job numbers and rates-of-pay. The loading Procedure uses a variable named KOUNT to count the number of jobs that were loaded. After the table is loaded, the main logic routine calls the sort Procedure with the statement CALL S100_SORT;. The sort Procedure uses KOUNT to control the sort, as

DO SUB = 1 TO KOUNT − 1;

An outer DO WHILE loop stores the value zero in a Bit variable named SWITCHED. Processing is to continue as long as SWITCHED contains the value 1. (Note that the DCL statement initializes SWITCHED to 1.) The inner DO-loop establishes SUB as the subscript for each lower table entry. The logic begins by comparing successively entry-1 against entry-2, entry-2 against entry-3, 3 against 4, and so forth. If an exchange is made, SWITCHED is set to 1 to indicate that entries are still being exchanged; the DO WHILE loop sets SWITCHED to zero and the entire DO-loop is repeated. If no exchange is made, SWITCHED remains at zero, causing the DO WHILE (and the sort) to terminate.

Suggestion: Devise some imaginary table entries, such as 15, 12, 11, 10, 07, 05, and 04, and check how the sort logic works.

SHELL-METZNER SORT

Although relatively simple to understand, the preceding sort is inefficient, especially for large tables. A more efficient sort routine for any number of entries is the Shell-Metzner sort.:*

The Shell sort takes a binary approach. The first step is to determine the midpoint of the table entries. For example, assume that the table contains 10 entries with alphabetic data in the following sequence:

1	K
2	J
3	H
4	G
5	F
6	E
7	D
8	C
9	B
10	A

*A technical explanation of the Shell-Metzner sort is in *Creative Computing,* November-December, 1976.

The sort compares entry-1 to entry-6, entry-2 to entry-7, entry-3 to entry-8, entry-4 to entry-9, and entry-5 to entry-10. After this pass, the table appears as follows:

1	E	⎫
2	D	⎪
3	C	⎬ *Five lower values*
4	B	⎪
5	A	⎭
6	K	⎫
7	J	⎪
8	H	⎬ *Five higher values*
9	G	⎪
10	F	⎭

The lower half of the table now contains the lowest five entries, and the upper half now contains the highest five entries. The Shell sort then processes smaller sections of the table: 4, 2, and 1.

The flowchart in Figure 18–3 provides the sort logic in structured style (processing goes down the page). The variable KOUNT is the number of table entries. MID is the initial midpoint entry and in each iteration of the outer DO-loop is divided by 2; when MID equals zero, the sort is completed. SUB and MIDPLUS are used respectively as subscripts for comparison of the lower table entry to the higher entry. J determines initial values for SUB, while SUB and MID determine the values for MIDPLUS. The variable K is always the difference between KOUNT and MID and controls the first inner DO-loop.

Suggestion: Work through the entire sort step-by-step using the ten example entries; you should complete it with 12 exchanges. Do not be alarmed by the number of tests—it is still much faster than the bubble sort. Figure 18–4 contains the PL/I code for this flowchart. The routine was tested simply by replacing the bubble sort in Figure 18–1. For debugging purposes, initial test runs included a count of the number of exchanges and a dump of the table after the sort—a recommended practice because of the ease of making coding errors.

BINARY SEARCH

If you were to search for a telephone number in a large directory starting with the first name on page one, locating the number would be enormously time consuming. You usually open the directory toward the center and flip the pages forward or backward as you approach the required name. To locate an argument in a large table there is an equivalent programming method called binary search.

If a table contains 100 entries, then a standard table search requires an average of 50 compares to locate an entry. A binary search can reduce this number considerably. The technique begins at the middle of the table to determine in which half is the required entry. The next step checks the midpoint of the half,

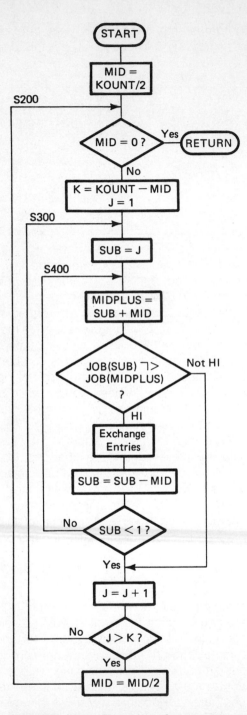

FIGURE 18–3 Flowchart for Shell-metzner Sort.

```
DCL        (J, K, MIDPLUS)
           KOUNT, MID, MIDPLUS) BIN FIXED (15) ;

           MID = KOUNT / 2 ;
S200:      DO WHILE (MID ¬= 0) ;
           K = KOUNT - MID ;
           J = 1 ;
S300:      DO UNTIL (J > K) ;
               SUB = J ;
S400:          DO UNTIL (SUB < 1) ;
                   MIDPLUS = SUB + MID ;
                   IF JOBN_TAB(SUB) ¬> JOBN_TAB(MIDPLUS) THEN LEAVE;
                   ENTRY_SAVE = JOB_RATE_TABLE(MIDPLUS) ;
                   JOB_RATE_TABLE(MIDPLUS) = JOB_RATE_TABLE(SUB) ;
                   JOB_RATE_TABLE(SUB) = ENTRY_SAVE ;
                   SUB = SUB - MID ;
               END S400 ;
               J = J + 1 ;
           END S300 ;
           MID = MID / 2 ;
       END S200 ;
```

FIGURE 18–4 Shell-metzner Sort.

and so forth, thereby quickly closing in on the required entry. As an illustration, assume a table of 20 job numbers and their associated rates-of-pay:

ENTRY	JOB	RATE	ENTRY	JOB	RATE	ENTRY	JOB	RATE	ENTRY	JOB	RATE
1	01	8.50	6	13	9.25	11	30	9.25	16	56	10.30
2	03	9.25	7	15	9.25	12	32	9.95	17	63	10.20
3	04	9.35	8	16	10.30	13	47	10.30	18	72	9.95
4	06	9.35	9	20	10.30	14	50	8.50	19	74	9.95
5	07	9.25	10	27	10.30	15	52	10.30	20	76	9.35

To locate the middle entry, average the first position (assumed to start at zero for the search) and the last position (20):

$$Mid\text{-}point = (0 + 20) \div 2 = 10$$

Consequently, the search begins at the 10th entry, which contains job 27. Comparing the search argument to the value 27 reveals the following:

Equal	The required entry is found.
Lower	The required entry is in the lower half of the table.
Higher	The required entry is in the upper half of the table.

If an input record contains job 47, then the first compare of 47 against 27 is high, and you can immediately eliminate searching the lower half of the table. Now compute the midpoint of the upper half: $(10 + 20) \div 2 =$ entry 15, which contains job 52. A comparison of job 47 to 52 gives a low condition indicating that the required entry is in the third quarter of the table.

The midpoint of the third quarter is $(10 + 15) \div 2 = 25 \div 2 = 12\frac{1}{2}$, rounded to 13. Because the job number of entry 13 is 47, the comparison reveals that the correct entry has been found. The rate-of-pay for job 47 is $10.30, located with only three compares.

There are two ways to initialize the calculation of the midpoint:

1.   (0 + highest entry) $\div$ 2, rounding this and all subsequent calculations.
2.   (1 + highest entry + 1) $\div$ 2, with no rounding of this or subsequent calculations. The preceding example could have been $(1 + 21) \div 2$.

Either rule applied consistently works for a table of any number of entries. Other calculations, such as not rounding method 1 or rounding method 2, will cause the search to miss the first or last entry in the table.

The formula to calculate each midpoint is

$$MID = (LO + HI) \div 2$$

LO is the low entry position, and HI is the high entry. To move up or down the table, place the previously calculated midpoint (MID) in LO or HI. If the comparison of the search argument to the table is low, place MID in HI to check lower in the table. If the comparison is high, place MID in LO to check higher in the table.

The previous example initially calculated MID as $(0 + 20) \div 2 = 10$. The first comparison of job 47 to entry 10, job 27, was high. Therefore, to check higher in the table, store the contents of MID (10) in LO. The next comparison is $(10 + 20) \div 2 = 15$.

Missing Entries

One danger in a search for a unique entry is that the entry may be missing. A conventional table search can detect a missing entry by a low comparison or by reaching the end of the table, but a binary search does not proceed sequentially through a table. But there is one device that does work: if two successive calculations result in the same midpoint, then the entry is not in the table. For example, assume the same table of job numbers and rates-of-pay, and assume that the input record contains job 12. The calculations of midpoints and the compares are as follows:

STEP	MIDPOINT	COMPARISON SEARCH : TABLE	RESULT
	(LO + HI) $\div$ 2		
1	(0 + 20) $\div$ 2 = 10	12 : 27	Low
2	(0 + 10) $\div$ 2 = 5	12 : 07	High
3	(5 + 10) $\div$ 2 = 7½ or 8	12 : 16	Low
4	(5 + 8) $\div$ 2 = 6½ or 7	12 : 15	Low
5	(5 + 7) $\div$ 2 = 6	12 : 13	Low
6	(5 + 6) $\div$ 2 = 5½ or 6	12 : 13	

Midpoint 6 has now been calculated twice in a row and will continue to be calculated unless you provide a test, as shown in the flowchart in Figure 18–5.

The Maximum Number of Compares

The following table compares the use of sequential search with binary search. The table assumes that a sequential search on the average requires processing half way through the table.

NUMBER OF ENTRIES	MAXIMUM SEQUENTIAL	AVERAGE SEQUENTIAL	MAXIMUM BINARY
20	20	10	5
50	50	25	6
100	100	50	7
400	400	200	9
800	800	400	10
2,000	2,000	1,000	11
10,000	10,000	5,000	14

The figures for "maximum binary search" are based on the formula

$$2^n > \text{number of table entries}$$

where n is the maximum number of compares required. For example, if there are 50 table entries, then select the smallest n necessary:

$$2^5 = 32 \text{ (too small, because } 32 < 50)$$
$$2^6 = 64 \text{ (correct, because } 64 > 50)$$

As a result, searching a table from 32 to 63 entries in size involves a *maximum* of six compares. But since a binary search generates more machine instructions than a sequential search, it is best used with tables containing about 60 or more entries.

Example Binary Search

In Figure 18–1, the employee processing procedure, B100_PROC, CALLs the binary search Procedure with the statement

CALL C100_SEARCH;

The following is the binary search routine from the program:

```
/*       B I N A R Y   S E A R C H              */
C100_SEARCH: PROCEDURE ;
         FOUND = '0'B ;
         HI, MID = KOUNT+1 ;
         LO, PREVMID = 1 ;
C200:    DO WHILE (¬FOUND & MID ¬= PREVMID) ;
             PREVMID = MID ;
             MID = (LO + HI) / 2 ;
             IF JOBNIN < JOBN_TAB(MID) THEN
               HI = MID ;
             ELSE IF JOBNIN > JOBN_TAB(MID)
                  THEN LO = MID ;
                  ELSE FOUND = '1'B ;
         END C200 ;
      END C100_SEARCH ;
```

The binary search routine initializes a FOUND indicator to zero (defined as BIT (1)) and initializes HI to KOUNT+1 and LO to 1. The purpose of PREVMID is to check if a job is not in the table: the DO WHILE loop will terminate if a job

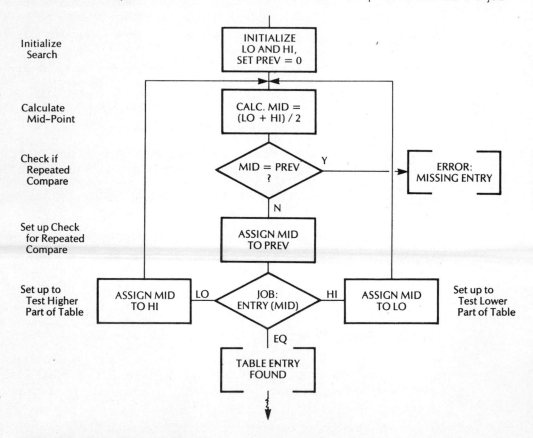

FIGURE 18–5 Binary Search.

is FOUND or if MID = PREVMID. On return from the binary search, the employee processing Procedure checks if the job was FOUND; if FOUND, the wage is calculated, and if not FOUND, an error message is printed.

MERGING ARRAYS

Assume that a program is to merge two arrays, A and B, into one array, C. Arrays A and B may be any length, but the merged array C must be at least the length of A plus the length of B. Data in both arrays must be in ascending sequence, and equal element values are permitted.

As shown in Figure 18–6, the program compares elements from A to elements in B and stores the lower value in C. The subscript for A or B is incremented depending on which one is stored, and the subscript for C is always incremented.

To facilitate determining the end of the arrays, each array contains 999 in its last element. Once the program assigns 999 to array C, the merge terminates. At the end, a PUT statement prints the contents of array C.

FILE SORTING

Programming for sorting files is quite complex and is almost always handled by manufacturer-supplied programs. A PL/I program can interface with a utility sort program using a routine PLISRT. You must notify the routine as to the length and format of control fields, ascending or descending sequence, and other required information. The PL/I sort statement has the following general format:

CALL PLISRTn (options);

PLISRT has four options:

1. PLISRTA specifies that the unsorted input data is on a data set and that the sorted output data is to be placed on a data set.
2. PLISRTB accepts input data from a subroutine and places sorted data on a data set.
3. PLISRTC accepts input data from a data set and supplies sorted data to a subroutine.
4. PLISRTD accepts input data from a subroutine and supplies sorted data to a subroutine.

```
1   PROG18B:
         PROCEDURE OPTIONS(MAIN) ;

2   DCL      (I, J, K)           BIN FIXED (15) INIT (1B) ;
3   DCL      A(10)               DEC FIXED (3)  INIT (03,04,07,10,13,
                                                15,16,20,30,999);
4   DCL      B(10)               DEC FIXED (3)  INIT (01,02,05,07,11,
                                                18,19,22,23,999);
5   DCL      C(20)               DEC FIXED (3)  INIT ( (20) 0) ;
6   DCL      MERGED              BIT (1)        INIT ('0'B) ;

    /*       MERGE ARRAY-A AND ARRAY-B       */
7            DO UNTIL (MERGED) ;
8              IF A(I) <= B(J) THEN
                 DO;
9                  C(K) = A(I);
10                 I = I + 1 ;
11               END;
12             ELSE
                 DO;
13                 C(K) = B(J);
14                 J = J + 1 ;
15               END;
16             IF C(K) = 999 THEN MERGED = '1'B ;
17             K = K + 1 ;
18           END;

    /*       PRINT MERGED ARRAY-C            */
19           PUT DATA (C) ;
20           SIGNAL FINISH ;
21       END PROG18B ;
```

FIGURE 18–6 Merging Arrays.

The latter three options provide user exits for special handling of records before and after sorting. A simple example for OS PL/I follows:

```
CALL PLISRTA (' SORT FIELDS=(1,5,CH,A) ',
              ' RECORD TYPE=F,LENGTH=(100) ',
              60000,
              RETCODE) ;
```

The program is to sort a file based on the parameters in SORT FIELDS: the control field is columns 1 to 5 and is character (CH) format to be sorted into ascending (A) sequence. One or more blanks are required after a starting apostrophe and before an ending apostrophe. Record type is fixed-length (F), and length of records is 100 bytes. The sort is provided with 60,000 bytes of storage. RETCODE is any variable name defined as BINARY FIXED (31) used by PLISRT to indicate the success or failure of the sort. A return code of zero means that the sort was successful. If the program is to terminate in the event of a failed sort, you could code a routine such as the following:

```
IF RETCODE ¬= 0 THEN
   DO ;
      PUT DATA (RETCODE) ;
      SIGNAL ERROR ;
   END ;
```

Data sets for the sort are handled through job control entries for SORTLIB (the library where the sort resides), SORTIN (for the input data set, if any), SORTOUT (for the output data set, if any), and SORTWK01, SORTWK02, and SORTWK03 (for sort work data sets).

Details of PLISRT specifications, the use of subroutines for special handling of records, and job control requirements are in the PL/I Programmer's Guide for your installation.

DECIMAL ACCUMULATION

In repetitive computations, rounding sometimes introduces a small error. For example, assume that a department sells three categories of hardware. Total sales by category and percentage of the total are as follows:

CATEGORY	SALES		PERCENT OF TOTAL (ROUNDED)
A	$155.47	0.2184180	21.84%
B	236.92	0.3328463	33.28
C	319.41	0.4487355	44.87
Total	711.80	0.9999998	99.99%

The total percent is 99.99%. In order to ensure 100.00%, you can use for rounding the decimal positions that are normally rounded off, as follows:

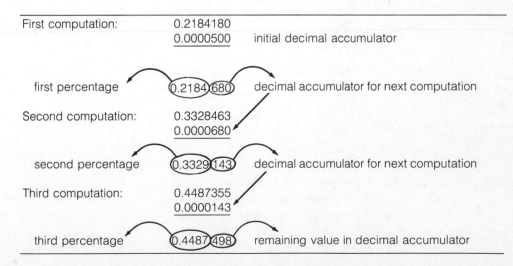

First computation:	0.2184180	
	0.0000500	initial decimal accumulator
first percentage	0.2184 680	decimal accumulator for next computation
Second computation:	0.3328463	
	0.0000680	
second percentage	0.3329 143	decimal accumulator for next computation
Third computation:	0.4487355	
	0.0000143	
third percentage	0.4487 498	remaining value in decimal accumulator

The three calculated percentages total 100.00% as follows:

FRACTION	PERCENTAGE
0.2184	21.84%
0.3329	33.29
0.4487	44.87
1.0000	100.00%

Each related group of computations begins with a decimal accumulator initialized to 0.0000500 (the precision will vary by application).

Negative Values

Although the percentages in this example are positive, in some applications results can be negative. In such cases, define a positive accumulator initialized to +5 and a separate negative accumulator initialized to −5. Add the positive accumulator to positive values and the negative accumulator to negative values.

Programming for Decimal Accumulation

Figure 18–7 illustrates the PL/I coding for the preceding example. The program initializes DEC_ACCUM and processes an array, SALE_TAB, containing three sales amounts. Let's examine the logic using the first element of SALE_TAB containing 155.47:

1. Divide SALE_TAB (1) by TOTAL_SALES: 0.2184180
   Then add DEC_ACCUM, store in QUOTIENT: 0.2184680
2. Store QUOTIENT IN SALE_PCT (note the precision of the two
   variables)   0.2184
3. Subtract SALE_PCT from QUOTIENT and store the result in DEC
   ACCUM: 0.0000680

The program performs the loop for each of the three elements of SALE_TAB.

DEBUGGING TIPS

- A table search that exits through the bottom of a DO-loop (but not DO UNTIL) causes the subscript to be too large by 1.
- If a table consists of unique table arguments in ascending sequence, a table search can exit immediately if the search argument is lower than the table argument—the item is not in the table.

```
 3   DCL      SALE_TAB(3)        DEC FIXED(7,2) INIT(155.47,
                                                     236.92,
                                                     319.41),

              DEC_ACCUM          DEC FIXED(7,7),
              QUOTIENT           DEC FIXED(8,7),
              SALE_PCT           DEC FIXED(5,4),
              K                  BIN FIXED(15),
              TOTAL_SALES        DEC FIXED(7,2) INIT(711.80),
              TOTAL_PCT          DEC FIXED(5,4) INIT(0);

 4            DEC_ACCUM = .0000500;
 5            DO K = 1 TO 3;
 6                QUOTIENT = (SALE_TAB(K) / TOTAL_SALES) + DEC_ACCUM;
 7                SALE_PCT = QUOTIENT;
 8                DEC_ACCUM = QUOTIENT - SALE_PCT;
 9                PUT SKIP LIST (SALE_TAB(K), SALE_PCT) ;
10                TOTAL_PCT = TOTAL_PCT + SALE_PCT;
11            END;
12            PUT SKIP(2) (TOTAL_SALES, TOTAL_PCT);
```

```
          155.47              0.2184
          236.92              0.3329
          319.41              0.4487

          711.80              1.0000
```

FIGURE 18–7 Decimal Accumulation.

- If a table consists of arguments in steps such as an income tax table, the last table argument should contain nines if arithmetic or HIGH characters if CHAR to force termination of a search. Usually, all search arguments are valid, and an equal or low compare indicates that the item is found.
- Loading a table from an external device should be coded carefully. Check that the table does not overload, and if necessary check that the items are in sequence.
- As a check on accuracy in early program tests, print the contents of a loaded or sorted table using, for example, a statement such as PUT LIST (TABLE);.
- Double-check a sort and a binary search after coding; a simple error can cause a disaster at execution-time.

PROBLEMS

18–1.   Define a sales table for twelve months. Each month's sales can total up to $250,000.00. Initialize entries to zero.

18–2.   Under what circumstances would table arguments not be in ascending sequence for table lookup?

18–3.   For table searches, there are two basic types of tables. What are these types and how do they differ?

18–4. Specify two ways to ensure that a table search will always terminate.

18–5. Define the following table as an array of structures for quantities sold and discount rate. A quantity up to 10 has no discount; from 11 to 25, a discount of 2% (.02), and so on.

QUANTITY	DISCOUNT RATE
10	.000
25	.020
100	.025
250	.040
500	.080
over 500	.105

18–6. Using the discount table in Problem 18–5, code a routine that calculates discount (DISCOUNT) based on quantity-sold (QTYSOLD) and amount of sale (AMTSOLD). The routine uses QTYSOLD to search the table for low or equal quantity and uses the corresponding discount rate to calculate the amount of discount as follows:

Amount of discount = amount of sale × discount rate (rounded).

18–7. When is it preferable to load table entries from external storage?

18–8. Define a table that is to be loaded from external storage with a maximum of 25 elements. The table requires entries for stock numbers (arguments) and prices (functions). Stock number is five characters, and price is of the form xxx.xx.

18–9. Code a routine that reads records containing stock numbers and prices and stores them in the table defined in Problem 18–8. Ensure that the table does not overload. The last stock number in the file is 99999.

18–10. Using the stored table from the previous problem, code a routine that sorts the table entries into sequence by stock number.

18–11. Use the sorted table from Problem 18–10 to perform a binary search routine. Input records contain a stock number, STOCKIN, to use for the search. Use QTYIN from the input record to calculate stock value:

Stock value = quantity × price

18–12. Combine the previous four problems into one program. Provide enough stock input records to test the table thoroughly, being sure to have stock numbers that are equal to the first and to the last table arguments. Suggestion: To help debug, print the contents of the table after loading and after sorting using a statement such as PUT LIST (STOCKTABLE).

CHAPTER 19

STRING DATA HANDLING

OBJECTIVE:

To cover the statements that manipulate Character and Bit String data.

INTRODUCTION

This chapter extends and completes the coverage of string data introduced in Chapter 4. Included are the various special *attributes* POSITION and VARYING, and the various *built-in functions.* Many of these features are especially useful for text-editing applications and for validating input data. This chapter covers the DATE built-in function, introduces two important features—concatenation and the SUBSTR built-in function—and then covers the remaining operations in alphabetic sequence.

The two types of string data are *Character string,* a contiguous sequence of characters, and *Bit string,* a contiguous sequence of binary integers (bits 0 and 1). A Character string may contain any computer-recognizable character, including blanks. For both Declaratives and assignment statements, PL/I assigns the Character or Bit string one byte at a time, from left to right .

THE DATE BUILT-IN FUNCTION

It is often necessary to use the current date in programming, for example to calculate finance charges, or to print the current date on a report. The current date as initialized by the computer operator is stored in the "communications region" in the Supervisor area. The DATE built-in function is used to extract this date and return it in the six character format *yymmdd*. DATE and TIME should be declared as BUILTIN to avoid confusion because many programs use such names as variables. For example:

```
DCL DATE BUILTIN ,
        TODAY CHAR(6) ;
    TODAY = DATE ;
```

The assignment statement causes the current date to store in TODAY as yymmdd. This format is not always desirable on a report heading, where ddmmyy or mmddyy may be more conventional.
    The following statements arrange the date so that the program can access any field yy, mm, or dd to facilitate separate processing of them:

```
DCL     TODAY      CHAR(6) ;
DCL 1 DATSTRUC   DEFINED TODAY,
        3 YEAR     CHAR(2),
        3 MONTH    CHAR(2),
        3 DAY      CHAR(2);

    TODAY = DATE ;
```

It is now possible to assign DAY, MONTH, or YEAR to the print area, in the required sequence. Note: a statement

```
DATSTRUC = DATE ;
```

would generate three assignment statements that store the first two characters of DATE in YEAR, MONTH, and DAY. The result is yy stored in each 2-character element.

CONCATENATION

Concatenation means "joining together" and in PL/I involves connecting separately defined Character strings and Bit strings. Concatenation may also join arithmetic fields, but PL/I converts them to string data according to the rules of conversion. The symbol for concatenation is two bar characters: ‖ . Assume the following character data:

```
DCL     CHARA     CHAR(9)      INIT ('DECEMBER') ,
        CHARB     CHAR(4)      INIT ('12TH') ,
        CHARC     CHAR(13) ;
```

The following statement joins the contents of CHARA with that of CHARB and assigns the result to CHARC:

```
CHARC = CHARA ‖ CHARB ;
```

CHARC now contains the Character string 'DECEMBER 12TH'. CHARA and CHARB need not be defined adjacent. It is also possible to concatenate Bit string data in a similar fashion.

THE SUBSTR BUILT-IN FUNCTION

The Substring built-in function, SUBSTR, has the ability to extract portions of a Character or Bit string. The format is

$$SUBSTR (x_1 , x_2 [, x_3])$$

- x_1 is the name of the string variable from which characters or bits are to be extracted or placed.
- x_2 is an expression that signifies the starting position (numbered from the left) of the string. The leftmost position is number 1 and so on.
- x_3 is an optional expression that gives the number of characters or bits that are referenced. If x_3 is omitted, the function assumes that the length is from the starting position, x_2, to the end of the string. Under the Subset, x_3 may be only a decimal integer. For example:

```
DCL TITLE CHAR(25) INIT ('PROGRAMMING IN PL/I') ,
    SAVE CHAR(5) ;
    SAVE = SUBSTR (TITLE, 16, 4) ;
```

The assignment statement extracts four characters from TITLE, beginning with the 16th character. SAVE now contains 'PL/I'. Since the extracted string contains the last characters of TITLE, a SUBSTR statement that omits x_3 works equally well; the extraction begins at the 16th character and continues for four characters until reaching the end of the string, as follows:

```
SAVE = SUBSTR (TITLE, 16) ;
```

SUBSTR is also known as a *pseudovariable,* which can be used in a receiving field. Other pseudovariables are COMPLETION, COMPLEX, IMAG, ON-CHAR, ONSOURCE, REAL, STATUS, STRING, and UNSPEC. The example illustrates use of variables (I and J) in the SUBSTR expression. The effect is to assign the first four characters of STOREB ('WORD') to the first four characters of STO-REA, generating 'WORD PROCESSING'.

```
DCL  STOREA    CHAR(13)  INIT ('DATA PROCESSING'),
     STOREB    CHAR(09)  INIT ('WORD LIST') ;
DCL (I, J)     BIN FIXED(15) ;

     I = 1 ;
     J = 4 ;
     SUBSTR(STOREA, I, J) = SUBSTR(STOREB, I, J) ;
```

The SUBSTR function may also be combined with concatenation. The next example uses the DATE built-in function to extract from the computer communications region the day, month, and year. DATE delivers the current date in the 6-character format *yymmdd.* The following SUBSTR operation converts this date to the format *ddmmyy:*

```
DCL  DATE     BUILTIN,
     DT       CHAR(6),
     TODAY    CHAR(6);

     DT = DATE ;
     TODAY = SUBSTR(DT,5,2) || SUBSTR(DT,3,2) || SUBSTR(DT,1,2);
```

The result is that DT contains yymmdd, and TODAY contains ddmmyy.

SUBSTR requires that the starting position of the string (x_2) and the number of characters (x_3) are valid, that is within the length of the string. For example, assume that the coding in the preceding SUBSTR statement is SUBSTR (DT,7,10). The starting position (7) is beyond the string length, and the number of characters to move (10) exceeds the string length. The error causes the STRINGRANGE condition, as described in Chapter 23.

THE ALL AND ANY BUILT-IN FUNCTIONS

The ALL and the ANY built-in functions are used on Bit-string arrays. ALL, which is equivalent to Boolean AND, determines if *all* bits are '1'B in the corresponding position of each element. If true, the operation returns the value '1'B, and if not true, the operation returns the value '0'B. ANY, which is equivalent to Boolean OR, checks if *any* bit is '1'B in the corresponding position of each element. If true, the operation returns the value '1'B, and if not true, the operation returns '0'B.

Assume the following Declaratives and assignment statements:

```
DCL   BITSTR      BIT(8),
      BITARR(3) BIT(8)      INIT ('11110000'B,
                                  '10111010'B,
                                  '11011000'B) ;

      BITSTR = ALL(BITARR) ;   /* BITSTR = '10010000'B */
      BITSTR = ANY(BITARR) ;   /* BITSTR = '11111010'B */
```

For the ALL example, the corresponding bits in each element that are all '1' are (from the left) the first and fourth bits. For the ANY example, the corresponding bits that have at least one '1' are bits one, two, three, four, five, and seven. The comment to the right of each example shows the result stored in BITSTR.

THE BIT BUILT-IN FUNCTION

BIT converts data or an expression to Bit format. The general format for BIT is as follows:

$$\text{bit-result} = \text{BIT} (x_1 [,x_2]) ;$$

- x_1 is the data or expression to be converted to Bit.
- x_2 is an optional expression that can designate the length of the resulting Bit string. Omission of x_2 causes the conversion operation to determine the length.

THE BOOL BUILT-IN FUNCTION

The BOOL built-in function gives a programmer more capability of processing Bit data. The Boolean operators are AND, OR, and XOR (Exclusive OR). AND means that if both compared bits are '1', the result is a '1' bit. OR means that if either or both bits are '1', the result is '1'. XOR means that if either bit, but not both, is '1', the result is '1'. The following illustrates Boolean comparison of two Bit strings:

	AND	OR	XOR
String-1	0 0 1 1	0 0 1 1	0 0 1 1
String-2	0 1 0 1	0 1 0 1	0 1 0 1
	─ ─ ─ ─	─ ─ ─ ─	─ ─ ─ ─
Result	0 0 0 1	0 1 1 1	0 1 1 0

The format for the BOOL function is

$$\text{Result} = \text{BOOL} (x_1, x_2, x_3) ;$$

- x_1 and x_2 are the two Bit strings. The operation compares bits in x_1 with corresponding bits in x_2.
- x_3 is a string of four bits that defines the Boolean operation. Each bit specifies the result of the comparison bit-by-bit of x_1 with x_2, according to the following rules:
  1. The first (leftmost) bit—the required result (0 or 1) of a comparison of bits where both compared bits are 0.
  2. The second bit—the required result (0 or 1) of a comparison where the x_1 bit is 0 and the x_2 bit is 1.
  3. The third bit—the required result (0 or 1) of a comparison where the x_1 bit is 1 and the x_2 bit is 0.
  4. The fourth bit—the required result where the compared bits are both 1.

For example, assume that a program wants to perform a comparison operation on two bit strings, BITA and BITB. In this example, x_3 of the BOOL operation is:

x_3	EXPLANATION
①0 0 1	The result of comparing 0 with 0 is to be ①
1 ⓪ 0 1	The result of comparing 0 with 1 is to be ⓪
1 0 ⓪ 1	The result of comparing 1 with 0 is to be ⓪
1 0 0 ①	The result of comparing 1 with 1 is to be ①

```
DCL  BITA      BIT(8)      INIT ('10101010'B),
     BITB      BIT(8)      INIT ('11110000'B),
     BITC      BIT(8) ;

     BITC = BOOL(BITA, BITB, '1001'B) ; /* BITC = '10100101' */
```

BOOL performs the comparison of BITA with BITB bit-by-bit according to the rules of x_3. The result assigned to BITC is the bit string shown. For example, comparing bit-1 of BITA with bit-1 of BITB ('1' with '1') according to rule 4, yields a '1' in the first position of BITC, and so forth.

Extended BOOL Example

A students' quiz consists of ten true or false questions. The students' answers are recorded in STUDANS as '0' for false and '1' for true. The correct (model) answer is in MODELANS. The example uses BOOL to match the students' answers against the model answer. The operation stores a string of ten bits in RESULT—a '0' means wrong and a '1' means correct:

```
DCL  STUDANS    BIT(10),                        /* STUDENTS' ANSWER    */
     MODELANS   BIT(10) INIT('1100101101'B),/* CORRECT MODEL ANS   */
     RESULT     BIT(10),                        /* RESULT OF BOOL OPN */
     CORRECTNO  DEC FIXED(3) INIT (0),          /* COUNTER FOR CORRECT*/
     N          BIN FIXED(15) ;                 /*  ANSWERS            */

     RESULT = BOOL(MODELANS, STUDANS, '1001'B) ;
```

Next, the example has to add the number of '1's in RESULT. It steps through RESULT one bit at a time. If the tested bit is '1', the program adds 1 to the number of correct answers in CORRECTNO.

```
DO N = 1 TO 10 ;
   IF SUBSTR(RESULT, N, 1) = '1'B THEN
      CORRECTNO = CORRECTNO + 1 ;
END ;
```

On completion of the loop, CORRECTNO will contain the number of answers that the student has correct.

THE CHAR BUILT-IN FUNCTION

CHAR converts a variable or an expression to Character format. The general format for CHAR is

$$\text{character-result} = \text{CHAR}(\ x_1\ [,x_2]\ )\ ;$$

- x_1 is the data or expression to be converted to Character.
- x_2 is an optional expression that can designate the length of the resulting Character string. Omission of x_2 causes the conversion operation to determine the length.

THE HIGH AND LOW BUILT-IN FUNCTIONS

The HIGH and LOW built-in functions are useful to determine the highest and the lowest byte value on the computer. Since such values vary by computer, HIGH and LOW permit the same program to be compiled on different computers.

On the 360 and 370 the lowest value in the 8-bit byte is all bits = 0(hexadecimal '00'), and the highest is all bits = 1 (hexadecimal 'FF'). LOW is lower than character '0', and HIGH is higher than '9' or 'Z'.

LOW is often used, for example, to establish the control word of the first record of a run with the lowest possible value, and HIGH to establish the control word of the last record with the highest value. Assume the following statements:

```
DCL   FIRSTCUSTOMER   CHAR(5),
      LASTCUSTOMER    CHAR(5);

      FIRSTCUSTOMER = LOW(5) ;
      LASTCUSTOMER  = HIGH(5) ;
```

Both FIRSTCUSTOMER and LASTCUSTOMER are 5-byte fields. LOW(5) asks for five bytes of the lowest character value, and HIGH(5) asks for five of the highest value. The function (n) specifying the number of bytes must be coded.

THE INDEX BUILT-IN FUNCTION

INDEX has the facility to compare a Character (or Bit) string ("argument-2") against a portion of another string ("argument-1"). The value in the operation looks for a combination of identical characters. The string in argument-2 may or may not be found in argument-1. INDEX is particularly useful, for example, for searching name lists for blanks in order to reverse first and last names. The general format of INDEX is

> value = INDEX (argument-1, argument-2) ;

---

argument-1:	the first argument, the name of a string to be searched.
argument-2:	the second argument, containing the string checked against argument-1.

The following code illustrates the use of INDEX:

```
DCL  FIELDA    CHAR(10)  INIT ('SECONDHAND'),
     FIELDB    CHAR(04)  INIT ('HAND'),
     K         BIN FIXED(15) ;

     K = INDEX(FIELDA, FIELDB) ;
```

The INDEX function compares the value in FIELDB ('HAND') against FIELDA, from left to right, looking for the same combination of characters. The same string is found in FIELDA beginning at the seventh character. INDEX then delivers the binary value 7 to K. If no equal is found, INDEX inserts 0 in K. (If there is more than one identical string in argument-1, INDEX locates only the first one.)

Now, suppose it is necessary to change this found argument ('HAND') to the string 'FOOT'. K contains the starting position, but it is not permissible to use K as a subscript, since FIELDA is not an array. But SUBSTR can be used as follows:

> IF K ¬ = 0 THEN SUBSTR (FIELDA, K, 4) = 'FOOT' ;

THE LENGTH BUILT-IN FUNCTION

At times, the specific length of a Character or Bit string may be unknown, although the maximum possible length is known. You can use the VARYING attribute (not in the Subset) to determine the actual character field length, as follows:

```
DCL FIELD CHAR(25) VARYING ;
```

In this case, the program may assign any length string up to 25 characters into FIELD. The operation automatically records the length of the assigned field in a 2-byte prefix preceding the string.

For Character or Bit strings with the VARYING attribute, you can access the length of the string currently stored. The LENGTH built-in function provides this length as a Binary Fixed value:

```
DCL   NAME        CHAR(25) VARYING,
      J           BIN FIXED(15) ;

NAME = 'ANALOG' ;
J = LENGTH(NAME) ;
```

Since the string assigned to NAME is six characters, LENGTH inserts the value 6 in J.

THE POSITION ATTRIBUTE

Assume the following declarative statements:

```
DCL   AMTPIC    PIC '9999V99' ;
DCL   AMTCHAR   CHAR (7) DEFINED AMTPIC ;
```

The DEFINED attribute defines AMTCHAR beginning at the first position of AMTPIC. Occasionally you may need to define string data beginning at some position other than the first one. The POSITION attribute (not in the Subset) permits redefining at any position, as

```
DCL AMTCHAR CHAR (2) DEFINED AMTPIC POSITION(5) ;
```

AMTCHAR now references bytes 5 and 6 of AMTPIC:

9999V$\boxed{99}$

Note that the decimal point specifier (V) does not count as a character.

THE REPEAT BUILT-IN FUNCTION

REPEAT can be used to define string constants that have to be repeated a specified number of times. The general format for REPEAT is

$$string = REPEAT \ (\ x_1, \ x_2 \ ) ;$$

- x_1 is the Character or Bit expression to be repeated.
- x_2 is an expression designating the number of times to repeat the string.

For example:

```
DCL  FIELD      CHAR(100) ;

 1.    FIELD = (100)'*' ;              /* USE OF REPETITION */
 2.    FIELD = REPEAT('*', 99) ;      /* USE OF REPEAT     */
```

In case (1), the compiler generates a constant that requires 100 storage positions. In case (2), the compiler generates only a 1-byte constant; at execution-time, the program repeats the '*' through the 100-character string. For large, repeated values, REPEAT can save storage at some loss of execute speed.

THE STRING BUILT-IN FUNCTION

STRING, like SUBSTR, acts both as a built-in function and as a pseudovariable. STRING extracts and concatenates all the specified elements of a structure or array:

$$STRING (X)$$

x references a structure or array containing all Character or Bit string data.
Assume the following declaratives:

```
DCL 1 A,
      2 AB       CHAR(8),
      2 AC       CHAR(4);

DCL   B          CHAR(12) ;
```

Based on the preceding Declares, the statement

$$B = A ;$$

is an error, since it is invalid to assign a structure to a variable. The built-in function STRING can remedy this problem by concatenating all the elements of A and assigning them to B:

$$B = STRING (A) ;$$

Also, the statement A = B ; incorrectly generates

```
AB = B ;
AC = B ; .
```

STRING solves this problem with the following statement that assigns all twelve characters:

STRING(A) = B ;

Built-in functions gererate code to perform the operation, and there are often alternative ways to solve a problem without their use. For example, the use of DEFINED to redefine the structure A as a 12-character variable may be more efficient than using STRING (although PL/C users will have to use STRING):

```
DCL C CHAR(12) DEFINED A ;
C = B ;          /*VALID ASSIGNMENT*/
B = C ;          /*VALID ASSIGNMENT*/
```

STRING is useful in an IF statement where you want to compare data in a major or minor structure level.

THE TIME BUILT-IN FUNCTION

On computer models with a timing facility, the TIME built-in function can return a 9-character string in the format hhmmssttt, where

hh = hours   mm = minutes
ss = seconds   ttt = milliseconds

The following example defines TIME as a BUILTIN function and assigns it to a 9-character variable:

```
DCL     TIME     BUILTIN ,
        NOW      CHAR(9) ;

NOW = TIME ;
```

Assignment of TIME directly to a structure would cause an invalid result just as for DATE.

THE TRANSLATE BUILT-IN FUNCTION

The purpose of the TRANSLATE built-in function is to change specified characters to some other characters. The general format for TRANSLATE is

string = TRANSLATE ($x_1, x_2 [,x_3]$) ;

- x_1 is a string in which specified characters are to be translated.

- x_2 is a table containing replacement characters that are to be selected from x_1 for translation.
- x_3 is a lookup table containing the characters to be translated and replaced in x_1. Omitting x_3 causes the compiler to assume a string of 256 characters in ascending sequence (eight 0-bits through eight 1-bits).

The TRANSLATE function checks each character in x_1 against the x_3 table. If an equal is found, the x_2 character corresponding to the one in x_3 is replaced in the receiving string. For example, the following replaces blanks and commas in FLDA with a '0' character and a '.' respectively:

```
DCL   FLDA      CHAR(5)    INIT (' 1,23'),/* STRING TO CHANGE */
      FLDB      CHAR(2)    INIT ('0.');   /* ZERO & DEC POINT */

      FLDA = TRANSLATE(FLDA, FLDB, ' ,');/* FLDA NOW '01.23' */
```

TRANSLATE extracts the first character of x_1 (FLDA), a blank, and checks x_3 for this character. Since the first character of x_3 is a blank, the operation places the first character of x_2 (FLDB) into the first position of FLDA. The second character in FLDA is a '1', which is not in x_3, so TRANSLATE moves the '1' into the second position of FLDA. The function continues in this manner until FLDA is exhausted. At this point, FLDA contains '01.23'.

THE UNSPEC BUILT-IN FUNCTION

The purpose of the UNSPEC built-in function is to provide the bit configuration of any byte or variable. The general format for UNSPEC is

Bit-string = UNSPEC (x) ;

where x is an expression coded in any format.

The attribute of x determines the length of the returned Bit string, which requires eight bits for each byte in x. UNSPEC acts also as a pseudovariable. Note: the bit configuration of a byte is in EBCDIC format, as explained in Chapter 1. A programmer who knows how to interpret the bit configuration may find UNSPEC occasionally useful in debugging, where the contents of a variable contains bit values for which there is no printer character.

A useful application for UNSPEC is conversion of a lowercase character to uppercase, and vice versa. In EBCDIC, an upper case letter has a 1 in the second bit, whereas a lowercase letter has a 0. For example:

| Uppercase | A = 1100 0001 | J = 1101 0001 | S = 1110 0010 |
| Lowercase | a = 1000 0001 | j = 1001 0001 | s = 1010 0010 |

A text-editing application may require conversion of uppercase to lowercase. You could perform the conversion by means of the TRANSLATE built-in function or by a table lookup routine; UNSPEC can convert characters by use of logic: AND the uppercase character(s) with a bit string '10111111'B, which will convert bit-2 to a zero.

```
DCL   UNSPEC    BUILTIN ;
DCL   UPPER     CHAR(10),
      LOWER     CHAR(10);

UNSPEC(LOWER) = UNSPEC(UPPER) & (10)'10111111'B ;
```

The expression on the right ANDs the bit values in UPPER (a 10 byte string) with the ten bit strings. The *receiving* character string LOWER uses UNSPEC as a pseudovariable because the statement has to assign a bit string to a bit string in order to avoid conversion errors. (Assigning a bit string to a character string causes bits 0 and 1 to convert directly to *character* 0 and 1.)

A program may also have to convert lowercase letters to uppercase. For example, an operator may use a typewriter console to key a request in lowercase into a program. Actually the request could be in either lowercase or uppercase. An UNSPEC statement could OR the request with ten repetitions of '0100000000'B, as follows:

```
UNSPEC(UPPER) = UNSPEC(LOWER) | (10)'01000000'B ;
IF UPPER = 'CANCEL' THEN SIGNAL FINISH ;
```

THE VERIFY BUILT-IN FUNCTION

The VERIFY function checks for invalid or specific bits or characters. The function gives the position in a string x_1 of the first character or bit not in a control string x_2. The control string contains the characters or bits that are "valid." If no mismatch occurs (all the characters in x_1 are listed in x_2), the returned value is zero. The general format for VERIFY is

$$\text{Value} = \text{VERIFY} (x_1, x_2) ;$$

• x_1 is the string that the function scans for characters not in x_2.
• x_2 is the control string, containing a table of characters to scan in any sequence.

The VERIFY operation scans x_1 for any of the characters not listed in x_2. The value returned is the position of the first character identified. The following checks if a field contains only the characters 0 through 9:

```
DCL   VERIFY     BUILTIN ;
DCL   VALUE      CHAR(5),   INIT ('12.34'),
      K          BIN FIXED (15) ;

K = VERIFY (VALUE, '0123456789') ;
```

The third character of VALUE contains a decimal point (.), which does not occur in the verification string x_2. The result returned to K is therefore the fixed binary value 3. The SUBSTR function could be used subsequently to change the contents of the "invalid" character, for example, as

$$\text{SUBSTR(VALUE, K, 1)} = \text{'0'};$$

PROGRAM: VALIDATION OF INPUT RECORDS

The program in Figure 19–1 illustrates many of the features that this chapter discusses. The program first processes a Date record, then reads and "validates" any number of Account records. The objective is to check that each record contains only valid data. The example is illustrative only and is not intended to represent the way a program is normally written or should be written. The following explains various features by statement number:

STATEMENT	FEATURE		
8	POSITION	AMOUNTIN is a 6-character field, redefined such that AMOUNTCHAR defines the first five characters, and AMOUNTSIGN defines the sixth (rightmost) character.	AMOUNTCHAR AMOUNTSIGN
14	INDEX	The Date record contains the identification "DATE =" beginning in an unspecified position. INDEX is used to locate this character string. The length of the following alphabetic date (e.g., 31 AUGUST, 19xx) is unknown. To determine this length, Statement 17 locates the last (rightmost) character of the date; it begins at the end of the input record and scans from right to left looking for a nonblank character.	
19	SUBSTR	SUBSTR moves the located alphabetic date to DATEFIELD, starting at I + 6. The length of the substring is calculated as the difference between J and I, plus 5. As seen in the example, I is assumed to be in position 5, and J in 26. The length of date is J-(I+5)=26−(5+5)=16.	

DATE = 31 AUGUST, 19xx

I   J
5   11   26

(16 characters)

STATEMENT	FEATURE	
25	LOW	The program initializes PREVACCT to low-values to ensure that the first record sequenced against PREVACCT is higher.
30	CONCATENATION	ACCTIN ‖ AMOUNTCHAR creates a string consisting of the contents of ACCTIN and the first five characters of AMOUNTIN.
30	VERIFY	VERIFY checks that the concatenated string contains only the valid characters 0 through 9. Any invalid character causes an error message to print.
31	VERIFY	The statement checks that the sixth character of AMOUNTIN contains only 0–9 or $\overline{0}$–$\overline{9}$ (for negative values). In the control string table, J–R represents $\overline{1}$ through $\overline{9}$; $\overline{0}$ is a multipunch that not all printers can print.

```
1    PROG19:
          PROCEDURE OPTIONS(MAIN) ;

2    DCL     SYSIN    FILE STREAM INPUT ENV( BUFFERS(2) ) ;
3    DCL     SYSPRINT FILE PRINT;
4            DEFAULT RANGE(*) STATIC;
5    DCL     (INDEX, LOW, SUBSTR, VERIFY) BUILTIN ;
6    DCL     DATEREC          CHAR(80) ;

7    DCL 1   RECIN,
             2 RECODEIN         CHAR(2),
             2 ACCTIN           CHAR(5),
             2 AMOUNTIN         CHAR(6),
             2 FILLER           CHAR(67) ;

8    DCL     AMOUNTCHAR        CHAR(5) DEFINED AMOUNTIN POSITION(1),
             AMOUNTSIGN        CHAR(1) DEFINED AMOUNTIN POSITION(6);
9    DCL     RECORDIN          CHAR(80) DEFINED RECIN ;

10   DCL     (I, J)            BIN FIXED(15),
             DATEFIELD         CHAR(20)  INIT (' '),
             PREVACCT          CHAR(05),
             END_OF_FILE       BIT (01)  INIT ('0'B);

11           ON ENDFILE(SYSIN) END_OF_FILE = '1'B;
12           OPEN  FILE(SYSIN),
                   FILE(SYSPRINT);

     /*      PROCESS DATE RECORD           */
     /*      *******************           */
13           GET EDIT (DATEREC) ( A(80) ) ;
14           I = INDEX(DATEREC, 'DATE =');
15           IF I ¬= 0
                THEN DO;
16                    DO J = 80 TO I BY -1 ;
17                       IF SUBSTR(DATEREC,J,1) ¬= ' ' THEN LEAVE;
18                    END;
19                    DATEFIELD = SUBSTR(DATEREC, I+6, J-(I+5));
20                    PUT SKIP LIST (DATEFIELD);
21                 END;
22              ELSE PUT SKIP LIST ('DATE NOT FOUND');
```

FIGURE 19–1 Data Validation.

```
      /*          PROCESS ACCOUNT RECORDS        */
      /*          ***********************        */
23              PUT SKIP(2) LIST ('ACCOUNT NO.', 'AMOUNT') ;
24              PUT SKIP ;
25              PREVACCT = LOW(5);
26              GET EDIT (RECORDIN) ( A(80) ) ;

27              DO UNTIL (END_OF_FILE) ;
28                 IF ACCTIN < PREVACCT THEN
                      PUT SKIP LIST (ACCTIN, 'OUT OF SEQUENCE');
29                 ELSE PREVACCT = ACCTIN ;

30                 IF VERIFY(ACCTIN||AMOUNTCHAR, '0123456789') ¬= 0 THEN
                      PUT SKIP LIST (ACCTIN, AMOUNTIN, 'INVALID ACCT OR AMT');

31                 IF VERIFY (AMOUNTSIGN, '0123456789 JKLMNOPQR') ¬= 0 THEN
                      PUT SKIP LIST (ACCTIN, AMOUNTIN, 'INVALID AMOUNT');
32                 GET EDIT (RECORDIN) ( A(80) ) ;
33              END;

34              CLOSE FILE(SYSIN) ,
                      FILE(SYSPRINT) ;
35      END PROG19 ;
```

Output:-

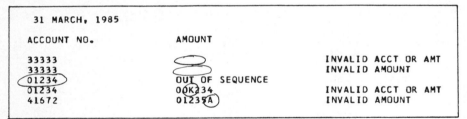

```
   31 MARCH, 1985

   ACCOUNT NO.                AMOUNT

   33333                                          INVALID ACCT OR AMT
   33333                                          INVALID AMOUNT
   01234                      OUT OF SEQUENCE
   01234                      00K234              INVALID ACCT OR AMT
   41672                      01235A              INVALID AMOUNT
```

FIGURE 19–1 (cont.)

SCANNING FOR CHARACTERS: FOUR WAYS

There are many situations in which a program has to scan a string for a specific character or group of characters. For example, a special "delimiter" character may follow variable-length name and address records. Or, a word processing program may have to locate a special character that indicates converting of uppercase to lowercase. The following section discusses four different ways to scan a character string. The examples scan for the end of a character string to determine its length. In all cases, the variable LEN is BIN FIXED (15) for storing the calculated length.

1.   Use of SUBSTR. The SUBSTR pseudovariable is one of PL/I's most useful

functions for handling character strings. The following scans from right to left until locating the first nonblank character:

```
DCL  NAME        CHAR(25);

     DO LEN = 25 TO 1 BY -1;
          IF SUBSTR(NAME, LEN, 1) ¬= ' ' THEN LEAVE;
     END;
```

An alternative solution is

```
     DO LEN = 25 TO 1 BY -1 WHILE (SUBSTR(NAME,LEN,1)) = ' ';
     END;
```

2. Use of a DEFINED Array. The character string can be redefined as an array, and a DO-loop can scan the array from right to left as follows:

```
DCL  NAME        CHAR(25),
     NAMARR(25) CHAR(1)  DEFINED NAME;

     DO LEN = 25 TO 1 BY -1;
          IF NAMARR(LEN) ¬= ' ' THEN LEAVE;
     END;
```

You may also recode the loop using WHILE in the DO statement.

3. Use of VARYING and LENGTH. The VARYING attribute and the LENGTH built-in function can also solve this problem, although they are limited to this particular use.

```
DCL  NAME        CHAR(25) VARYING;
     LEN = LENGTH(NAME);
```

If the character string is not currently in a VARYING string, you could assign it to a VARYING string and then use LENGTH.

4. Use of INDEX. The INDEX built-in function scans from left to right for a character or group of characters. In this case, NAME may validly contain embedded blanks such as JP SMITH, and consequently INDEX should not scan for a single blank. INDEX could scan for a pair of blanks—except that the name may be 24 or 25 characters long. A solution is to concatenate NAME with blanks as in the following. Note that since INDEX locates the position following the end of the name, the expression deducts 1 from the result.

```
     LEN = INDEX(NAME||'  ', '  ') - 1;
```

A clearer solution is to assign NAME to a 27-character string that is certain to contain following blanks:

```
DCL  NAME27     CHAR(27);

     NAME27 = NAME;
     LEN = INDEX(NAME27, '  ') - 1;
```

DEBUGGING TIPS

- Assign the DATE built-in function to a six-character variable rather than to a structure consisting of three two-character elements.
- Use concatenation only to link together Character strings and Bit strings.
- For SUBSTR, ensure that the starting position and the length are within the length of the referenced string.
- INDEX returns a binary value indicating a position where a matching string is located. Test the returned value for zero before assuming that there was a matching string.
- Use REPEAT for large string literals that contain repetitions of the same character(s).

PROBLEMS

19–1. Use the following declaratives to determine the result in the receiving field after each unrelated assignment statement. Assume that FLDA always initially contains blanks.

```
DCL         K              BIN FIXED(15);
DCL         FLDA           CHAR(20)       INIT (' ') ,
            FLDB           CHAR(07)       INIT ('PULSAR') ,
            FLDC           CHAR(11)       INIT ('CONSULTANTS') ;
DCL 1       STRUC,         CHAR(07)       INIT ('QUASAR') ,
            2 STRA         CHAR(05)       INIT ('DATA') ,
            2 STRB         CHAR(10)       INIT ('PROCESSING') ;
            2 STRC
```

- (a) FLDA = FLDB ‖ STRC;
- (b) FLDA = SUBSTR(FLDC, 8);
- (c) FLDA = SUBSTR(STRUC, 8, 9);
- (d) SUBSTR(FLDA, 3, 6) = SUBSTR(STRA,1,3) ‖ SUBSTR(FLDC,9,3);
- (e) FLDA = HIGH(20);
- (f) FLDA = LOW(20);
- (g) K = INDEX(FLDB, SUBSTR(STRA, 4, 3));
- (h) FLDA = REPEAT('-', 19);
- (i) FLDA = STRING(STRUC);
- (j) FLDA = TRANSLATE(FLDB, 'QA', 'PL');
- (k) UNSPEC(FLDA) = UNSPEC(FLDB) & (7)'10111111'B;
- (l) K = VERIFY(FLDB, STRA);

19–2. Use the following declaratives to determine the result in the receiving field after each *unrelated* assignment statement. Assume that BITA is always initialized with zeros.

```
DCL BITA      BIT(8) INIT ('00000000'B),
              ARRAY(2) BIT(8) INIT ('01010101'B, '11001100'B);
```

(a) BITA = ALL (ARRAY);
(b) BITA = ANY (ARRAY);
(c) BITA = BIT ('A');
(d) BITA = BOOL (ARRAY(1), ARRAY(2), '0111'B);

19–3. Refer to the DO loop in Figure 19–1 that scans from right to left looking for a nonblank character in the date record. Change the logic two ways: (a) Give DATEFIELD the VARYING attribute and use LENGTH; (b) Redefine DATEREC as DATEARRAY(80) CHAR(1) and scan the array.

19–4. An on-line program delivers to a PL/I program messages that can be any length up to 50 characters. The program is to print the message centered on a page. (In practice, the message could be displayed centered on a screen.) Use the following declaratives to center MESSAGE in PRINT. Hint: You can use a midpoint of 60 for PRINT and can calculate the length of MESSAGE and a starting position; for example, a 20-character string begins at position 60 − (20/2) = 50.

```
DCL MESSAGE   CHAR(50) VARYING,
    PRINT     CHAR(120);
```

19–5. Revise Problem 19–4 so that MESSAGE does not contain the VARYING attribute.

19–6. A word processing routine is to *right-adjust* character strings for printed columns, as follows:

```
JL BROWN
MN RICHARDS
FR MILLER
```

An input routine delivers the names into a declarative AUTHOR, which is to be stored consecutively in an array ARRNAMES. Complete the program using GET LIST (AUTHOR) to read each name. Code a loop that reads the names and stores the right-adjusted name into ARRNAMES until either end-of-file or the table is full. Code any other necessary declaratives. At end-of-file, code a DO-loop to print each stored name from the array. Hint for right-adjusting: Scan the name from right to left until locating a nonblank character. That position gives the string length, which you can use to determine the starting position.

```
DCL AUTHOR CHAR(25);
DCL ARRNAMES(100) CHAR(25) INIT ( (100)(25) ' ' );
```

19–7. Code a program to scan for frequency of nonblank characters in input data. Each character should have a separate counter. You could code an array of structures such as the following:

```
DCL 1 CHARCTR(n),
        2 CHARAC   CHAR(1)        INIT('0','1', . . . 'A', . . . ,'Z', etc),
        2 CHARCTR DEC FIXED(5)    INIT( (n) 0 );
```

The table should include the characters 0 through 9, A through Z, and any other common expected character. Provide for other characters that are not defined in the table. For each input character located in CHARAC, add 1 to the corresponding element of CHARCTR. For input, you could use a PL/ I program. At end-of-file, print the contents of the array.

CHAPTER 20

PROCEDURE AND BEGIN BLOCKS

OBJECTIVE:
To discuss Procedure and Begin blocks and their uses.

INTRODUCTION

A PL/I program consists of at least one Procedure, the main Procedure, as follows:

program-name: PROCEDURE OPTIONS(MAIN) ;

(PL/I statements)

END [program-name] ;

A Procedure is a unique type of *block;* the other type is a Begin block. By definition, a *block* is a "delimited sequence of statements that constitutes a section of a program." This chapter explains what blocks are, when to use them, and how to organize them in a program.

Among the purposes of blocks are the following:

* To limit the use ("scope") of declaratives within blocks.

- To limit the extent ("scope") of certain ON-conditions, as covered in the next chapter. This is the main purpose of Begin blocks.
- To facilitate coding separately written sections, possibly by different programmers. Such sections may be compiled separately and linked together before execution into one working program. (The system performs this "linking" as a separate step, called *linkage-editing*.) This is the main purpose of procedure blocks.

The use of multiple blocks is largely optional, and many programmers code PL/I programs using only the required main Procedure block. However, a knowledge of blocks can aid in more effective program organization and debugging.

COMPARISON OF BEGIN AND PROCEDURE BLOCKS

The following are examples of a Begin and a Procedure block:

I—USE OF A BEGIN BLOCK	II—USE OF A PROCEDURE BLOCK
[label:] BEGIN ;	label: PROCEDURE ;
.	.
.	.
.	.
END [label] ;	END [label] ;

A Begin block starts with a BEGIN statement with an optional label and terminates with END. The label following END is optional, but if a label exists, it must match the BEGIN label.

A Procedure block starts with a required label preceding a PROCEDURE statement and terminates with END. The label following END is optional, but if a label exists, it must match the PROCEDURE label.

The important distinction between a Begin block and a Procedure block is the following: *Program execution enters a Begin block through normal program flow, but enters a Procedure block only by means of a CALL statement.*

The following examples compare a Begin block with a Procedure block:

```
PROGBEG: PROCEDURE OPTIONS(MAIN) ;

    DCL  (HRS, OT) DEC FIXED(5,2) ;
         HRS = 5.00 ;

  ┌─AB:   BEGIN ;
  │             OT = HRS * 1.5;
  └─      END AB ;

    END PROGBEG ;
```

```
PROGPRO: PROCEDURE OPTIONS(MAIN) ;

    DCL  (HRS, OT) DEC FIXED(5,2) ;
         HRS = 5.00 ;

  ┌─BC:   PROCEDURE ;
  │             OT = HRS * 1.5 ;
  └─      END BC ;

    END PROGPRO ;
```

In PROGBEG, the first statement to execute assigns the value 5.00 to HRS. The program then enters the Begin block AB where it multiplies the contents of HRS by 1.5 and assigns the product HRS × 1.5 to OT. On encountering END AB, the program leaves the Begin block and terminates processing at END PROGBEG.

PROGPRO contains a Procedure block instead of a Begin block. It may help to understand Procedures by remembering that the compiler removes each Procedure to a separate part of the compiled program. In PROGPRO, the first statement to execute is also HRS = 5.00. Then program flow, rather than entering Procedure block BC, bypasses it. The next statement encountered is END PROGPRO, where the program terminates. After PROGBEG, the value in OT is 7.5; whereas after PROGPRO, OT has not been assigned any value. Execution of Procedure BC would require a CALL statement in PROGPRO.

NESTED BLOCKS

Blocks can contain one or more other blocks; each contained block must be contained *completely.* For example, the Procedure PROGBEG completely contains the Begin block AB, and the Procedure PROGPRO completely contains the Procedure block BC. Both main procedures, PROGBEG and PROGPRO, are external procedures because they are not contained in any other block and are separate compilations. The name of an external Procedure is limited to seven characters.

In PROGBEG, the Begin block AB is an *internal (nested) Begin block* and is entirely contained in PROGBEG. In PROGPRO, the Procedure BC is an *internal (nested) Procedure block,* entirely contained in PROGPRO. Internal names have a limit of 31 characters. By definition, Begin blocks are always internal and contained in some other block; Procedure blocks may be either internal or external.

In Figure 20–1, blocks B and C are contained in A and are at the first level of nesting. D, contained in C, is at the second level. The maximum number of levels under full PL/I is 50, and under the Subset is 3. There is, however, seldom reason to exceed three levels of nesting.

ACTIVATION OF BLOCKS

Program flow entering a block for execution causes *activation* of the block. A program activates a Begin block in the normal flow of program execution. A program activates a Procedure block however only by means of the CALL statement. The basic format for the CALL statement is

        CALL name [argument-list] ;

In a CALL statement, "name" can be only the name of a Procedure (the "primary entry-point") or of a designated entry-point within the Procedure ("secondary

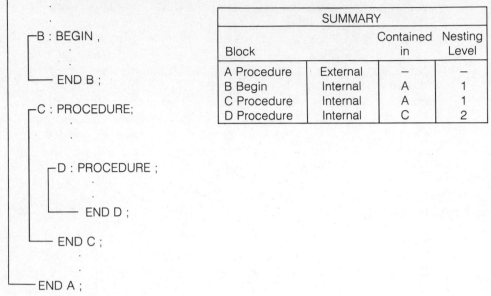

A : PROCEDURE OPTIONS(MAIN) ;

　　　.

　B : BEGIN ,

　　　.

　　　 END B ;

　C : PROCEDURE;

　　　.

　　　.

　　 D : PROCEDURE ;

　　　　.

　　　　 END D ;

　　　 END C ;

　　　.

　 END A ;

SUMMARY			
Block		Contained in	Nesting Level
A Procedure	External	–	–
B Begin	Internal	A	1
C Procedure	Internal	A	1
D Procedure	Internal	C	2

FIGURE 20–1 Nested Blocks.

entry-point"). This chapter covers only the simplest and most common use of CALL. Chapter 22 covers the use of the "argument-list."

In Figure 20–2, both CALL statements activate the Procedure CD. CALL CD causes execution to begin at CD, the primary entry-point, whereas CALL CDENT causes execution to begin at CDENT, an entry-point within Procedure CD. Note that CDENT is designated as ENTRY rather than PROCEDURE.

When the program completes execution of the called Procedure (in this case at END CD), it returns control to the statement immediately following the CALL statement.

Certain rules govern the CALLing of Procedures:

1.　A Procedure can CALL any internal Procedure nested one level within it. But it cannot CALL a Procedure nested two or more levels lower.
2.　A Procedure can CALL an inactive Procedure that is at the first level of nesting within an active Procedure.
3.　Any internal or external Procedure can always CALL an external Procedure (generally one that is separately compiled).
4.　Under full PL/I, a Procedure can CALL any active Procedure. This practice requires use of the RECURSIVE attribute. For example, Procedure A calls Procedure B, which in turn calls Procedure A. This practice can be dangerous and should be used with caution.

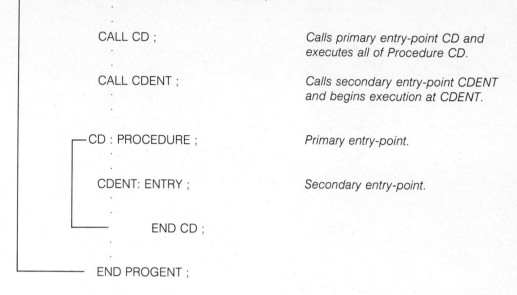

```
┌─ PROGENT: PROCEDURE OPTIONS (MAIN) ;
│                    .
│
│              CALL CD ;                        Calls primary entry-point CD and
│                    .                          executes all of Procedure CD.
│
│              CALL CDENT ;                     Calls secondary entry-point CDENT
│                    .                          and begins execution at CDENT.
│                    .
│                    .
│        ┌─ CD : PROCEDURE ;                    Primary entry-point.
│        │         .
│        │
│        │  CDENT: ENTRY ;                      Secondary entry-point.
│        │         .
│        │         .
│        └──────        END CD ;
│                    .
│                    .
└──────────── END PROGENT ;
```

FIGURE 20–2 Entry-points to an Internal Procedure.

The program in Figure 20–3 is illustrative and is not intended to be realistic. In the example, PROGINV is the main Procedure and contains Procedures DE and DF. Procedure DF contains Procedure DG. At the beginning of execution, the program starts at the main Procedure and activates it. The main Procedure remains active throughout the entire program execution. If a statement in PROGINV says CALL DE, then DE is active only until the end of its execution. This program illustrates rules 1 and 2; rule 3 is covered in Chapter 22.

PROCEDURE	ACTION
D	At the start of Procedure PROGINV are three statements that CALL respectively DE, DF, and DG. CALL DE and CALL DF are valid because the Procedures are nested one level within PROGINV (Rule 1). But CALL DG is invalid because DG is nested within the inactive Procedure DF.
DE	CALL DF is valid because DF is at the first level of nesting within the active Procedure PROGINV (Rule 2). CALL DG is invalid because DG is nested within the inactive Procedure DF.
DF	CALL DE is valid because DE is at the first level of nesting within the active Procedure PROGINV (Rule 2). But CALL DE may violate Rule 4 (Recursion) because DE also CALLs DF. CALL DG is valid because DG is nested one level within DF (Rule 1).
DG	CALL DE is valid (Rule 2).

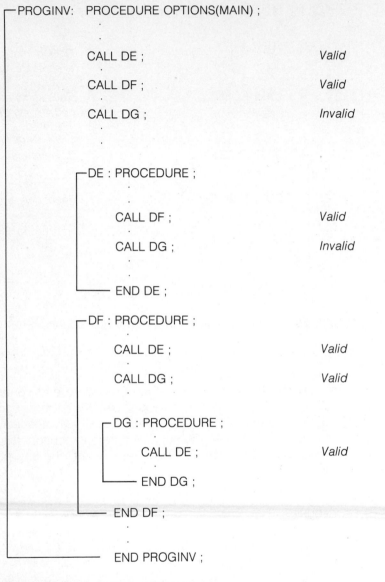

```
PROGINV:   PROCEDURE OPTIONS(MAIN) ;
               .

               CALL DE ;                              Valid
               .
               CALL DF ;                              Valid
               .
               CALL DG ;                              Invalid
               .
               .


       DE : PROCEDURE ;
               .

               CALL DF ;                              Valid
               .
               CALL DG ;                              Invalid
               .
               .
           END DE ;

       DF : PROCEDURE ;
               .
               CALL DE ;                              Valid

               CALL DG ;                              Valid
               .


           DG : PROCEDURE ;

                   CALL DE ;                          Valid
                   .
               END DG ;

           END DF ;
               .

           END PROGINV ;
```

FIGURE 20–3 Invoking Procedures.

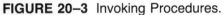

Once a block is called, it remains active as long as (a) the program is executing statements within the block or in any block contained in that block, or (b) within the block a statement has CALLed another Procedure.

TERMINATION OF BLOCKS

Except for a temporary exit using CALL, leaving a nested block causes termination of the block and all blocks contained in it. The following are four ways that execution terminates ("deactivates") a block. (Under certain conditions, other statements such as ON conditions may cause termination.) The normal exit, however, should be at the end of a block.

1. Control reaches the block's END statement:

BEGIN	Control continues with the next statement following the block.
PROCEDURE	Control returns to the statement following the original CALL.

2. Control reaches a RETURN statement. RETURN acts like END in this regard, but may be placed anywhere in the block:

BEGIN	Transfers control out of the block and out of its containing procedure.
PROCEDURE	Returns control to the statement following the CALL in the calling block. If RETURN is in the main Procedure, the program terminates execution (this is a valid normal termination).

3. Execution of a GO TO statement:

BEGIN and PROCEDURE	Execution of a GO TO out of the block to some other *active* block (a practice that violates structured programming conventions).

4. Execution of a STOP statement:

BEGIN and PROCEDURE	An abnormal termination of the program. The entire program itself may terminate execution on encountering END, SIGNAL FINISH or RETURN (normal), or STOP (abnormal).

Example Program Execution

The sample program in Figure 20–4 illustrates many of the preceding points concerned with activation and termination of blocks.

		SEQUENCE OF EXECUTION
1 PROGSTP:	PROCEDURE OPTIONS (MAIN) ;	1 Procedure PROGSTP activated.
	DCL (X, Y) ;	2 and 3 executed.
2	statement	4 Calls B10.
3	statement	11 B10 activated.
4	CALL B10;	12 Executes.
5	statement	13 If X = 0 terminates B10,
		returns to 5.
6	A10: BEGIN ;	14 If X ≠ 0, calls C10.
7	statement	16 C10 activated.
8	statement	17 C10 terminated, return to 15.
9	END A10 ;	15 Executes, then bypasses C10.
		18 B10 terminates, return to 5.
10	statement	5 Executes.
11	B10: PROCEDURE ;	6 A10 activated.
12	statement	7 and 8 execute.
13	IF X = 0 THEN RETURN ;	9 A10 terminated.
14	ELSE CALL C10 ;	10 Executes, then bypasses
15	statement	procedure B10.
		19 Executes.
16	C10: PROCEDURE ;	20 Termination of PROGSTP.
	.	
	.	
	.	
17	END C10 ;	
18	END B10 ;	
19	statement	
20	END PROGSTP ;	

FIGURE 20–4 Activation and Termination of Blocks.

THE SCOPE OF IDENTIFIERS

All statements in a block are *contained* in that block, including statements in nested blocks, from the start of the block to its END. The exception is the name of the block itself and the name of any ENTRY statement. The following explanation is based on Figure 20–4:

BLOCK	STATEMENTS CONTAINED IN THE BLOCK
PROGSTP	All statements in the program except the name PROGSTP.
A10	All of A10 through to its END except the name A10.
B10	All of B10 except the name B10, including all of C10.
C10	All of C10 except the name C10.

Two or more *structures* may contain elements with duplicate names, provided that references to the names are qualified to make them unique. But other than structures, within a block duplicate names are "ambiguous references," which the compiler treats as errors. However, different *blocks* within a program may define an identifier with the same name. The causes of the situation, which may or may not be valid, are:

* Several programmers are engaged in coding separate sections of the same program and may not know the names used by other programmers.
* A program may include precoded common routines that are available to all programs in the system.
* The duplicate names could be coded that way in error.

Figure 20–5 contains an identifier, A, that is explicitly declared in three different blocks. *The scope of an explicitly declared identifier is the block in which it is declared, and all contained blocks except those which have the same name declared.* Note the following in Figure 20–5:

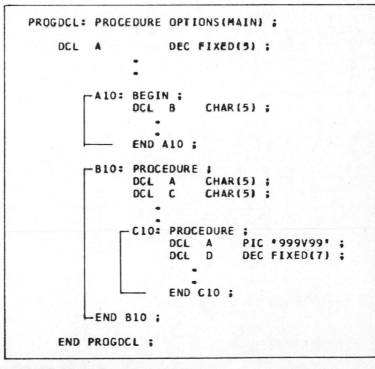

```
PROGDCL: PROCEDURE OPTIONS(MAIN) ;

     DCL   A          DEC FIXED(5) ;
                      .
                      .
    ┌─A10: BEGIN ;
    │     DCL  B     CHAR(5) ;
    │                .
    │                .
    └──── END A10 ;
    ┌─B10: PROCEDURE ;
    │     DCL  A     CHAR(5) ;
    │     DCL  C     CHAR(5) ;
    │                .
    │                .
    │    ┌─C10: PROCEDURE ;
    │    │     DCL  A    PIC '999V99' ;
    │    │     DCL  D    DEC FIXED(7) ;
    │    │              .
    │    │              .
    │    └──── END C10 ;
    └─END B10 ;
     END PROGDCL ;
```

FIGURE 20–5 Scope of Identifiers.

When coding blocks, you may intentionally or accidentally define duplicate names. It is important to understand the effect because the PL/I compiler treats

IDENTIFIER	SCOPE OF IDENTIFIER
A DEC FIXED	Declared in PROGDCL and known as DEC FIXED throughout PROGDCL and its contained block A10. But contained blocks B10 and C10 contain identifiers also named A. A reference to A within B10 and C10 are to these identifiers.
B CHAR	Declared in block A10 and known only in A10. Since the scope of B is block A10, any reference to an identifier B outside of A10 is not recognized as this identifier.
A CHAR	Declared in B10; the scope of this A is B10 but not contained block C10 which defines another A.
C CHAR	Declared in B10; the scope of C is B10 and its contained block C10.
A PIC	Declared in C10 and its scope is C10.
D DEC FIXED	Declared in C10 and its scope is C10.

each duplicate name as unique and valid and you must be sure which identifier the program will access.

It is also common (intentionally or not) to *implicitly declare* identifiers. This situation occurs when you reference a name that has no DCL or is not the name of any statement, procedure, or entry. If an identifier is not explicitly declared, the compiler checks if it is "contextually declared" (that is, can it tell from the context in which it is used?). If not contextually declared, the compiler treats the identifier as an implicit declare. For example, in Figure 20–5 assume that a statement L = 5; occurs in the block B10. The identifier L is nowhere explicitly declared. *The compiler acts as if the implicitly declared identifier L were declared in PROGDCL.* Therefore, PROGDCL and every block contained in it recognize that a reference to L is to the same identifier. The scope of an implicit declare is all contained blocks in the program, except any block where the same name is explicitly declared.

In summary, subject to explicit declaration of the same name in other blocks, a program recognizes an explicitly declared name in the block in which it is declared and in its contained blocks and recognizes implicitly declared names in all blocks.

PROGRAM: EXPENSE ALLOCATIONS

Problem Definition

Certain departments in a company provide services to other departments. For example, costs of maintenance—cleaning, heat, and power—are allocated at monthend to users based on floor area. Also, the computer department produces information for Marketing, Production, and Finance; its expenses are allocated to them at monthend based on computer usage. For example, the Computer department (code 007) has paid computer rentals (expense code 197) of $14,226.27, which a program is to allocate to the following three departments according to their percentages:

DEPARTMENT	PERCENTAGE
216	64.27%
275	33.73
416	2.00
	100.00%

The expenses allocated to departments 216, 275, and 416 will be respectively $9,143.22, $4,798.52, and $284.53.

Program Solution

Groups of input records can be designed to contain the "allocate from" fields (department number, expense code, and expense amount) and their associated "allocate to" fields (department code and percentage). The program in Figure 20–6 provides a solution and consists of the following routines:

- Main Processing routine initializes, performs repetitive looping, and terminates at end-of-file.
- B100_STORE Procedure stores the "allocate from" department, expense code, and expense amount from the first record of a group, and stores in an array the rest of the group; the "allocate to" department numbers and percentages. The routine stores the number of "allocate to" departments in a counter named K.
- C100_CALC Procedure computes the allocated amounts for each department that is stored in the array. The Procedure executes when an entire related group of allocation records is stored and the program reads a new group (with a different department and expense code) and also executes when the program reaches end-of-file in order to process the last stored group. (Note that B100_STORE calls C100_CALC on a change of department/expense code; since the first input record causes this condition, a test if counter K contains zero assumes that the first record has just been read and C100_CALC is not to execute.)

  C100_CALC uses decimal accumulation (explained in Chapter 18) to ensure that the "allocate from" amount is fully allocated, and uses the count K from B100_STORE to determine the number of departments for the group stored in the array.

The main processing routine calls B100_STORE, and both the main processing routine and B100_STORE call C100_CALC. All declaratives except two are defined in the main processing routine and are accordingly known in all

```
 1   PROG20:
         PROCEDURE OPTIONS(MAIN);
 2   DCL     SYSIN FILE INPUT STREAM ENV(MEDIUM(SYSIPT) BUFFERS(2));
 3   DCL     SYSPRINT FILE PRINT ENV(BUFFERS(2) ) ;
 4           DEFAULT RANGE(*) STATIC ;

 5   DCL     ALLOC_RECIN            CHAR (80);
 6   DCL 1   RECORDIN DEFINED ALLOC_RECIN,
             3    DEPT_FROMIN    CHAR (3) ,
             3    EXP_CODEIN     CHAR (3) ,
             3    FROM_AMTIN     PIC  '99999V99',
             3    DEPT_TOIN      CHAR (3) ,
             3    PCT_AMTIN      PIC  '999V99',
             3    FILLER         CHAR (59);

 7   DCL     PRINT                 CHAR (120)INIT (' ') ;
 8   DCL 1   PRDETAIL DEFINED PRINT ,
             3    FILL1          CHAR (34) ,
             3    DEPT_FROMPR    CHAR (3) ,
             3    FILL2          CHAR (3) ,
             3    EXP_CODEPR     CHAR (3) ,
             3    FILL4          CHAR (3) ,
             3    FROM_AMTPR     PIC  'ZZ,ZZ9V.99-' ,
             3    FILL6          CHAR (10) ,
             3    DEPT_TOPR      CHAR (3) ,
             3    FILL7          CHAR (3) ,
             3    PCT_PR         PIC  'ZZ9V.99-' ,
             3    FILL8          CHAR (2) ,
             3    ALLOC_PR       PIC  'ZZZ,ZZ9V.99-';

 9   DCL     PREV_DEPT             CHAR (3),
             PREV_EXP              CHAR (3);
10   DCL 1   WORK_TABLE (10) ,
             3    WORK_DEPT      CHAR (3) ,
             3    WORK_PCT       DEC FIXED (5,2) ;

11   DCL     K                     BIN FIXED (15)  INIT (0);
12   DCL     EOF                   BIT (1)   INIT ('0'B);

13   DCL     EXP_CTL_AMT           DEC FIXED (8,2) INIT (0) ,
             (AMT_ALLOC,
              CALC_PCT)            DEC FIXED (7,2) INIT (0) ,
             SAVE_PCT              DEC FIXED (5,2) INIT (0) ,
             POS_ACCUM             DEC FIXED (7,6) INIT (0) ,
             NEG_ACCUM             DEC FIXED (7,6) INIT (0) ,
             CALC_AMT              DEC FIXED (14,6)INIT (0) ;

     /*       M A I N   P R O C E S S I N G           */

14           OPEN FILE(SYSIN), FILE(SYSPRINT);
15           ON ENDFILE(SYSIN) EOF = '1'B;
16           PUT PAGE EDIT ('ALLOCATION REPORT') (COL(56), A);
17           PUT SKIP EDIT ('ALLOCATE FROM') (COL(40), A)
                           ('ALLOCATE TO')   (COL(75), A);
18           PUT SKIP EDIT ('DEPT   EXP')        (COL(35), A)
                           ('AMOUNT          DEPT') (COL(50), A)
                           ('PCT.   AMT. ALLOC.') (COL(75), A);
19           PUT SKIP;
```

FIGURE 20–6 Expense Allocations

```
20              GET EDIT (ALLOC_RECIN) (A(80));
21              DO WHILE (¬EOF) ;
22                   CALL B100_STORE;
23                   GET EDIT (ALLOC_RECIN) (A(80));
24              END ;
25              CALL C100_CALC;
26              CLOSE FILE(SYSIN), FILE(SYSPRINT);
27              SIGNAL FINISH ;

    /*        S T O R E   A L L O C   A M O U N T   &   P C T S     */

28  B100_STORE:
        PROCEDURE;
29              IF DEPT_FROMIN¬=PREV_DEPT | EXP_CODEIN¬=PREV_EXP THEN
                  DO;
30                   IF K ¬= 0 THEN CALL C100_CALC;
31                   EXP_CODEPR, PREV_EXP   = EXP_CODEIN;
32                   DEPT_FROMPR, PREV_DEPT = DEPT_FROMIN;
33                   FROM_AMTPR, AMT_ALLOC  = FROM_AMTIN;
34                   K = 1;
35                  END ;
36              WORK_DEPT(K) = DEPT_TOIN ;
37              WORK_PCT(K)  = PCT_AMTIN ;
38              K = K + 1;
39      END B100_STORE;

    /*        A L L O C A T I O N   L O G I C            */

40  C100_CALC:
        PROCEDURE;
41      DCL (KOUNT, J)              BINARY FIXED (15);
42          POS_ACCUM =  0.005 ;
43          NEG_ACCUM = -0.005 ;
44          KOUNT = K - 1;
45  C200:   DO J = 1 BY 1  WHILE (KOUNT ¬= 0) ;
46              SAVE_PCT, PCT_PR = WORK_PCT(J);
47              CALC_AMT = AMT_ALLOC * SAVE_PCT * 0.01;
48              IF CALC_AMT ¬= 0 THEN
                  DO;
49                       CALC_AMT  = CALC_AMT + POS_ACCUM ;
50                       CALC_PCT  = CALC_AMT ;
51                       POS_ACCUM = CALC_AMT - CALC_PCT ;
52                  END;
53                ELSE
                  DO;
54                       CALC_AMT  = CALC_AMT + NEG_ACCUM ;
55                       CALC_PCT  = CALC_AMT ;
56                       NEG_ACCUM = CALC_PCT - CALC_AMT ;
57                  END;
58              DEPT_TOPR = WORK_DEPT(J) ;
59              ALLOC_PR = CALC_PCT;
60              PUT SKIP EDIT (PRINT) (COL(1), A(120));
61              PRINT = ' ';
62              EXP_CTL_AMT = EXP_CTL_AMT + CALC_PCT;
63              KOUNT = KOUNT - 1 ;
64          END C200;
65          PUT SKIP(2) EDIT (EXP_CTL_AMT) (COL(82), P'ZZZ,ZZ9V.99-')
                             ('*')             (COL(93), A);
66          PUT SKIP;
67          EXP_CTL_AMT = 0;
68      END C100_CALC;

69      END PROG20;
```

FIGURE 20–6   (cont.)

Input
data:-

Dpt	Exp	Amount	Dpt	Percent
007	196	0692745	146	00555
007	196		193	02000
007	196		218	01865
007	196		964	05580
007	197	1422627	216	06427
007	197		275	03373
007	197		416	00200
009	195	0621430	116	06667
009	195		146	01277
009	195		216	02056

Output:-

```
                          ALLOCATION REPORT
          ALLOCATE FROM                    ALLOCATE TO
     DEPT  EXP      AMOUNT         DEPT     PCT.     AMT. ALLOC.

     007   196    6,927.45         146     5.55         384.47
                                   193     20.00      1,385.49
                                   218     18.65      1,291.97
                                   964     55.80      3,865.52

                                                      6,927.45 *


     007   197   14,226.27         216     64.27      9,143.22
                                   275     33.73      4,798.52
                                   416     2.00         284.53

                                                     14,226.27 *

     009   195    6,214.30         116     66.67      4,143.07
                                   146     12.77        793.57
                                   216     20.56      1,277.66

                                                      6,214.30 *
```

FIGURE 20–6   (cont.)

Procedures. C100_CALC contains two declaratives, KOUNT and J, that are known and used only in that Procedure.

The program could contain other features to validate the input data: The first record of each group should contain the "allocate from" percentage; the "allocate to" percentages for a group should equal 100.0%; and no group should contain more than ten "allocate to" departments (since the array is limited to ten).

PROLOGUES AND EPILOGUES

Blocks are expensive in use of storage and execute-time. For Procedures, the CALL statement generates special code to provide linkage to the Procedure and to facilitate return. Also, preceding both Begin and Procedure blocks is a set of instructions called a *prologue,* and following each block is a set of instructions called an *epilogue.*

A program executes the prologue immediately on activation of a block. The prologue is concerned with such duties as assessing which currently active blocks are known to this block, allocating dynamic storage for automatic variables, and initializing constants where necessary. These features are explained in Chapter 22.

A program executes the epilogue as the last step on termination of a block. The epilogue is concerned with such duties as reinitializing the condition of a program prior to activation of a block and releasing a block's dynamic storage area.

Because extensive use of blocks can make a program inefficient, avoid using them extravagantly. The next two chapters cover the practical uses of blocks. Chapter 21 shows blocks used to delimit the scope of ON-Conditions, and Chapter 22 illustrates how to construct a program with separately compiled external Procedures.

DEBUGGING TIPS

- Be sure to activate a Procedure only by means of a CALL statement, and conversely use CALL only for that purpose.
- As a structured programming convention, enter a Procedure only at its top, and exit through its END.
- Be careful of defining a declarative in a nested block since it will be known only in that block (and in any contained block).
- Ensure that a contained block is completely contained.
- After a compilation, check the diagnostics for any implicitly declared identifier; the diagnostics may explain reasons for execution errors.

PROBLEMS

20–1. Under what circumstances would you use a Begin block?

20–2. How does a program execute a Begin block and a Procedure block?

20–3. How is a block activated?

20–4. What is the purpose of the ENTRY statement?

20–5. Compare the use in a Procedure of the END statement and the RETURN statement. When would you use RETURN?

20–6. How does the RETURN statement differ from the LEAVE statement?

20–7. Assume the following skeleton program and answer the questions.

```
 1       0   PROG: PROCEDURE OPTIONS(MAIN) ;
 2    1  0          ;
 3    1  0      DCL   M ;
 4    1  0              CALL K10 ;
 5    1  0              CALL F10 ;
 6    1  0          ;
 7    1  0   E10: PROCEDURE ;
 8    2  0              CALL F10 ;
 9    2  0              N = 0 ;
10    2  0          ;
11    2  0          ;
12    2  0      END E10 ;

13    1  0   F10: PROCEDURE ;
14    2  0      DCL   P ;
15    2  0              CALL G10 ;
16    2  0          ;
17    2  0   G10: PROCEDURE ;
18    3  0      DCL   Q ;
19    3  0          ;
20    3  0      END G10 ;
21    2  0          ;
22    2  0      END F10 ;

23    1  0   H10: BEGIN ;
24    2  0          ;
25    2  0      END H10 ;

26    1  0   K10: PROCEDURE ;
27    2  0          ;
28    2  0      END K10 ;

29    1  0      DCL   R ;
30    1  0          ;
31    1  0      END PROG;
```

(a) Starting with statement 4, in what sequence are the statements executed? (Exclude declaratives from your answer.)

(b) In which blocks are the following identifiers known? M, N, P, Q, R.

(c) Assume that statement 4 is changed first to CALL G10 and then to CALL H10. Explain if each CALL is legal or not. (Ignore logical processing.)

CHAPTER 21

ON CONDITIONS AND DEBUGGING

OBJECTIVE:

To cover ON conditions for error recovery and debugging.

INTRODUCTION

During compilation, the PL/I compiler checks if a program violates any punctuation and spelling errors and ensures that the program follows the conventions of naming and conversions. The compiler generates routines that check for certain conditions that can occur during execution, such as conversion of invalid data or generating values too large for the defined field size. Then when executing, the program automatically checks for these conditions. Not all such conditions are errors; one valid condition that we have already used is the ON ENDFILE condition.

This chapter describes in detail some of the more important conditions and explains how a programmer may cause a compiled program to check or not check the conditions and how to make use of this knowledge for more effective debugging and program control.

COMMON EXECUTION ERRORS: CONVERSION, SIZE, AND FIXEDOVERFLOW

The following describes three of the most common of many execution-time errors: CONVERSION, SIZE, and FIXEDOVERFLOW.

Conversion

An attempt to assign invalid character or bit string data causes (*raises*) the CONVERSION condition, as shown:

```
DCL   CHARA      CHAR(7)   INIT ('$123.45'),
      BITA       BIT (8),
      PICA       PIC '999V99' ;

1.    BITA = CHAR ;        /* CHARACTER TO BIT */
2.    PICA = CHARA ;       /* CHARACTER TO PIC */
```

Statement (1) is a CONVERSION error because a BIT string can receive only characters 0 and 1. Statement (2) is also a conversion error because arithmetic fields can receive only the digits 0 through 9, decimal point and sign, but not the character dollar sign ($).

Size

An attempt to assign decimal or binary fixed-point data to a field that is defined too short causes loss of leftmost significant digits. Such an operation causes the SIZE error condition (if SIZE is "enabled," as explained later). The following illustrates:

```
DCL   DECA       DEC FIXED (3,1) INIT (99.0),
      DECB       DEC FIXED (3,1) ;

DECB = DECA + 1 ;   /* SUM IS TOO LARGE */
```

The sum of DECA + 1 (99.0 + 1.0) is 100.0, which exceeds the capacity (99.9) of the receiving field, DECB. The operation truncates the leftmost digit 1 from the sum causing a SIZE error. But unless you explicitly request error handling, the program does not signal an error and will produce incorrect results. You can also cause a SIZE error on a Binary Fixed variable, for example, by assigning a value exceeding 32,767 to a Binary Fixed variable with precision (15).

Fixedoverflow (FOFL)

PL/I has its own exclusive work areas for performing fixed-point arithmetic. A programmer has no access to these areas. For each type of data there is a maximum permissible length for the field that is generated in the work area:

FORMAT	MAXIMUM LENGTH OF WORK-AREA (MOST PL/I VERSIONS)
DECIMAL FIXED	15 decimal digits
BINARY FIXED	31 binary digits

A PL/I program generates field lengths in the work area depending on

1. The arithmetic format.
2. The length of the arithmetic fields.
3. The arithmetic operations being performed.

With p the field length in digits and q the number of decimal or binary places, the formulas for the generated field lengths in the PL/I work area are given in Figure 21–1.

OPERATION	FORMULA
Addition or Subtraction	$p = 1 + MAX(p_1 - q_1 , p_2 - q_2) + q$ $q = MAX(q_1 , q_2)$
Multiplication	$p = p_1 + p_2 + 1 \ (MAX\ 15)$ $q = q_1 + q_2$
Division: Decimal	$p = 15$ $q = 15 - ((p_1 - q_1) + q_2)$
Binary	$p = 31$ $q = 31 - ((p_1 - q_1) + q_2)$
(MAX means select the larger of the choices given)	

FIGURE 21–1 Work Area Sizes for Fixed-point Arithmetic.

For exponentiation, you can determine computed precision for either decimal or binary values by

$$p = (p_1 + 1) * n - 1$$
$$q = q_1 * n$$

where n is the exponent. For example, a Decimal Fixed variable with precision (9,3) and an exponent of 2 will generate six positions after the decimal point.

For example, assume the following data:

```
DCL   AMTA      DEC FIXED (7,2),
      AMTB      DEC FIXED (5,2) INIT (123.45),
      AMTC      DEC FIXED (5,3) INIT (12.345);

      AMTA = AMTB + AMTC ;
```

The assignment statement generates code that adds the contents of AMTB and AMTC in the PL/I work area before assigning the sum to AMTA. The precision of AMTB is $(p_1, q_1) = (5,2)$, and the precision for AMTC is $(p_2, q_2) = (5,3)$. To calculate the length of the generated field in the PL/I work area, simply insert these precision values in the formula for addition:

$$q = MAX (q_1, q_2) = MAX (2,3) = 3$$

$$p = 1 + MAX (p_1 - q_1 , p_2 - q_2) + q$$

$$= 1 + MAX (5\text{-}2 , 5\text{-}3) + 3 = 1 + 3 + 3 = 7$$

The precision of the generated PL/I workarea field is therefore $(p, q) = (7, 3)$, well within the maximum of 15 significant decimal digits. The result (123.45 + 12.345 = 0135.795) when assigned to AMTA becomes 00135.79. (Note that truncation of a fractional digit on the right is not a SIZE error.) A FIXEDOVERFLOW error occurs because of truncation of a leftmost significant digit in the work area, whereas a SIZE error occurs when a statement that assigns a value to a field that is defined too short causes truncation of a leftmost significant digit.

The next example involving more extensive arithmetic shows how a generated value can exceed the work area maximum and cause FIXEDOVERFLOW:

```
DCL   AMTD      DEC FIXED (9,1) INIT (12345678.9),
      AMTE      DEC FIXED (7,3) INIT (1234.567),
      AMTF      DEC FIXED (7,1) INIT (100000.0),
      AMTG      DEC FIXED(15,1) ;

      AMTG = (AMTD + AMTE) * AMTF ;
```

1. Perform the sum in parentheses (AMTD + AMTE):

    $$(p_1, q_1) + (p_2, q_2) = (9,1) + (7,3)$$

    $$q = MAX(1,3) = 3$$

    $$p = 1 + MAX(8,4) + 3 = 1 + 8 + 3 = 12$$

    $(p, q) = (12, 3)$. The sum = 012346913.467 .

2. Multiply this sum by AMTF (Sum * AMTF) :

    $$(p_1, q_1) * (p_2, q_2) = (12, 3) * (7, 1)$$

    $$p = p_1 + p_2 + 1 = 12 + 7 + 1 = 20, \text{ reduced to 15}$$

    $$q = q_1 + q_2 = 3 + 1 = 4$$

The final (p, q) is (15, 4) but the result exceeds the work area maximum:

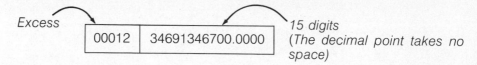

Excess

00012	34691346700.0000

15 digits
(*The decimal point takes no space*)

Because the result exceeds 15 significant digits, the program raises the FIXEDOVERFLOW condition and does not assign the result to AMTG. To avoid this error, you could use the built-in arithmetic functions ADD, MULTIPLY, and DIVIDE, or you could simply code the expression in two statements. The first statement can perform the arithmetic and can reduce the generated precision, as follows:

```
DCL  AMTH       DEC FIXED (9,0) ;

AMTH = AMTD + AMTE ;    /* ADD & ASSIGN TO TEMP FIELD */
AMTG = AMTH + AMTF ;    /* MPY WITH REDUCED PRECISION */
```

ON CONDITIONS

The CONVERSION, SIZE, and FIXEDOVERFLOW conditions are only three of many conditions. The system acts upon a condition if it is *enabled* and ignores conditions that are *disabled*. For example, the CONVERSION and FIXEDOVER-FLOW conditions are normally enabled for a system. Consequently, if the condition occurs, the system executes an error message routine and terminates the program. You have, however, two other alternatives:

1.   You can provide special coding so that the program attempts to correct the error (covered in ON STATEMENT later); or
2.   You can disable the conditions so that the system does not check for them (covered under CONDITION PREFIX later).

Since the SIZE condition is normally disabled, a compiled program does not check for it; if a SIZE error occurs, there is an invalid result with no warning. You can, however, enable the SIZE condition so that the system will check for it. A later section, "The Condition Prefix," covers enabling and disabling.

Normally enabled means that the compiler generates code to check for the condition, but you may disable the condition. *Normally disabled* means that the compiler generates code to check for the condition only if you enable the condition. *Always enabled* means that the compiler always checks for the condition and that you cannot disable it.

The six classes and types of ON conditions are as follows.

1.   COMPUTATIONAL CONDITIONS. These conditions are concerned with arithmetic operations.

   •   CONVERSION or CONV. Normally enabled. As explained earlier, this is an invalid conversion of String data.
   •   FIXEDOVERFLOW or FOFL. Normally enabled. As explained earlier, an expression generates a field whose length exceeds the maximum (decimal 15, binary 31), and there is loss of a leftmost significant digit.
   •   SIZE. Normally disabled. As explained earlier, the receiving (target) field is too short to receive leftmost significant decimal or binary digits.
   •   OVERFLOW or OFL. Normally enabled. The magnitude of a floating-point number has exceeded the permitted maximum (about 10^{75}).
   •   UNDERFLOW or UFL. Normally enabled. The magnitude of a floating-point number is lower than the permitted minimum (about 10^{-78}).

2.   INPUT/OUTPUT CONDITIONS. These conditions are concerned with the transmission of data between main storage and an external device.

   •   ENDFILE. Always enabled. A valid condition, raised when the systemencounters the end of the input data file. Coded as ON ENDFILE (file-name). . . ; .
   •   ENDPAGE. Always enabled. A valid condition under Stream I/O, raised when a PUT statement attempts to write on the printer device past the limit for a page. Coded as ON ENDPAGE (print-device-name). . . ; .
   •   KEY. Always enabled. A disk device error is raised during an operation on "keyed" records for a file organized as Indexed Sequential, Keyed-sequence VSAM, or Direct. Coded as ON KEY (filename). . . ; .
   •   NAME. Always enabled. Under Data-directed Stream I/O, a GET encounters a record with an unrecognizable data item. Coded as ON NAME (filename). . . ; .
   •   RECORD. Always enabled. An actual record does not agree in length with the RECSIZE or BLKSIZE entry.
   •   TRANSMIT. Always enabled. Caused by a permanent transmission error during any I/O operation. Coded as ON TRANSMIT (filename) . . . ; .
   •   UNDEFINEDFILE or UNDF. Always enabled. An unsuccessful attempt to OPEN a file. This condition is most often raised by a tape or disk file where the job control entries such as DLBL and EXTENT are incorrect. Coded as ON UNDF (filename). . . ; .

3.   PROGRAM CHECKOUT CONDITIONS. These conditions are designed to aid during program debugging.

   •   CHECK. Normally disabled. Used to provide a "trace" of execution, for programs with difficult bugs. This condition is explained in more detail in a later section.

- STRINGRANGE or STRG. Normally disabled. Caused by violation of the rules of the built-in function SUBSTR regarding argument lengths. The system prints a warning and forces a revised operation.
- STRINGSIZE or STRZ. Normally disabled. The receiving (target) string field is shorter than the assigned string. The operations for String data assign characters or bits from left to right, as many as possible. The system prints a warning message and resumes processing. (Not available in PL/C.)
- SUBSCRIPTRANGE or SUBRG. Normally disabled. (Enabled in PL/C.) An evaluated subscript is outside its defined bounds. The result is unpredictable. (Not available in the Subset.) For example:

```
DCL TABLE (10) . . . ;     /* DEFINE ARRAY WITH 10 ELEMENTS */
       TABLE (11) = 0 ;     /* SUBSCRIPT (11) OUTSIDE BOUNDS */
```

4. SYSTEM ACTION CONDITIONS. The ERROR and FINISH conditions provide facilities to extend the standard system action that is taken after raising of a condition or completion of the program.

- ERROR. Always enabled. Certain ON conditions print a message and raise this condition. ERROR also occurs if there is an error and the program provides for no ON condition. ERROR raises the FINISH condition.
- FINISH. Always enabled. Raised by RETURN, END, or SIGNAL FINISH in the main Procedure (normal termination), by STOP (abnormal termination), and by ERROR.

5. PROGRAMMER-NAMED CONDITION.

- CONDITION or COND. Always enabled. Covered in detail later.

6. STORAGE CONTROL CONDITION.

- AREA. Always enabled.

THE CONDITION PREFIX

To enable or disable a condition simply requires use of a *condition prefix,* in which the condition, enclosed in parentheses, precedes a block or a statement. The examples in Figure 21–2 use a condition prefix to enable the SIZE condition for three cases: an entire program, one block only, and a single statement within a program. The SIZE condition is enabled as (SIZE): with a following colon.

ENTIRE PROGRAM	ONE BLOCK ONLY	ONE STATEMENT ONLY

(SIZE):
PROGA: PROC OPTIONS
    (MAIN) ;
 	
.
.
.
.
 	
END PROGA ;
	PROGB: PROC OPTIONS
	    (MAIN) ;
	
	.
	(SIZE):
	    BEGIN ;
	.
	    END ;
	.
	END PROGB ;
		PROGC: PROC OPTIONS
		    (MAIN) ;
		
		.
		(SIZE)
		    WAGE = HRS*RATE ;
		.
		.
		.
		END PROGC ;

The program checks every arithmetic statement in the program, including nested blocks, for SIZE errors.	The program checks only in the BEGIN blocks for SIZE errors.	The program checks only the one arithmetic statement for a SIZE error.

FIGURE 21–2 Enabling the SIZE Condition.

Note: Under normal circumstances, it is more efficient to enable conditions such as SIZE and SUBSCRIPTRANGE only during the debugging stage. The compiler generates additional code to perform this checking, resulting in more use of storage and execute-time. Once a program is fully working, you should take out all such enabled conditions.

ENTIRE PROGRAM	ONE BLOCK ONLY	ONE STATEMENT ONLY

(NOFOFL):
PROGA: PROC OPTIONS
    (MAIN) ;
 	
.
.
.
.
 	
END PROGA ;
	PROGB: PROC OPTIONS
	    (MAIN) ;
	.
	(NOFOFL):
	SAM: PROC ;
	.
	    END SAM ;
	.
	END PROGB ;
		PROGC: PROC OPTIONS
		    (MAIN) ;
		.
		(NOFOFL):
		    WAGE = HRS*RATE ;
		.
		.
		END PROGC ;

The compiler generates no code to check for FOFL throughout the entire program, including any nested blocks.	The compiler generates no code to check for FOFL in the Procedure SAM only. FOFL is normally enabled for all other statements.	There is no check for FOFL for the one arithmetic statement. FOFL is normally enabled for all other statements.

FIGURE 21–3 Disabling the FIXEDOVERFLOW Condition.

The *disabling* of a condition simply requires the use of a condition prefix preceded by NO, as (NOSIZE): or (NOCONVERSION):. The three examples in Figure 21–3 disable FIXEDOVERFLOW with the condition prefix (NOFOFL):.

Enabling or disabling more than one condition at a time simply requires multiple condition prefixes, coded as

(SIZE): (SUBRG): (STRG): or (SIZE, SUBRG, STRG):

Such conditions may be enabled or disabled at any point throughout the program. However, you should be cautious about disabling conditions because serious errors may occur without warning.

THE ON STATEMENT

For a disabled ON condition, the compiler generates no code to check for the condition. For an enabled condition, however, the compiler generates code that always checks for the condition. If the enabled condition is found to exist, then in the absence of an ON-unit, the system takes standard action. The *ON-unit* results from a programmer ON statement that tells the compiler in effect: Do not take the standard (default) action; instead, execute the statements that follow. For example, the statement

ON ENDFILE (SYSIN) EOF = '1'B ;

is an ON statement in which the ON-unit "EOF = '1'B" tells the compiler what action to take when the condition is raised by the system recognizing the end-of-data.

There may be an ON statement for any enabled ON condition. Figure 21–4 shows a program with two contained BEGIN blocks. Both blocks enable the SIZE condition and provide ON-units that execute error message routines. The reason for the separate blocks is that the program can better inform you where a SIZE error occurs.

The general form of the ON statement is

ON condition-name [SNAP] [On-unit or SYSTEM];

The condition-name is the name of any enabled condition, such as SIZE.

• SNAP is an optional entry that causes a program to list all the currently active procedures (not available in the Subset). Depending on the PL/I implementation and other available features such as GOSTMT and FLOW, SNAP may be used to provide the statement number that caused an interrupt and the name of the calling procedure (if there was one) and the number of the CALL statement.

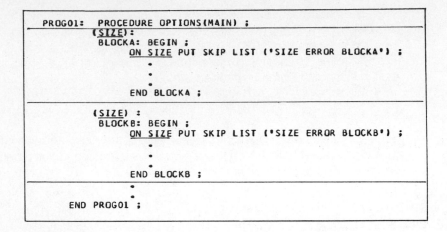

FIGURE 21–4 Enabled SIZE Condition in Blocks.

- For On-unit, the first statement may be GO TO. . ., BEGIN. . ., CALL. . ., and SIGNAL. . . (But specifically not DO, IF, ON, PROCEDURE, RETURN, END, DECLARE, and FORMAT.)
- SYSTEM is an alternative to the use of ON-unit and designates that the system is to take standard default action, such as action to override a previous ON statement.

The raising of an ON condition causes it to remain in effect within its block and in all its activated blocks until

1.   There is another ON statement raised for the same condition, or
2.   The program executes a REVERT statement. REVERT condition-name re-establishes the ON condition to its condition at the time the block was activated.

For all computational conditions except CONVERSION, a program, after executing the ON unit, normally returns to the instruction immediately following the interrupt. For CONVERSION, the program returns to the interrupted statement in order to reattempt the conversion. The coding in an ON-unit may correct the invalid condition (by use of ONCHAR and ONSOURCE, covered in a later section). If the coding does not amend the CONVERSION error, the program raises the ERROR condition to prevent a permanent program loop—conversion error to ON-unit to conversion error and so on.

Some example ON statements follow:

```
ON CONVERSION CALL . . . ;
ON ERROR BEGIN . . . ;
ON ERROR SNAP SYSTEM . . . ;
ON SIZE ;          /* NULL ON-UNIT */
```

The last example with a "null ON-unit" means that the system checks for the error, but takes no action. The error is not signaled, and the program continues with the next statement. A null ON-unit is not the same as disabled. If a condition is disabled, the program does not even check for it.

Absence of ON-Units

In the absence of a programmer ON condition, the system has standard action for enabled conditions, as follows:

- CONVERSION, FIXEDOVERFLOW, KEY, OVERFLOW, RECORD, SIZE, SUB-SCRIPTRANGE, TRANSMIT, UNDEFINEDFILE, ZERODIVIDE—The system prints a message specifying the condition and raises the ERROR condition. A program could therefore provide an ON-unit for the ERROR condition, for error recovery from any or all the preceding: ON ERROR . . . ; .
- ERROR—The system prints a message and raises the FINISH condition, which terminates the program.
- ENDPAGE—The system automatically begins a new page.
- NAME—The system ignores the invalid data, prints a warning message, and resumes the GET statement.
- STRINGSIZE, STRINGRANGE, and UNDERFLOW—The system prints a message and resumes processing the statement.

USE OF ON CONDITIONS IN DEBUGGING

During the debugging stage, it is often useful to enable the SIZE condition and whichever other conditions are appropriate, such as SUBSCRIPTRANGE if there is much subscripting. It is the programmer's discretion to elect the use of ON-units. Test data should include extremely large and small values. It is possible to avoid or at least to minimize certain conditions:

- SIZE—Define field lengths for the largest possible values that could ever occur in the program.
- FIXEDOVERFLOW—Consider the maximum generated field lengths with the formulas given earlier in this chapter. If necessary, use several statements for long fixed-point arithmetic calculations. Also, the built in functions ADD, MULTIPLY, and DIVIDE are useful in controlling the precision of arithmetic data.
- SUBSCRIPTRANGE—In a program that calculates subscript values, it may be wise to code statements that test for their validity. The following tests if a subscript value is within the bounds (1 to 20) of the array:

```
DCL   AMT        DEC FIXED(5) ;
DCL   TABLE(20) DEC FIXED(5) ;

GET LIST (K, AMT) ;
IF K < 1 | K > 20 THEN
     PUT SKIP LIST ('CODE ERROR') ;
ELSE TABLE(K) = AMT ;
```

•   ZERODIVIDE—If the contents of input data are unpredictable, test for a zero divisor prior to dividing. This practice generates less code than the ZERODIVIDE condition and provides better control:

```
IF QUANTITY = 0
     THEN PUT SKIP LIST ('ZERO DIVISOR') ;
     ELSE COST = VALUE / QUANTITY ;
```

ON ERROR System

In the following partial code, an error may occur during execution of the BEGIN block:

```
ON ERROR SNAP
     BEGIN ;
          . . .
     END ;
```

If an error occurs, the system will cause automatic reexecution of the BEGIN block, which again causes the error, and so forth. To prevent the program from looping indefinitely, code an ON ERROR SYSTEM statement in the BEGIN block, as follows:

```
ON ERROR SNAP
     BEGIN ;
          ON ERROR SYSTEM ;
          . . .
     END ;
```

The SIGNAL Statement

It is possible to force (or "simulate") an enabled condition with the use of the SIGNAL statement:

```
SIGNAL condition-name ;
```

For example, the following causes the ENDPAGE interrupt to occur if the number of lines printed exceeds 45. The program will execute the procedure P100HDG (not shown).

```
DCL  SYSPRINT FILE PRINT ;
     ON ENDPAGE(SYSPRINT) CALL P100HDG ;
                •
                •
                •
     IF LINECOUNT > 45 THEN SIGNAL ENDPAGE ;
```

There are two other SIGNAL options: SIGNAL FINISH causes normal termination of program execution, and SIGNAL CHECK is covered in the next section.

OTHER CONDITIONS: CHECK, CONDITION, ONCODE, AND CONVERSION

Other useful PL/I debugging aids include the CHECK condition, the CONDITION condition, the ONCODE built-in function, and the CONVERSION condition.

The CHECK Condition

The CHECK condition is one of the most useful PL/I debugging aids (not in the Subset). Sometimes a program has a serious bug and because of sudden termination with little or no output leaves no clue as to the cause. The CHECK condition provides a trace of the sequence of blocks and statements as they are executed, as shown in Figure 21–5.

In the block named FIRST, CHECK specifies that during execution of this block, the system is to print the contents of HOURS and RATE (the "designated variables") whenever their values change.

```
PROGCHK: PROCEDURE OPTIONS(MAIN) ;
    DCL (HOURS,
         RATE,
         WAGE)      DEC FIXED(7,2) ;
                •
    (CHECK (HOURS, RATE)) :            (Designated variables)
    FIRST: BEGIN ;
                •
                •
         END FIRST ;
    (CHECK) :                          (No designated variables)
    SECOND: BEGIN ;
                •
                •
         END SECOND ;
                •
                •
                •
    END PROGCHK ;
```

FIGURE 21–5 Enabling the CHECK Condition.

In the block named SECOND, the CHECK condition prefix has no designated variables. It says in effect: During execution of this block, print the contents of any changed variable or the name of any label to which the program passes control. Note: with CHECK, unlike other conditions and built-in functions, omission of designated variables causes the condition for *all* variables.

After the program prints the contents of the variable or label name, it resumes normal processing. CHECK may be inserted before any statement or block. It is also possible to code SIGNAL CHECK at any point to force the program to print the contents of the required variables. For example, SIGNAL CHECK coded in the block FIRST would cause the contents of HOURS and RATE to print at that point, whether they had changed or not. SIGNAL CHECK coded in SECOND would print the contents of all variables that are known in that block (in this case HOURS, RATE, and WAGE).

The "CONDITION" Condition

CONDITION is always enabled and is occasionally useful in program debugging. Assume the Procedure in Figure 21–6.

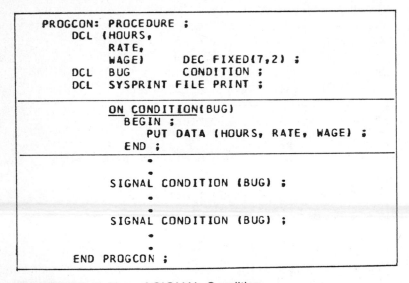

FIGURE 21–6 Use of SIGNAL Condition.

Statement-2 explicitly declares a name BUG with the CONDITION attribute. Statement-4 provides the CONDITION ON-unit. In this program, it is necessary to print the contents of X, Y, and Z at specified points. The coding as shown in Statements-7 and 8 is SIGNAL CONDITION (name); . In this example, the condition is named BUG. When program execution reaches the SIGNAL statement, CONDITION is raised, and the CONDITION ON-unit beginning at Statement-4 is executed.

Condition Codes and the ONCODE Built-in Function

There are many errors that can cause conditions such as ERROR, KEY, or RE-CORD. For example, over 50 different errors can raise the ERROR condition. One problem when the condition is raised is to determine exactly which error raised it. PL/I provides a solution because each condition has one or more condition code (ONCODE) numbers that the system automatically displays if

1.   The condition is enabled, and
2.   There is no programmer's ON-unit to direct some other action.

The program can contain ON-unit coding that tests and prints a condition code. The code, a fixed binary value, is available through the ONCODE built-in function. (The complete list of ONCODE numbers is available in the PL/I manual for each version of the compiler.) For example, among the KEY condition codes for the OS and DOS Optimizer are the following:

51	A key specified cannot be found. (For example, the system is unable to find a specific disk record that a program has asked for.)
52	An attempt has been made to add a duplicate key (one with the same control number) to a disk file.
56	An attempt has been made to access a record with a key that is outside the limits of a file as defined.
57	There is no space available on disk to add a keyed record.

Assume the following program reads input from disk:

```
DCL   DISKFL FILE RECORD INPUT KEYED ENV(VSAM) ;
DCL   DISKIN CHAR(200) ;
DCL   ONCODE BUILTIN ;

ON KEY (DISKFL)
  BEGIN ;
    IF ONCODE = 51 THEN
      PUT LIST (ONCODE, 'INVALID KEY') ;
    ELSE ... ;
  END ;

READ FILE (DISKFL) INTO (DISKIN) KEY(CUSTNO) ;
```

The statement ON KEY provides an ON-unit for the KEY condition, which is always enabled. If the condition is raised during the READ operation, the program branches to the ON-unit to test if the specific ONCODE condition is 51. If so, the program processes a routine that prints the ONCODE number and any suitable warning message. The Begin block can also test for any of the other KEY codes as required.

The CONVERSION Condition

Basically, CONVERSION is raised by an attempt to assign invalid Character or Bit string data. either through an assignment statement or through an I/O operation. Since PL/I converts string data one character at a time from left to right, the first (leftmost) invalid character encountered raises the condition. PL/I provides the facility to determine

1.   The contents of an offending field, with the ONSOURCE built-in function, and

2.   An offending character (or bit) itself, with the ONCHAR built-in function.

The following example shows how to assign the contents of both built-in functions to your own variables:

```
DCL  SAVESOUR  CHAR(20) VARYING,
     SAVECHAR  CHAR(01) ;
DCL  (ONSOURCE, ONCHAR)  BUILTIN ;

     ON CONVERSION SNAP
       BEGIN ;
           SAVESOUR = ONSOURCE ; /* OFFENDING FIELD */
           SAVECHAR = ONCHAR   ; /* OFFENDING CHARACTER */
           .
           .
           .
       END ;
```

The routine gives SAVESOUR the attribute VARYING because (it is assumed) the length of the offending string is unknown, but will never exceed 20 characters. Both ONCHAR and ONSOURCE are pseudovariables because it is permissible to use them in the receiving field of a statement to correct an offending character. The next example illustrates printing of both ONSOURCE and ONCHAR and correcting an invalid character arbitrarily to '0':

```
ON CONVERSION SNAP               /* ON-UNIT FOR CONVERSION */
  BEGIN ;
      SAVESOUR = ONSOURCE ;      /* ASSIGN OFFENDING FIELD */
      SAVECHAR = ONCHAR   ;      /* ASSIGN OFFENDING CHAR  */
      PUT DATA (SAVESOUR, SAVECHAR) ; /* ERROR MESSAGE      */
      ONCHAR = '0' ;             /* RESET INVALID CHAR      */
  END ;
```

After printing and correcting the invalid character, the program automatically returns to reattempt the conversion statement. Possibly there is more than one invalid character in the field, but the program will now correct each one, from left to right.

Other Condition Built-in Functions

The following built-in functions are often useful in program debugging:

ONLOC	For any ON condition, ONLOC gives the name of the entry-point of the Procedure in which the condition was raised. ONLOC can be used in any ON-unit and is useful in helping to isolate an error.
ONFILE	ONFILE gives the name of the file that caused an I/O or a conversion error. ONFILE is especially useful where a program has several input files, and any one of them could have invalid data.
ONKEY	ONKEY is useful for VSAM, ISAM, and Regional files where a key for a record raises an I/O error condition. The purpose of ONKEY is to extract the contents of an offending key (see the ON ERROR statement in the following example).

Figure 21–7 gives a generalized error recovery routine that prints the cause and location of errors raised by conditions and continues processing. There are ON-units for FIXEDOVERFLOW, SIZE, STRINGRANGE, SUBSCRIPTRANGE, and CONVERSION. STRINGSIZE is not enabled because the condition assigns as many characters as possible to a string field that is too short; whether the effect is incorrect depends on the application. ON ERROR captures all other conditions for which there is no ON-unit.

```
(SIZE)=(STRG)=(SUBRG):
PROGREC= PROCEDURE OPTIONS(MAIN) ;
    DCL (ONCODE, ONLOC, ONSOURCE,
         ONFILE, ONCHAR, ONKEY) BUILTIN ;

        ON FOFL  PUT DATA (ONCODE, ONLOC) ;
        ON SIZE  PUT DATA (ONCODE, ONLOC) ;
        ON STRG  PUT DATA (ONCODE, ONLOC) ;
        ON SUBRG PUT DATA (ONCODE, ONLOC) ;
        ON CONVERSION
          BEGIN ;
            PUT DATA (ONCODE, ONCHAR, ONSOURCE, ONFILE) ;
            ONCHAR = '0' ;
          END ;
        ON ERROR SNAP
          BEGIN ;
            PUT DATA (ONCODE, ONLOC, ONFILE, ONKEY) ;
            /* .
               .         ERROR RECOVERY ROUTINE
               .         TO RESUME PROCESSING   */
          END ;
             .
             .
    END PROGREC ;
```

FIGURE 21–7 Generalized Error Recovery Routine.

There are many possible variations for each condition in the routine. Note that the PUT DATA statements show ONCODE and ONLOC coded within the data-list. Some PL/I versions do not permit them to appear in a data-list; if so, you must assign these built-in functions to ordinary variables (such as SAVESOUR and SAVECHAR used in the previous examples) and then PUT the variables.

DEBUGGING TIPS

- A knowledge of ON conditions is essential for efficient program debugging. For each enabled condition, the PL/I compiler generates additional code to check for the condition. As a rule, normally disabled conditions such as SIZE and SUBSCRIPTRANGE should be enabled only when necessary, and only during the debugging stage. Once a program is thoroughly tested (if such a state exists!), then the enabling condition prefixes should be taken out. A program in production will run more efficiently (in terms of execution-time and use of storage) without the code generated by enabled conditions. This does not mean, however, that you should therefore disable conditions that are normally enabled.
- Declare built-in functions such as ONCODE, ONLOC, and ONKEY as BUILTIN. In an undeclared reference to these functions, such as PUT DATA (ONKEY), some compilers default to a DECIMAL FLOAT variable.
- The PL/I PROCESS statement and the *PL/C statement provide other useful debugging aids—see Chapter 29 for details.

PROBLEMS

21–1. Certain conditions such as SIZE are normally disabled. In your own words, explain what this statement means. Use an example.

21–2. Show for an entire Procedure how the STRINGSIZE condition may be enabled, and how the FIXEDOVERFLOW condition may be disabled.

21–3. Explain by an example how the STRINGSIZE condition may be raised.

21–4. Assume that all conditions such as STRZ, SIZE, FOFL, STRG, and SUBRG are enabled. Explain clearly the effect of the following:

```
(a)  DCL   NAME                   CHAR(15)        INIT  (DATA  PROCESSORS')

     DCL   NAMEOUT                CHAR(12);
           NAMEOUT = NAME;
(b)  DCL   K                      BIN FIXED(15),
           N                      BIN FIXED(15)    INIT(15),
           TABLE(12)              DEC FIXED(05),
           COUNT                  DEC FIXED(03)    INIT (1);
           TABLE = 0;
           DO K = 1 TO N;
              TABLE(K) = TABLE(K) + COUNT;
           END;
```

(c) DCL VALUE   DEC FIXED(5,2),
          PRICE   DEC FIXED(4,2)   INIT (25.00),
          QUANTITY   DEC FIXED(3)   INIT (100);
          VALUE = PRICE * QUANTITY;
(d) DCL TIME   DEC FIXED(9,2)   INIT (5000000.00),
          RATE   DEC FIXED(7,2)   INIT (50000.00),
          DISTANCE   DEC FIXED(15);
          DISTANCE = TIME * RATE;

21–5. Show two ways to revise the executable code to prevent the error in Problem 21–4 (d). Define any other necessary declaratives.

CHAPTER 22

EXTERNAL PROCEDURES

OBJECTIVE:

To explain the requirements for coding External Procedures and for linking separately compiled programs.

INTRODUCTION

Many situations require the organization of a program into separate Procedures that often are separately compiled. Among the causes of such organization are the following:

- A program has to incorporate specially prewritten routines that are available to all programs in the system.
- Several programmers may independently code large sections of the same program.
- A program may exceed the capacity of main storage (although computer systems with Virtual Storage are less likely to encounter insufficient main storage area). If you cannot reduce the program to several small programs, then you may have to reduce the program to separate *phases*, one to *overlay* another at execution-time.

EXTERNAL PROCEDURES

Consider the following three program outlines in Figure 22–1. Example I illustrates a conventional program outline with a Main Procedure, PROCA1, containing one internal Procedure, PROCB1. Any data declared in PROCA1 is automatically known in PROCB1 (but not vice versa). The handling of declaratives causes little difficulty in such a program.

Example II introduces a new situation because the program consists of a Main Procedure, PROCA2, and a second Procedure, PROCB2, that is not contained in the main Procedure. Both PROCA2 and PROCB2 are *external Procedures*. But note that PROCA2 has the OPTIONS(MAIN) attribute, but not PROCB2, because a program may have only one Main Procedure. There is no great difficulty coding and compiling such a program with external Procedures. But there is one problem: data declared in PROCA2 is not known (without additional declarations) in PROCB2, and vice versa. Indeed, a program consisting of separate external Procedures would make sense only if both were processing some common data.

Example III shows a third type of program consisting of two external Procedures that are *separately compiled*. Once again the problem is that data defined in one external Procedure is not known automatically in the other one. Additional coding is required to make data names common to both Procedures and also to load the separately compiled Procedures into main storage for execution. Many PL/I programs are organized like one of these three, with variations of external and internal Procedures. There has to be some way to make data known commonly to external Procedures. Indeed, PL/I has such capability, as the next sections describe.

Previous examples have already covered the situation in Example I in which an external Procedure contains an internal Procedure. The next section, "External Procedures," covers Example II, and the section "Phases and Overlays" covers Example III.

An external Procedure is one that is not contained in any other Procedure. Its name is an external identifier and is limited to seven characters (six under PL/C and the Subset) and may not contain the break character (_). A program may consist of any number of external Procedures, each containing internal Procedures. Within a program, only the first external Procedure has the OPTIONS(MAIN) attribute. One of the chief purposes of external Procedures is that they may be separately compiled and cataloged so that they are available for inclusion in other programs.

Since data defined in one external Procedure is not automatically known in another, PL/I has provided two ways of making the address of a data item known in more than one external procedure:

Example I One External Procedure, one Internal Procedure	Example II Two External Procedures	Example III Two separately link-edited External Procedures
* PROCESS ; PROCA1: PROCEDURE OPTIONS (MAIN) ; PROCB1: PROCEDURE . . END PROCB1; . . END PROCA1;	* PROCESS ; PROCA2: PROCEDURE OPTIONS (MAIN) ; DCL PROCB2 EXTERNAL ENTRY; . . END PROCA2; * PROCESS; PROCB2: PROCEDURE; . . END PROCB2;	* PROCESS NAME('name1') ; PROCA3: PROCEDURE OPTIONS (MAIN) ; DCL PROCB3 EXTERNAL ENTRY; . . END PROCA3; * PROCESS NAME('name2'); PROCB3: PROCEDURE; . . END PROCB3;

FIGURE 22-1 Internal and External Procedures.

1. Through the use of the EXTERNAL attribute, and
2. By means of *arguments* and *parameters.*

THE EXTERNAL ATTRIBUTE

Other than file names, which are usually EXTERNAL, the compiler automatically gives the INTERNAL attribute to all names that do not have the EXTERNAL attribute. INTERNAL means that the name is known only in the declaring block and any blocks that it may contain. The way to make a declarative known outside of its own Procedure is to give it the EXTERNAL attribute and declare it identically in each required external Procedure. In this way, the EXTERNAL attribute makes a declarative known outside of its own Procedure.

Figure 22–2 depicts a Main Procedure PROCEXA that CALLs an external Procedure PROCEXB. Under the Optimizing compiler, PROCEXA must declare PROCEXB as ENTRY so that the Linkage Editor will establish the correct storage address for CALL PROCEXB; during execution.

Both Procedures contain three declaratives: DIST, TEMP, and PRESS. DIST and TEMP have the EXTERNAL attribute in both external Procedures, PROCEXA and PROCEXB. A reference to DIST or TEMP in either external Procedure is to the *same declaratives.* PRESS, declared in both PROCEXA and PROCEXB, does not have the EXTERNAL attribute. The compiler therefore gives each declaration

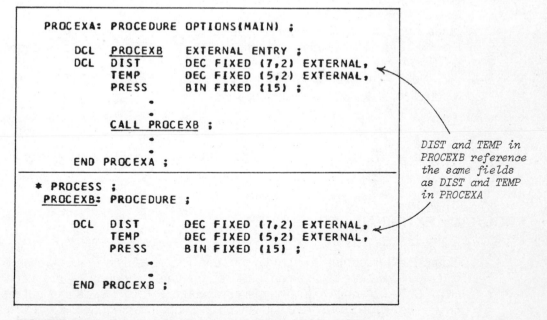

```
PROCEXA: PROCEDURE OPTIONS(MAIN) ;

    DCL    PROCEXB    EXTERNAL ENTRY ;
    DCL    DIST       DEC FIXED (7,2) EXTERNAL,
           TEMP       DEC FIXED (5,2) EXTERNAL,
           PRESS      BIN FIXED (15) ;
                •
                •
           CALL PROCEXB ;
                •
                •
    END PROCEXA ;
─────────────────────────────────────────────
 * PROCESS ;
 PROCEXB: PROCEDURE ;

    DCL    DIST       DEC FIXED (7,2) EXTERNAL,
           TEMP       DEC FIXED (5,2) EXTERNAL,
           PRESS      BIN FIXED (15) ;
                •
                •
    END PROCEXB ;
```

DIST and TEMP in PROCEXB reference the same fields as DIST and TEMP in PROCEXA

FIGURE 22–2 External Declaratives in External Procedures.

of PRESS the INTERNAL attribute, resulting in two separate fields, each unique in its own Procedure.

The external declares, DIST and TEMP, each generate one field in storage. The fields are actually in the *calling* Procedure PROCEXA; the EXTERNAL attribute makes their addresses known to other external Procedures. To initialize these declaratives, you need only code the INITIAL attribute in the main Procedure, PROCEXA. The compiler in effect ignores INIT for DIST and TEMP if it appears in PROCEXB. Otherwise matching declaratives should be identical in each external Procedure.

In addition, the compiler generates certain code for each use of EXTERNAL. In a large program with many declares, it is more efficient to minimize the number of separately defined EXTERNAL declarations. A standard practice is to define all such declares in a single structure that has the EXTERNAL attribute. Each declarative will then have the EXTERNAL attribute, but the compiler generates an external address only for the entire structure. The following illustrates:

```
DCL 1 COMMON EXTERNAL,
      2 DIST    DEC FIXED (7,2),
      2 TEMP    DEC FIXED (5,2);
```

All the elements in the structure COMMON now contain the EXTERNAL attribute. To ensure that each called Procedure has declaratives with identical attributes, simply duplicate the declaratives (or catalog them on disk and INCLUDE them) and insert them in the appropriate Procedures. *Other than INIT, each structure in each Procedure must be identically declared, with matching names and attributes, and in the same sequence.* The same file used in more than one external Procedure must be declared identically, but need not be explicitly coded as EXTERNAL.

Note: If you use the PL/I Optimizing compiler, insert a PROCESS statement before each external Procedure, as

* PROCESS

with the asterisk in column one. PROCESS may contain various options as explained in Chapter 29

PROGRAM: EXTERNAL PROCEDURES

Figure 22–3 illustrates a program that consists of a main Procedure and two external Procedures. Common data for the three Procedures are variables HOURS, RATE, and WAGE. The main Procedure, PROCA, reads an input record containing HOURS and RATE and CALLs an external Procedure, PROCB. PROCB in turn calculates WAGE (HOURS * RATE) and CALLs PROCC. PROCC prints

```
            /*        MAIN PROCEDURE      */
1       0  PROCA:
                PROCEDURE OPTIONS(MAIN) ;

2    1  0       DCL  SYSIN FILE INPUT STREAM ;
3    1  0       DCL  1 COMMON        EXTERNAL ,
                       2 HOURS       DEC FIXED (5,1) ,
                       2 RATE        DEC FIXED (5,2 ) ,
                       2 WAGE        DEC FIXED (9,2) ;
4    1  0       DCL  PROCB           EXTERNAL ENTRY ;

5    1  0            GET LIST (HOURS, RATE) ;
6    1  0            CALL PROCB ;
7    1  0            SIGNAL FINISH ;
8    1  0       END PROCA ;


            /*      EXTERNAL PROCEDURE: PROCB      */
1       0  PROCB:
                PROCEDURE OPTIONS(MAIN) ;

2    1  0       DCL  1 COMMON        EXTERNAL ,
                       2 HOURS       DEC FIXED (5,1) ,
                       2 RATE        DEC FIXED (5,2 ) ,
                       2 WAGE        DEC FIXED (9,2) ;
3    1  0       DCL  PROCC           EXTERNAL ENTRY ;

4    1  0            WAGE = HOURS * RATE ;
5    1  0            CALL PROCC;
6    1  0       END PROCB ;


            /*       EXTERNAL PROCEDURE: PROCC      */

1       0  PROCC:
                PROCEDURE ;

2    1  0       DCL  SYSPRINT FILE PRINT ;
3    1  0       DCL  1 COMMON        EXTERNAL ,
                       2 HOURS       DEC FIXED (5,1) ,
                       2 RATE        DEC FIXED (5,2 ) ,
                       2 WAGE        DEC FIXED (9,2) ;

4    1  0            PUT DATA (HOURS, RATE, WAGE) ;
5    1  0       END PROCC ;
```

Output:-

COMMON.HOURS=   123.0   COMMON.RATE=   9.25   COMMON.WAGE= 1137.75;

FIGURE 22-3 Linkage to External Procedures.

the three external variables. PROCC then returns to PROCB, which returns to PROCA. Processing terminates at this point.

The program illustrates the use of common data and linkage between external Procedures. Needless to say, such simple processing would normally be done in one main Procedure.

ARGUMENTS AND PARAMETERS

A program may make common data known to more than one external Procedure by means of the EXTERNAL attribute, or by use of *arguments* and *parameters,* or by a mixture of both. Figure 22–4 illustrates passing arguments from the calling Procedure PROCARA to the called Procedure PROCARB.

Whereas Figure 22–2 used the EXTERNAL attribute to make DIST and TEMP known in more than one Procedure, Figure 22–4 supplies DIST and TEMP as arguments in the CALL statement:

CALL PROCARB (DIST, TEMP) ;

This CALL statement tells the compiler that the storage addresses of these two fields (DIST and TEMP) declared in the calling procedure (PROCARA) are to be known also in the external Procedure PROCARB. In turn, PROCARB must allow for receiving the addresses of the arguments by means of parameters in its PROCEDURE (or ENTRY) statement:

```
PROCARA: PROCEDURE OPTIONS(MAIN) ;

    DCL  PROCARB    EXTERNAL ENTRY ;
    DCL  DIST       DEC FIXED (7,2),
         TEMP       DEC FIXED (5,2) INIT (0),
         PRESSURE   BIN FIXED (15) ;
                  .
                  .
         CALL PROCARB (DIST, TEMP) ;          (Arguments)
                  .
                  .
         END PROCARA ;

PROCARB: PROCEDURE (DISTANCE, TEMPER) ;    (Parameters)

    DCL  DISTANCE  DEC FIXED (7,2),
         TEMPER    DEC FIXED (5,2),
         PRESSURE  BIN FIXED (15) ;
                  .
                  .
         END PROCARB ;
```

FIGURE 22–4 Passing of Arguments between Procedures.

PROCARB: PROCEDURE (DISTANCE, TEMPER) ;

In the called procedure PROCARB, the parameters do not have the same names as the passed arguments (they may or may not—it makes little difference); technically, CALL delivers the storage addresses, not the names. In PROCARB, a reference to DISTANCE is to the same storage location as DIST, and a reference to TEMPER is to TEMP. Note: the compiler relates the arguments with the parameters, from left to right. As a result,

1. Arguments and corresponding parameters must be in the same sequence.
2. There must be the same number of arguments and parameters.
3. Each matched argument/parameter should have identical attributes. However, the compiler ignores the INIT attribute in the declaration of a parameter in the called Procedure, so you may code or omit INIT. Further a parameter may not have the attributes AUTOMATIC, STATIC, BASED, DEFINED, or EXTERNAL.
4. If it is necessary to pass a structure, ensure that both argument and parameter are level-1.

In Figure 22–4, DISTANCE and TEMPER are defined identically to DIST and TEMP respectively. Both Procedures contain a field defined as PRESSURE, but since the definitions do not have the EXTERNAL attribute, nor is PRESSURE passed as an argument, each PRESSURE references a different field in main storage.

Chapter 29 provides the DOS and OS job control for compile, link-edit, and execute of external Procedures.

PHASES AND OVERLAYS

There are three main stages in a PL/I program's life:

1. *Compilation,* through the job control statement

// EXEC PLIOPT or //STEP EXEC PLIXCLG

(depending on the compiler version). This step involves the translation from source PL/I language to the low-level machine language, reorganization of procedures and declaratives, and assignment of relative storage locations.
2. *Linkage-editing,* through the Linkage Editor control statement

// EXEC LNKEDT or //LKED

This stage involves incorporating required precompiled input/output modules and any other required program modules into one working program. Since a program may consist of more than one compilation ("phase"), the Linkage Editor determines the relative location of each phase. It converts the machine-language program into executable format and under DOS stores it in the "Core Image Library," or under OS in the "Load Library."

3. *Execution,* by means of the job control statement // EXEC (under DOS). This statement "loads" the main ("root") phase of the program from the Core Image Library or Load Library into main storage and initiates execution at its entry-point. This phase may be the entire program (if only one phase) or only part of the program (the first, or "root," phase).

This section of the text is concerned with the organizing of a PL/I program into separate phases (also called "overlays"), the means of making common declaratives known throughout these phases, and the way to load program phases from the library into main storage during execution.

Up to this point, every program has consisted of a single phase, with one or more external Procedures. But is also possible to code a PL/I program that consists of more than one phase. The main purpose of a multiphase program is to permit *program overlays*—if a program is too large to fit into available storage, you may organize it into separate phases that may overlay one another at execution-time. This feature is less important on virtual storage systems.

The compiler treats each phase as independent of the other phases, in effect as separate compilations. When processing each phase, the Linkage Editor relates entry-points and common data for the phases. Then it writes the phases separately in the Core Image Library or Load Library.

A program that consists of more than one phase requires considerable work on the part of the Linkage Editor, but fortunately little from the programmer. Each phase requires a PROCESS statement entry called NAME to notify the Linkage Editor of the name and origin of each phase. The program also requires a special CALL statement to load a copy of each phase (other than the first "root" phase) into storage during execution. The NAME entry is coded as follows:

```
OS:   * PROCESS NAME ('name') ;
DOS: * PROCESS NAME ('phase-name,origin') ;
```

Under OS, each phase (or "module") must simply have a unique name. The DOS NAME entry, however, is more complicated. The following explains:

Phase-name,ROOT	The phase-name is limited to eight characters. For identification, the first four characters must be identical in each phase of the program, but otherwise the name is unique. ROOT means that this phase is to be the main (root) phase. It must be the *first* and the *only* entry to contain the origin ROOT. Its origin is the lowest available storage position assigned for execution of the program.

Phase-name,*	The first four characters of "phase-name" are identical to all other phases. The asterisk (*) means that the origin of this phase immediately follows the previous phase.
Phase-name, symbol	The first four characters of "phase-name" are identical to all other phases. "Symbol" is the name of a previous phase (not the ROOT) that this phase is to overlay during program execution. In effect, this phase is the same initial storage position at execution-time as the other phase specified in the "symbol" part of the Phase entry statement.

Figure 22–5 illustrates the use of each type of phase: OVERONE is the ROOT phase, and OVERTWO is the next phase that immediately follows. At some point during execution, as explained in the next section, OVERTHRE, the third phase, is to overlay and erase OVERTWO.

Under OS, you could establish the overlay facility as a PARM entry:

```
//STEP1 EXEC PLIXCLG,PARM.LKED = 'OVLY'
```

and link-edit the separate modules with the Linkage Editor control statements OVERLAY and INSERT.

The DOS CALL OVERLAY Statement

The // EXEC job control entry loads the root phase into storage from the Core Image Library, but does not load the other phases. The programmer has to determine at what point to load the other phases for execution. The statements that load a phase during execution are

DOS PL/I:	CALL PLIOVLY ('phasename');
Subset:	CALL OVERLAY ('phasename');

The CALL overlay statement causes the named phase to load into storage, beginning at the entry-point designated in the Phase entry on the PROCESS statement or the PHASE statement. CALL overlay does not cause the program to link to the phase for execution—the statement CALL entry-point performs that function.

The standard practice is to code the common data and the CALL overlay statements in the root phase, which controls the main program logic. It is not feasible to overlay the root phase itself.

The overlay program in Figure 22–5 is illustrative and is not intended to be realistic (or even sensible!). The job control statement // EXEC loads a copy of

```
        /*  MAIN PHASE - LINK TO OVERLAY TO PROCESS & PRINT */

1   PROCA:
        PROCEDURE OPTIONS(MAIN) ;

2       DCL  SYSIN FILE INPUT STREAM ;
3       DCL  1 COMMON        EXTERNAL ,      /* DATA COMMON TO PHASES */
                 2 HOURS      DEC FIXED (5,1) ,
                 2 RATE       DEC FIXED (5,2 ) ,
                 2 WAGE       DEC FIXED (9,2) ;

4       DCL (PROCB,
             PROCC)          EXTERNAL ENTRY ;

5           GET LIST ( HOURS, RATE ) ;

6           CALL PLIOVLY ('OVERTWO') ;   /* LOAD PHASE TWO */
7           CALL PROCB ;                 /* EXECUTE PHASE 2 AT ENTRY */

8           CALL PLIOVLY ('OVERTHRE') ;  /* LOAD PHASE THREE */
9           CALL PROCC ;                 /* EXECUTE PHASE 3 AT ENTRY */

10      END PROCA ;
```

```
        /*  PHASE2 -   CALCULATE  AND RETURN TO MAIN PHASE */

1   PROCB:
        PROCEDURE ;

2       DCL  1 COMMON        EXTERNAL ,      /* DATA COMMON TO PHASES */
                 2 HOURS      DEC FIXED (5,1) ,
                 2 RATE       DEC FIXED (5,2 ) ,
                 2 WAGE       DEC FIXED (9,2) ;

3           WAGE = HOURS * RATE ;

4       END PROCB ;
```

```
        /* PHASE3 -    PRINT WAGE CALCULATION & RETURN TO MAIN PHASE */

1   PROCC:
        PROCEDURE ;

2       DCL  SYSPRINT FILE PRINT ;
3       DCL  1 COMMON        EXTERNAL ,      /* DATA COMMON TO PHASES */
                 2 HOURS      DEC FIXED (5,1) ,
                 2 RATE       DEC FIXED (5,2 ) ,
                 2 WAGE       DEC FIXED (9,2) ;

4           PUT DATA (HOURS,RATE,WAGE) ;  /* WRITE RESULT */

5       END PROCC ;
```

Output:-

```
COMMON.HOURS=    123.0   COMMON.RATE=    9.25   COMMON.WAGE=     1137.75;
```

FIGURE 22–5 Overlay Program.

the Root Phase, OVERONE, into storage and begins its execution. At this point, main storage could appear in concept as follows:

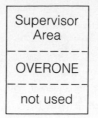

OVERONE reads records containing hours worked (HOURS) and rate-of-pay (RATE). It then executes the statement

CALL PLIOVLY ('OVERTWO') ;

to load a copy of the next phase, OVERTWO, into storage. The statement CALL PROCB then causes program control to link to the entry-point of this phase, at PROCB. At this point, main storage appears as follows:

PROCB simply multiplies HOURS by RATE to get the product WAGE. Note that these three variables have the EXTERNAL attribute in each phase. PROCB then returns (by means of its END statement) to PROCA, following CALL PROCB. PROCA next executes

CALL PLIOVLY ('OVERTHRE')

in order to load the next phase, OVERTHRE, into storage. OVERTHRE loads on top of, and erases, OVERTWO. The statement CALL PROCC then causes program control to link to the entry-point of OVERTHRE, at PROCC. At this point, main storage appears as follows:

In PROCC, the program prints HOURS, RATE, and WAGE and then returns to the main procedure, PROCA (by means of the END statement). PROCA continues reading input records and loading and executing the phases until every input record is read, processed, and printed.

Note: The statement CALL PLIOVLY ('OVERTWO') loads the phase OVER-TWO into storage where it remains until overlaid by the phase OVERTHRE. Once a phase is loaded, it is possible to call its entry-point at any time for execution and any number of times without reloading it.

You can organize a program with many phases overlaying other phases. A multiphase program should be organized very carefully because the loading of a phase can require additional processing time. It is also important to realize that phases vary in size and may need careful planning in their organization. For example, consider the following program that consists of four phases, arranged as follows:

(PHASEA,ROOT)	The Root phase
(PHASEB,*)	Follows PHASEA
(PHASEC,*)	Follows PHASEB
(PHASED,PHASEB)	Overlays PHASEB during program execution

Assume that the program has loaded copies of PHASEB and PHASEC. If PHASED is larger than PHASEB and overlays PHASEB during program execution, then PHASED may erase part of PHASEC and cause a serious execution error.

LINKAGE TO AN ASSEMBLER MODULE

The coding and job control for linking PL/I and Assembler programs is similar to linking two PL/I programs. The PL/I statement that defines the name of the Assembler module that is to be called is

DCL module-name ENTRY OPTIONS(ASSEMBLER, INTER), parameter-name attributes

The INTER option allows PL/I to handle any program interrupt that occurs in the Assembler module. The CALL statement that calls the module-name optionally provides the name of the parameter that is defined in the above ENTRY statement. PL/I supplies in register-1 the address of the parameter to the Assembler program.

The Assembler module requires precise coding and for program linkage defines a register savearea of 20 fullwords (instead of the usual 18). Also, the Assembler module should avoid use of register-12, which PL/I error-handling routines use if a program check interrupt occurs.

Figure 22–6 illustrates linking a PL/I program to an Assembler module. The PL/I program is to pass the variables HOURS, RATE, and WAGE. In order to pass

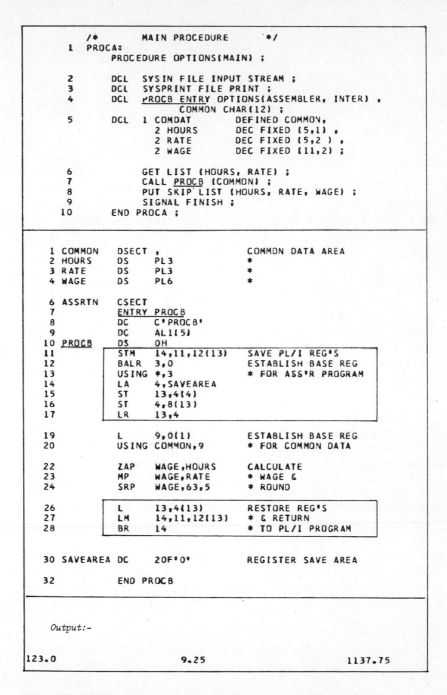

```
            /*        MAIN PROCEDURE        */
        1   PROCA:
                PROCEDURE OPTIONS(MAIN) ;

        2       DCL  SYSIN FILE INPUT STREAM ;
        3       DCL  SYSPRINT FILE PRINT ;
        4       DCL  PROCB ENTRY OPTIONS(ASSEMBLER, INTER) ,
                          COMMON CHAR(12) ;
        5       DCL  1 COMDAT        DEFINED COMMON,
                       2 HOURS       DEC FIXED (5,1) ,
                       2 RATE        DEC FIXED (5,2 ) ,
                       2 WAGE        DEC FIXED (11,2) ;

        6           GET LIST (HOURS, RATE) ;
        7           CALL PROCB (COMMON) ;
        8           PUT SKIP LIST (HOURS, RATE, WAGE) ;
        9           SIGNAL FINISH ;
       10       END PROCA ;
```

```
    1 COMMON    DSECT  ,                COMMON DATA AREA
    2 HOURS     DS     PL3             *
    3 RATE      DS     PL3             *
    4 WAGE      DS     PL6             *

    6 ASSRTN    CSECT
    7           ENTRY PROCB
    8           DC     C'PROCB'
    9           DC     AL1(5)
   10 PROCB     DS     0H
   11           STM    14,11,12(13)    SAVE PL/I REG'S
   12           BALR   3,0             ESTABLISH BASE REG
   13           USING  *,3             * FOR ASS'R PROGRAM
   14           LA     4,SAVEAREA
   15           ST     13,4(4)
   16           ST     4,8(13)
   17           LR     13,4

   19           L      9,0(1)          ESTABLISH BASE REG
   20           USING  COMMON,9        * FOR COMMON DATA

   22           ZAP    WAGE,HOURS      CALCULATE
   23           MP     WAGE,RATE       * WAGE &
   24           SRP    WAGE,63,5       * ROUND

   26           L      13,4(13)        RESTORE REG'S
   27           LM     14,11,12(13)    * & RETURN
   28           BR     14              * TO PL/I PROGRAM

   30 SAVEAREA  DC     20F'0'          REGISTER SAVE AREA

   32           END PROCB
```

```
    Output:-


    123.0              9.25                      1137.75
```

FIGURE 22–6 Linkage of PL/I and Assembler Programs.

389

them as a single parameter, the variables are defined in a structure with the name COMDAT (any valid PL/I name). The DCL statement that declares the ENTRY point in the Assembler program, PROCB, also defines a parameter COMMON (any valid PL/I name). COMDAT is DEFINED on COMMON, which is the parameter in the CALL statement

CALL PROCB (COMMON);

The CALL statement passes to the Assembler module the address of COMMON, which is the same address as COMDAT. Note that the lengths of HOURS, RATE, and WAGE are respectively 3, 3, and 6 bytes, which equal the length (12) of COMMON. Your compiler may print a warning diagnostic about defining decimal variables on a character string, but generates correct machine code.

The Assembler module multiplies HOURS by RATE and stores the result in WAGE. Note the following:

- The common data, called COMMON in this example, is a DSECT that contains HOURS, RATE, and WAGE *in the same sequence and format as the PL/I program.*
- The entry point to the Assembler module is PROCB (the first executable instruction).
- The two related statements

DC C'PROCB'
DC AL1(5)

define the name and length of the Assembler module name so that the system can print the name in error messages and PLIDUMP.
- The Assembler instructions to save the PL/I registers on entry and to reload them on return are shown in boxes. Some of this code is necessary only if the Assembler module in turn CALLs another program, but strict adherence to Assembler linkage conventions will ensure fewer bugs.
- The Assembler module uses register-3 as its base register, although any other valid register is acceptable.
- The PL/I CALL statement delivers in register-1 the address of a DC that contains A(COMMON). The Assembler module loads the contents of this address constant into register-9 (any other valid register is acceptable) and establishes register-9 as the base register for the common data in the DSECT.

If the Assembler module incurs a program interrupt such as a Data Exception, the resulting diagnostic message may reference the statement number of the PL/I CALL statement; the message informs you that the error is in the called program, not the CALL statement. You may want to force a dump of the program's partition or insert your own trace routine in the Assembler program.

The *IBM PL/I Programmer's Guide* provides other features for linking PL/I and Assembler programs. Note that at the time of this writing, the Guide makes no reference to the fact that the parameter address is delivered in register-1.

DEBUGGING TIPS

- A program may contain only one MAIN procedure. Other subsidiary external Procedures do not contain the MAIN option but cause the compiler (depending on compiler version) to generate an I-level (informatory) diagnostic

    NO MAIN OPTION ON EXTERNAL PROCEDURE

    that merely notifies you of the fact; the message does *not* mean that you should therefore convert the Procedure to OPTIONS(MAIN).
- A called external Procedure may consist of various internal Procedures. A common error is to code all of its statements as internal Procedures, as

```
PROCO2: PROCEDURE;
  DCL statements;
  PROCA: PROCEDURE;

  CALL PROCB;

  END PROCA;
  PROCB: PROCEDURE;

  END PROCB;
END PROCO2;
```

In this case, PROC02 when called will perform nothing. Since there is no statement to CALL PROCA, program control goes around PROCA and PROCB, encounters END PROC02, and returns to the calling Procedure. The solution is to code CALL PROCA or to eliminate the statements PROCA: PROCEDURE and END PROCA.

- If a called Procedure has a main logic routine and a number of internal Procedures, for clarity code RETURN in the main Procedure to return to the calling Procedure.
- If two external Procedures use the same file (such as a printer), declare the file identically in both Procedures. Since a file is automatically EXTERNAL, you need not explicitly define that attribute, but for other than SYSIN or SYSPRINT the compiler must know whether the file is input or output, tape, disk, and so on.
- A variable with the EXTERNAL attribute may not be defined as AUTOMATIC or as DEFINED. The compiler defaults all EXTERNAL variables to the STATIC attribute.

PROBLEMS

22–1. For what reasons may a program be divided into separate external Procedures?

22–2. Assume that a program consists of a main Procedure and one external procedure. The main Procedure contains the declaratives DIST, TIME, and RATE that are to be known in the external Procedure. Complete the coding so that PROCB knows the three declaratives by means of the EXTERNAL attribute.

```
PROCA: PROCEDURE OPTIONS(MAIN) ;

    DCL   DIST        DEC FIXED(7,3),
          TIME        DEC FIXED(7,3),
          RATE        DEC FIXED(7,3);

          CALL PROCB ;
          PUT LIST (DIST, TIME, RATE) ;
    END PROCA ;

PROCB: PROCEDURE ;
                  .
                  .
          RATE = DISTANCE * TIME ;
    END PROCB ;
```

22–3. Revise Problem 22–2 so that PROCB knows the three declaratives by means of passed parameter(s).

22–4. What other statement is required in PROCA in Problem 22–2 concerning PROCB?

CHAPTER 23

STORAGE CLASSES

OBJECTIVE:

To cover the four PL/I storage classes:
AUTOMATIC, STATIC, BASED, and
CONTROLLED.

INTRODUCTION

A data name references a location in main storage where the data is stored. The association of a data name with a storage location means that the storage is *allocated,* that is, made available for processing. PL/I permits the allocating of storage at different times, depending on the storage class of the data. There are four storage classes: AUTOMATIC, STATIC, BASED, and CONTROLLED.

AUTOMATIC STORAGE

For any Declarative such as

DCL AMOUNT DEC FIXED (5) ;

the compiler assigns the AUTOMATIC attribute. The significance of the AUTO-MATIC attribute is shown in Figure 23–1. Each variable—TABLEA, TABLEB, and

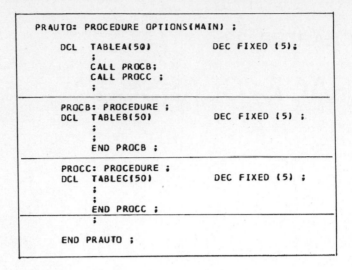

```
PRAUTO: PROCEDURE OPTIONS(MAIN) ;
      DCL  TABLEA(50)         DEC FIXED (5);
           ;
           CALL PROCB;
           CALL PROCC ;
           ;
      PROCB: PROCEDURE ;
      DCL  TABLEB(50)         DEC FIXED (5) ;
           ;
           ;
           END PROCB ;
      PROCC: PROCEDURE ;
      DCL  TABLEC(50)         DEC FIXED (5) ;
           ;
           ;
           END PROCC ;
           ;
      END PRAUTO ;
```

FIGURE 23–1 Automatic Storage.

TABLEC—has the AUTOMATIC attribute and is defined and used in one Procedure and not in any other. PL/I can therefore allocate at different times during program execution the same storage space to different variables. This use of main storage is called *dynamic storage allocation*. PL/I allocates storage for such variables during program execution—and allocates storage for a variable as long as the Procedure in which it is declared remains active.

For example, in Figure 23–1 when the Main Procedure, PRAUTO, is activated, the program allocates an automatic Dynamic Storage Area (DSA) for TABLEA (declared in PRAUTO), but not at that time for TABLEB or TABLEC (in contained Procedures):

PRAUTO	
PROCB	
PROCC	
TABLEA (Automatic)	Dynamic Storage Area (DSA)

Note that statements that are internal to PRAUTO are stored first, followed by contained Procedures PROCB and PROCC, then the Dynamic Storage Area for

TABLEA. Since PRAUTO is the main Procedure and is always active, the storage for TABLEA is always allocated during program execution.

Next, assume that CALL PROCB activates the Procedure PROCB. The program then allocates storage for TABLEB in a Dynamic Storage Area following TABLEA. On termination of PROCB (through END or RETURN to PRAUTO), the program releases TABLEB, making that storage area available.

```
┌─────────────────────────────┐
│ PRAUTO                       │
│ ─ ─ ─ ─ ─ ─ ─ ─ ─ ─ ─ ─ ─   │
│ PROCB                        │
│ ─ ─ ─ ─ ─ ─ ─ ─ ─ ─ ─ ─ ─   │
│ PROCC                        │
│ ─ ─ ─ ─ ─ ─ ─ ─ ─ ─ ─ ─ ─   │
│ TABLEA              DSA      │
│ ─ ─ ─ ─ ─ ─ ─ ─ ─ ─ ─ ─ ─   │
│ TABLEB              DSA      │
└─────────────────────────────┘
```

Next, assume that CALL PROCC activates the Procedure PROCC. The program then releases storage for TABLEB and allocates storage for TABLEC. These may be the same locations, and the contents of TABLEB may be lost.

```
┌─────────────────────────────┐
│ PRAUTO                       │
│ ─ ─ ─ ─ ─ ─ ─ ─ ─ ─ ─ ─ ─   │
│ PROCB                        │
│ ─ ─ ─ ─ ─ ─ ─ ─ ─ ─ ─ ─ ─   │
│ PROCC                        │
│ ─ ─ ─ ─ ─ ─ ─ ─ ─ ─ ─ ─ ─   │
│ TABLEA              DSA      │
│ ─ ─ ─ ─ ─ ─ ─ ─ ─ ─ ─ ─ ─   │
│ TABLEC              DSA      │
└─────────────────────────────┘
```

The purpose of dynamic storage allocation is to provide automatic reduction of a program's use of main storage. However, the values in TABLEB and TABLEC may not be saved when PROCB and PROCC are reactivated.

If an AUTOMATIC variable has the INITIAL attribute, the compiler sets up the constant outside the main program. Each time the program enters the block during execution, it allocates storage in the dynamic storage area and then initializes the constant. The initialization is performed by assigning the "hidden" constant to the variable in the DSA.

For example, assume that in Figure 23–1, TABLEA, TABLEB, and TABLEC each have the INITIAL attribute. The compiler sets up their constants outside the main program. When the program PRAUTO is initiated for execution, the program assigns the constants to TABLEA. Then when the program calls PROCB, the program allocates a DSA and assigns TABLEB's constants. When it calls PROCC, the program allocates a DSA and assigns TABLEC's constants. As a result, each time you CALL a Procedure, the program reinitializes any AUTOMATIC variables that have the INITIAL attribute.

STATIC STORAGE

If you want to save the values in variables such as TABLEB and TABLEC through-out different activations of their Procedures, declare them with the STATIC attri-bute, as follows:

```
DCL TABLEA (50) DEC FIXED (5) STATIC ; (in PRAUTO)
DCL TABLEB (50) DEC FIXED (5) STATIC ; (in PROCB )
DCL TABLEC (50) DEC FIXED (5) STATIC ; (in PROCC )
```

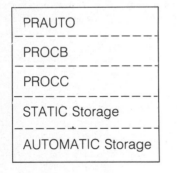

Main storage is now arranged with permanent STATIC areas for variables with the STATIC attri-bute. TABLEB and TABLEC have storage allo-cated during the entire program execution.

—*For TABLEA, TABLEB, and TABLEC*

—*For other variables that are AUTOMATIC*

If an AUTOMATIC variable has the INITIAL attribute, the compiler sets up the constant concealed outside the main program. When the program enters the block in which the automatic variable is declared, the program then allocates storage and initializes the variable. But if you code a variable with the STATIC attribute, the program simply inserts the constant directly in the variable at com-pile-time. Thus, the use of the STATIC attribute causes no extra program overhead (the space for the concealed constant and the process of initializing are AU-TOMATIC features).

When you CALL a Procedure that contains STATIC variables with INITIAL constants, the constants are already stored. You may therefore CALL the Pro-cedure any number of times; the variable is not reinitialized, and you may ac-cumulate a value in the variable safely throughout the program's execution. It is therefore a common efficient practice to define as STATIC all variables that have the INITIAL attribute. For example:

DCL AMOUNT DECIMAL FIXED (5,2) INIT (0) STATIC ;

Alternatively, you may code a DEFAULT statement prior to the Declaratives to force all variables to be STATIC:

DEFAULT RANGE(*) STATIC ;

But any variables that have dynamic bounds (that is, not known at compile-time) must have the AUTOMATIC (or CONTROLLED) attribute. Also, any POINTER with the INITIAL attribute must be AUTOMATIC.

BASED STORAGE

The system determines the address of a STATIC variable when the program loads into main storage for execution and determines the address of an AUTOMATIC variable when the program activates a block. The system stores the address of a BASED variable in a *pointer variable,* subject to the program's direction. (BASED storage is not available in PL/C.)

The POINTER Attribute and the ADDR Built-in Function

BASED storage, like DEFINED, uses no storage, but provides an image of an area of storage. Figure 23–2 contrasts the use of the DEFINED attribute with the use of a BASED variable and POINTER attribute.

In Example I, the DEFINED attribute aligns the structure VALUES on the structure AMOUNT. The limitations are that DEFINED is a permanent overlay, and both the base and defined variables require the same base/scale/precision attributes (although you may define Character on Picture and vice versa).

In Example II, the first statement declares a variable called PTR with the POINTER attribute. The structure VALUES has the BASED attribute instead of DEFINED. As a result, the program allocates no storage to VALUES, but instead bases the *address* of VALUES on whatever address is in PTR—just yet there is none. The last statement uses the ADDR built-in function that assigns to PTR the

```
      Example i—Use of DEFINED                    Example II—Use of BASED

                                          DCL     PTR               POINTER;
 DCL 1 AMOUNTS,                           DCL 1 AMOUNTS,
         2 TIME         DEC FIXED(5,2),           2 TIME         DEC FIXED(5,2),
         2 RATE         DEC FIXED(5,2),           2 RATE         DEC FIXED(5,2),
         2 DISTANCE     DEC FIXED(7,2);           2 DISTANCE     DEC FIXED(7,2);
 DCL 1 VALUES DEFINED AMOUNTS,            DCL 1 VALUES  BASED (PTR),
         2 HOURS        DEC FIXED(5,2),           2 HOURS        DEC FIXED(5,2),
         2 MPH          DEC FIXED(5,2),           2 MPH          DEC FIXED(5,2),
         2 MILES        DEC FIXED(7,2);           2 MILES        DEC FIXED(7,2);

                                          PTR = ADDR(AMOUNTS) ;
```

FIGURE 23–2 Use of DEFINED and BASED.

beginning address of AMOUNTS. Now, any reference to VALUES, HOURS, MPH, or MILES references respectively the variables AMOUNTS, TIME, RATE, or DISTANCE. The result is similar to that for Example I using DEFINED, but with two important differences:

1.   Unlike DEFINED, BASED does not require that variables "overlay defined" have the same base/scale/precision.
2.   The pointer for BASED (in this example PTR) may be changed to reference the address of any area of storage.

Before referencing a pointer variable, ensure that it contains a valid address. The following operations set a pointer variable: the ADDR built-in function, the NULL built-in function, the ALLOCATE statement, and the READ and LOCATE statements (covered next).

Processing Records in Buffers

File declarative statements enable you to designate the number of buffers with the entry BUFFERS(n). A buffer is simply an area in storage that the system may allocate for holding input and output records in order to overlap input/output with processing. The next section discusses a conventional use of buffers.

Move Mode.   The following example assumes that a tape file contains one record per block (unblocked):

```
DCL    TAPE FILE RECORD INPUT ENV( RECSIZE(244) BUFFERS(2) );
DCL 1 TAPEAREA,
       2 IDENTIN        CHAR (05),          5 BYTES
       2 NAMEIN         CHAR (25),         25
       2 BALCIN         DEC FIXED(7,2),     4
       2 FILLIN         CHAR(210);        210
                                         ---
                        TOTAL            244 BYTES
                                         ---

       READ FILE(TAPE) INTO (TAPEAREA) ;
```

For the tape file, BUFFERS(2) allocates two buffers for input, each 244 bytes long. The READ statement causes the system to deliver the first record into buffer 1 and to transfer it to the workarea TAPEAREA. While the program processes the record, the system reads ahead and stores the next tape record in buffer-2:

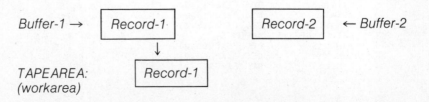

This reading into buffer-2 occurs while the program processes record-1 in buffer-1. When the program executes the next READ statement, record-2 is (probably) already in storage in buffer-2; the system simply *moves* record-2 from buffer-2 directly to TAPEAREA so that there is little delay waiting for a record to be read. Then, while the program processes record-2 in TAPEAREA, the system reads record-3 into buffer-1:

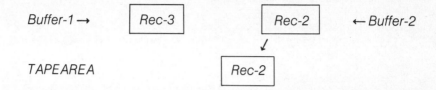

This method is called *Move Mode* because the operation moves a record from a buffer to the work area. More than one buffer provides faster input and output. It is also possible to reduce storage (and slow I/O) by specifying BUFFERS(1). In fact, it may be a good idea to code BUFFERS(1) if a block contains many records because the reduction in space is considerable but the loss in time may be trivial.

LOCATE Mode for Input.   Although buffers are normally concealed from a programmer, with long tape and disk records, it is sometimes desirable to reduce storage by eliminating the work area and processing records directly in a buffer. The following uses the SET option to locate the address of the current buffer:

```
DCL    PIN             POINTER ;
DCL 1 TAPEAREA         BASED (PIN),
       2 IDENTIN       CHAR (05),
       2 NAMEIN        CHAR(25),
       2 BALCIN        DEC FIXED(7,2),
       2 FILLIN        CHAR(210);
       READ FILE(TAPE) SET (PIN) ; /* USE OF SET OPTION */
```

In the example, the READ statement does not move a record to a work area. Instead, the SET option sets the pointer PIN to the address of whichever buffer contains the current record that was read. Any reference now to a variable in TAPEAREA is to the address in PIN, and you process the tape record directly in the buffer (you don't know which one). The method is called *Locate Mode* because the SET option locates the buffer that contains the record:

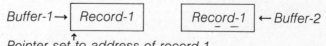

Pointer set to address of record-1

Since TAPEAREA is based on PIN, you may now reference any variable in the structure. Just like Move Mode, the system reads ahead and stores record-2 into buffer-2. The next READ executed sets PIN to the address of buffer-2, where record-2 will be located.

If there is more than one type of record format, such as Name and Address records and Sales records, it is possible to define each type of record based on the same pointer variable.

LOCATE Mode for Output.   It is also possible to write a record directly from a buffer. In this case, instead of WRITE, you use the LOCATE statement with the SET option:

LOCATE based-variable FILE(filename) SET(pointer-variable) ;

The partial program in Figure 23–3 illustrates the use of LOCATE for a tape file. The tape area, TAPEOUT, is a BASED variable, based on the pointer POUT. The LOCATE statement does not *initially* write a tape record—it reserves storage in an output buffer for TAPEOUT and sets the pointer POUT to the address of this area. The READ reads a record into RECORDIN, and the program assigns the record to TAPEOUT in a buffer. The program then loops back to execute another LOCATE. This time, LOCATE writes the contents of the first buffer (record-1) and sets the pointer to the address of the second buffer. The program will continue in this fashion with a delayed write operation.

A PL/I program may consist of input/output in any combination of Move and Locate mode. Locate mode should be used with caution, however, because its use requires a knowledge of how the compiler aligns data in storage (see the section on Data Alignment at the end of Chapter 16).

Note that a base variable (one that is referenced by a DEFINED attribute

```
DCL   FLIN FILE RECORD   INPUT ENV( RECSIZE(080)BUFFERS(2) ),
      TAPE FILE RECORD OUTPUT ENV( RECSIZE(244) BUFFERS(2) );
DCL   RECORDIN           CHAR (80) ;
DCL   TAPEOUT            CHAR(244) BASED (POUT) ;
DCL   POUT               POINTER ;
DCL   EOF                BIT (1)   INIT ('0'B) ;

      ON ENDFILE(FLIN) EOF = '1'B ;
      OPEN  FILE(FLIN), FILE(TAPE) ;
      READ  FILE(FLIN) INTO (RECORDIN) ;
      DO WHILE (¬EOF) ;
          LOCATE TAPEOUT FILE(TAPE) SET (POUT) ;
          ;
          ;
          TAPEOUT = RECORDIN ;
          READ FILE(FLIN) INTO (RECORDIN) ;
      END ;
      CLOSE FILE(FLIN), FILE(TAPE) ;
```

FIGURE 23–3 Use of LOCATE Mode.

in another variable) cannot contain the BASED attribute. Also, a variable with the DEFINED attribute cannot be defined as INITIAL, AUTOMATIC, BASED, CONTROLLED, or STATIC.

CONTROLLED STORAGE (NOT IN PL/C)

If you define a variable with the CONTROLLED attribute, you are notifying the compiler that

1.   You intend to allocate the storage area when you actually need it, and
2.   You will free the area when you are finished with it, using the FREE statement.

Controlled storage can be useful if a program contains a large array with adjustable extents. The following routine can adjust the size of an array according to the exact amount of required storage and release the storage space when it is no longer required.

```
DCL ARRAY(K) DEC FIXED (7,2) CONTROLLED;
    . . .
GET LIST (K);
ALLOCATE ARRAY;
    .

    (process ARRAY)

    .
FREE ARRAY;
```

The example defines ARRAY as CONTROLLED storage with its extents defined by the contents of variable K. Initially, the program reserves no space for ARRAY. The program reads in a value for K—the extent of ARRAY. The ALLOCATE statement is used to make a CONTROLLED variable available for use; ARRAY can only be referenced after execution of an ALLOCATE statement. In this case, ALLOCATE allocates K spaces for ARRAY. For example, if K contains 10, then the size of ARRAY will be 10 elements. The program may then store data in ARRAY and perform any other processing on it. Storage for ARRAY remains allocated until either 1. Execution of a FREE statement, or 2. Termination of the program.

LOCATOR QUALIFICATION

A *locator qualifier* consists of a composite symbol: a minus sign immediately followed by a "greater than" symbol, as $->$. The value to the left of a locator qualifier must be a locator variable, and the value to its right must be a based variable.

Assume the following based variable, INTERVAL:

DCL INTERVAL BIN FIXED (15) BASED (INT_PTR);

INTERVAL contains an optional locator variable called INT_PTR. You can use locator qualification to reference INTERVAL, for example, as

ALLOCATE INTERVAL;
INT_PTR –> INTERVAL = INT_PTR –> INTERVAL + 1;

The ALLOCATE statement sets a value (actually an address) in the locator variable INT_PTR so that a reference to INTERVAL applies to allocated storage. The effect of the second statement is to add 1 to INTERVAL—that is, to the currently allocated area to which INT_PTR points (INT_PTR contains the address of INTERVAL). Since INTERVAL is already defined as BASED (INT_PTR), you could also code the statement as

INTERVAL = INTERVAL + 1;

You *must* use a locator qualifier, however, if the BASED variable does not have a locator qualifier, as

DCL INTERVAL BIN FIXED (15) BASED;

PROGRAM: CREATING A LIST

In simple terms, a *list* is a series of related data items that are not necessarily adjacent in storage but are linked by pointers. Consequently, each list item contains both regular data as well as a pointer address. The pointer may contain the address of the immediately preceding item (if any) in the list, or the immediately following item (if any), or may even contain pointers for both the preceding and he following item.

The program in Figure 23–4 uses BASED storage, POINTER declaratives, ALLOCATE, FREE, and locator qualification to create a list. The list, a structure called LIST_PILE, is defined as BASED and contains elements for customer number, customer name, and a pointer for the preceding list item. The list may contain any number of data groups. Although the original declaration of a BASED variable reserves no storage, each execution of

ALLOCATE LIST_PILE;

allocates a storage area for one list group.

```
1        0    PROG23:
                   PROCEDURE OPTIONS(MAIN) ;

2    1   0    DCL      SYSIN     FILE INPUT ;
3    1   0    DCL      SYSPRINT FILE PRINT ;

4    1   0    DCL      1 LIST_PILE              BASED (CUST_PTR),
                         3 LISTNO               CHAR (05),
                         3 LISTNAME             CHAR (20),
                         3 LIST_PTR             POINTER ;

5    1   0    DCL      (TOP_PTR,
                       CUST_PTR,
                       SAVE_PTR)                POINTER ;
6    1   0    DCL      NULL                     BUILTIN ;

7    1   0    DCL      CUSTNOIN                 CHAR (05),
                       CUSTNAMEIN               CHAR (20),
                       EOF                      BIT  (1) INIT ('0'B) ;

              /*       BUILD LIST          */
8    1   0             TOP_PTR = NULL ;
9    1   0             ON ENDFILE(SYSIN) EOF = '1'B ;
10   1   0             GET LIST (CUSTNOIN, CUSTNAMEIN) ;
11   1   0             DO UNTIL (EOF) ;
12   1   1                 ALLOCATE LIST_PILE ;
13   1   1                 LISTNO   = CUSTNOIN ;
14   1   1                 LISTNAME = CUSTNAMEIN ;
15   1   1                 IF TOP_PTR = NULL THEN
                               LIST_PTR = NULL ;
16   1   1                 ELSE LIST_PTR = TOP_PTR ;
17   1   1                 TOP_PTR = CUST_PTR ;
18   1   1                 GET LIST (CUSTNOIN, CUSTNAMEIN) ;
19   1   1             END ;

              /*       PRINT LIST          */
20   1   0             DO UNTIL (TOP_PTR = NULL) ;
21   1   1                 PUT SKIP LIST (TOP_PTR -> LISTNO,
                                          TOP_PTR -> LISTNAME) ;
22   1   1                 SAVE_PTR = TOP_PTR ;
23   1   1                 TOP_PTR = TOP_PTR -> LIST_PTR ;
24   1   1                 FREE SAVE_PTR -> LIST_PILE ;
25   1   1             END ;

26   1   0         END PROG23;
```

FIGURE 23–4 Processing a List.

The objective of the program is to read and store any number of customer numbers and names—they could, for example, be received from on-line customer inquiries. The program stacks in allocated storage the customer number, name, and a pointer to the preceding list group. Note the following:

- ALLOCATE LIST_PILE allocates a storage area for one list group and sets CUST_PTR to the address of this particular edition of LIST_PILE, implicitly using the pointer CUST_PTR.

- IF TOP_PTR = NULL tests if the pointer TOP_PTR contains no address. (TOP_PTR was initialized to the NULL built-in function earlier.) The *first* time through the routine, TOP_PTR contains NULL, and the program assigns NULL to the pointer LIST_PTR in the list group. Since LIST_PTR is supposed to contain the address of the previous list group and there is none, then NULL indicates that there is no preceding list group. (The case whereTOP_PTR does not equal NULL is discussed later.)

- TOP_PTR = CUST_PTR assigns the current pointer value into another pointer that will be used to store the "preceding" address in LIST_PTR. The first edition of LIST_PILE resembles the following:

LIST_PILE #1

The program reads the next customer number and name, ALLOCATEs another edition of LIST_PILE, and stores the customer number and name in the list group. Since TOP_PTR now contains the address of the previous list group, it does not contain NULL. Consequently, the ELSE statement stores TOP_PTR in the current edition of LIST_PILE. The second and third edition look like the following:

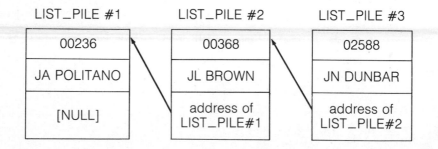

The program can continue storing data in this manner, with each new edition linked to each preceding edition. After reaching end-of-file, the program prints the stored editions of LIST_PILE in reverse sequence. In this case, locator qualification is necessary to reference each edition because only the last stored LIST_

PILE is "current." The FREE statement releases to the computer system the storage area for each edition of LIST_PILE as it is printed. The three stored list groups print as follows:

```
02588   JN DUNBAR
00368   JL BROWN
00236   JA POLITANO
```

If you want to print the list groups in their original sequence, store the address of the *first* edition in a pointer and store in each LIST_PTR the address of the *following* list group, using locator qualification.

PROBLEMS

23–1. What are the four storage classes?

23–2. PL/I causes variables to default to the AUTOMATIC attribute. In what way can this default attribute be inefficient? What can you do to make the program more efficient?

23–3. Assume the following declaratives:

```
DCL CHARSTR      CHAR(9);
DCL PICSTR       PIC'999' DEFINED CHARSTR;
```

Show how to accomplish the same results by defining PICSTR as a BASED variable.

23–4. Find and explain the three errors in the following declaratives.

```
DCL FLDA    CHAR(10) BASED(PTR),
    FLDB    CHAR(10) DEFINED FLDA,
    FLDC    CHAR(10) DEFINED FLDB,
    FLDD    CHAR(10) DEFINED FLDA AUTOMATIC,
    PTR     POINTER;
```

23–5. Revise the example program in Figure 23–4 so that it prints customer numbers and names beginning from the bottom of the list.

PART VI

FILE PROCESSING

CHAPTER 24

TAPE AND DISK CONSECUTIVE FILES

OBJECTIVE:
To describe the characteristics of magnetic tape and disk, and to cover processing of tape and disk Consecutive files.

INTRODUCTION

Most computer installations maintain large volumes of data requiring a storage medium such as magnetic tape or disk. These devices provide a highly condensed storage medium with fast input/output and have a number of important features:

- Tape and disk can store large amounts of data in a small storage space.
- Input and output is extremely fast.
- Tape and disk storage involves little manual handling, and records are well protected from external damage.
- Sorting of tape and disk records is rarely inaccurate.
- Tape reels are an easy and inexpensive way of mailing large volumes of data and of storing in archives.
- Disk devices facilitate direct access to any record in a file without the need to process every preceding record.

This chapter first discusses magnetic tape characteristics, uses, and programming requirements. Then it introduces direct access storage device (disk) features and covers programming for sequential (consecutive) disk file organization. Since the topic of this book is PL/I, it does not attempt to cover the details of tape and disk in depth. Such a discussion would require an entire book alone. Compared especially to Assembler language, PL/I greatly facilitates programming for tape and disk. Therefore, although a good knowledge of tape and disk is imperative for their efficient planning and organization, it is possible to code a PL/I program with surprisingly little such detailed knowledge.

Record I/O is normally used for tape and disk processing. The READ and WRITE statements and structures for input/output areas are similar to earlier program examples. The only major difference is in the file declaratives and the job control statements. Otherwise, it may simplify programming to think of tape and disk as only other input/output devices.

MAGNETIC TAPE

Magnetic tape is a convenient way to store large volumes of data. The computer system records data on tape much the same way the common tape recorder records sound. A program may write data on tape, erasing any previous data, and subsequently another program may read the tape as input. In this way, tape may be used and reused almost indefinitely.

Typically, magnetic tape is $\frac{1}{2}$ inch wide and consists of a thin ferromagnetic coating on flexible plastic. The length of a reel may vary from 200 to 2400 feet. Just as a byte in computer main storage contains a character of data, so a tape reel stores data in bytes. Tape density is measured in the number of bytes stored per inch (bpi), such as 800 bpi, 1600 bpi, and 6250 bpi. Accordingly, a 2400 foot reel of 6250 bpi can theoretically contain

$$2400' \times 12'' \times 6250 = 180,000,000 \text{ bytes}$$

However, tape file organization does not permit storing data on every inch of tape—some space is reserved for nondata such as "interblock gaps" and "tape labels."

TAPE BLOCKING

Whether an application is business or scientific, almost invariably data is in the form of records. So that a computer can distinguish a record on tape, a blank space, called an *interblock gap (IBG),* separates each block of data, as shown:

UNBLOCKED TAPE RECORDS

In this case, one block stores a single record. The word *block* in this context means a block of data, not a Begin or Procedure block. When a program writes a record from main storage onto tape, the tape drive automatically erases the old record (if any) and writes the new record one byte at a time on the tape. It then leaves a blank gap of about 0.6 inch. The IBG has two purposes:

1.   The IBG provides the start and end for each block of data. On reading tape data, the computer reads one byte at a time. It continues reading until encountering the IBG, which terminates the read operation.
2.   The IBG provides space for the tape device to slow down and stop after a read or write, and to start up on the next read/write—"stop/start time."

On tape with density of 800 bpi, an IBG of 0.6 inch takes the space of 480 bytes of data. Accordingly, if each record were 120 bytes long, then the tape would hold four times as much blank space for IBG's as for data blocks. But tape storage is made more efficient by the use of *blocked* records. The computer system permits each block to contain more than one record. The following shows tape blocked with three records per block (that is, the *blocking factor* = 3):

BLOCKED TAPE RECORDS

There is virtually no additional programming effort involved in blocking records. The computer system for *input* reads an *entire block* into storage (from IBG to IBG). As far as the program is concerned, it reads a record—the system may have read a block of three records, but delivers only the first record to the program. The next read instruction by the program causes the system to deliver the second record, and so forth. Similarly with *output,* the program "writes" one record at a time, but the system gathers three into a block (assuming a blocking factor of 3) and then writes the *block* onto the tape reel.

TAPE ORGANIZATION

Tape files (*data sets*) are normally organized as Consecutive with one block of records following another according to ascending sequence on some control word located in a specific field in each record. A file may be so large that it requires more than one tape reel; there is no practical limit to the number of reels a file may use. To locate a particular record, the program must read each preceding record. If the program is to add, change, or delete a record, it normally must rewrite the entire updated tape file onto some other tape reel.

Tape Labels

IBM and other manufacturers supply and support *tape labels* to identify and protect tape files. The use of such tape (and disk) labels is optional but recommended since they provide considerable protection at negligible cost. In some cases, files may be unlabeled or have labels that the system does not check. This section describes IBM standard tape labels.

At the beginning of each reel is a *volume label* that describes the tape reel, not the file. (Some systems provide for more than one label.) The volume label is an 80-byte record that contains the *volume serial number,* a permanent unique number assigned to each reel for identification.

Following the volume label is a *header label* that describes the file that follows. Also 80 bytes, the header label contains fields such as

- *File identifier,* a unique name for the file, such as "PAYROLL MASTER". (This name is not necessarily the declared file name in the program, which is limited to seven characters.) Job Control checks the file identifier when the file is opened.
- *Creation date,* the year and day the file was written.
- *Expiration date,* the year and the day the file may be erased and rewritten.

At the end of each reel is a *trailer label* that is identical to the header label, with one additional field—a *block count* that contains the number of blocks in the reel.

The operating system provides the processing and updating of file labels. You need to be familiar with the labels because the tape job control statement (TLBL under DOS and DD under OS) allows (and sometimes requires) you to reference and change fields on the labels.

TAPE FILE DECLARATIVES

File declaratives vary by PL/I version; this section covers OS and DOS versions.

IBM OS

The following provides the DCL statement for a magnetic tape data set under the OS PL/I Optimizer:

DCL filename FILE INPUT or OUTPUT RECORD ENV (F(blksize, recsize)) ;

- F—Indicates fixed-length (instead of V, variable-length) records.
- blksize—Provides the size of a block of records.
- recsize—Provides the size of a single record.

For example, if records are 500 bytes in length and the blocking factor is 4, then the ENV entry is F(2000, 500). The ENV options may also be entered through DD job control statements.

IBM DOS

The following provides the DCL statement for a magnetic tape file under the DOS PL/I Optimizer:

DCL filename FILE INPUT or OUTPUT RECORD ENV(MEDIUM(SYSnnn,devicenumber)

format RECSIZE(m) BLKSIZE(n) BUFFERS(p)) ;

MEDIUM	Designates the device type: • SYSnnn—gives the symbolic device name assigned to the tape drive. This entry varies by installation, but includes SYSIPT, SYSLST, SYSPCH, and SYS000 through SYS221. • Device number—IBM magnetic tape drive entries include 2400, 3410, and 3420.
format	Indicates that records may be "fixed" in length (record lengths all the same) or "variable" (record lengths vary). Formats are F = Fixed, Unblocked FB = Fixed, Blocked V = Variable, Unblocked VB = Variable, Blocked
RECSIZE(m)	Gives the length in bytes of each record if fixed-length.
BLKSIZE(n)	Gives the length in bytes of each block. For example, if the file is Fixed, Blocked (FB), with RECSIZE(200) and three records per block, then the entry is BLKSIZE(600). For FB, BLKSIZE is a multiple of RECSIZE; for F, BLKSIZE and RECSIZE are the same. For F records only, if BLKSIZE is omitted, the compiler defaults BLKSIZE to the length of RECSIZE.
BUFFERS(p)	Provides the number of buffers, (1) or (2) for DOS. Specifying BUFFERS(2) ensures faster I/O. However, each buffer in main storage stores the contents of an entire block of records. Records may be both long and blocked, such as 1000 bytes long × 10 records = 10,000-byte block. Since each buffer requires 10,000 bytes of storage, then if main storage is restricted, it may be better to specify BUFFERS(1), which is the default if omitted.

OTHER TAPE OPTIONS

PL/I provides additional options for magnetic tape in the file DCL statement:

- BACKWARDS (DOS and OS) for reading tape backward, from last record to first.
- LEAVE (DOS and OS) for files with the BACKWARDS attribute to cause no rewinding on OPEN or CLOSE.
- REWIND (OS) for designating what action to take when the tape is closed.

OS PL/I provides additional attributes in the OPEN statement:

BUFFERED or UNBUFFERED
BACKWARDS

PROGRAM: CREATING A TAPE FILE

Problem Definition

It is necessary to convert a file of customer cards to a magnetic tape file. Input records contain customer number, name, balance, and credit limit. Record length is to be reduced from 80 characters to 40 and formatted on tape with ten records per block. The program is to convert the customer balance and credit limit to Decimal Fixed format on the tape record. Keep in mind that Decimal Fixed format stores two decimal digits per byte and requires a half-byte for the sign. Consequently, precision of (7, 2) for the balance requires only four bytes of storage, and precision of (5, 0) for credit limit requires only three bytes.

Figure 24–1 gives the complete program.

THE OPEN STATEMENT

The OPEN statement has a number of options relevant to tape and disk processing.

DOS OPEN

Under DOS, you may omit INPUT or OUTPUT from the DCL statement of a CONSECUTIVE file and code them in the OPEN statement as

OPEN FILE(CUSDISK) OUTPUT . . . ;

```
1    PROG24A:
          PROCEDURE OPTIONS(MAIN) ;

2    DCL       FILEIN FILE RECORD    INPUT
                                     ENV( MEDIUM(SYSIPT)
                                          F
                                          RECSIZE(80)
                                          BUFFERS(02) ) ;

3    DCL       FILETP FILE RECORD    OUTPUT
                                     ENV( MEDIUM(SYS009,3410)
                                          FB
                                          RECSIZE(40)
                                          BLKSIZE(400)
                                          BUFFERS(02) ) ;

4    DCL       1 RECDIN ,
                3 CUSTIN            CHAR (05) ,
                3 NAMEIN            CHAR (25) ,
                3 BALANCEIN         PIC '9999V9R',
                3 CRLIMIN           PIC '9999',
                3 UNUSED            CHAR (40) ;

5    DCL       1 TAPEOUT ,
                3 CUSTOUT           CHAR (05),
                3 NAMEOUT           CHAR (25),
                3 BALANCEOUT        DEC FIXED (7,2),
                3 CRLIMOUT          DEC FIXED (5,0),
                3 UNUSED            CHAR (03) ;

6    DCL       EOF                 BIT  (01) INIT ('0'B) ;

7              ON ENDFILE(FILEIN) EOF = '1'B ;
8              OPEN FILE(FILEIN),
                    FILE(FILETP) ;
9              READ FILE(FILEIN) INTO (RECDIN) ;

10             DO WHILE (¬EOF) ;
11                CUSTOUT = CUSTIN ;
12                NAMEOUT = NAMEIN ;
13                BALANCEOUT = BALANCEIN ;
14                CRLIMOUT = CRLIMIN ;
15                WRITE FILE(FILETP) FROM (TAPEOUT) ;
16                READ FILE (FILEIN) INTO (RECDIN) ;
17             END ;

18             CLOSE FILE(FILEIN),
                     FILE(FILETP) ;
19             SIGNAL FINISH ;
20        END PROG24A ;
```

FIGURE 24–1 Creating a Tape File.

In this way, you could, for example, create a file as OUTPUT and on completion CLOSE it. Subsequently, in the same program you could re-OPEN the file in order to read it as

        OPEN FILE(CUSDISK) INPUT . . . ;

OS OPEN

OS provides many more options in the OPEN statement. In fact, most OS users code standard file DCL options in the OPEN or in DD job control. The following are some common OS tape and disk options:

              DIRECT/SEQUENTIAL/TRANSIENT
              BUFFERED/UNBUFFERED
              STREAM/RECORD
              INPUT/OUTPUT/UPDATE
              BACKWARDS

For example, you could OPEN a disk file as DIRECT UPDATE, update it directly, CLOSE it, and re-OPEN it as SEQUENTIAL INPUT in order to read the file.

DIRECT ACCESS STORAGE DEVICES

A Direct Access Storage Device (DASD), commonly a disk storage device, stores data on disks coated with magnetic oxide. A DASD has unique capabilities:

1.   A DASD can process input and output data *sequentially* just like cards and tape. A later section, "Consecutive Disk Files," covers this method.
2.   A DASD can also process data *directly (randomly)* so that a program may seek and extract any specified record on the disk file without having to search sequentially through the entire file. There are three main ways of direct processing: Indexed-Sequential, Regional, and Virtual Storage Access Method (VSAM).

A DASD consists of a number of disks that rotate on a shaft. Records are stored on the surfaces of the disks in concentric *tracks,* as shown in Figure 24–2. Each track is a circle, completely contained one inside the other. Although track lengths vary because inside tracks are shorter than outside ones, each track contains the same number of bytes. There are tracks on both the top and bottom surface of each disk, except the outer top and bottom surface. The number of tracks and surfaces, the data density, and access speed vary considerably by disk model.

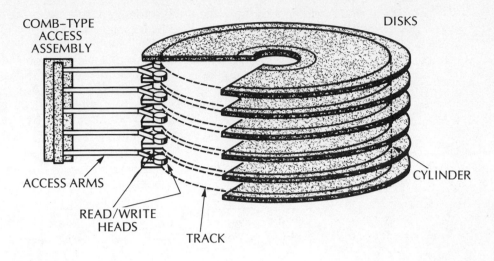

FIGURE 24–2 Disk Storage Device.

     The DASD has a number of access arms, each with two read/write heads. Each head accesses either an upper or lower disk surface; therefore, if the DASD has six disks as in Figure 24–2, then there are ten surfaces, and it needs only five access arms. To write data on a specific track, the DASD moves the arm if necessary inward or outward until it locates the track. Then the device activates the head for the correct surface.

     Disk processing involves little additional programming effort; the hardware and programming software support handle almost all the complexities.

Track Format

Every track contains certain information about its address and condition. Between the different records on the track are gaps; these vary by device and their location on the track. The basic format for a track is as follows:

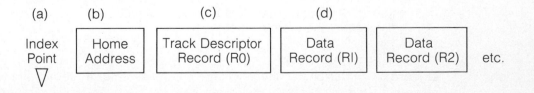

(a)	(b)	(c)	(d)	
Index Point ▽	Home Address	Track Descriptor Record (R0)	Data Record (RI)	Data Record (R2)	etc.

(a)   The Index Point tells the read/write device that this point is the physical beginning of the track—data is recorded following the Index Point.

(b) The Home Address tells the system the address of the track (the cylinder and head, or surface, number) and whether the track is a primary or alternate track, or defective.

(c) The Track Descriptor Record (R0) immediately follows the Home Address. The system stores information about the track in this record. There are two separate fields: a Count Area and a Data Area. The Count Area contains '0' for record number and '8' for data length. It is otherwise similar to the Count Area described next for Data Record under item (d). The Data Area contains eight bytes of information used by the system. The Track Descriptor Record is not normally accessible to the programmer.

(d) Data Record Formats (R1 through Rn). Following the Track Descriptor (R0) record is one or more of your data records, each consisting of the following:

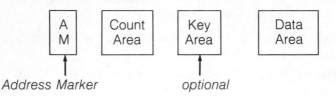

Address Marker. The I/O control unit stores a two-byte Address Marker prior to each block of data. When reading records, the control unit uses the Address Marker to locate the beginning of data.

Count Area. The system also stores and uses this field. Included are the following:

- An Identifier field gives the cylinder/head number (similar to that in the Home Address) and the sequential record number (0–255) in binary, representing R0 through R255. (The Track Descriptor Record, R0, contains zero for record number.)
- The Key Length field is explained in the next section, Key Area.
- The Data Length is a binary value 0 through 65,535 that specifies the number of bytes in the Data Area field (the length of your block of data). For the end-of-file, the system generates a last ("dummy") record containing a length of zero in this field. When the system reads the file, this zero length indicates that there are no more records.

Key Area. Under DASD, the *key* is the control field for the records in the file, such as customer or inventory number. The key, if stored in this separate Key Area, can facilitate locating of records. The key area is *optional*. If omitted, then the file is called *formatted without keys* (Count-Data-Format). The key length in the Count Area contains zero. If the file is *formatted with keys* (Count-Key-Data-Format), then the Key Length contains the length of the Key Area.

Data Area.   You store data blocks in this area in any format—unblocked or blocked, fixed length or variable, just as on magnetic tape.

Under normal circumstances, a programmer is not concerned with the Home Address and Track Descriptor record, nor with the Address Marker, Count Area, and Key Area portions of the Data Record field. The system completely handles the processing of these fields. As shown in the following example programs, it is simply necessary to specify appropriate entries in the DCL and the job control statements. You can then read and write sequential disk records much like cards and tape.

The system stores as many records on the track as possible. Usually, records are stored completely (intact) on a track. A record overflow feature permits records to overlap from one track to the next.

THE CYLINDER CONCEPT

A disk file normally begins with the first record on the highest surface of the outermost track. The number of records stored depends on the length of each record and the number of bytes that a track holds. The disk device fills the first track, then stores data on the outermost track directly beneath, and so on to the bottom outermost track. When the device has filled these tracks, it then moves the read/write heads to the next inner track. Beginning at the highest surface of this track, the device then fills these tracks successively from the highest to the lowest.

Each series of vertical tracks is called a *cylinder*. The outermost set of tracks is cylinder-0, the next inner one is cylinder-1, and so forth. Under the cylinder method of storing data, the disk device minimizes access motion because if it is sequentially reading or writing down the tracks of a cylinder, the device needs only to switch from head to head. The only access motion involved is when the device moves the read/write heads to the next cylinder (inner set of tracks). If data were stored from track to track across a surface, there would be considerably more access motion involved.

Disk files also have labels to identify the "volume" (disk pack) and the file. Cylinder-0, track-0 is reserved for this purpose. The volume label is similar to that for tape. Disk file labels are 140 bytes long and have fields in addition to "file identifier," "creation date," and "expiration date." Details of disk labels are available in the appropriate IBM manuals.

DASD CAPACITY

If you know the length of records (assuming fixed-length) and the number of records, you can calculate the number of records on a track, the number of records in a cylinder, and the number of cylinders for the entire file. Based on the values in Figure 24–3, the formula for the number of *blocks* of data per track is

$$\text{blocks per track} = \frac{\text{track capacity}}{\text{overhead} + C + KL + DL}$$

Device	Max. Block Size	Data Blocks	Key Overhead		Track Capacity
3330	13,030	135 + C + KL + DL	C = 0 when KL = 0	C = 56 when KL ≠ 0	13,165
3340	8,368	167 + C + KL + DL	C = 0 when KL = 0	C = 75 when KL ≠ 0	8,535
3350	19,069	185 + C + KL + DL	C = 0 when KL = 0	C = 82 when KL ≠ 0	19,254

FIGURE 24–3 Track Capacity by Device.

In the figure, C is a constant overhead value for keyed records, KL is key length, and DL is data (block) length. The following two examples illustrate:

• Example 1. Device is 3350, records are 300 bytes, four records per block, formatted without keys.

$$\text{Blocks per track} = \frac{19,254}{185 + 4(300)} = \frac{19,254}{1,385} = 13.9 = 13$$

Records per track = 4 × 13 = 52.

• Example 2. Same as Example 1, but formatted with keys (key length is 15).

$$\text{Blocks per track} = \frac{19,254}{185 + 82 + 15 + 1200} = \frac{19,254}{1,482} = 12.99 = 12.$$

Records per track = 4 × 12 = 48.

Note that you cannot store 13.9 or 12.99 blocks on a track; the fraction is truncated. Based on Figure 24–4, you can calculate the total number of records on a cylinder. If the number of records per track is 52 as in Example 1 above, then the number

Device	Bytes per Track	Tracks per Cylinder	No. of Cylinders	Total Bytes
3330-1	13,030	19	404	100,000,000
3330-11	13,030	19	808	200,000,000
3340-1	8,368	12	348	35,000,000
3340-2	8,368	12	696	70,000,000
3350	19,069	30	555	317,000,000

FIGURE 24–4 Capacity by Device.

of records on a 3350 cylinder is 52 × 30 = 1,560. Using these figures, you can now calculate the number of cylinders that a file requires. For example, a file that contains 100,000 records for the data supplied in Example 1 would require 100,000 ÷ 1,560 = 64.1 cylinders.

Two other devices, the 3375 and the 3380, contain 819 million and 1.25 billion bytes respectively.

DEVICES WITH FIXED-LENGTH BLOCKS

The IBM 3310 and 3370 DASD's are designed for the 4331 and 4341 computers. Instead of cylinders, they store records in fixed-length blocks of 512 bytes. The devices are designed to facilitate Virtual Storage and VSAM data sets.

The 3310 has 126,016 fixed blocks, providing 64 million bytes of storage. The 3370 has 1,116,000 fixed blocks, providing 571 million bytes of storage. (Internally, the 3370 contains two devices each with 558,000 blocks.)

DISK FILE ORGANIZATION

There are several ways to organize a DASD file. The choice of method is a systems, not a programming, problem, and therefore this text gives a limited description of organization methods. The four main methods of DASD file organization are as follows:

1. *Consecutive Organization.* In the Consecutive method, also used by cards and magnetic tape, each record follows another successively according to a predetermined key (control field). You would adopt Consecutive if you do not require online processing, and if most records are processed when the file is read. Advantage: Consecutive provides simplest design and programming and minimizes DASD storage space. Disadvantage: it is difficult to locate a unique record and to insert a new record without rewriting the entire file.

2. *Regional (Direct) Organization.* The Regional method stores records based on a relationship between the key (control field) and the track address where the DASD record is stored. The program performs a calculation on the key number to locate the address of the record. Advantage: Regional access provides fast and efficient use of DASD storage for directly accessing any record. Disadvantages: (1) The file keys must lend themselves to the calculation; (2) A calculation for more than one key may generate the same track address ("synonyms"); (3) The file may be arranged in a sequence other than sequential and require special programming to produce sequential reports; and (4) You must provide special programming to locate a record.

3. *Indexed Sequential Organization.* Under Indexed Sequential Organization, records are stored sequentially, permitting normal sequential processing. In addition, this method has indexes related to the file; you may use these indexes to locate records directly. Advantage: Indexed Sequential permits both sequential and direct processing of files with little special programming effort. Disadvantage: Indexed Sequential may use more DASD storage and process more slowly under some conditions.

4. *Virtual Storage Access Method.* VSAM is a more recent development for IBM systems and permits both sequential and direct processing.

CONSECUTIVE DISK FILES

Disk files are often organized as Consecutive. Under Consecutive organization, processing of disk records is similar to magnetic tape. Each record follows others depending on a control word (or key) placed in a specific field on the record. In order to locate a particular record, the program has to read all the preceding records, testing for an equal condition. To add, change, or delete a record, the program normally rewrites the entire file onto some other disk area ("extent").

Consecutive disk records may be unblocked or blocked, and fixed-length or variable-length. An interblock gap (IBG) separates and distinguishes each block.

CONSECUTIVE DISK FILE DECLARATIVES

File declaratives vary by PL/I version; this section covers OS and DOS versions.

IBM OS

The following provides the DCL statement for a Consecutive disk data set under the OS PL/I Optimizer:

```
DCL filename FILE INPUT or OUTPUT or UPDATE RECORD ENV (F(blksize, recsize)) ;
```

The DCL is similar to the one for tape. The program can determine the type of device through DD job control entries. An additional entry is UPDATE to indicate that the program is to "update" records by changing and rewriting them in place on disk.

IBM DOS

The following provides the DCL statement for a Consecutive disk file under the DOS PL/I Optimizer:

DCL filename FILE INPUT or OUTPUT or UPDATE RECORD ENV(MEDIUM(SYSnnn,devicenumber)

format RECSIZE(m) BLKSIZE(n) BUFFERS(p)) ;

DOS also provides a VERIFY option to cause a disk device to reread and check the validity of a record just written.

INPUT or OUTPUT or UPDATE	Tells the compiler if the file is to be read (INPUT) or written (OUTPUT). If UPDATE, the file is to be updated—that is read and changed in place on disk.
MEDIUM	Designates the device type: • SYSnnn—gives the symbolic device name assigned to the disk drive. This entry varies by installation, but includes SYSIPT, SYSLST, SYSPCH, and SYS000 through SYS221. • Device number—IBM disk devices include 2314, 3330, 3340, 3350, and 3370.
Format	The same entry as for tape: F = Fixed, Unblocked FB = Fixed, Blocked V = Variable, Unblocked VB = Variable, Blocked
RECSIZE(m)	Provides the length of each record (the same as tape).
BLKSIZE(n)	Provides the length of each block (the same as tape).
BUFFERS(p)	Provides the number of buffers. Under DOS the number is either (1) or (2). If omitted, the default is (1).

PROGRAM: CREATING A CONSECUTIVE DISK FILE

Problem Definition

To convert a magnetic tape file containing customer records into a disk file and to reblock records from ten to fifteen per block.

Solution

The only new feature is a DCL statement for tape input and a DCL for disk output. Figure 24–5 gives the program using the tape file created in Figure 24–1. The DCL statements do not specify BUFFERS(2) because the high blocking factors cause efficient input/output processing, whereas additional buffers result in much more main storage space used. With a default to BUFFERS(1), the storage area is 400 + 600 = 1000 bytes. BUFFERS(2) would require 2000 bytes.

```
1    PROG24B:
          PROCEDURE OPTIONS(MAIN) ;

2    DCL      FILETP FILE RECORD   INPUT
                              ENV( MEDIUM(SYS008,3410)
                                   FB
                                   RECSIZE(40)
                                   BLKSIZE(400) ) ;

3    DCL      FILEDK FILE RECORD   OUTPUT
                              ENV( MEDIUM(SYS009,3350)
                                   FB
                                   RECSIZE(40)
                                   BLKSIZE(600) ) ;

4    DCL      TAPEIN               CHAR (40),
              DISKOT               CHAR (40),
              EOF                  BIT  (01) INIT ('0'B) ;

5             ON ENDFILE(FILETP) EOF = '1'B ;
6             OPEN FILE(FILETP),
                   FILE(FILEDK) ;
7             READ FILE(FILETP) INTO (TAPEIN) ;

8             DO WHILE (¬EOF) ;
9               DISKOT = TAPEIN ;
10              WRITE FILE(FILEDK) FROM (DISKOT) ;
11              READ  FILE(FILETP) INTO (TAPEIN) ;
12            END ;

13            CLOSE FILE(FILETP),
                    FILE(FILEDK) ;
14            SIGNAL FINISH ;
15            END PROG24B ;
```

FIGURE 24–5 Creating a Consecutive Disk File.

VARIABLE-LENGTH RECORDS

Tape and disk files provide for variable-length records that are unblocked or blocked. The use of variable-length format can reduce the amount of unused tape or disk storage, but a disadvantage is in additional programming steps. A record may be variable length because it contains one or more variable-length fields or a variable number of fixed-length fields.

Variable-Length Fields

Some fields, such as name and address, may vary considerably in length. In the normal fixed-length format, you define the length as that of the longest possible content. But with variable length, it is possible to store only the significant characters of the field. For example, an address such as 123 W. 35TH ST. requires only 15 characters, whereas an address such as 1234 SOUTH HOLLINGSWORTH DRIVE requires 30 characters.

Variable Number of Fields

Certain applications require some data fields for one record but not for another. For example, a utility company sells both electricity and gas, and customers may adopt paying by budget. For any given customer, the *basic* subrecord could be customer number, customer name, address, and balance owed. Optionally, the customer may have an *electric* subrecord containing rate and history of consumptions and a *budget* subrecord containing payment record. Customers may have any combination of these subrecords, but their record need not provide space for all possibilities. If a customer buys only electricity and does not pay by budget, then only the basic subrecord and electric subrecord are stored.

Variable Unblocked and Blocked Records

The input/output system processes variable-length records similar to its processing of fixed-length records. However, both the system and the programmer must know the length of each *record* that is being read or written. Therefore, immediately preceding each record a 4-byte *record control word* containing the length of the record is stored. For example, if the record is 310 bytes long, then the record control word contains the value 314 (310 plus 4 bytes required by the record control word itself). Further, the system must know the length of each

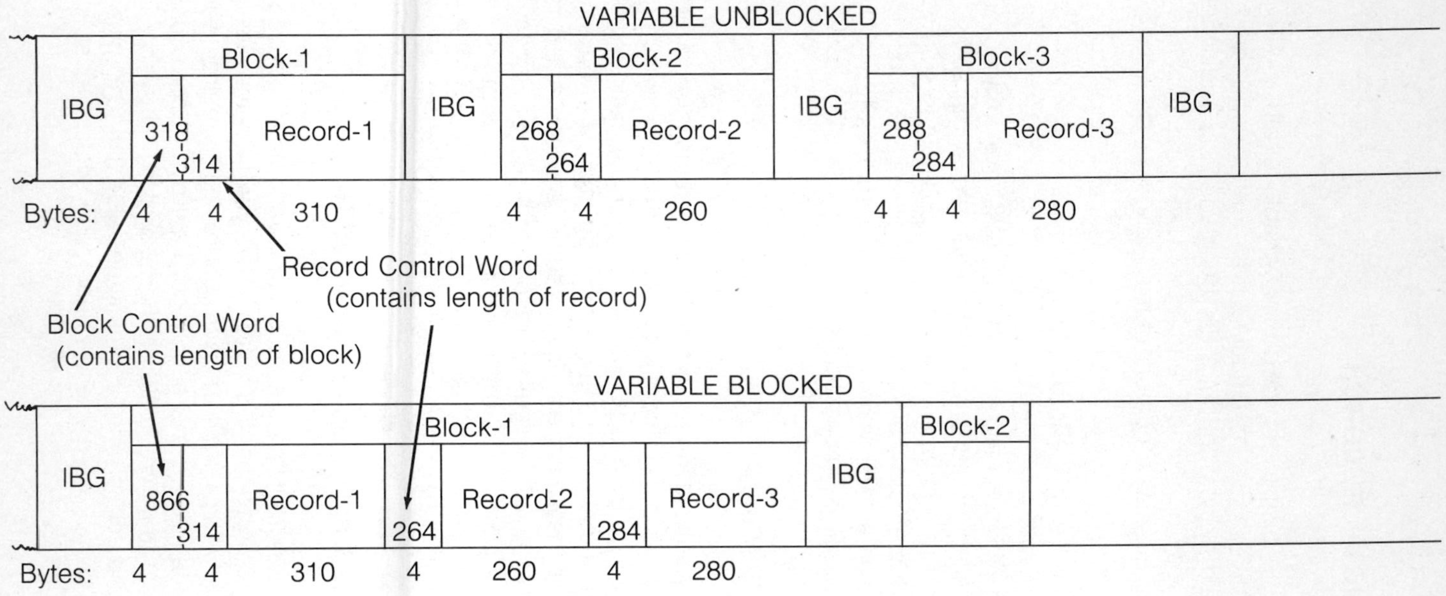

FIGURE 24–6 Variable Unblocked and Blocked Record Formats.

block. Therefore, immediately preceding each block is a 4-byte *block control word* containing the length of the block. You calculate and store the record length; the system calculates and stores the block length.

Figure 24–6 illustrates both variable unblocked and variable blocked records. For *variable unblocked* note the following:

1. The first record (Rec-1) is 310 bytes long and its record control word contains 314. The block control word contains 318, which is the length of the entire block.
2. The second record (Rec-2) is 260 bytes long, its record control word contains 264, and the block control word contains 268.

For *variable blocked,* Figure 24–6 shows three records stored in the first block. A record control word precedes each record, and a block control word (containing 866) precedes the block. The system calculates the length in the block control word as follows:

$$
\begin{array}{lll}
\text{Length of record-1: } 310 + 4 & = & 314 \text{ bytes} \\
\text{Length of record-2: } 260 + 4 & = & 264 \\
\text{Length of record-3: } 280 + 4 & = & \underline{284} \\
& & 862 \text{ bytes} \\
\text{Add length of block control word:} & & \underline{4} \\
\text{Total length of block:} & & \underline{866 \text{ bytes}}
\end{array}
$$

Programming Considerations

You designate a maximum block length in the file DCL entry BLKSIZE, and the system fits as many records into this block length as possible. For example, in Figure 24–6, the block length may have been defined as (maximum) 900. If it were defined as 800, only the first two records would fit in this block, and the system would begin the next block with the third record. The actual block length and number of records per block will vary depending on the lengths of the records.

Although the system performs most of the processing required for variable-length records, you must provide the record length. PL/I handles both the record control word and the block control word.

The program in Figure 24–7 creates a disk file of variable-length records. Each input record contains customer number, customer name, address, and city in conventional fixed-length format. The program inserts an asterisk (*) delimiter at the immediate end of name, address, and city and compresses them to variable length as follows:

Fixed-length:

| JL BROWN   2765 BEACH AVE.   SPRINGFIELD, ORE. |

Variable-length:

| JL BROWN*2765 BEACH AVE.*SPRINGFIELD, ORE.* |

The output record, RECOUT, is defined as 83 characters long, whereas the input record, RECIN, is 80 characters long. The length of 83 is the maximum possible length to accommodate the three asterisks, although most records will be shorter.

The program writes the variable-length records onto a disk file named WRKOUT1, which has the following attributes:

VB	VB defines variable-length blocked record format.
RECSIZE(RECLEN)	At the time of compilation, the length of each record is unknown. The program calculates and stores each record length in a variable named RECLEN (any valid PL/I name). When the program writes a record, the system uses the length in RECLEN to determine the length of the record. A variable used for the RECSIZE attribute must contain the attributes BINARY FIXED (31) STATIC.
BLKSIZE(440)	The value in BLKSIZE includes the lengths of records in the block plus four bytes for the block control word. In this program, the number 440 is arbitrary; the system stores as many variable-length records as possible in a block of this length before writing the entire block onto disk. The file DCL attribute for variable unblocked under the Optimizing complier is V BLKSIZE(n) or V RECSIZE(n).

After writing all records onto disk, the program then reads and prints the contents of the disk file. This procedure is done to check the validity of the stored records and does not suggest that this is otherwise a normal practice. DOS PL/I requires separate definitions of the input and output disk files with separate DLBL/EXTENT job statements. OS PL/I permits you to declare one file that you OPEN as OUTPUT for writing, CLOSE, and OPEN as INPUT for reading.

Job control for variable-length records is identical to that for fixed-length records. Also, you may encounter programs that use the VARYING attribute to handle variable-length records.

DEBUGGING TIPS

- Ensure that the record length and blocking factor are the same for all programs that process a tape or disk file.

```
PROG24C:
    PROCEDURE OPTIONS(MAIN) ;

DCL      SYSIN    FILE STREAM INPUT ENV ( BUFFERS(2) ) ;
DCL      SYSPRINT FILE STREAM PRINT ENV ( BUFFERS(2 ) ) ;
DCL      WRKOUT1 FILE RECORD OUTPUT ENV( MEDIUM(SYS033,3350)
                     VB RECSIZE(RECLEN) BLKSIZE(440) ) ;
DCL      WRKIN1  FILE RECORD  INPUT ENV( MEDIUM(SYS033,3350)
                     VB RECSIZE (087)    BLKSIZE(440) ) ;
DEFAULT  RANGE(*) STATIC ;

DCL      RECIN              CHAR(80) ;
DCL 1    RECDEF             DEFINED RECIN,
         3 CUSTNOIN         CHAR(05),
         3 NAMEIN           CHAR(25),
         3 ADR1IN           CHAR(25),
         3 ADR2IN           CHAR(25);

DCL 1    RECOUT,
         3 CUSTNOUT         CHAR(05),
         3 NAMADDOUT        CHAR(78) ;

DCL      RECLEN             BIN FIXED(31) INIT (0),
         (K, J)             BIN FIXED(15) ;
DCL      EOF                BIT (01)       INIT('0'B) ;
DCL      SUBSTR             BUILTIN ;
```

```
/*  CREATE VARIABLE-LENGTH RECORDS, WRITE ON DISK  */

        ON ENDFILE(SYSIN) EOF = '1'B ;
        OPEN FILE(SYSIN),
             FILE(SYSPRINT),
             FILE(WRKOUT1) ;
        GET EDIT (RECIN) (A(80)) ;
        DO WHILE (¬EOF) ;
             CALL B100_CREATE;
             GET EDIT (RECIN) (A(80)) ;
        END ;
        CLOSE FILE(SYSIN),
             FILE(WRKOUT1) ;
        OPEN FILE(WRKIN1) ;
        CALL P100_PRINT;
        CLOSE FILE(WRKIN1) ,
             FILE(SYSPRINT) ;
        SIGNAL FINISH;
```

FIGURE 24-7 Creating Variable-length Records.

```
B100_CREATE: PROCEDURE;
         CUSTNOUT = CUSTNOIN ;
         NAMADDOUT = ' ' ;
         DO K = 25 TO 1 BY -1 ;
            IF SUBSTR(NAMEIN,K,1) ¬= ' ' THEN LEAVE ;
       . END ;
         SUBSTR(NAMADDOUT,1,K+1) = SUBSTR(NAMEIN,1,K)||'*';

         J = K + 2 ;
         DO K = 25 TO 1 BY -1 ;
            IF SUBSTR(ADR1IN,K,1) ¬= ' ' THEN LEAVE ;
         END ;
         SUBSTR(NAMADDOUT,J,K+1) = SUBSTR(ADR1IN,1,K)||'*';

         J = J + K + 1 ;
         DO K = 25 TO 1 BY -1 ;
            IF SUBSTR(ADR2IN,K,1) ¬= ' ' THEN LEAVE ;
         END ;

         SUBSTR(NAMADDOUT,J,K+1) = SUBSTR(ADR2IN,1,K)||'*';
         RECLEN = J + K ;
         WRITE FILE(WRKOUT1) FROM (RECOUT) ;
      END B100_CREATE;

   /* READ & PRINT VARIABLE-LENGTH RECORDS     */
   P100_PRINT: PROCEDURE;
         EOF = '0'B ;
         ON ENDFILE(WRKIN1) EOF = '1'B ;
         READ FILE(WRKIN1) INTO (RECOUT) ;
         DO WHILE (¬EOF) ;
              PUT SKIP LIST (RECOUT) ;
              READ FILE(WRKIN1) INTO (RECOUT) ;
         END ;
      END P100_PRINT;
      END PROG24C ;
```

Fixed-length input:-

```
00275HP ALDRICH            426 W. BROADWAY ST.     RESTON, VA
01547AL BROOKER            1427 LAKE BOULEVARD     SPRINGFIELD, MO
23658RP MIDDLETON          R.R. 205                CLEVEDALE, WY
02995JR HUGHES             425-2637 N. CARRINGTON STELLIOT LAKE, FLA
```

Variable-length output:-

```
00275          HP ALDRICH*426 W. BROADWAY ST.*RESTON, VA*
01547          AL BROOKER*1427 LAKE BOULEVARD*SPRINGFIELD, MO*
23658          RP MIDDLETON*R.R. 205*CLEVEDALE, WY*
02995          JR HUGHES*425-2637 N. CARRINGTON ST*ELLIOT LAKE, FLA*
```

FIGURE 24-7 (cont.)

- Check the record length carefully. Decimal Fixed variables are packed two digits per byte, plus sign. Accordingly, a 1-digit field requires one byte, 2- and 3-digit fields require two bytes, 4- and 5-digit fields require three bytes and so on.

- Ensure that binary and floating-point fields defined in records have the UNALIGNED attribute to prevent the compiler from erroneously aligning them in storage.

- Records with a large blocking factor may require considerable main storage for buffers. For example, if records are 800 bytes long and the blocking factor is 10, a buffer requires 8,000 bytes of storage. It may be preferable to designate only one buffer.

- For variable-length records, calculate the length as a BINARY FIXED (31) STATIC value. If you use the VARYING attribute and have to redefine it, provide for the 2-byte length preceding the VARYING character string, as follows:

```
DCL    VARFLD   CHAR(50)  VARYING ;
DCL 1 VARSTR   DEFINED VARFLD,
      2 LENFLD BIN FIXED (15)  UNALIGNED,
      2 RECFLD CHAR(50);
```

PROBLEMS

24–1.   What are the major uses of magnetic tape?

24–2.   Distinguish between a record and a block.

24–3.   What indicates the beginning and the end of a block of data on tape?

24–4.   Code a program to create a tape file. Customer input records are on cards, with the following fields:

COL.		COL.		
1–3	Branch number	35–40	Current amount due	(XXXX.XX)
4–8	Customer number	41–46	31–60 days due	(XXXX.XX)
9–28	Customer name	47–52	61–90 days due	(XXXX.XX)
31–34	Credit limit (no cents)	53–58	Over 90 days due	(XXXX.XX)

Amount fields are for balances owed, aged by month. Store arithmetic fields on the tape record in Decimal Fixed format. Ensure that records are in ascending sequence by customer number. Accumulate and print total amounts owed.

24–5.   Code a program to print the contents of the tape file created in Problem 24–4. Format the print area for clarity, allowing for decimal points and negative current amount owed (caused by overpayments). Show with asterisks any customer whose total amount owed (current, 31, 61, plus over 90) exceeds the credit limit.

24–6. What advantage does disk storage have compared with magnetic tape?

24–7. What is a *cylinder*?

24–8. Determine the method of disk storage in your system.

   (a) If the disk devices store records by track and cylinder as do many IBM devices, determine the number of bytes that one track and one cylinder can contain.

   (b) If the devices store data by sectors, determine the amount of storage in one sector and the entire disk.

24–9. Revise problem 24–4 so that the output is on disk.

24–10. Code a program to age customer balances. Disk records are those created by the previous problem, in sequence of customer number.

   At the end of each month, the program has to "age" each customer's balances. (Subsequently during the month, another program updates the balances by adding sales to current due and deducting payments from the oldest balance(s)—see problem 25–6.) For each customer, age balances as follows:

   • Add 61–90 to over 90.
   • Move 31–60 to 61–90.

   Move current due only if positive to 31–60 and clear current due. Negative balances are not aged. Accordingly, the current due field will now contain either zero or negative balances. For example:

	CURRENT DUE	31–60	61–90	OVER 90
Before aging:	$50	$75	$45	$20
After aging:	0	50	75	65

   Write a new aged master file. Suggestion: To check the contents of output records, also print each record's contents.

24–11. What is the advantage of using variable length records?

24–12. Revise the program in Figure 24–7: change the routine at the end that reads and prints the variable-length records in order to print the name, street, and city separately (without the asterisk delimiters) beginning in columns 25, 49, and 73 respectively. Hint: INDEX and SUBSTR could be useful.

CHAPTER 25

FILE MERGING AND UPDATING

OBJECTIVE:
To cover the logic and programming for merging
and updating files.

INTRODUCTION

Most computer systems have disk storage or tape or both. Such systems do not need to merge master and transaction records into the same file. The computer can read the tape or disk files from different input devices. This capability simplifies the system but complicates programming. Fortunately, there is a standard strategy in flowcharting multiple inputs regardless of the number of input files.

The standard procedure for processing more than one input is called the *balance line method.* The initial step is to read the first record of each file and determine which record has the lowest control field (some call this *low key*). The program then processes the file or files with the low control field.

There are two basic approaches to processing multiple inputs: *file merging* and *file updating.* Typically, a merge combines several transaction files into one file, whereas an update applies transaction records against a master file.

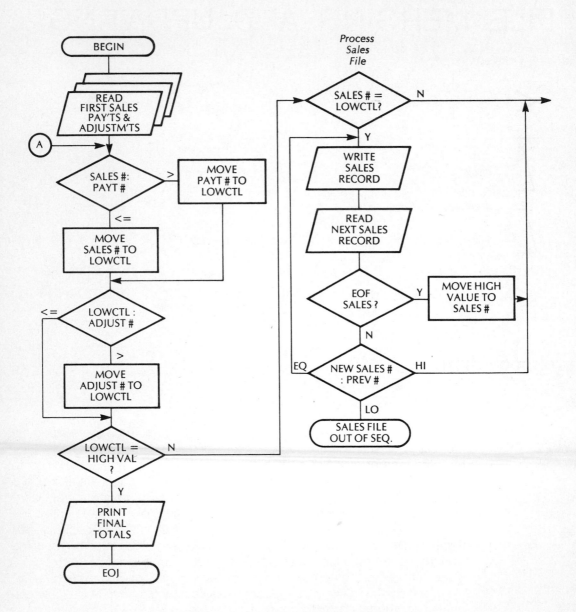

434

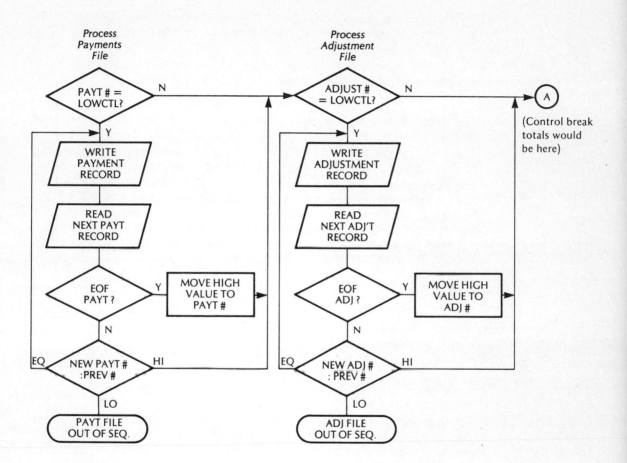

FIGURE 25-1 Balance Line Method—Merging Three Input Files.

FILE MERGING

The flowchart in Figure 25–1 *merges* three transaction input files (Customer Sales, Payments, and Adjustments) into one output file. In this case, each file is in ascending sequence by customer, with any number of transactions for a customer. Any file can contain the lowest control field at any time. Note the following after the program reads the first record of each file (at BEGIN):

1. The program selects the lowest customer number from among the three files and stores the number in a field called LOWCTL.
2. The program checks if LOWCTL contains the highest possible value. This check is an end-of-job test, explained in steps 4 and 6.
3. The program then checks the Sales file, the Payment file, and the Adjustment file in turn and processes the file whose customer number equals LOWCTL. (One, two, or all three files could equal LOWCTL.) If a file's customer number is equal to LOWCTL, its record is written on an output tape or disk file, and the next input record for that file is read and checked for sequence. Each record when read is sequenced against the previously processed record for the file:

LOW	Out of sequence customer, error (not shown in detail on the flowchart).
EQUAL	Same customer number—write the record.
HIGH	Go to process the next file.

4. If a read operation encounters an end-of-file, the program assigns the computer's HIGH value into its customer number field. This procedure is to prevent the program from attempting to read another record for that file. But the program must continue processing the other files not at end-of-file.
5. After reading and writing all the records for a customer, the program then returns to step 1 to determine which file now has the lowest customer number.
6. Each input file that reaches an end-of-file stores the HIGH value in its customer number. Once all files reach their end, each will contain the HIGH value. When this occurs, the comparison for the "lowest" customer number in step 1 will result in storing this HIGH value in LOWCTL; at this point step 2 discovers that all files have been read and processed. You can then print any final totals and terminate the run.

The balance line method works equally well for more than three inputs. For each additional file, simply insert another test to find the "low" control word, and one more vertical column to process the file. The input files may be on any combination of tape or disk devices.

PROGRAM: FILE MERGE

The flowchart is conventional and should be treated as illustrative of the approach to solving a typical merge problem in any language. The example program in Figure 25–2 depicts merging two input files into one output file. It uses the flowchart as a guide, with some adaptations for structured programming conventions. The two disk files, PAYTIN and SALEIN, merge into one output disk file, TRANOUT. The merge is based on the Customer number in the first seven positions of each record:

COMPARISON	ACTION
Payment Customer lower	Write the Payment record, read next Payment record.
Sales Customer lower	Write the Sales record, read next Sales record.
Payment and Sales equal	Write the Payment first, read next Payment. Write Sales when Payment becomes higher.

The program assigns HIGH(7) into the control field of a file that reaches ON ENDFILE, and when both files contain HIGH(7) as their last record, the program terminates. On IBM computers, the HIGH built-in function returns all 1-bits, or hex 'F's, to the receiving string. In this case, the receiving string attribute is CHAR(7).

FILE UPDATING

Quite often, one input file is a master file and the others are transactions, and a program has to *update* the master file balances with the current transactions. The logic requires that there must be only one record for each master, but none or any number for the transactions. Also, the lowest control word must be that of the master file, otherwise a transaction has no matching master to update. The solution is similar to that for merging files, but with several important differences.

```
1    PROG25A: PROCEDURE OPTIONS(MAIN);

2    DCL      PAYTIN  FILE RECORD INPUT ENV(MEDIUM(SYS016,3350)
                      FB RECSIZE(100) BLKSIZE(1000) ),
                      SALEIN  FILE RECORD INPUT ENV(MEDIUM(SYS017,3350)
                      FB RECSIZE(100) BLKSIZE(1000) ),
                      TRANOUT FILE RECORD OUTPUT ENV(MEDIUM(SYS018,3350)
                      FB RECSIZE(100) BLKSIZE(1600) );

3    DCL 1    PAYTRECIN,                              /* PAYT INPUT AREA    */
              2 PAYCTLIN          CHAR(07),           /* PAYT CTL KEY       */
              2 FILLER            CHAR(93);           /* UNUSED PART OF RECORD*/

4    DCL 1    SALERECIN,                              /* SALE INPUT AREA    */
              2 SALCTLIN          CHAR(07),           /* SALE CTL KEY       */
              2 FILLER            CHAR(93);           /* UNUSED PART OF RECORD*/

5    DCL 1    TRANRECOUT,                             /* OUTPUT RECORD AREA */
              2 TRACTLOT          CHAR(07),           /* TRAN'N CTL KEY     */
              2 FILLER            CHAR(93);           /* UNUSED PART OF RECORD*/

6    DCL      LOW_CTL_KEY         CHAR(7);            /* AREA FOR SELECTED LOW*/
                                                      /*    CTL KEY         */

     /*       M A I N   P R O C E S S I N G                                 */
7            OPEN FILE(PAYTIN), FILE(SALEIN), FILE(TRANOUT);
8            ON ENDFILE(PAYTIN) PAYCTLIN = HIGH(7);
9            ON ENDFILE(SALEIN) SALCTLIN = HIGH(7);

10           READ FILE(PAYTIN) INTO (PAYTRECIN);/* INITIAL READ PAYT       */
11           READ FILE(SALEIN) INTO (SALERECIN);/* INITIAL READ SALE       */

12           IF PAYCTLIN <= SALCTLIN             /* PAYT LOWER CTL KEY ? */
               THEN LOW_CTL_KEY = PAYCTLIN;      /*  YES- STORE PAYT KEY */
13             ELSE LOW_CTL_KEY = SALCTLIN;      /*  NO - STORE SALE KEY */

14           DO WHILE(LOW_CTL_KEY ¬= HIGH(7));   /* READ & PROCESS FILES */
15             CALL B000_PROCESS;                /* UNTIL BOTH REACH END */
16           END;

17           CLOSE FILE(PAYTIN), FILE(SALEIN), FILE(TRANOUT);
18           SIGNAL FINISH;

     /*       S E L E C T   &   W R I T E   L O W   R E C O R D            */

19   B000_PROCESS: PROCEDURE;
20           IF PAYCTLIN = LOW_CTL_KEY               /* PAYT LOWER CTL KEY ? */
               THEN DO;
21                   TRANRECOUT = PAYTRECIN;    /*  YES- MOVE PAYT TO OP*/
22                   READ FILE(PAYTIN) INTO (PAYTRECIN);
23                 END;
24             ELSE DO;
25                   TRANRECOUT = SALERECIN;    /*  NO - MOVE SALE TO OP*/
26                   READ FILE(SALEIN) INTO (SALERECIN);
27                 END;                          /* WRITE SELECTED RECORD*/
28           WRITE FILE(TRANOUT) FROM (TRANRECOUT);

29           IF PAYCTLIN <= SALCTLIN             /* PAYT LOWER CTL KEY ? */
               THEN LOW_CTL_KEY = PAYCTLIN;      /*  YES- STORE PAYT KEY */
30             ELSE LOW_CTL_KEY = SALCTLIN;      /*  NO - STORE SALE KEY */
31       END B000_PROCESS;

32       END PROG25A;
```

FIGURE 25–2 Merging Files.

438

Figure 25–3 illustrates a program that updates an Inventory Master file with two transaction files: Stock Receipt records and Stock Issues. Restrictions regarding this inventory file update are (1) There is only one Master File record for each Stock Item; (2) There may be none or any number of Receipts and Issues for a Stock Item; and (3) Each file is in Stock Item sequence.

The flowchart logic is as follows:

1. At the start, the program reads the first record for each input file.
2. The program determines which file has the lowest Stock number and stores it in LOWCTL, as before. In this problem, the Master file must contain every valid Stock number. The Master, therefore, must be equal to or lower than Receipts or Issues Stock numbers.
3. The contents of LOWCTL are tested for the HIGH value, as in the previous flowchart. At this point, LOWCTL contains the low Stock number (the Master's).
4. The flowchart proceeds to the next column to process the Master file. The program stores the various fields of the Master record and sets up the output record for the new Master file.
5. The next Master is then read. If it is at the end-of-file, the program stores the HIGH value into the input Master Stock number. This procedure prevents the program from attempting to read more Master records. If not the end-of-file, the new Master just read is compared to the previous Master Stock number. In this problem it must be *higher;* low and equal conditions are errors.
6. The flowchart now goes to the next column to process the *Receipts* file. The Receipts Stock number is compared to LOWCTL, the current lowest Stock number. The Receipts should not be low. If high, then there are no Receipts for this Stock, and the program goes to process Issues (in the next column).
7. If Receipts Stock number equals LOWCTL, the program adds the Receipt quantity to the stored Master quantity and to total receipts. The next Receipt record is then read. If at the end-of-file, the program stores HIGH value into the input Receipt Stock number.
8. If not the end-of-file, the new Receipt Stock number just read is compared to the previous Receipt. A low comparison is an out-of-sequence error. Equal means that this new record is for the same Stock number; the program branches back to process the record (step 7) and to read the next Receipt. A high comparison means that this record is for a higher Stock number; the program goes to the next column to process the *Issues* file.
9. Processing of Issues is similar to that for Receipts. At the end-of-file, the program stores the HIGH value into the input Issues Stock number.
10. After processing all Issues for the Stock Item, the program proceeds to the next column to check the sequence of the output and to write the new updated Inventory Master record. This procedure could also perform a control break and print totals on Branch or Region number, as required. The program returns to the beginning (step 2) to test and process the newly read records.

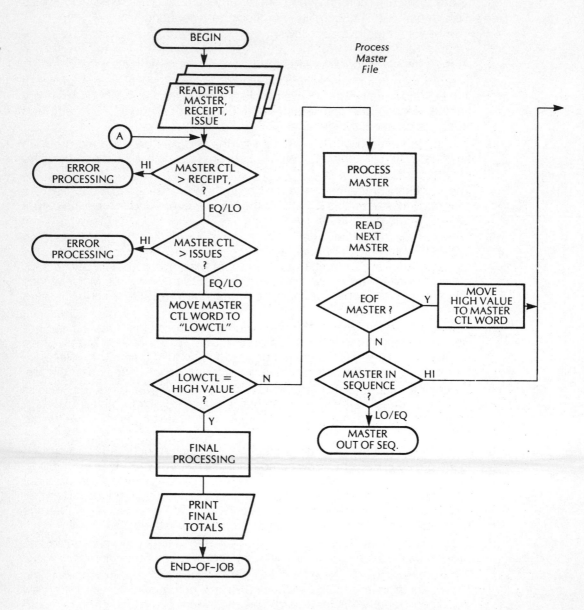

Process Master File

440

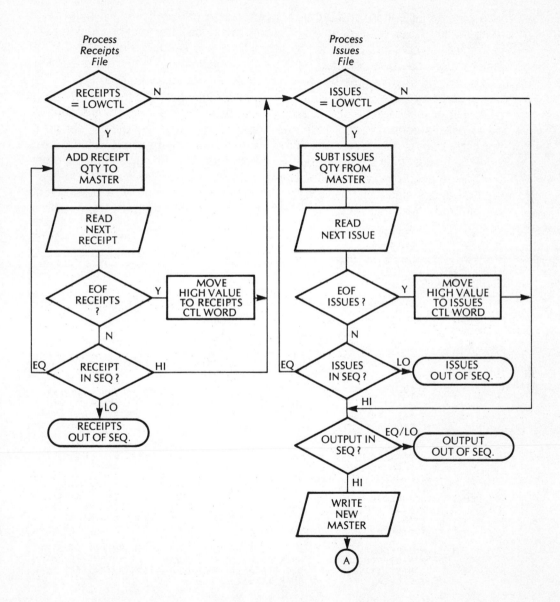

FIGURE 25–3 Balance Line Method—File Updating.

Mismatched Transactions

It is a common situation for a program to encounter transactions for which there are no Master records. The causes of such mismatched transactions include (1) the transaction contains an incorrect control field, such as Stock number; (2) the Master record has been deleted because it is obsolete; and (3) the transaction is for a new Stock Item, but the Master record has not yet been entered.

In some systems, the decision is to reject the mismatched transactions and print an error message. In other cases, the decision is to accept the transaction and to use its control field(s) (such as Branch and Stock number) to set up a temporary *dummy* Master record. In this case, any one of the input files (Master, Receipts, Issues) may contain the low Stock number, and the flowchart logic must be modified accordingly. Note: The dummy Master is written as a new "updated" Master, but contains a special code to indicate that it is a dummy. A subsequent program may overwrite the dummy with the correct data record or may delete the dummy if necessary.

```
1    PROG25B:
        PROCEDURE OPTIONS(MAIN) ;

2    DCL      MASTIN FILE RECORD INPUT  ENV(MEDIUM(SYS015,3350) FB
                         RECSIZE(150) BLKSIZE(750) ),
             TRANIN FILE RECORD INPUT  ENV(MEDIUM(SYS018,3350) FB
                         RECSIZE(100) BLKSIZE(1000)),
             ADJTIN FILE RECORD INPUT  ENV(MEDIUM(SYS019,3350) FB
                         RECSIZE(100) BLKSIZE(1000)),
             MASOUT FILE RECORD OUTPUT ENV(MEDIUM(SYS015,3350) FB
                         RECSIZE(150) BLKSIZE(750) );

3    DCL 1    MASTRECIN ,                              /* MASTER INPUT AREA*/
             2 MAST_CTL_IN        CHAR (7) ,          /* MASTER CTL KEY   */
             2 MAST_AMT_IN        DEC FIXED (7,2),    /* MASTER AMOUNT    */
             2 FILLER             CHAR (139);

4    DCL 1    TRANRECIN,                               /* TRAN'N INPUT AREA*/
             2 TRAN_CTL_IN        CHAR (7),           /* TRAN'N CTL KEY   */
             2 TRAN_AMT_IN        DEC FIXED (7,2),    /* TRAN'N AMOUNT    */
             2 FILLER             CHAR (89) ;

5    DCL 1    ADJURECIN,                               /* ADJUST INPUT AREA*/
             2 ADJU_CTL_IN        CHAR (7),           /* ADJUST CTL KEY   */
             2 ADJU_AMT_IN        DEC FIXED (7,2),    /* ADJUST AMOUNT    */
             2 FILLER             CHAR (89);

6    DCL 1    MASTRECOUT,                              /*MASTER OUTPUT AREA*/
             2 MAST_CTL_OUT       CHAR (7),           /*MASTER OUTPUT KEY */
             2 MAST_AMT_OUT       DEC FIXED (7,2),    /*MASTER OUTPUT AMT */
             2 FILLER             CHAR (139);

7    DCL      LOW_CTL_KEY         CHAR (7);
8    DCL      HIGH                BUILTIN ;
```

FIGURE 25-4 Updating a File.

```
    /*        M A I N   P R O C E S S I N G                     */

 9          OPEN  FILE(MASTIN),
                  FILE(TRANIN),
                  FILE(ADJTIN),
                  FILE(MASOUT) ;
10          ON ENDFILE(MASTIN) MAST_CTL_IN = HIGH(7) ;
11          ON ENDFILE(TRANIN) TRAN_CTL_IN = HIGH(7) ;
12          ON ENDFILE(ADJTIN) ADJU_CTL_IN = HIGH(7) ;
13          READ FILE(MASTIN) INTO (MASTRECIN);
14          READ FILE(TRANIN) INTO (TRANRECIN);        /* INITIAL READS   */
15          READ FILE(ADJTIN) INTO (ADJURECIN);
16          CALL C000_SELECT_LOW;                      /*CHECK FOR LOW KEY */

17          DO WHILE(LOW_CTL_KEY ¬= HIGH(7));          /*READ & PROCESS    */
18            CALL B000_PROCESS;                       /*UNTIL ALL AT END  */
19          END;

20          CLOSE FILE(MASTIN),
                  FILE(MASOUT),
                  FILE(TRANIN),
                  FILE(ADJTIN) ;
21          SIGNAL FINISH;

    /*        P R O C E S S   &   R E A D   F I L E S            */

22   B000_PROCESS: PROCEDURE;
23          MASTRECOUT = MASTRECIN;                    /*MOVE MASTER TO OP */
24          READ FILE(MASTIN) INTO (MASTRECIN);

25          DO WHILE(TRAN_CTL_IN = LOW_CTL_KEY);       /*PROCESS EQ TRANSNS*/
26            MAST_AMT_OUT = MAST_AMT_OUT + TRAN_AMT_IN;
27            READ FILE(TRANIN) INTO (TRANRECIN);
28          END;
29          DO WHILE(ADJU_CTL_IN = LOW_CTL_KEY);       /*PROCESS EQ ADJUSTS*/
30            MAST_AMT_OUT = MAST_AMT_OUT + ADJU_AMT_IN;
31            READ FILE(ADJTIN) INTO (ADJURECIN);
32          END;

33          WRITE FILE(MASOUT) FROM (MASTRECOUT);      /*WRITE UPDATED MAST*/
34          CALL C000_SELECT_LOW;                      /*CHECK FOR LOW KEY*/
35          END B000_PROCESS;

    /*        C H E C K   F O R   L O W   K E Y                  */

36   C000_SELECT_LOW: PROCEDURE;
37          IF MAST_CTL_IN <= TRAN_CTL_IN & MAST_CTL_IN <= ADJU_CTL_IN
                THEN LOW_CTL_KEY = MAST_CTL_IN;        /*MASTER IS LOW KEY */
38            ELSE DO;
                  /* MISSING MASTER - PRINT MESSAGE, TERMINATE RUN       */
39                END;
40          END C000_SELECT_LOW;

41      END PROG25B ;
```

FIGURE 25–4 (cont.)

PROGRAM: FILE UPDATE

Figure 25–4 illustrates a program that updates a Master file with two files, Transactions and Adjustments (the Transaction file is the one created in the previous example). The program reads the Master and transfers its contents to an output area. For Transaction and Adjustment records with the same control key as the Master, the amount (TRAN_AMT_IN and ADJU_AMT_IN) is added to the Master amount (MAST_AMT_OUT).

COMPARISON	ACTION
Master Customer equal/lower	Move Master record to output, read next Master.
Transaction or Adjustment lower	Error, missing Master—run is terminated (detailed coding omitted for brevity).
Transaction or Adjustment equal to Master	Add input amount to Master output.

The solution also uses the Balance Line Method and is similar to the previous example. However, whereas the previous program may have a low Customer number in either control key, in this example the Master must always contain the low key.

Note that on the input/output records the amount fields are defined as DEC FIXED, so that the program can perform arithmetic directly on the fields. The only complication in the program is handling transactions for which no master record exists. The program bypasses such unmatched transactions and prints a warning message. There is also a special test to ensure that there are no transactions still left unprocessed after the master file has reached end-of-file.

DEBUGGING TIPS

Clearing a Record

It is sometimes necessary to clear an output record area; character fields should be blank, and arithmetic fields should be zero. A null string can perform this clearing. In the following, assume that RECORDAREA is a level-1 structure that contains character and arithmetic elements:

RECORDAREA = ''; (no blank between the apostrophes)

Testing Multiple Inputs—Something to Ponder

A program with multiple inputs often involves complex logic. Assume that you want to continue processing until both files, FILEA and FILEB, reach end-of-file. There are two end-of-file bit indicators, EOFA and EOFB, respectively for the files. A DO WHILE statement requires the "not" operator. Which of the following is the correct logic,

DO WHILE (¬ EOFA & ¬ EOFB) or DO WHILE (¬ EOFA | ¬ EOFB) ?

Since processing must continue until *both* files are ended, many people would reply that the first example is correct. However, because the question was worded using "until" instead of "while," the logic could be recast using DO UNTIL:

DO UNTIL (EOFA & EOFB)

Since DO UNTIL is opposite to DO WHILE, DeMorgan's Rule prevails: EOFA and EOFB become respectively ¬ EOFA and ¬ EOFB, and the logical operator & becomes |. The second DO WHILE is the correct answer. You can check the logic by supplying EOFA and EOFB with all four combinations of 0 and 1: 0 and 0, 0 and 1, 1 and 0, and 1 and 1. The DO loop should terminate only when both EOFA and EOFB are 1.

PROBLEMS

25–1. What is the standard method for processing more than one input file in a program?

25–2. In what way can updating a disk master file differ from updating a tape master file?

25–3. Draw the flowchart to merge four disk files into one. The four files contain customer transactions for week 1, week 2, week 3, and week 4. The control field is customer number. For each customer, merge the transactions for week 1 ahead of week 2, week 2 ahead of week 3, and so on.

25–4. Code the program for the preceding problem. Record format is as follows:

COL.	
1–2	Record code
3–7	Customer number
8–13	Date
14–19	Amount of transaction ($\pm$)
20–25	Unused

Each file contains transactions with code 15 for payments and 16 for sales. Assume any suitable blocking factor.

25–5. In what particular way does a file update differ from a file merge?

25–6. Code the program that updates customers' aged balances with sales and payments. The customer master file is the one created in problem 24–9 and aged in 24–10. Input is in sequence of customer number.

The program applies sales and payments to the master file. The transaction file contains any number of (or no) transactions per customer. The format is as follows:

COL.	
1	Transaction code
2–4	Branch number
5–9	Customer number
10–15	Transaction date
16–21	Source document code
22–27	Amount of transaction ($\pm$)

Transaction codes are 'S' for sales and 'P' for payments. On the master, only the current balance may be negative because of overpayments. Transaction amounts may be negative because of correcting entries and NSF checks. For sales, add sales amounts to the master current due. If a payment is negative, subtract it from current due. If the payment is positive, subtract from the oldest balance first. For example:

	CURRENT DUE	31–60	61–90	OVER 90
Before payment:	$25	$30	$25	0
After payment of $50:	25	5	0	0

Normally, such a program would write a new updated customer master file. For this program, print the updated balances and detail for each customer, including total owed by customer. "Flag" any customer whose total owed exceeds credit limit. Print final totals of all customer balances.

CHAPTER 26

VIRTUAL STORAGE ACCESS METHOD—VSAM

OBJECTIVE:

To examine the Virtual Storage Access Method and its programming requirements.

INTRODUCTION

Sequential processing involves reading each record from a file successively. In many cases, however, there are a number of reasons why a more efficient processing is direct (or random) accessing of records. For example, there may be relatively few records in a file to update. Or, the transactions may be in unsorted sequence. Also, an online system may require that remote terminals have direct and immediate access to any record in the file.

The methods that permit direct accessing are Virtual Storage Access Method (VSAM), covered in this chapter, Indexed Sequential Access Method, covered in Chapter 27, and Regional file organization, covered in Chapter 28. (PL/C does not support these file organization methods.)

Virtual Storage Access Method (VSAM) is a relatively recent file organization method for users of IBM OS/VS and DOS/VS. VSAM facilitates both sequential and direct processing and is more efficient and simpler to understand than Indexed Sequential (ISAM). When referencing VSAM files, IBM literature uses the term *data set* instead of file. The term *file* is somewhat ambiguous since it may mean a device or the records that a device processes. This chapter uses the term data set.

There are three types of VSAM data sets:

1.   *Key-Sequenced data set.* Records are in sequence by key (such as employee or part number). This type, the most commonly used, is covered in detail in this chapter.
2.   *Entry-Sequenced data set.* Records are in sequence by which they were entered.
3.   *Relative Record data set.* Records are in order of relative record number.

These organizations are roughly equivalent to, respectively, INDEXED (Indexed Sequential), CONSECUTIVE (Sequential), and REGIONAL(1) (Direct). An advantage of VSAM is data security: a program may be required to supply a correct password to access the data set.

CONTROL INTERVAL

Regardless of the type of data set, VSAM stores records in groups (one or more) in *control intervals.* The user may select the control interval size, but if VSAM does, it optimizes the size based on record length and the type of disk device to be used. The maximum size is 32,768 bytes. A convenient size would be the length of a track, although VSAM is not dependent on the disk storage device.

At the end of each control interval is control information that describes the data records:

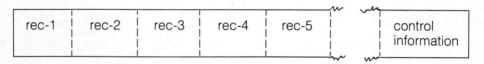

FIGURE 26–1 VSAM Control Interval.

VSAM addresses a data record by its displacement in bytes from the beginning of the data set—the *relative byte address (RBA).* Thus, the first record in the data set is at RBA zero, and if records are 200 bytes long, the second is at RBA 200.

KEY-SEQUENCED DATA SETS

A control interval contains one or more data records. (Technically, an extremely large record could spread across more than one control interval, a "spanned record.") A specified number of control intervals comprises a control area. Figure 26–2 depicts a simplified overview of a Key-Sequenced data set organization.

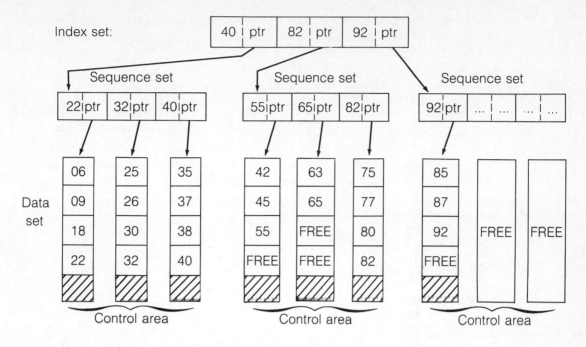

FIGURE 26–2 Key-sequenced Organization.

In Figure 26–2, the control intervals that contain the data records are shown vertically, and three control intervals comprise a control area. A *sequence set* contains an entry for each control interval in a control area. Entries in a sequence set consist of the highest key for each control interval and the address of the control interval; the address acts as a pointer to the beginning of the control interval. In Figure 26–2, the highest keys for the first control area are respectively 22, 32, and 40. VSAM stores these high keys as well as an address pointer in the sequence set for the first control area.

At a higher level, an *index set* (various levels depending on the size of the data set) contains high keys and address pointers of sequence sets. In Figure 26–2, the highest key for the first control area is 40. VSAM stores this value and an address pointer for the first sequence set in the index set.

If a program wants to directly access a record in the data set, VSAM locates the record by means of the index set and the sequence set. For example, a program requests record key 63. VSAM first checks the index set as follows:

RECORD KEY		INDEX SET	
63	:	40	Record key is high, not in first control area.
63	:	82	Record key is low, in second control area.

VSAM has determined that key 63 is in the second control area. It next examines the sequence set for the second control area to locate the correct control interval as follows:

RECORD KEY		SEQUENCE SET	
63	:	55	Record key is high, not in first control interval.
63	:	65	Record key is low, in second control interval.

VSAM has determined that key 63 is in the second control interval of the second control area. The address pointer in the sequence set directs VSAM to the correct control interval. VSAM then reads the keys of the data set and locates key 63 as the first record which it delivers to the program.

Free Space

When creating a Key Sequenced data set, you can tell VSAM to allocate free space in two ways:

1. Leave space at the end of each control interval, or
2. Leave some control intervals vacant.

If a program deletes or shortens a record, VSAM reclaims the space by shifting to the left all following records in the control interval. If the program adds or lengthens a record, VSAM inserts the record in its correct space and moves to the right all following records in the control interval. VSAM updates RBA's and indexes accordingly.

Control Interval Splits

Perhaps you wondered what would happen if the control interval did not contain enough free space for the inserted record. Assume the following four control intervals in a control area:

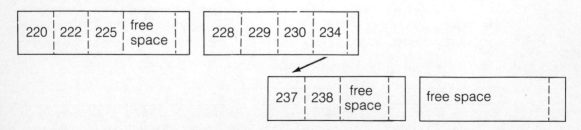

The program now has to insert a new record with key 233. Because there is insufficient space in the control interval, VSAM causes a *control interval split:*

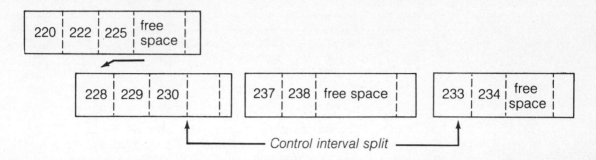

Control interval split

VSAM removes about half the records to a vacant control interval in the same control area. Although records are now no longer precisely in key order, the updated sequence set index controls the sequence for retrieval.

What if there is no vacant control interval in the control area? VSAM causes a *control area split,* using free space outside the control area.

Under normal conditions, such a split will seldom occur. In fact, a VSAM data set is to a large degree self-organizing and does not require reorganization as often as an ISAM file.

ACCESS METHOD SERVICES (AMS)

Before you physically write records in a VSAM data set, you must catalog its structure. IBM supplies a program package, Access Method Services (AMS), that enables you to supply such details to VSAM as the name of the data set, record length, block length, and password. Since VSAM will subsequently know the physical characteristics of the data set, the ENV option of the file DCL statement normally needs to contain only ENV(VSAM).

The following is a brief description of the more important features of AMS. Full details are in the *IBM OS and DOS PL/I Programmer's Guide* and in the IBM AMS manual. You catalog a VSAM structure using a program named IDCAMS, as follows:

```
OS:    //STEP EXEC PGM = IDCAMS
DOS:   // EXEC IDCAMS,SIZE = AUTO
```

Immediately following the above statement are the various entries that define the data set. The first statement, DEFINE CLUSTER, provides the various required and optional entries in parentheses. A hyphen follows each entry to indicate continuation; the last entry has no hyphen following.

```
DEFINE CLUSTER (NAME(data-set-name) -
   VOLUME(volume-serial-number) -
   INDEXED/NONINDEXED/NUMBERED -
   KEY(length offset) -
   RECSIZE(average maximum) -
   password options) -
   DATA (TRACKS/CYLINDERS/RECORDS (prime-alloc second-alloc)) -
   INDEX (TRACKS (prime-alloc second alloc)) -
CATALOG (cat-name/password)
```

- DEFINE CLUSTER provides the various definitions, all in parentheses; in this example from NAME through "password options." The word CLUSTER implies more than one component: a data component and an index component.
- NAME provides the name of the data set, up to 44 characters with a period for each eight characters or less, for example, (EMPLOYEE.WAGE.V255). The first character following a period must be a letter, @, or #. The name will correspond to the OS DD entry or DOS DLBL entry:

```
OS:     //FILEVS DD DSNAME = EMPLOYEE.WAGE.V255, etc.
DOS:    // DLBL FILEVS,'EMPLOYEE.WAGE.V255',0,VSAM
```

The name FILEVS is whatever name that you assign to the DCL for the VSAM data set in your program, such as

```
DCL FILEVS FILE RECORD . . . ENV(VSAM);
```

- VOLUME designates the name of the DASD volume(s) where the data set is to reside.
- INDEXED defines a Key-Sequenced data set, NONINDEXED defines an Entry-Sequenced data set, and NUMBERED defines a Relative Record data set. (The default is INDEXED.)
- KEY specifies the length and position for a key for Key-Sequenced. For example, KEY(7 0) indicates a key that is 7 characters long and begins in position zero (the first byte) of the record. Note that a blank separates the entries for length and position.
- RECSIZE provides the size of records in terms of average size and maximum size. For fixed-length records, the two entries are identical, as RECSIZE (150 150).
- DATA defines the amount of disk space for the data set. TRACKS, CYLINDERS, or RECORDS reserves space that you can allocate according to number of tracks, cylinders (not if 3370 DASD), or records. You indicate a *primary allocation* and a *secondary allocation.* For example, TRACKS (50 25) notifies VSAM to allocate 50 tracks for the data set; when the 50 tracks are filled, VSAM is to allocate 25 more tracks.
- INDEX allocates primary and secondary storage for a Key-Sequenced index set.
- CATALOG stipulates the disk address where the data set is to be stored.

An explanation of other DEFINE items is in the PL/I Programmers' Guide and in the Access Method Services manual for your installation.

PROGRAMMING VSAM DATA SETS

Since VSAM entirely handles its indexes and insertion of new records, little added programming effort is involved in the use of a VSAM data set. There are, however, different processing modes that involve special requirements in the declaring of the data set and in the use of READ and WRITE:

- Creating a VSAM data set.
- Sequential reading of a VSAM data set.
- Sequential updating of a VSAM data set.
- Direct retrieval and updating of a VSAM data set.

The programming differences between one mode and another are usually minor, but critical.

File Declare Statement

The basic file declare statement for VSAM data sets is as follows:

```
                              | SEQUENTIAL | INPUT
DCL filename FILE RECORD       |            | OUTPUT      [KEYED] ENV(VSAM);
                              | DIRECT     | UPDATE
```

The two options SEQUENTIAL and DIRECT indicate the *processing* mode. For example, you normally create a VSAM data set sequentially, but may update it sequentially or directly (if Key-Sequenced).

The options INPUT, OUTPUT, and UPDATE depend on how the VSAM data set is to be used:

- INPUT: The program is to read the data set only.
- OUTPUT: For SEQUENTIAL only, the program is to create the data set or is to insert new records only.
- UPDATE: The program is to use the data set as *both* input and output and may change old records or insert new records.

The KEYED option is used when a READ or WRITE statement contains any of the options KEY, KEYTO, or KEYFROM. The use of DIRECT implies KEYED.

Under OS, you may code various attributes in the OPEN statement for the data set, as

```
OPEN FILE (filename) INPUT DIRECT . . . ;
```

ENVIRONMENT Options.   Since a VSAM data set is preformatted by Access Method Services, the only required entry in the ENV clause is ENV(VSAM). Other options include the following:

```
ENV(VSAM PASSWORD ('password') |SKIP|  REUSE BUFND GENKEY);
                                |SIS |
```

VSAM Input/Output Statements

The basic READ and WRITE statements for VSAM are

```
READ FILE(filename) INTO (inarea) [KEY(key)];
WRITE FILE(filename) FROM (outarea) KEYFROM (key);
```

In addition, VSAM requires a REWRITE statement for UPDATE files. For SEQUENTIAL processing, REWRITE causes the last record that was read to be rewritten. For DIRECT processing, you may REWRITE any record directly (provided that it exists) using the KEY option. The basic REWRITE statement is as follows:

```
REWRITE FILE(filename) FROM (area) [KEY (key)];
```

Other READ, WRITE, and REWRITE options include SET, EVENT, and IGNORE.

Deleting Records

PL/I has a DELETE statement used to delete unwanted records from a Key-Sequenced data set. The file DCL must contain the UPDATE attribute. The format for DELETE is as follows:

```
DELETE FILE(filename) [KEY (key)];
```

For SEQUENTIAL UPDATE, you may omit the KEY option; VSAM then deletes the last record that was read. For DIRECT UPDATE, the KEY option is required.

ON KEY Conditions

Invalid READ, WRITE, REWRITE, and DELETE operations can raise the KEY condition. The system stores a value in ONCODE to indicate the cause of the error. Some possibilities include the following:

51	Key specified cannot be found.
55	Invalid key.
56	Key is outside the limits of the data set (READ).
57	No space available to add a record.
58	Key is outside the limits of the data set (WRITE).

Also, codes 92 and 93 are concerned with errors on opening and closing a VSAM data set.

CREATING A KEY-SEQUENCED DATA SET

After using Access Method Services to format a Key-Sequenced data set (KSDS), you may write records to create the data set. Input records should be in ascending sequence by control field (key), and all keys are normally unique. The file DCL statement should specify SEQUENTIAL, OUTPUT, and KEYED.

The program in Figure 26–3 creates a VSAM data set of customer records. The WRITE statement uses the KEYFROM option to notify VSAM of the location of the key, since VSAM requires the keys in order to establish its indexes.

SEQUENTIAL READING OF A KEY-SEQUENCED DATA SET

For ordinary sequential reading, the file DCL statement does not need to indicate KEYED. The DCL could be coded as follows:

```
DCL filename FILE RECORD SEQUENTIAL INPUT ENV (VSAM);
```

The READ statement is conventional:

```
READ FILE(filename) into (inarea);
```

```
PROG26A:
     PROCEDURE OPTIONS(MAIN) ;

DCL      FILEIN FILE RECORD  INPUT
                             ENV( MEDIUM(SYSIPT)
                                  F
                                  RECSIZE(80)
                                  BUFFERS(02) ) ;
DCL      FILEVS FILE RECORD  SEQUENTIAL
                             OUTPUT
                             KEYED
                             ENV (VSAM ) ;

DCL    1 RECORDIN,
          3 CUSTIN            CHAR (05) ,
          3 NAMEIN            CHAR (22) ,
          3 FILLER           CHAR (03) ,
          3 BALANIN          PIC '9999V9R',
          3 CRLIMIN          PIC '9999',
          3 UNUSED           CHAR (40) ;

DCL    1 RECORDVS,
          3 CUSTVS            CHAR (05) ,
          3 NAMEVS           CHAR (22),
          3 BALANVS          DEC FIXED (7,2),
          3 CRLIMVS          DEC FIXED (5,0),
          3 UNUSED           CHAR (06) INIT (' ') ;

DCL      EOF                 BIT (1) INIT ('0'B) ;

         ON ENDFILE(FILEIN) EOF = '1'B ;
         OPEN FILE(FILEIN),
              FILE(FILEVS) ;
         READ  FILE(FILEIN) INTO (RECORDIN) ;

         DO UNTIL (EOF) ;
             CUSTVS  = CUSTIN ;
             NAMEVS  = NAMEIN ;
             BALANVS = BALANIN ;
             CRLIMVS = CRLIMIN ;
             WRITE FILE(FILEVS) FROM (RECORDVS) KEYFROM (CUSTVS);
             READ FILE(FILEIN) INTO (RECORDIN) ;
         END ;

         CLOSE FILE(FILEIN),
               FILE(FILEVS) ;
         SIGNAL FINISH ;
     END PROG26A ;
```

FIGURE 26–3 Creating a Key-sequenced Data Set.

In order to begin reading at a particular key, use the KEY option in a READ statement as

```
READ FILE(filename) INTO (inarea) KEY (key);
```

The file DCL must then include the KEYED attribute. The key may be a variable or a character-string. You may then continue processing using a READ with no KEY option.

SEQUENTIAL UPDATING OF A KEY-SEQUENCED DATA SET

If there are many transactions that are to update a VSAM data set, it may be more efficient to sort them and then perform a sequential update (rather than a direct update). The file DCL is as follows:

```
DCL filename FILE RECORD SEQUENTIAL UPDATE [KEYED] ENV (VSAM);
```

You can both READ and REWRITE records as

```
READ FILE(filename) INTO (inarea);
REWRITE FILE(filename) FROM (area);
```

In order to REWRITE a record, you must first READ it. You may change any field in the record except its key before you REWRITE the record.

You may also begin reading at a particular key using the KEY option in a READ, as described in the previous section.

DIRECT UPDATING OF A KEY-SEQUENCED DATA SET

A main purpose of defining a Key-sequenced data set is to facilitate direct processing of records. The file DCL should be as follows:

```
DCL filename FILE RECORD DIRECT UPDATE KEYED ENV (VSAM);
```

The statements to READ (random retrieval), WRITE (add a new record), and REWRITE (change a stored record) are as follows:

```
READ FILE(filename) INTO (inarea) KEY (key);
WRITE FILE(filename) FROM (outarea) KEYFROM (key);
REWRITE FILE(filename) FROM (area) KEY (key);
```

```
PROG26B:
     PROCEDURE OPTIONS(MAIN) ;

DCL      FILEIN FILE RECORD  INPUT
                             ENV( MEDIUM(SYSIPT)
                                      F
                                      RECSIZE(80)
                                      BUFFERS(02) ) ;
DCL      FILEVS FILE RECORD  DIRECT
                             UPDATE
                             KEYED
                             ENV( VSAM ) ;
DCL      FILEV2 FILE RECORD  SEQUENTIAL
                             INPUT
                             KEYED
                             ENV( VSAM ) ;


DCL 1    RECORDIN,
         3 CODEIN            CHAR (01),
         3 CUSTIN            CHAR (05),
         3 NAMEIN            CHAR (22),
         3 FILLER1           CHAR (03),
         3 BALANIN           PIC '9999V9R',
         3 CRLIMIN           PIC '9999',
         3 FILLIN            CHAR (39) ;

DCL 1    RECORDVS,
         3 CUSTVS            CHAR (05),
         3 NAMEVS            CHAR (22),
         3 BALANVS           DEC FIXED (7,2),
         3 CRLIMVS           DEC FIXED (5,0),
         3 FILLVS            CHAR (06) INIT (' ') ;

DCL      ONCODE             BUILTIN ;
DCL      EOF                BIT (01) INIT ('0'B) ;

         ON KEY(FILEVS)
           BEGIN ;
             SELECT(ONCODE) ;
                  WHEN (51) PUT SKIP LIST ('NOT FOUND', CUSTIN) ;
                  WHEN (52) PUT SKIP LIST ('DUPLICATE', CUSTIN) ;
                  OTHERWISE PUT SKIP LIST ('ONCODE =' , ONCODE,
                                                       CUSTIN) ;
             END ;
           END ;

         /*  M A I N  L O G I C    */
         CALL A100_UPDATE ;
         CALL B100_PRINT ;
         SIGNAL FINISH ;
```

FIGURE 26-4 Direct Updating of a Key-sequenced Data Set.

```
            /*  U P D A T E   O F   D A T A   S E T  */
A100_UPDATE:
    PROCEDURE ;
        OPEN FILE(FILEIN),
             FILE(FILEVS) ;
        ON ENDFILE(FILEIN) EOF = '1'B ;
        READ  FILE(FILEIN) INTO (RECORDIN) ;

A200:   DO UNTIL (EOF) ;
            CUSTVS  = CUSTIN ;
            NAMEVS  = NAMEIN ;
            BALANVS = BALANIN ;
            CRLIMVS = CRLIMIN ;
A300:       SELECT(CODEIN) ;
                WHEN ('A')
                    WRITE FILE(FILEVS) FROM (RECORDVS)
                        KEYFROM (CUSTVS) ;
                WHEN ('C')
                    REWRITE FILE(FILEVS) FROM (RECORDVS)
                        KEY (CUSTVS) ;
                WHEN ('D')
                    DELETE FILE(FILEVS) KEY (CUSTVS) ;
                OTHERWISE PUT SKIP LIST ('INVALID CODE', CUSTIN);
            END A300 ;
            READ FILE(FILEIN) INTO (RECORDIN) ;
        END A200 ;

        CLOSE FILE(FILEIN),
              FILE(FILEVS) ;
    END A100_UPDATE ;

            /*  P R I N T O U T   O F   D A T A   S E T  */
B100_PRINT:
    PROCEDURE ;
        EOF = '0'B ;
        ON ENDFILE(FILEV2) EOF = '1'B ;
        OPEN FILE(FILEV2) ;
        READ FILE(FILEV2) INTO (RECORDVS) ;

B200:   DO UNTIL(EOF) ;
            PUT SKIP LIST (RECORDVS) ;
            READ FILE(FILEV2) INTO (RECORDVS) ;
        END B200 ;

        CLOSE FILE(FILEV2) ;
    END B100_PRINT ;

    END PROG26B ;
```

Updated output:-

Cust. No.	Cust. Name	Balance	Cr.Limit
00688	ANDERSON, AL	567.20	3500
00752	HOWIE, RH	95.60	1200
05248	SMITH, BP	55.00	1000
10254	SANDERSON, DG	68.94	500
12544	POLLARD, BJ	250.25	1500
15324	BROWN, JL	752.36	1500

FIGURE 26–4 (cont.)

For most updating, you normally READ directly, change the required record fields (but not the key), and then REWRITE the record. REWRITE must contain a KEY clause.

If a program is to READ directly only (and not update), code the file DCL as INPUT instead of UPDATE. The READ statement is otherwise identical. Remember that OS permits attributes such as INPUT and DIRECT in the OPEN statement.

The program in Figure 26–4 uses a *transaction file* to update the Key-sequenced data set created in the previous example. The program provides for three types of changes according to a code in the transaction records:

1. A—Add the transaction record (a new customer record) to the data set.
2. C—Change a present VSAM record according to the contents of the transaction record.
3. D—Delete a present record in the data set.

The program ensures that the transaction code is valid and tests for the common ON KEY conditions; any ON KEY condition not tested for will cause the ONCODE to print.

ENTRY-SEQUENCED AND RELATIVE RECORD DATA SETS

These VSAM organization methods have more specialized uses than Key-Sequenced. The following is a list comparing the three types:

FEATURE	KEY-SEQUENCED	ENTRY-SEQUENCED	RELATIVE RECORD
Record Sequence	By key.	In sequence in which entered.	In sequence of relative record number.
Record Length	Fixed or Variable.	Fixed or Variable.	Fixed length only.
Access of Records	By key through index or RBA.	By RBA.	By relative record number.
Change of Address	Can change record RBA.	Cannot change record's RBA.	Cannot change relative record number.
New Records	Distributed free space for new records.	Space at end of data set for new records.	Empty slots in data set for new records.
Recovery of Space	Reclaims space if record deleted.	Does not delete, but can overwrite a new record over old.	Can reuse deleted space.

PROCESSING ENTRY-SEQUENCED DATA SETS

An Entry-Sequenced data set (ESDS) acts like a Consecutive (Sequential) data set but has the advantages of being under control of VSAM, password facilities, and some use of keys. Basically, the data set is in the sequence in which it is written, and normal processing involves conventional READ and WRITE statements with no KEY option. You can cause ESDS to provide keyed access to the data set—see the *IBM PL/I Reference Manual* for this feature.

File Creation

For creation of an ESDS, the file DCL and the WRITE are conventional:

```
DCL filename FILE RECORD SEQUENTIAL OUTPUT ENV(VSAM);
WRITE FILE(filename) FROM (outarea);
```

Sequential Reading

For sequential reading of an ESDS, VSAM delivers records one at a time in the sequence in which they were originally written regardless of any "key" that you may think they have. The file DCL and the READ for reading ESDS sequentially are

```
DCL filename FILE RECORD SEQUENTIAL INPUT ENV(VSAM);
READ FILE(filename) INTO (inarea);
```

Sequential Updating

You may update an ESDS sequentially; the following file DCL applies:

```
DCL filename FILE RECORD SEQUENTIAL UPDATE ENV(VSAM);
```

The READ and WRITE statements do not involve a KEY option. WRITE stores a new record at the end of the data set. A REWRITE statement needs no KEY option; it replaces the record that the previous READ accessed. There is no DELETE statement.

PROCESSING RELATIVE RECORD DATA SETS

File Creation

For creation of a Relative Record data set, the file DCL contains the attributes SEQUENTIAL or DIRECT, and OUTPUT. For SEQUENTIAL, the WRITE statement may omit the KEYFROM option in order to WRITE records consecutively. For DIRECT, the WRITE contains KEYFROM to indicate the key in the data set.

Sequential Access

The file DCL contains the attributes SEQUENTIAL, INPUT or UPDATE, and KEYED (if you use the KEY, KEYTO, or KEYFROM options).

If a READ has no KEY option, the system delivers records in ascending relative record number (key). If a READ contains the KEY option, the system delivers the specified record; you could then code succeeding READ statements with no KEY to read sequentially from that point.

If a WRITE has no KEYFROM option, the system writes at the next data set position (relative to the current position), which must be empty. If a WRITE has a KEYFROM option, the program can insert a record anywhere in the data set, but only where there is an empty position.

REWRITE permits revision of actual records according to the usual REWRITE rules (see Key-sequenced). The DELETE statement is used to delete records from the data set.

Direct Access

For DIRECT access, the file DCL contains the attributes DIRECT, KEYED, and INPUT or OUTPUT or UPDATE. Processing statements are similar to those for SEQUENTIAL access.

VSAM SORT

You can sort a VSAM data set into another sequence, such as descending sequence of employee salaries. SORT writes the sorted data set into a vacant VSAM area that must be already formatted by DEFINE CLUSTER. A typical SORT specification follows:

1.   // EXEC SORT,SIZE = 64K

2.   SORT FIELDS = (1,5,CH,A,9,4,PD,D)
3.   RECORD TYPE = F,LENGTH = (150)
4.   INPFIL VSAM
5.   OUTFIL ESDS
6.   END
7.   /*

- Statement 1 is a DOS statement that causes the SORT program to execute.
- Statement 2 specifies the fields to be sorted. The major sort field begins in position 1 (RBA zero under VSAM) and is five bytes long in character (CH) format to be sorted in ascending (A) sequence. The minor sort field begins in position nine and is four bytes long in packed (PD) format to be sorted in descending (D) sequence.
- Statement 3 indicates record type (fixed-length) and record length (150 bytes).
- Statement 4 informs SORT that the input file is VSAM; SORT can determine the type of data set from VSAM itself.
- Statement 5 defines the type of output file; in this case Entry-Sequenced. (This entry should match the DEFINE CLUSTER for this data set: NONIN-DEXED.)

Job control statements for SORTIN and SORTOUT provide the data-set-names. Job control for SORT varies by operating system and by installation; check with your installation before attempting the SORT utility.

VSAM UTILITY PRINT

IDCAMS provides a convenient utility program that can print the contents of a VSAM data set. The following illustrates:

```
OS:   //STEP EXEC PGM = IDCAMS or DOS: // EXEC IDCAMS,SIZE = 64K
         PRINT INFILE(filename) CHARACTER or HEX or DUMP
      /*
```

The options for PRINT are CHARACTER to print the contents in character format, HEX to print the contents in hexadecimal format, and DUMP (the standard default) to print hexadecimal format on the left and character format on the right. Hexadecimal format is useful because it can represent the contents of packed and binary fields.

INFILE(filename) matches the name in the OS DD job statement or the DOS DLBL statement, with any valid name such as FILEVS as long as the two are identical. The data-set-name in the DD or DLBL statement tells IDCAMS which data set to print.

DEBUGGING TIPS

Errors occur in processing VSAM data sets because of the need to match the program, job control, and defined VSAM area.

- If fixed-length, the record length that a program defines must be the same as the RECSIZE entry in the DEFINE CLUSTER.
- For Key - sequenced, the length and starting position of the key in a record must agree with the KEY entry in the DEFINE CLUSTER.
- The name of the DCL data set in the program (such as FILEVS) must agree with the name in job control: the name given in the DD statement (OS) or in the DLBL statement (DOS).
- The data-set-name in the job control (such as CUSTOMER.INQUIRY.XRQ) must agree with the NAME(data-set-name) entry in the DEFINE CLUSTER. This name is the only one by which VSAM recognizes the data set. VSAM relates the file DCL name in the program to the job control name, the job control name to the data-set-name in the job control, and the data-set-name in job control to the VSAM data set, as follows:

```
File declarative:    DCL FILEVS FILE . . . ENV (VSAM);
Job control:         FILEVS . . . CUSTOMER.INQUIRY.XRQ . . .
VSAM data set:                    CUSTOMER. INQUIRY.XRQ
```

- Ensure that every program that references the data set defines the fields with similar formats and lengths in the same positions; the actual field names need not be identical. Technically, you can define as CHARACTER any input field(s) in a record that the program does not need to reference. The simplest practice is to catalog all record definitions in the source library and use %INCLUDE to copy the definition into the program during compilation.
- During testing, you may have changed the contents of a VSAM data set and now want to reload (recreate) the original data set. Except for updating with new keys, VSAM does not permit you to WRITE records into a data set that contains records. You have to use IDCAMS to DELETE and reDEFINE the entire data set as follows:

```
DELETE (data-set-name) CLUSTER PURGE CATALOG(disk-name)
DEFINE CLUSTER (NAME(data-set-name) -
    etc . . .
```

PROBLEMS

26–1. What is a control interval?

26–2. A VSAM program is required to insert a new record, key 532, but there is insufficient space in the following control interval:

/ 527 / 529 / 558 / 562 /

How does VSAM handle this situation?

26–3. What does VSAM do if there is no vacant control interval in a control area?

26–4. Create a Key-Sequenced data set using the same record format and requirements as the tape file in Problem 24–4.

26–5. Randomly update the VSAM data set created in Problem 26–4 using the sales records in Problem 25–6.

26–6. Print the contents of the VSAM data set in Problem 26–5. Allow for editing of decimal point and possible negative amount owed. Print a total for the customer amount owed field.

CHAPTER 27

INDEXED SEQUENTIAL ACCESS METHOD—ISAM

OBJECTIVE:

To examine the Indexed Sequential Access Method and its programming requirements.

INTRODUCTION

Indexed Sequential Access Method (ISAM) is an older file organization method. IBM no longer supports ISAM on some systems and is gradually replacing it with VSAM. This text covers ISAM because older IBM systems still support it and because many other manufacturers use ISAM extensively. (PL/C does not support ISAM.)

Indexed Sequential Access Method provides the benefits of both sequential and direct processing. Whereas sequential processing requires the program to read every record consecutively, direct processing enables the program to access any record in the file more or less directly.

There is a distinct difference between updating a file sequentially and updating a file directly. A sequential update rewrites the entire file. Although this feature involves more disk space and possibly more I/O operations, it does leave the original file as a convenient "backup" file in case the job must be rerun. A direct update rewrites records directly in place, thereby providing no automatic backup. A user of the system must provide backups by periodically copying the file onto tape or another disk area.

The flexibility of Indexed Sequential Access Method has a price in both storage space and accessing time. First, the system requires various levels of indexes to locate records randomly. Second, because the system does not rewrite the entire file when updating records, it stores new records in special reserved overflow areas.

INDEXED SEQUENTIAL CHARACTERISTICS

Under ISAM, records are stored sequentially (at least initially) and can be accessed sequentially or directly. The features that provide this flexibility are indexes to locate the correct cylinder and track, and keys to locate the record on the track.

Keys

ISAM writes each record with a *key* preceding each block. The key is the record control field, such as employee number or inventory stock number, which the system uses to locate a record directly. Records are arranged in order of key to permit sequential processing. A READ operation reads the data block, not the key, into main storage. For unblocked records, the key may or may not be embedded within the data record. It usually is, however, because most programs need the key for processing (such as printing the employee number). For blocked records, the key preceding the block is the key number of the last record in the block, as shown in Figure 27–1. Each blocked record must contain an embedded key because a READ operation must be able to locate a specific record within the block.

Indexes

ISAM maintains *indexes* on the disk to facilitate the locating of records directly. There are three levels of indexes: The track index, the cylinder index, and optionally a master index.

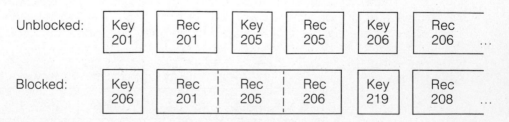

FIGURE 27–1 Keys for Unblocked and Blocked Records.

The Track Index.   When ISAM creates a file, it stores a track index in track-0 of each cylinder that the file uses. The track index contains the highest key number for each track on the cylinder. For example, if a DASD has ten tracks per cylinder, then there are ten key entries for each track index, in ascending sequence.

The Cylinder Index.   When creating a file, ISAM stores a cylinder index on a separate cylinder. The cylinder index contains the highest key number for each cylinder. For example, assume a program has as its key a stock number stored in a declarative called STOCK. The program uses this key to locate a specific inventory stock number on an ISAM file.

The Master Index.   The optional master index is generally used if the cylinder index is so large that it exceeds four cylinders. Its use is to facilitate locating the appropriate cylinder index.

PROCESSING AN ISAM FILE

Let's examine a small indexed file that uses tracks 01, 02, and 03 of cylinder 05. There are five "prime data" records on tracks 01 and 02, and four on track 03. Track 01, for example, contains records with keys 205, 206, 208, 210, and 213.

Track					
01	205	206	208	210	213
02	214	219	220	222	225
03	226	227	230	236	unused

Prime data records on cylinder 05

Track 0 of cylinder 05 contains the track index for the cylinder, with an entry for each track indicating the high key for each track. The first track index entry, for example, specifies that 213 is the highest key on cylinder 05, track 01:

	Key	cyl/tr	Key	cyl/tr	Key	cyl/tr
Track index	213	0501	225	0502	236	0503

The cylinder index contains an entry for each cylinder that contains prime data, indicating the high key for each cylinder. The first (and, in this case, only) cylinder index entry specifies that 236 is the highest key on cylinder 05 (the track number is not important here):

	Key	cyl
Cylinder index	236	0500

If a processing program needed to directly locate a record with key 227, a READ statement would cause the system to perform the following:

1. Checks the cylinder index (assuming no master index) comparing key 227 against the first entry. Since 227 is lower than high key 236 in the entry, the required record should be on cylinder 05.
2. Accesses the track index in cylinder 05, track 00, comparing key 227 successively against each entry: 213 (low), 225 (low), and 236 (high). According to the entry for 236, the required record should be on cylinder 05, track 03.
3. Checks the keys on track 03 where it finds key 227 and delivers the record to the program's input area. If the key (and the record) does not exist, the system raises the KEY condition.

As can be seen, locating a record involves a number of additional processing steps, although there is little extra programming effort. Even more steps are involved if a new record is stored in an "overflow area."

Overflow Areas

When a program first creates a file, ISAM stores the records sequentially in the prime data area. Subsequently, it may be necessary to insert new records into the file. Unlike tape and CONSECUTIVE disk files, ISAM does not need to rewrite the entire file to insert records. Instead, ISAM stores them in an *overflow area* and maintains links to point to these areas. For example, if a record with key 209 is to be added to the file in the previous example, the system "bumps" key 213 into an overflow area, moves 210 into its place, and inserts 209 in the place vacated by 210. The track index is changed to high key 210, with a pointer now to key 213 in the overflow area.

Because there is a limit to the number of records that an overflow area can store, a special program can be used periodically to rewrite ("reorganize") the file into sequence. (This simply involves reading the records sequentially and writing them into another disk area, dropping deleted records.)

There are two types of overflow areas:

1. *Cylinder overflow areas* reserve tracks on a cylinder for all the overflow data that are stored on the specific cylinder. Each cylinder has its own overflow track area. The advantage is less seek time because there is no access motion to find records on a different cylinder. The disadvantage concerns the distribution of overflow records: there may be too many overflow records on one cylinder, and very few on others.
2. *Independent overflow areas* reserve a number of separate cylinders for overflow records. All cylinders in the file use this area for storing overflow records. The advantage is that the distribution of overflow records does not matter. The disadvantage is in additional access time to seek the overflow area.

Many systems adopt both types: the cylinder overflow area for initial overflows, and the independent area in case the cylinder area itself overflows.

PROGRAMMING ISAM FILES

Since ISAM entirely handles the indexes and overflow areas, little added programming effort is involved in the use of indexed files. There are different processing modes that involve special requirements in declaring of the file and in the use of READ and WRITE:

*   Creating an indexed file.
*   Sequential reading of an indexed file.
*   Sequential updating of an indexed file.
*   Direct reading and updating an indexed file.

The programming differences between one mode and another are usually minor but critical and are similar to VSAM.

File Declare Statement

The basic file declare statement for the PL/I Optimizer compiler follows (the declare for other compilers is similar):

```
                              | SEQUENTIAL  | INPUT  |
DCL filename FILE RECORD      |             | OUTPUT |  [KEYED] ENV ( . . . ) ;
                              | DIRECT      | UPDATE |
```

The options SEQUENTIAL and UPDATE indicate the *processing* mode. For example, you normally create an ISAM file sequentially, but update it directly or sequentially. Omission of either entry causes a default to SEQUENTIAL.

The options INPUT, OUTPUT, and UPDATE depend on how the file is to be used:

INPUT:	The program is to read the file only.
OUTPUT:	For SEQUENTIAL only, the program is to create the file or insert new records.
UPDATE:	The program is to use the file as both input and output and may change old records and insert new records.

The KEYED option is used when the READ/WRITE/REWRITE statements contain any of the options KEY, KEYTO, or KEYFROM. The use of DIRECT implies KEYED.

OS allows these options to appear in the OPEN statement.

ENVIRONMENT Options.   Figure 27–2 lists the various ENVIRONMENT options by PL/I version. Following sections explain the options in detail. Entries for DOS PL/I D are identical to the DOS Optimizer except for record format which is coded as

F(blksize[,recsize])

ISAM INPUT/OUTPUT STATEMENTS

The basic READ and WRITE statements for Indexed Sequential files are as follows:

```
READ FILE (filename) INTO (inputarea)      ⎡KEY (key)⎤
                                           ⎣KEYTO    ⎦
WRITE FILE (filename) FROM (outputarea)    [KEYFROM (key)]
```

In addition, ISAM requires a REWRITE statement for UPDATE files. For SEQUENTIAL processing, REWRITE causes the last record read to be rewritten. Between the READ and the REWRITE, no other I/O operation for that file must occur. (For example, a program has read a customer record, update its balance with current sales and payments, and has to REWRITE the new updated record back on disk.) For DIRECT processing, it is permissible to REWRITE any record on the file directly (assuming that it exists) using the KEY option. The basic REWRITE statement is

REWRITE FILE (filename) FROM (recordarea) [KEY(key)] ;

	DOS OPTIMIZER ENV Options	OS PL/I F ENV Options	OS PL/I OPTIMIZER ENV Options	OS Job Control Options
Record Format	F FB BLKSIZE (m) RECSIZE (n)	F (blksize [,recsize]) V (blksize [,recsize])	F FB V VB BLKSIZE (m) RECSIZE (n)	RECFM = F FB V VB BLKSIZE = m LRECL = n
Key Format	KEYLOC (n) KEYLENGTH (n)	GENKEY	KEYLOC (n) KEYLENGTH (n) GENKEY	RKP = n KEYLEN = n
Storage Control	EXTENTNUMBER (n) OFLTRACKS (n)			DD job entry CYLOFL = n OPTCD = Y
Optimization	BUFFERS (n) ADDBUFF (n) INDEXAREA (n) NOWRITE	BUFFERS (n) INDEXAREA (n) NOWRITE	BUFFERS (n) ADDBUFF (n) INDEXAREA (n) NOWRITE	BUFNO = n
Index Control	INDEXMULTIPLE HIGHINDEX (device)			OPTCD = M UNIT = device
Write Verification	VERIFY			OPTCD = W

FIGURE 27–2 ISAM ENVIRONMENT Options by PL/I Version.

472

DELETING RECORDS

OS PL/I has a DELETE statement used to delete records from an ISAM file that has the UPDATE attribute. Its format is

DELETE FILE (filename) [KEY (key)] ;

For SEQUENTIAL UPDATE, you may omit the KEY option; ISAM deletes the last record that was read. For DIRECT UPDATE, the KEY option is required.

Normally, you reserve the first byte of each record as a delete byte. When a program DELETEs a record, ISAM inserts HIGH(1) (or eight '1' bits) into the delete byte. The record remains temporarily intact until the file is *reorganized.*

A program that reads *sequentially* automatically bypasses any record flagged as deleted. A program that reads *directly* delivers a deleted record to the input area; consequently, your program should test the first byte for the delete code:

IF DELETE_CODE = HIGH(1) THEN . . . ;

DOS PL/I does not support the DELETE statement; instead, you must dispose of unwanted records according to installation standards. The common practice is to reserve the first byte of each record (like OS) for a delete byte. To "delete" a record, you could insert HIGH(1) into the delete byte, as follows:

```
IF (record is to be deleted) THEN
   DO;
      DELETE_CODE = HIGH(1);
      REWRITE FILE(FILEIS) FROM (RECORDIS) KEY(CUSTIS);
   END;
```

On a READ, since DOS ISAM delivers a "deleted" record like an actual record, the program must check for the presence of HIGH(1) in the delete byte.

THE KEY CONDITION

A READ statement uses a key to locate an ISAM record directly. Assume that a file name is DISKISQ, the input structure is DISKIN, and a variable STOCK contains the KEY. The READ statement is

READ FILE (DISKISQ) INTO (DISKIN) KEY (STOCK) ;

If the key actually exists on a track, ISAM reads the record into the storage area DISKIN. If the key is not found, the system raises the KEY condition, prints an error message, and terminates processing. Programs using ISAM may provide an ON-unit for the key condition and test the ONCODE, such as the following:

```
ON KEY(DISKISQ)
      BEGIN ;
            IF ONCODE = 51 THEN
                PUT DATA (ONCODE, ONLOC, ONFILE, ONKEY) ;
            ELSE check other ONCODEs . . . ;
      END ;
```

Key condition codes include the following:

51	Key specified cannot be found (READ or REWRITE).
52	An attempt to add a record to a file that already contains the same key (WRITE).
53	During sequential creation of an ISAM File, a key is out of sequence (WRITE).
56	An attempt to access a record using a key that is outside the limits of the file area (READ or REWRITE).
57	No space available to add a keyed record (WRITE).
58	An attempt to write a record outside the limits of the file area (WRITE).

When reading directly, ISAM searches through the indexes to locate the cylinder and the track. The disk system starts at the home address of the track and scans the key that precedes each block. Since the block key is the key of the last record on the block, the system simply has to compare the input key to the block key. If the input key is higher, the system checks the next block key; if the input key is lower, the system reads the entire block into main storage and delivers the record for the requested key to the program. (If no record in the block contains the requested key, the system raises the KEY condition.)

Other READ/WRITE options include SET, EVENT, and IGNORE.

CREATING AN ISAM FILE

For creating an ISAM file, input records must be in ascending sequence by control field (key), and all keys must be unique. The file DCL statement should specify SEQUENTIAL, OUTPUT, and KEYED. The program in Figure 27–3 creates an ISAM file of customer records. Note the following EVIRONMENT attributes:

FB	FB specifies fixed-blocked records. The letter F indicates fixed-unblocked. OS also supports V (variable-unblocked and VB (variable-blocked).
RECSIZE(40)	RECSIZE provides the length of each record.
BLKSIZE(600)	BLKSIZE provides the length of each block and should be a multiple of RECSIZE (in this case 15).
INDEXED	INDEXED signifies Indexed-Sequential File organization.
KEYLOC(2)	KEYLOC is required when you create an ISAM file of blocked records. The key location is the first byte of the embedded key (for example customer number) in the data records. Under DOS, the leftmost byte of a record is numbered 1, and under OS it is 0.
KEYLENGTH(5)	KEYLENGTH provides the length of the key. ISAM requires the location and length of the key in order to insert it separately before each block of records.
EXTENTNUMBER(2)	An ISAM file may be arranged in more than one area (*extent*) on the same disk or on different disks. EXTENTNUMBER for DOS indicates the number of extents that the file uses, including all data area extents and cylinder index extents.
OFLTRACKS(2)	OFLTRACKS stipulates the number of tracks per cylinder that ISAM is to reserve for overflow records. The entry is for output files and is ignored if coded for input files.

Other ENV options for DOS could include BUFFERS(n) to indicate the number of buffers to use (1 or 2), and VERIFY. VERIFY causes the disk system to read and check each record as it is written. The feature provides an additional check on data validity but at a cost of more processing time.

Note in Figure 27–3 that the first byte of the ISAM record is reserved for a delete character which the program initializes to LOW(1). Also, the WRITE statement contains a KEYFROM option to indicate the location of the key for the file. ISAM ensures that records are in ascending sequence (or it raises the KEY condition) and copies the key number of the last record in each block into a key field preceding each block.

SEQUENTIAL READING OF AN ISAM FILE

For ordinary sequential reading, the file DCL does not need to indicate KEYED. DCL entries should be

```
DCL filename FILE RECORD SEQUENTIAL INPUT ENV ( . . .) ;
```

```
1    PROG27A:
        PROCEDURE OPTIONS(MAIN) ;

2    DCL      FILEDK FILE RECORD  INPUT
                                  ENV( MEDIUM(SYS008,3340)
                                  FB
                                  BLKSIZE(600)
                                  RECSIZE(040) ) ;
3    DCL      FILEIS FILE RECORD SEQUENTIAL OUTPUT KEYED
                                  ENV( MEDIUM(SYS008,3340)
                                  FB
                                  RECSIZE(40)
                                  BLKSIZE(600)
                                  INDEXED
                                  KEYLOC(2)
                                  KEYLENGTH(5)
                                  OFLTRACKS(2) ) ;

4    DCL   1 RECORDIN,
              3 CUSTIN          CHAR (05),
              3 RESTIN          CHAR (35);

5    DCL   1 RECORDIS,
              3 DELETIS         CHAR (01),
              3 CUSTIS          CHAR (05),
              3 RESTIS          CHAR (34) ;

6    DCL      EOF              BIT (1) INIT ('0'B) ;
7    DCL      LOW              BUILTIN ;

8             ON ENDFILE(FILEDK) EOF = '1'B ;
9             OPEN  FILE(FILEDK),
                    FILE(FILEIS) ;
10            READ  FILE(FILEDK) INTO (RECORDIN) ;

11            DO UNTIL (EOF) ;
12                 DELETIS = LOW(1) ;
13                 CUSTIS = CUSTIN ;
14                 RESTIS = RESTIN ;
15                 WRITE FILE(FILEIS) FROM (RECORDIS) KEYFROM (CUSTIS);
16                 READ FILE(FILEDK) INTO (RECORDIN) ;
17            END ;

18            CLOSE FILE(FILEDK),
                    FILE(FILEIS) ;
19            SIGNAL FINISH ;
20       END PROG27A ;
```

FIGURE 27–3   Creating an ISAM Data Set.

ENV options may include record format (F/FB/V/VB), RECSIZE, BLKSIZE, IN-DEXED, and BUFFERS(2) for DOS.

The READ statement does not normally indicate any key:

READ (filename) INTO (inputarea) ;

In order to begin reading at a particular key, code KEYED in the file DCL and use the KEY option in the READ:

READ FILE (filename) INTO (inputarea) KEY (key) ;

Continue reading then with a READ that has no KEY option.

SEQUENTIAL UPDATING OF AN ISAM FILE

If there are many transactions that are to update an ISAM file, it may be more efficient to sort them and perform a sequential update. The file DCL is

DCL filename FILE RECORD SEQUENTIAL UPDATE [KEYED] ENV (. . .) ;

You can READ and REWRITE records as

READ FILE (filename) INTO (recordarea) ;
REWRITE FILE (filename) FROM (recordarea) ;

In order to REWRITE a record, you must first READ it. You may change any field in the record except its key. You may also begin reading at a particular key using the KEY option, as described in the previous section.

DIRECT UPDATING OF AN ISAM FILE

The main purpose of organizing a file as Indexed Sequential is to facilitate direct accessing of records. The file DCL statement should be as follows:

DCL filename FILE RECORD DIRECT UPDATE KEYED ENV (. . .) ;

OS assumes UNBUFFERED for DIRECT files because the system cannot overlap processing with input/output. ENV options may include record format (F/FB/V/VB), RECSIZE, BLKSIZE, INDEXED, KEYLOC, KEYLENGTH, ADDBUFF, and INDEX-AREA.

```
1    PROG27B:
         PROCEDURE OPTIONS(MAIN) ;
2    DCL       FILEIN FILE RECORD   INPUT
                                    ENV( MEDIUM(SYSIPT) F
                                         RECSIZE(80)
                                         BUFFERS(02) ) ;

3    DCL       FILEIS FILE RECORD   DIRECT UPDATE KEYED
                                    ENV( FB
                                         MEDIUM(SYS008,3340)
                                         RECSIZE(40)
                                         BLKSIZE(400)
                                         INDEXED
                                         KEYLOC(02)
                                         KEYLENGTH(05)
                                         INDEXAREA(143) ) ;
4    DCL 1     RECORDIN,
               3 CODEIN              CHAR (01),
               3 CUSTIN              CHAR (05),
               3 NAMEIN              CHAR (25),
               3 BALANIN             PIC '9999V9R',
               3 CRLIMIN             PIC '9999',
               3 UNUSED              CHAR (39) ;

5    DCL 1     RECORDIS,
               3 DELETIS             CHAR (01),
               3 CUSTIS              CHAR (05),
               3 NAMEIS              CHAR (25),
               3 BALANIS             DEC FIXED (7,2),
               3 CRLIMIS             DEC FIXED (5,0),
               3 FILLIS              CHAR (03) ;

6    DCL       EOF                   BIT (01) INIT ('0'B) ;
7    DCL       (LOW, ONCODE)         BUILTIN ;

8              ON KEY(FILEIS)
                  BEGIN ;
9                   IF ONCODE = 51 THEN
                          PUT SKIP LIST ('NOT FOUND', CUSTIN) ;
10                  ELSE IF ONCODE = 52  THEN
                          PUT SKIP LIST ('DUPLICATE', CUSTIN) ;
11                  ELSE PUT SKIP LIST ('ONCODE =', ONCODE, CUSTIN) ;
12                END ;

13             OPEN  FILE(FILEIN), FILE(FILEIS);
14             ON ENDFILE(FILEIN) EOF = '1'B ;
15             READ  FILE(FILEIN) INTO (RECORDIN) ;
16             DO UNTIL (EOF) ;
17                 DELETIS = LOW(1) ;
18                 CUSTIS  = CUSTIN ;
19                 NAMEIS  = NAMEIN ;
20                 BALANIS = BALANIN ;
21                 CRLIMIS = CRLIMIN ;
22                 IF CODEIN = 'A' THEN
                          WRITE FILE(FILEIS) FROM (RECORDIS) KEYFROM(CUSTIS);
23                 ELSE IF CODEIN = 'C' THEN
                          REWRITE FILE(FILEIS) FROM (RECORDIS) KEY(CUSTIS) ;
24                 ELSE IF CODEIN = 'D' THEN
                          DELETE FILE(FILEIS) KEY(CUSTIS) ;
25                 ELSE PUT SKIP LIST ('INVALID CODE', CUSTIN) ;
26                 READ FILE(FILEIN) INTO (RECORDIN) ;
27             END ;
28             CLOSE FILE(FILEIN), FILE(FILEIS);
29             SIGNAL FINISH ;
30       END PROG27B ;
```

FIGURE 27–4 Direct Updating of an ISAM Data Set.

ADDBUFF	The ADDBUFF option can be used for efficiency when adding records to an ISAM file. ISAM allocates an area in main storage for shifting records from a track. Under DOS, ADDBUFF(n) indicates the amount of main storage, usually the number of bytes on a track. Under OS, ADDBUFF causes the system to assume the size of the workspace to be equivalent to one disk track.
INDEXAREA	The INDEXAREA option causes the cylinder index (DOS) or the highest index (OS) to be loaded into main storage at execution-time to reduce disk accessing time. Under OS, you may specify the amount of main storage; if omitted, the highest index is stored automatically in main storage. Under DOS, you must specify the amount of storage space as INDEXAREA(n) using the formula

$$n = (m + 3) \text{ (keylength} + 6)$$

where m is the number of index entries. (Since there is one index entry per cylinder of data, m is the number of cylinders of prime data.) For example, assume 10 cylinders and a key length of 5:

$$n = (10 + 3) \times (5 + 6) = 13 \times 11 = 143$$

The statements to READ, WRITE (add a new record), and UPDATE (change a stored record) are as follows:

```
READ FILE (filename) INTO (IOarea) KEY (key) ;
WRITE FILE (filename) FROM (IOarea) KEYFROM (key) ;
REWRITE FILE (filename) FROM (IOarea) KEY (key) ;
```

In order to REWRITE a record, you normally first READ it, change any field in the record except its key, and then REWRITE the record. You must include the KEY option.

If you want the program only to READ directly (and not update), code the file DCL as INPUT instead of UPDATE. The READ is otherwise identical.

The program in Figure 27–4 uses a "transaction file" to update the ISAM file created in the previous example. The program provides for three types of changes according to a code on transaction records:

A	*Add* the transaction record—a new customer record—to the ISAM data set.
C	*Change* a present ISAM record according to the contents of the transaction record.
D	*Delete* a present ISAM record.

The program ensures that the code is valid and tests for the common ON KEY conditions (any ON KEY condition not tested for will cause the program to terminate).

FILE REORGANIZATION

ISAM inserts added records into an overflow area and leaves deleted records in place. As a result, many additions and deletions may cause processing to become inefficient. An installation *reorganizes* ISAM files periodically depending on the amount of changes. One common method is simply to code a program that reads records sequentially and writes them on a separate ISAM output file. Under OS PL/I, sequential reading automatically bypasses deleted records, and ISAM transfers all records from the overflow area into sequence in the new prime data area. Consequently, deleted records are physically dropped, and overflow areas are emptied. Under DOS PL/I, the program must check for the presence of a delete condition and accordingly not WRITE a "deleted" record.

PROBLEMS

27–1. What is the main processing difference between a disk file organized as sequential and a disk file organized as indexed sequential?

27–2. The following block of five records shows the key values only. What is the key that the system stores for the entire block?

/ 842 / 844 / 852 / 853 / 857 /

27–3. Where are the following stored, and what is their purpose?
(a) Track index.
(b) Cylinder index.
(c) Master index.

27–4. Given the following prime data on cylinder 08, show the contents of the track index and the cylinder index:

TRACK	KEYS OF STORED RECORDS				
01	520	543	544	560	565
02	567	568	572	574	578
03	580	584	585	–	–

27–5. Using the stored keys in Problem 27–4, determine the effect on the stored records, the track index, and the cylinder index by adding
(a) first, a record with key 532;
(b) second, a record with key 579.

27–6. Code a program to create an indexed sequential file. Use the same record formats and requirements as in Problem 24–4 in Chapter 24.

27–7. Update the indexed file in Problem 27–6 with sales records as in Problem 25–6. In this case, however, perform *random updating*.

27–8. Code a program to print the contents of the updated file in Problem 27–7 as in Problem 24–5.

CHAPTER 28

REGIONAL FILE ORGANIZATION

OBJECTIVE:

To cover Regional file organization methods and their programming requirements.

INTRODUCTION

Sequential (CONSECUTIVE) and Indexed Sequential files have been the most common file organization methods. VSAM, an IBM method for OS/VS and DOS/VS, is intended to replace Indexed Sequential. Regional files, the topic of this chapter, are less commonly installed, but have some unique uses. Because you may encounter Regional files or have a particular use for one, this text covers them in some detail but does not attempt to be exhaustive. You should also examine the PL/I reference manual for your own installation for other features. (PL/C does not support Regional file organization.)

Regional records are divided into regions each containing one or more records. Each region is numbered in sequence beginning with zero. To retrieve a record, you supply a key containing region number or track number where the program is to begin a search for the record.

Direct access of Regional records is faster than VSAM or ISAM. But since records are not necessarily in sequence, the file does not lend itself to sequential processing. Also, because records are unblocked, disk storage may be inefficient.

Regional files, like ISAM, use two types of keys: A *recorded key* is a character string that immediately precedes each record for identification and has a maximum length of 255 bytes. A *source key* is a character string in a KEY or KEYFROM option of a READ, WRITE, or REWRITE. You notify the system of the length of a key by means of ENV (KEYLENGTH(n) . . .) or by KEYLEN in an OS DD job entry.

The three types of Regional files are

Regional (1)   Relative record organization, formatted *without* keys.
Regional (2)   Relative record organization, formatted *with* keys. (Not in DOS.)
Regional (3)   Relative track organization, a direct file method.

A *relative record* (called a region) is referenced by a number relative to the first record (record number zero) of the file. A *relative track* is a region that is relative to the first track (track number zero) for the file. All three types store records as unblocked, and only Regional(3) may be variable-length.

REGIONAL(1) ORGANIZATION

Regional(1) organization is based on the relative record, is fixed-length, and is formatted without keys. Since there is one record per region, the region number corresponds to the relative position of a record. Applications could include specialized situations such as sales records by month or year, or records by states (where Alabama begins at region zero). The following indicates the disk storage layout:

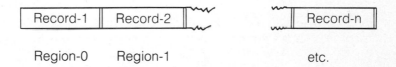

Region-0   Region-1   etc.

Keys

Valid keys contain only the digits 0 through 9 (leading blanks are treated as zeros). The maximum region number (and key) is 16,777,215.

Dummy Records

The system stores a dummy record in each unoccupied region, recognized by HIGH(1) in the first byte of each record.

File Creation

To create a Regional(1) file under DOS, you must *preformat* the disk area with dummy records using a utility program named CLRDSK—see the *DOS PL/I Programmer's Guide*. OS PL/I handles dummy records automatically. You can create a Regional(1) file either sequentially or directly. The file DCL statement is

DCL filename FILE RECORD │ SEQUENTIAL / DIRECT │ OUTPUT KEYED ENV (REGIONAL (1) . . .);

Typically, ENV options include F (for fixed-length unblocked), BLKSIZE(*n*), and RECSIZE(*n*) (where *n* is the same for both). Under OS you may include these options on DD job control.

For SEQUENTIAL output under OS, OPEN causes all tracks to be cleared and establishes a capacity record for each track to indicate available space. Records must be stored in *ascending sequence* by region number. The system fills dummy records if a region is omitted (for example, 1, 2, 3, dummy, 5, 6, . . .), and CLOSE causes unused regions at the end to be filled with dummies.

For DIRECT output under OS, OPEN fills the entire disk area with dummies. Input records may be in random sequence. The WRITE statement would appear as

WRITE FILE(filename) FROM (outarea) KEYFROM(key);

Sequential Access

When processing a Regional(1) file, the system delivers both actual and dummy records. The system could test for a dummy record using a statement such as

IF FIRST_BYTE = HIGH(1) THEN . . . ;

You may declare the file as INPUT or UPDATE, and with KEYED if a WRITE statement uses the KEYTO option, as

DCL filename FILE RECORD SEQUENTIAL │ INPUT / UPDATE │ [KEYED] ENV (REGIONAL(1) . . .);

The following are valid input/output statements for Sequential processing:

```
READ FILE(filename) INTO (inarea);
WRITE FILE(filename) FROM (outarea) [KEYTO(key)];
REWRITE FILE(filename) FROM (area);
```

Direct Access

If you declare a Regional(1) file as DIRECT, you may retrieve, add, delete, and replace records. The file DCL statement is as follows:

DCL filename FILE RECORD DIRECT | INPUT / UPDATE | KEYED ENV (REGIONAL(1) . . .);

Retrieval (READ) reads actual and dummy records. DELETE converts an unwanted record to a dummy. Their formats are

```
READ FILE(filename) INTO (inarea) KEY (key);
REWRITE FILE(filename) FROM (area) KEY (key);
WRITE FILE(filename) FROM (outarea) KEYFROM (key);
DELETE FILE(filename) KEY (key);
```

REGIONAL(2) ORGANIZATION

Regional(2) organization is based on the relative record, is fixed-length un-blocked, and is formatted with keys. You use the region number as a source key to locate a required record. Unlike Regional(1), Regional(2) records are not necessarily in specified regions; a specified region indicates a starting point for a record search. The maximum key value is 16,777,215. The following indicates disk storage layout:

The system automatically fills dummy records in unused regions. A dummy contains HIGH(1) in the first byte of the *key*. A READ operation returns only actual, not dummy, records.

File Creation

You can create a Regional(2) file either sequentially or directly. The system initializes each track with a capacity record to indicate available space. The file DCL statement is

DCL filename FILE RECORD | SEQUENTIAL / DIRECT | OUTPUT KEYED ENV (REGIONAL(2) . . .);

For SEQUENTIAL output, records must be stored in ascending sequence by region. The system fills dummy records if a region is omitted (for example, 1, 2, 3, dummy, 5, 6, . . .). CLOSE causes unused regions at the end to be filled with dummies.

For DIRECT output, OPEN fills the entire disk area with dummies. The system allows random sequence of records and duplicate keys.

Sequential Access

Sequential access is in the physical sequence of records on file, not necessarily in the order that they were added. The file DCL statement appears as

DCL filename FILE RECORD SEQUENTIAL $\left| \begin{array}{l} \text{INPUT} \\ \text{UPDATE} \end{array} \right|$ [KEYED] ENV (REGIONAL(2) . . .);

Direct Access

For processing a Regional(2) file directly, code the file DCL as

DCL filename FILE RECORD DIRECT $\left| \begin{array}{l} \text{INPUT} \\ \text{UPDATE} \end{array} \right|$ KEYED ENV (REGIONAL(2) . . .);

You can perform the following operations:

READ	Retrieves actual (not dummy) records only.
WRITE	Writes a new record on the first dummy on the track for the region.
DELETE	Converts the specified actual record to a dummy.
REWRITE	Allows you to REWRITE only an actual record, not a dummy.

READ, WRITE, DELETE, and REWRITE are used the same for Regional(2) as for Regional(1).

REGIONAL(3) ORGANIZATION

In Regional(3) files (a form of "relative track" organization), the system stores records according to keys. Records are unblocked, formatted with keys, and under OS may be variable-length. Typically, a program uses a *randomizing formula* to perform a computation on the key to determine the relative track (region) that contains the required record. Since a region is an entire track, a region may contain more than one record. The maximum region number is 32,767.

One feature of a Regional(3) file is that the range of possible key values may be greater than the available record spaces on the disk file. For example, a file contains 5,000 records, but the key values range from 01000 through 25000 (24,000 possible keys). A randomizing formula should *compress* the possible disk space (24,000) to an area closer to the space that is actually required (5,000). A common rule of thumb is to select a file space such that the records occupy 80 percent of the allocated space (a *packing factor* of 80 percent). In this case, 5,000 ÷ .80 = 6,250. Consequently, the disk space reserved for the file needs to be large enough for 6,250 records. The randomizing formula has to slot all 5,000 records randomly into this space.

As an example, a file of nine records is to be stored randomly in a disk area large enough for 12 records. The system can store three records on a track, so four regions are reserved: cylinder 08, tracks 00, 01, 02, and 03. The randomizing formula selected divides the key by the number of tracks; the *remainder* can contain only the values 00, 01, 02, and 03. The remainder stipulates the track address (and region) of each record, as follows:

KEY	TRACK (Key ÷ 4, Remainder)
122	02
208	00
269	01
324	00
359	03
366	02
441	01
523	03
622	02

The records are now distributed across the regions quite evenly, as follows:

TRACK (Region)	KEYS
00	208, 324
01	269, 441
02	122, 366, 622 (full)
03	359, 523

A file creation program would insert each record into these regions, and any other program that references the file must use the same formula.

Synonyms

You may have suspected a potential problem in this method: What if there were another record to add with key 374? Key 374 generates a remainder of 02, but region 02 is already full. The result is a *synonym:* there is no space in the region for the record. Technically, any key that generates the same address is a synonym, such as keys 122, 366, and 622 (which all generate region 02). The Regional(3) system will have to insert the record for key 374 into an overflow area.

There are two optional ways to minimize synonyms:

1. Increase the allocated disk space (for example, use a 70 or 60 percent packing factor). The cost of course is more unused disk space.
2. Change the randomizing formula. There is no rule that dictates a precise formula, and you may have to adopt a trial-and-error approach.

The Randomizing Formula

A randomizing formula should have two characteristics:

1. Every possible key must generate an address within the allocated disk space.
2. It should distribute records evenly throughout the regions, with a minimum number of synonyms.

In order to reduce the chances of synonyms, the division/remainder method usually divides the key by the largest *prime number* not greater than the number of regions allocated for the file. (A prime number is evenly divisible only by 1 and by itself, such as 2, 3, 5, 7, 11, and 13.) Therefore, if a file requires 500 regions, then the prime number to divide into each key would be 499.

The randomizing formula generates a relative track (region). Assume that the disk device has 20 tracks per cylinder. Region 02 is on cylinder 00, track 02; and region 22 is on cylinder 01, track 02, and so on. The program provides the region as a relative track, and the system converts the relative track to the actual cylinder/track.

Dummy Records

To indicate a dummy record, the system stores HIGH(1) in the first byte of the key. A READ operation delivers only actual records, not dummies.

File Creation

The file DCL statement used to create a Regional(3) file is as follows:

DCL filename FILE RECORD | SEQUENTIAL
DIRECT | OUTPUT KEYED ENV (REGIONAL(3) . . .);

ENV options could include F for fixed unblocked and KEYLENGTH(n). BLKSIZE and RECSIZE both specify the same size. OS PL/I supports variable-length records (V). Also, you can code these options on an OS DD job statement.

Under OS, the OPEN statement causes all tracks to be cleared and stores a capacity record for each track (region) to indicate available space. Under DOS, you must preformat the disk area with a utility program CLRDSK—see the *DOS PL/I Programmer's Guide.* You can create a Regional(3) file either sequentially or directly.

For SEQUENTIAL create, records must be in ascending sequence, but more than one record can be submitted for the same region number because the system can insert more than one record in a region (depending on the size of the record and of the track).

For DIRECT create, the system first fills the regions with dummies. Records can be in random sequence, and duplicate keys are allowed.

Regional(3) provides an overflow area for records that do not fit in their specified region, with linkages between the region and the overflow location.

Sequential Access

The file DCL statement for Sequential access is as follows:

DCL filename FILE RECORD SEQUENTIAL $\left|\begin{array}{l}\text{INPUT}\\\text{UPDATE}\end{array}\right|$ [KEYED] ENV (REGIONAL(3) . . .)

Processing is according to ascending relative tracks (regions). If the WRITE statement contains the KEYTO option, the DCL statement must contain KEYED.

Direct Access

The file DCL statement for Direct access is as follows:

DCL filename FILE RECORD DIRECT $\left|\begin{array}{l}\text{INPUT}\\\text{UPDATE}\end{array}\right|$ KEYED ENV (REGIONAL(3) . . .);

Direct accessing provides for various options:

Retrieval:	READ actual records only.
Add:	WRITE replaces a dummy record.
Replace:	REWRITE only an actual record, not a dummy.
Delete:	DELETE a specified actual record—converts to a dummy.

READ, WRITE, REWRITE, and DELETE are similar for Regional(1), Regional(2), and Regional(3).

PROBLEMS

28–1. Under what circumstances would you consider using Regional(1) data organization?

28–2. Create a Regional(1) data set from the following input record layout for an employee file. Test the program using records starting with employee 0001 through 0020.

COL.	
1–4	Employee number
5–24	Employee name
25–26	Department code
27	Job category code
28–29	Education code
30–35	Date of birth
36–41	Date hired
42	Marital status code
43	Male/female code

28–3. Write a program to read the file created in Problem 28–2. Print the contents of each record.

28–4. Under what circumstances would you consider using Regional(2) data organization?

28–5. Under what circumstances would you consider using Regional(3) data organization?

28–6. Assume that a file of 6,000 records is to be stored as a Regional(3) data set. The range of keys for the data set is 23000 through 64999 (42,000 possible keys). How much disk space in terms of number of records should be reserved for the data set?

28–7. Refer to the Regional(3) example in this chapter that stored records on tracks 0 through 3. Calculate the track addresses for the following keys and determine if there is any space left on the track: 160, 561, 231, 222.

28–8. What are two ways to reduce the number of synonyms in a Regional(3) data set?

28–9. The division/remainder randomizing formula uses a prime number to divide into the key. What prime number would you use if a data set of 5,000 records were to be stored on 200 tracks? What is the value that results from dividing the prime number into the key?

28–10. Revise Problem 28–2 to create a Regional(3) data set. Assume that there are ten tracks available for storing the data set randomly.

CHAPTER 29

JOB CONTROL AND COMPILER OPTIONS

OBJECTIVE:

To cover the requirements for job control, and compiler options for DOS, OS, and PL/C.

INTRODUCTION

This chapter provides a general description of an operating system, basic job control for DOS and OS, the PROCESS options for the optimizing compilers, the use of the %INCLUDE statement for copying PL/I source code into a program, and PL/C control statements. Enough information is included to enable a reader to handle most conventional situations and to provide insight into more specialized features covered in the appropriate manufacturer's manuals.

OPERATING SYSTEMS

An operating system consists of various interrelated programs that control the computer system. The main programs are Initial Program Load (IPL) and the Supervisor. IPL is used to load the Supervisor from disk into main storage. Frequently used Supervisor routines are stored in fixed locations in lower main storage, whereas less-used Supervisor routines are kept on disk to be loaded (in a transient area in Main Storage) when required. Technically, a computer can execute only one instruction at a time and is executing either in the *Supervisor state* or in the *Problem state* (executing a user program). The Supervisor controls the following functions:

- Which program is to be loaded into Main Storage (Job Management).
- Where each program is to be loaded (Task Management).
- Input/Output processing (Data Management).
- Diagnostic messages and canceling of jobs.

JOB MANAGEMENT

A job is a set of one or more related programs (each program is a *job step*). Particular job control statements control a job and each job step. Job Management loads each program (job step) one at a time into main storage for execution and terminates the job at its end. Job Management loads a program according to what main storage area is available; consequently, programs are *relocatable* and may be loaded into different main storage areas whenever executed.

TASK MANAGEMENT

Whereas the central processing unit executes in terms of microseconds and nanoseconds, input/output devices are relatively slow. The CPU can perform other processing while waiting for an input/output operation to be completed. Consequently, most operating systems provide for *multiprogramming*—processing of more than one program (or task) in main storage at one time. Task Management establishes priorities among tasks and protects the storage area of each task from other tasks.

As an example of multiprogramming, program A, executing in one area of storage, writes data on disk. Task Management can cause an exit from program A and begin processing program B elsewhere in storage. When the write operation for program A is completed, Task Management causes an exit from program B and resumes processing program A.

DATA MANAGEMENT

The part of the Supervisor that handles processing of data between main storage and external devices is Data Management (called Input/Output Control System, IOCS, under DOS). Its functions include blocking and deblocking records, handling variable-length blocks, handling opening and closing of data sets (files), and maintaining the various sequential and nonsequential access methods.

JOB CONTROL LANGUAGE (JCL)

The user of a computer system submits requests for special action by means of *job control language (JCL)*. Job control statements involve such functions as compilation and execution. Each manufacturer provides a job control language unique to its own computer systems. Although the languages are similar conceptually, the specific commands vary considerably. This chapter provides basic job control for the common IBM DOS and OS systems, although even these may vary slightly among installations and according to a particular job to be run. Consequently, this chapter is intended only as a guide; full job control details are available in the manufacturer's Programmer's Guide and job control manuals for your installation.

DOS JOB CONTROL

The three main DOS job statements—JOB, OPTION, and EXEC—all begin with a pair of slashes (//) in columns 1 and 2, followed by at least one blank.

The JOB Statement

The first entry of a job specifies the name of the job:

// JOB jobname

The jobname is 1–8 characters long; the first character must be a letter.

The OPTION Statement

A user indicates various options on an OPTION statement that the job is to perform. Some common PL/I options are as follows:

// OPTION LINK,XREF,PARTDUMP

LINK	Indicates that the compiled program is to be link-edited (see EXEC LNKEDT later); suppress with NOLINK.
XREF	Causes printing of a cross-reference of the symbolic names used in the program (or NOXREF). The Optimizing Compiler handles this option with the PROCESS statement.
PARTDUMP	Prints a hexadecimal dump of the program's partition on an abnormal program termination (DUMP on some systems).

The options may appear in any sequence. If omitted, an option will *default* to a value, depending on the installation. (One typical default would be NOLINK.) Other options for the PL/I Optimizer are available in the PROCESS statement.

The EXEC Statement

EXEC causes the system to load the specified program into main storage for execution. The following statement causes the DOS PL/I Optimizer compiler to begin execution:

// EXEC PLIOPT

To execute a program that has just been compiled and link-edited, omit the operand, as follows:

// EXEC

If there is no operand, the system loads into main storage the last link-edited program in the job stream and begins its execution.

Example. The following is a simple job stream that compiles a PL/I program with no execution. This procedure is useful for a first compilation, when there is a strong possibility of serious errors:

// JOB jobname	Job statement.
// EXEC PLIOPT	Execute the PL/I complier.
(PL/I source program)	
/*	End of the PL/I source program.
/&	End of the job.

Other DOS JCL Statements

Other DOS job control statements include /*, /&, and ACTION.

The /* Statement. A slash/asterisk (/*) in columns 1 and 2 tells the operating system that this point is the end-of-file—either of a PL/I source program or of a data file.

The /& Statement. A slash/ampersand (/&) in columns 1 and 2 tells the operating system that this point is the end of the job. A job may contain a number of /* entries, but only one /&, at the end.

The ACTION Statement.   ACTION denotes a Linkage Editor control statement. A common entry is:

ACTION MAP

The entry causes printing of a "map" of the link-edited program (suppress with NOMAP). The map is useful as an indication of the relative storage addresses of any External Procedures. It also prints error messages if the Linkage Editor is unable to locate an external Procedure or an input/output module that is supposed to be cataloged in the system library. Since the map's generation involves additional computer time, ACTION NOMAP is suggested for most simple PL/I processing.

DOS JCL EXAMPLES

The following are three DOS job streams:

1.   One Main Procedure.
2.   A main program with one subprogram.
3.   Card input and disk output.

DOS Example 1: JCL for One Main Procedure

This example provides typical job control for a program that consists of one Main Procedure and does not process tape or disk files.

```
// JOB jobname
// OPTION LINK,PARTDUMP        Supply options.
   ACTION NOMAP                Delete link-edit map.
// EXEC PLIOPT                 Begin execution of PL/I compiler.
*  PROCESS [options] ;
   (PL/I source program)
/*                             End of compilation.
// EXEC LNKTST                 Suppress link-edit/execute if there is a serious
                                   compile error.
// EXEC LNKEDT                 Perform link-edit: include input/output modules.
// EXEC                        Load compiled/linked program into main
                                   storage and begin its execution.
   (input data)
/*                             End of input data.
/&                             End of job, return control to
                                   Supervisor.
```

DOS Example 2: JCL for a Main Procedure and One External Procedure

This example provides for compiling, link-editing, and execution of a main Procedure and one external Procedure.

```
// JOB jobname
// OPTION LINK, etc.              Specify options.
   ACTION MAP                     Generate a link-edit map.
// EXEC PLIOPT                    Compile the main Procedure.
*  PROCESS [options] ;
   (PL/I main Procedure)
*  PROCESS [options] ;            Compile external procedure.
   (PL/I external Procedure)
/*                                End of compilations.
// EXEC LNKTST
// EXEC LNKEDT                    Link-edit Procedures and include input/output
                                     modules.
// EXEC                           Execute link-edited program.
   (input data)
/*                                End of input data.
/&                                End of job.
```

If each Procedure is to be a separately link-edited module, the PROCESS statement should include the NAME option, as follows:

| Main Procedure: | * PROCESS NAME ('name1, ROOT') ; |
| Second Procedure: | * PROCESS NAME ('name2, *') ; |

The Main Procedure must then load the second Procedure from the Core Image Library into main storage using

CALL PLIOVLY ('name2') ;

DOS Example 3: JCL for Disk Output

The following illustrates job control for writing disk records.

If a program uses nonsequential disk files, a LBLTYP entry is required before the LNKEDT. For example, if there are two nonsequential files, the entry is

// LBLTYP NSD(2)

```
//   JOB jobname
//   OPTION LINK, etc.              Specify options.
     ACTION NOMAP
//   EXEC PLIOPT
*    PROCESS [options] ;
     (PL/I source program)
/*                                  End of compilation.
//   DLBL filename, 'file-id',date,codes
          filename: name of the disk file in the file DCL statement.
          'file-id': 1–44 characters within apostrophes, such as 'CUSTOMER-FILE'.
          date, one of two formats:
                 dddd = retention period in days,
                 yy/ddd = date of retention.
          codes: type of file (e.g., SD = sequential disk, VSAM = Virtual storage
          access  method, DA = direct access).
//   EXTENT symbolic-unit, serial-no, type, sequence-no, relative-track, no-of-tracks
          symbolic-unit = SYSnn, in this case, SYS020.
          serial-no: the volume serial number for the disk volume.
          type: the type of disk extent (usually 1).
          sequence-no: the sequence number for the extent, if the file is on more than
          one disk area. Usually omitted.
          relative-track: the sequential track number, relative to zero, where the extent
          begins.
          no-of-tracks: tracks allocated for this extent (or file, if on one extent).
//   EXEC LNKTST
//   EXEC LNKEDT
//   EXEC
     (input data)
/*                                  End of data.
/&                                  End of job.
```

Magnetic tape requires a // LBLTYP TAPE entry and for each tape file a // TLBL entry.

OS JOB CONTROL

The three main OS job control statements—JOB, EXEC, and DD—all begin with a pair of slashes (//) in columns one and two, but unlike DOS job control, they are not followed by a space.

The JOB Statement

The first entry of the OS job specifies the name of the job and provides optional accounting information. Its general format is

//jobname JOB *options*

The *jobname* begins in column 3, starting with a letter and followed by up to seven alphanumeric characters. The *options* include account number, user name, job priority, job class, and message class. A simple example is

//PROG34 JOB (4275,25),'DEPRECIATION',CLASS = A

The items in parentheses are accounting information according to the installation's standards. 'DEPRECIATION' is an optional descriptive name to provide additional identification. CLASS = A indicates the priority class according to the installation's standards.

The EXEC Statement

EXEC causes execution of a specified program or procedure. The job control could provide separate EXEC entries for compile, link-edit, and execution. For example, to compile only:

//stepname EXEC PGM = PL/I (PGM means "program")

The stepname is 1–8 alphanumeric characters, the first of which must be a letter. To reduce coding and errors, most OS installations provide "cataloged procedures" in which commonly used job control is already cataloged. The statement to compile, link-edit ("load"), and execute ("go") under a cataloged procedure is

//stepname EXEC PLIXCLG

The portion CLG means the following:

* C = Compile.
* L = Link-edit the compiled program.
* G = Go, or execute the link-edited program.

PARM and Debugging Options

The EXEC PLIXCLG statement may contain PARM (parameter) entries, as

//stepname EXEC PLIXCLG,PARM.PLI = ('XREF,GOSTMT')

XREF causes printing of a cross-reference table of data names (or use NOXREF).

GOSTMT tells the compiler that the program is to print the number of any statement that causes an abnormal termination. This option is expensive in program size and should be used only for program testing. You also need a SYSDBOUT entry to direct the debugging message onto the system printer. For a dump of main storage, use the SYSUDUMP entry. Both statements precede other //GO entries:

```
//GO.SYSDBOUT DD SYSOUT=A
//GO.SYSUDUMP DD SYSOUT=A
```

For the PL/I optimizer, XREF, GOSTMT, and other compiler options are more commonly coded in the PROCESS statement.

The DD Statement

The DD (or Data Definition) statement describes the data sets (files) that the job uses. The general format is

```
//ddname DD operands
```

The *ddname* relates to the *system-name* in the file DCL statement, as

```
Program:          DCL PRINTER FILE. . . ;
Job control:      //GO. PRINTER DD SYSOUT=A
                         ↑
                      ddname
```

The GO entry in job control indicates an execute step. The operand SYSOUT=A is necessary to assign the data set to the printer device.
    A card file regardless of its file DCL name may be identified simply as

```
//GO.SYSIN DD *
```

An asterisk in the operand of a DD entry implies that input data for this file immediately follows in the job stream.

OS JCL EXAMPLES

The following are three OS job streams:

1.   One Main Procedure.
2.   A Main Procedure with one external Procedure.
3.   Card input and disk output.

OS Example 1: JCL for One Main Procedure

The following job stream uses a cataloged JCL procedure to compile, link-edit, and execute a program that consists of one Main Procedure and does not process tape or disk files. Assume that the program defines the printer data set as PRINTER.

```
//jobname JOB [optional entries]
//stepname EXEC PLIXCLG
```

//PLI.SYSIN DD *   The * denotes that the source program immediately follows in
                              the job stream.
  (PL/I source program)
/*   Indicates end of the compile.
//GO.PRINTER DD SYSOUT = A,DCB = (FBSM,LRECL = 133,BLKSIZE = 665)
  (some installations use just DD SYSOUT = A)
                         PRINTER specifies the name of the printer in the program's file
                              DCL.
                         FBSM means "fixed length, blocked" records (assuming that the
                              system temporarily writes output on disk prior to printing)
                         LRECL = 133 provides the "logical record length" of records.
                         BLKSIZE = 665 indicates blocking five records on disk prior to
                              printing.
//GO.SYSIN DD *   Data Definition for system input device. The * indicates that
                              input data immediately follows in the job stream.
/*   Denotes end of input data.
//   Denotes end of the job.

OS Example 2: JCL for a Main Procedure and One External Procedure

The following job control provides for compiling, link-editing, and execution of a Main Procedure and one external Procedure. It also illustrates the use of the GOSTMT option and the SYSDBOUT entry for debugging. Assume that the program defines the printer data set as PRINTER.

    The compilation may involve any number of PL/I modules each preceded by a PROCESS statement. The EXEC PLIXCG statement applies to all compiles. If each Procedure is to be a separately link-edited module, the PROCESS statement should include a NAME option, as

        * PROCESS NAME ('name') ;

```
//PROLINK JOB [optional entries]
//STEP1 EXEC PLIXCG,PARM = ('GOSTMT')
//PLI.SYSIN DD *
*PROCESS [options] ;
   (main PL/I module)
*PROCESS [options] ;
   (second PL/I module)
/*
```

//GO.SYSDBOUT	DD SYSOUT = A	Define debugging output.
//GO.PRINTER	DD SYSOUT = A,DCB = (*dcb entries*)	Printer data set.
//GO.SYSIN	DD *	Input data set.
(input data)		
/*		End of input data.
//		End of job.

OS Example 3: JCL for Disk Output

The following illustrates job control for writing disk records. Assume that the program defines the disk file as DISKOUT.

//CARDISK	JOB [*optional entries*]
//STEP1	EXEC PLIXCLG
//SYSIN	DD *
	(PL/I source program)
/*	
//GO.DISKOUT DD	DSN = dsname,
//	UNIT = 3350,
//	DISP = (NEW, CATLG),
//	SPACE = (TRK,(*no. of tracks*),RLSE),
//	DCB = (RECFM = FB,LRECL = *mm*, BLKSIZE = *nnn*,BUFNO = *p*)

(The preceding five entries could all be coded on one or two lines.)

DSN = dsname supplies the "data set name" used by the system to catalog the disk file.

UNIT identifies the particular disk device, in this case an IBM 3350.

DISP indicates "disposition": this is a new file and is to be cataloged.

SPACE defines the number of disk tracks (TRK) that the data set will require. (CYL would indicate the number of cylinders.) RLSE permits unused tracks to be released to the system.

DCB (Data Control Block) specifies the conventional entries: FB means "fixed, blocked", LRECL provides the logical length of each record, BLKSIZE is the length of each block (a multiple of record size), and BUFNO supplies the number of buffers.

//GO.SYSIN DD *	
/*	End of input data.
//	End of run.

OS AND DOS OPTIMIZER PROCESS OPTIONS

The PL/I compiler has a number of options and facilities. Among these is the *preprocessor,* an optional stage of the Optimizer compiler that executes only if you specify the PROCESS option MACRO. The preprocessor can modify the source statements, such as conversion of 48-character set into 60, and can insert cataloged PL/I source code into a program prior to compilation.

After the preprocessor step (if any), the compiler performs basic syntax checking. If successful (subject to PROCESS options), the compiler begins actual compilation, translating the PL/I source statements into Assembler routines.

The PROCESS statement optionally follows the EXEC PLIXCLG or EXEC PLIOPT job statement. Its format, beginning in Column 1, is

* PROCESS [options] ;

The options cause the compiler to provide more control during compilation and generate code to help control execution. These options include the following:

- AGGREGATE or NOAGGREGATE (AG or NAG). AGGREGATE lists a table showing the length in bytes of all structures and arrays.
- ATTRIBUTES or NOATTRIBUTES (A or NA). ATTRIBUTES lists a table of source program identifiers and their attributes. (See also XREF.)
- CATALOG ('name'). For DOS, CATALOG requests cataloging of the compiled program in a disk library.
- CHARSET. CHARSET specifies the character set in which the program is coded. The options are CHARSET(48) and CHARSET(60).
- COMPILE or NOCOMPILE (C or NC). COMPILE tells the compiler to complete compilation after syntax checking; NOCOMPILE tells the compiler to suppress compilation. In conjunction with the MACRO option, you can cause compilation to continue subject to severity of diagnostic messages in the preprocessor or syntax checking: NOCOMPILE(W)—no compilation if W, E, or S level diagnostic; NOCOMPILE(E)—no compilation if E or S diagnostic; and NOCOMPILE(S)—no compilation if S diagnostic. (See also MACRO.)
- COUNT or NOCOUNT (CT or NCT). COUNT lists a table indicating the number of times statements in the program are executed. Use of COUNT automatically implies the GOSTMT option (do not code both).
- DECK or NODECK (D or ND). DECK generates an object deck of a compiled program.
- FLOW(n,m) or NOFLOW. During execution, there may be an interrupt causing a diagnostic message. FLOW requests a list of the numbers of the last n branch-out and branch-in statements executed prior to the interrupt. m is the number of procedures through which a flow-trace is to be maintained at one time. Ommission of (n,m) causes a default to (25,10), adequate for most debugging purposes.

- GOSTMT or NOGOSTMT (GS or NGS). GOSTMT asks for generation of the source program statement numbers to print in execution diagnostic messages (an expensive but useful feature for debugging). (See also COUNT.)
- INCLUDE or NOINCLUDE (INC or NINC). INCLUDE requests the compiler to handle inclusion of PL/I cataloged code for programs using the %IN-CLUDE statement (see the next section). If using the MACRO option, omit INCLUDE.
- LINK or NOLINK. For DOS, LINK asks for a link-edit for all circumstances. NOLINK may be coded NOLINK(W or E or S) to suppress link editing depending on severity of diagnostic messages during compilation.
- LIST or NOLIST. LIST causes the compiler to list the generated Assembler code. For LIST(m,n), m is the statement where the list is to begin, and n the last statement.
- MACRO or NOMACRO (M or NM). MACRO causes inclusion of the preprocessor.
- MAP or NOMAP. MAP prints tables of dynamic and static storage. MAP is normally used with LIST.
- MARGINI('c'), abbreviated as MI('c'); or NOMARGINI, abbreviated as NMI. MARGINI defines a character 'c' for the compiler to print to reveal any code outside of columns 2 through 72. A common character is the bar character '|'.
- NAME('name') or N('name'). NAME supplies the name of a program phase for the Linkage Editor (covered in Chapter 22).
- NEST or NONEST. NEST causes printing of the level of nesting for each statement. This feature is useful for locating errors, especially those concerning missing END statements.
- OPTIMIZE(TIME) or NOOPTIMIZE (abbreviated as OPT(TIME) or NOPT). OPTIMIZE(TIME) causes slower compilation but less generated code and faster execution.
- OPTIONS or NOOPTIONS (OP or NOP). OPTIONS requests a list of all specified or default PROCESS statement options at the start of compilation.
- SIZE or SZ. In a multiprogramming system, available storage is limited to partition size. SIZE(64K) requests 64K storage, and SIZE(MAX) grabs all available storage in a partition. The DOS Optimizing compiler requires at least 44K of storage (1K = 1024 bytes).
- SOURCE or NOSOURCE (S or NS). SOURCE asks for a list of the PL/I source statements (the usual requirement).
- STORAGE or NOSTORAGE (STG or NSTG). STORAGE prints a table of the storage requirements of the compiled program.
- XREF or NOXREF (X or NX). XREF causes the compiler to list a cross-reference table of the identifiers used in the program and the statement numbers of the statements where they appear. Declare statements with the INITIAL attribute are assigned statement 1. Coding both ATTRIBUTES and XREF causes the compiler to combine the two tables, a recommended practice.

THE PL/I %INCLUDE STATEMENT

Most installations catalog commonly used source PL/I routines in a source library. A common example is file DCL statements and structures that define input/output records. Any program that needs to include the cataloged source statements simply provides a PROCESS statement containing the INCLUDE option:

* PROCESS INCLUDE ;

The PL/I program then contains a %INCLUDE statement

%INCLUDE library-member-name ;

at the place in the program where the source code is to be placed.

The advantages of including common source code are as follows:

1.   There is a reduction in repetitious coding and in errors.
2.   Maintenance is facilitated because a change to the routine has to be made only to the cataloged source code (although all programs that INCLUDE it must be recompiled).

PL/C CONTROL STATEMENTS

PL/C has its own unique job statements to specify compiler options. Otherwise, the usual job control for DOS or OS still applies. A PL/C control statement begins with an asterisk (*) in column 1 and a keyword following in column 2. Control statements include the following:

*PL/C	precedes each program of a job run and contains various options.
*DATA	precedes any input data records.
*INCLUDE	denotes that the program is to include cataloged PL/C source statements.

*PROCESS and *OPTIONS are covered later.

Example 1. One Procedure, no input data:

*PL/C [options]
PL/C source program

Example 2. One Procedure and input data:

```
*PL/C [options]
        PL/C source program
*DATA
        input data
```

Example 3. A main Procedure and an external Procedure:

```
*PL/C [options]
        PL/C main Procedure
*PROCESS [options]
        PL/C second (external) Procedure
*DATA
        input data
```

PL/C Options

You may stipulate options on any of the *PL/C, *PROCESS, or *OPTIONS statements, in any sequence, separated by commas or blanks. *PL/C is the commonly used statement that applies explicit and default options throughout an entire program. *PROCESS options apply only to an external Procedure that immediately follows. *OPTIONS options also apply to an external Procedure, but only to the section that immediately follows. An example of *PL/C options is

```
*PL/C ID = 'ident',ATR,ALIST,DUMPT(ARRAYS,FLOW,LABELS)
```

Except as noted, all options following may appear on *PL/C, *PROCESS, and *OPTIONS statements:

*   ATR (or NOATR).   Print a listing of attributes.
*   ALIST (or NOALIST).   Print a listing of the generated Assembler code.
*   DUMP or NODUMP (not on *PROCESS or *OPTIONS). DUMP is a useful option for debugging that produces an automatic printout at the end of execution. Its own options, coded as DUMP = (opt1,opt2,. . .) include

BLOCKS:	Print a trace of blocks active on job termination.
SCALARS:	Print values of scalar variables in active blocks on job termination.
ARRAYS:	Print final values of arrays in active blocks on job termination.
FLOW:	Print the last 18 transfers of control.
LABELS:	Print all labels and the frequency with which they were executed.
ENTRIES:	Print all entry-names and the frequency with which they were CALLed.
REPORT:	Print execution statistics of run time and main storage space,
UNREAD:	Print the remaining unread data cards (up to five).

Abbreviations for these options are respectively B, S, A, F, L, E, R, and U. Note that although most of the options generate a lot of machine code, they are powerful debugging aids. You may also code DUMP as DUMPE to cause printout diagnostics if the program encounters an error during execution, or as DUMPT if an error causes termination of execution.

- ERRORS = (c,r) (not on *PROCESS or *OPTIONS). Control execution based on number of errors. For example, ERRORS = (2,5) specifies suppress execution if there are 2 or more compiler errors or 5 or more execution-time (run) errors.
- FLAGW. Print compiler warnings and error messages. (FLAGE suppresses warnings.)
- ID = 'name' (not on *PROCESS or *OPTIONS). Provides up to 20 characters for program identification.
- LINES = n (not on *PROCESS or *OPTIONS). Indicates maximum number of lines to be printed (the usual default is 2000).
- PAGES = n (not on *PROCESS or *OPTIONS). Indicates maximum number of pages to be printed (usual default is 30).
- SOURCE (or NOSOURCE). Causes a printout of the PL/C source program.
- XREF (or NOXREF). Causes a cross-reference listing of variables.

The *PL/C User's Guide* supplies more options and features of the PL/C compiler.

APPENDIX A

KEYPUNCH PROCEDURE

This Appendix illustrates the punching of PL/I cards on an IBM 029 keypunch machine. The important keys are a follows:

- FEED—feeds a card from the read hopper into the punch area.
- REG—moves or "registers" a card into the punch station, ready for punching.
- SKIP—if there is a drum card initialized for automatic processing, advances the card to the next field according to the drum card format.
- DUP—duplicates information from the card immediately preceding (at the read station) into a card at the punch station. This feature is useful for correcting cards.
- REL—releases or ejects the card from the punch station.

Punched cards can be keypunched manually or keypunched automatically by using a program drum card.

MANUAL OPERATION

The following procedure is for the manual keying of punched cards and is recommended only if there is a small number of cards to be punched.

1. Insert blank cards in the input hopper with cards face forward and 9-edge down.
2. Turn on the power switch which is under the keyboard on the right front face of the cabinet.
3. Set all six switches, which are above the keyboard, to off (down) except PRINT, which prints the punched characters at the top of each card.
4. Turn off the program control lever, which is used for drum cards, by pressing it to the right. The lever is below the small window that indicates the card column being punched.
5. Press the FEED and REG keys to feed and register the first card.
6. Begin punching the card by entering the data from the program coding sheet position-for-position:

    •   To space one card column, press the space bar at the bottom of the keyboard.
    •   The keyboard is normally in alphabetic mode, as indicated by the characters printed on the lower part of each key: characters A through Z (all letters are capitals).
    •   For the characters 0 through 9 and the special characters shown on the upper part of the keys, press the numeric key to put the keyboard into numeric mode while punching.
    •   To backspace, press the backspace key.

7. When you have completed punching a card, press the REL key, the FEED key, and then the REG key. The punched card is now at the read station, and a new blank card is ready for punching at the punch station.
8. To duplicate all or part of a card, place the previously punched card in the read station and a blank card in the punch station. Press the DUP key for all positions to be duplicated.
9. To clear all cards from the read and punch stations, flip up the CLEAR switch (it should spring back down).
10. If you have a large number of cards to punch, you can automatically feed cards by turning on the AUTO FEED switch. Press the FEED key twice to feed the first and second card into the punch station. When you release a punched card, another card is automatically fed into the punch station.

AUTOMATIC OPERATION—DRUM CARD

The drum card facilitates the keypunching of a large amount of cards. The following is a typical PL/I drum card format that you can copy or modify for your own purposes:

COLUMN	PUNCH	PURPOSE
1	− (minus)	Skip column 1.
2–10	1AAAAAAAA	Start labels and declaratives.
11–15	1AAAA	Start names and statements.
16–20	1AAAA	Start of first indentation.
21–30	1 (followed by As)	Start of second indentation.
31–40	1 (followed by As)	Start of attributes.
41–72	1 (followed by As)	Start of INIT and comments.
73–80	− (followed by &s)	Skip to end of record.

Columns 2, 11, 16, 21, 31, and 41 all contain tab stops to separate punched fields. The card fits onto a drum that inserts onto a spindle that is inside the window that displays the column being punched. Be sure that the program control lever is turned off. It is best to have an experienced keypunch operator provide instruction in placing the program card on the drum and inserting it onto the spindle.

The procedure for operating the drum card is as follows:

1. Turn on the program control level (turn to the left), set the PROG SEL switch to ONE, and then turn on AUTO FEED and PRINT. All other switches should be off.

2. Depress the FEED key twice; the first card should advance directly to column 8. (If not, check the lever and switch settings. If these are correct, check if the drum card is correctly punched and properly inserted onto the drum.)

3. Either key in a value in column 2 or depress the SKIP key to advance to column 11. The drum card is designed to advance to columns 16, 21, 31, and 41 successively.

4. If you need to enter a character in column 1 (such as a zero or a hyphen), switch off the program control lever. Backspace from column 2 to column 1 and enter the required character.

5. Press the REL key to eject the punched card and feed another card automatically.

6. When you have finished, clean up your coding sheets and damaged cards. Switch off the program control lever (you may want to take off your drum card; do so carefully). Finally, turn off the machine power switch.

OS PL/I KEYWORDS

Keyword	Abbreviation	Use of Keyword
A[(w)]		format item
ABS(x)		built-in function
ACOS(x)		built-in function
%ACTIVATE	%ACT	preprocessor statement
ADD($x_1,x_2,x_3[,x_4$])		built-in function
ADDBUFF		option of ENVIRONMENT attribute
ADDR(x)		built-in function
ALIGNED		attribute
ALL [(character-string- expression)]		option of PUT statement
ALL(x)		built-in function
ALLOCATE	ALLOC	statement
ALLOCATION(x)	ALLOCN(x)	built-in function
ANY(x)		built-in function
AREA		condition
AREA[(size)]		attribute
ARGn		option of NOMAP, NOMAPIN, NOMAPOUT options
ASCII		option of ENVIRONMENT attribute
ASIN(x)		built-in function
ASSEMBLER	ASM	option of OPTIONS attribute
ATAN($x_1[,x_2]$)		built-in function
ATAND($x_1[,x_2]$)		built-in function
ATANH(x)		built-in function
ATTENTION	ATTN	condition
AUTOMATIC	AUTO	attribute
B[(w)]		format item
BACKWARDS		attribute, option of OPEN statement
BASED[(locator-expression)]		attribute
BEGIN		statement
BINARY	BIN	attribute
BINARY($x_1[,x_2[,x_3]]$)	BIN($x_1[,x_2[,x_3]]$)	built-in function
BIT[(length)]		attribute
BIT($x_1[,x_2]$)		built-in function
BKWD		option of ENVIRONMENT attribute
BLKSIZE(block-size)		option of ENVIRONMENT attribute
BOOL(x_1,x_2,x_3)		built-in function
BUFFERED	BUF	attribute
BUFFERS(n)		option of ENVIRONMENT attribute
BUFND(n)		option of ENVIRONMENT attribute
BUFNI(n)		option of ENVIRONMENT attribute
BUFSP(n)		option of ENVIRONMENT attribute
BUFOFF[(n)]		option of ENVIRONMENT attribute
BUILTIN		attribute
BY		option of DO statement, option of repetitive input/output specification
BY NAME	BYNAME	option of assignment statement
C(real-format-item [,real-format-item])		format item
CALL		statement, option of INITIAL attribute
CEIL(x)		built-in function
CHAR($x_1[,x_2]$)		built-in function
CHARACTER[(length)]	CHAR[(length)]	attribute

Keyword	Abbreviation	Use of Keyword
CHECK		statement
CHECK[(name-list)]		condition, condition prefix
CLOSE		statement
COBOL		option of ENVIRONMENT attribute, or OPTIONS option/attribute
COLUMN(n)	COL(n)	format item
COMPILETIME		preprocessor built-in function
COMPLETION(x)	CPLN(x)	built-in function, pseudovariable
COMPLEX	CPLX	attribute
COMPLEX(x_1, x_2)	CPLX(x_1, x_2)	built-in function, pseudovariable
CONDITION	COND	attribute
CONDITION(name)	COND(name)	condition
CONJG(x)		built-in function
CONNECTED	CONN	attribute
CONSECUTIVE		option of ENVIRONMENT attribute
%CONTROL		listing control statement
CONTROLLED	CTL	attribute
CONVERSION	CONV	condition, condition prefix
COPY[(file-expression)]		option of GET statement
COS(x)		built-in function
COSD(x)		built-in function
COSH(x)		built-in function
COUNT(file-expression)		built-in function
COUNTER		preprocessor built-in function
CTLASA		option of ENVIRONMENT attribute
CTL360		option of ENVIRONMENT attribute
CURRENTSTORAGE(variable)	CSTG(variable)	built-in function
D		option of ENVIRONMENT attribute
DATA		option of GET or PUT statement
DATAFIELD		built-in function
DATE		built-in function
DB		option of ENVIRONMENT attribute
%DEACTIVATE	%DEACT	preprocessor statement
DECIMAL	DEC	attribute
DECIMAL$(x_1[,x_2[,x_3]])$	DEC$(x_1[,x_2[,x_3]])$	built-in function
DECLARE	DCL	statement
%DECLARE	%DCL	preprocessor statement
DEFAULT	DFT	statement
DEFINED	DEF	attribute
DELAY		statement
DELETE		statement
DESCRIPTORS		option of DEFAULT statement
DIM(x_1, x_2)		built-in function
DIRECT		attribute
DISPLAY		statement
DIVIDE$(x_1, x_2, x_3[,x_4])$		built-in function
DO		statement, repetitive input/output data specification
%DO		preprocessor statement
E(w,d[,s])		format item
EDIT		option of GET or PUT statement
ELSE		clause of IF statement
%ELSE		clause of %IF statement
EMPTY		built-in function
END		statement
%END		preprocessor statement
ENDFILE(file-expression)		condition
ENDPAGE(file-expression)		condition
ENTRY		attribute, statement
ENVIRONMENT	ENV	attribute, option of CLOSE statement
ERF(x)		built-in function
ERFC(x)		built-in function
ERROR		condition
EVENT		attribute, option of CALL, DELETE, DISPLAY, READ, REWRITE, and WRITE statements

Keyword	Abbreviation	Use of Keyword
EXCLUSIVE	EXCL	attribute
EXIT		statement
EXP(x)		built-in function
EXTERNAL	EXT	attribute
F(w,[,d[,s]])		format item
F		option of ENVIRONMENT attribute
FB		option of ENVIRONMENT attribute
FBS		option of ENVIRONMENT attribute
FETCH		statement
FILE		attribute
FILE(file-expression)		option of CLOSE, DELETE, GET, LOCATE, OPEN, PUT, READ, REWRITE, UNLOCK, and WRITE statements
FINISH		condition
FIXED		attribute
FIXED(x$_1$[,x$_2$[,x$_3$]])		built-in function
FIXEDOVERFLOW	FOFL	condition, condition prefix
FLOAT		attribute
FLOAT(x$_1$[,x$_2$])		built-in function
FLOOR(x)		built-in function
FLOW		statement, option of PUT statement
FORMAT		statement, option of %CONTROL statement
FORTRAN		option of OPTIONS option/attribute
FREE		statement
FROM(variable)		option of WRITE or REWRITE statements
FS		option of ENVIRONMENT attribute
GENERIC		attribute
GENKEY		option of ENVIRONMENT attribute
GET		statement
GO TO	GOTO	statement
%GO TO	%GOTO	preprocessor statement
HALT		statement
HBOUND(x$_1$,x$_2$)		built-in function
HIGH(x)		built-in function
IF		statement
%IF		preprocessor statement
IGNORE(n)		option of READ statement
IMAG(x)		built-in function, pseudovariable
IN(element-area-variable)		option of ALLOCATE and FREE statements
%INCLUDE		preprocessor statement
INDEX(x$_1$,x$_2$)		built-in function
INDEXAREA [(index-area-size)]		option of ENVIRONMENT attribute
INDEXED		option of ENVIRONMENT attribute
INITIAL	INIT	attribute
INPUT		attribute, option of OPEN statement
INTER		option of OPTIONS option/attribute
INTERNAL	INT	attribute
INTO(variable)		option of READ statement
IRREDUCIBLE	IRRED	attribute
KEY(file-expression)		condition
KEY(x)		option of READ, DELETE, and REWRITE statements
KEYED		attribute, option of OPEN statement
KEYFROM(x)		option of WRITE statement
KEYLENGTH(n)		option of ENVIRONMENT attribute
KEYLOC(n)		option of ENVIRONMENT attribute
KEYTO(variable)		option of READ statement
LABEL		attribute
LBOUND(x$_1$,x$_2$)		built-in function
LEAVE		option of ENVIRONMENT attribute
LEAVE		statement
LENGTH(x)		built-in function
LIKE		attribute
LINE(n)		format item, option of PUT statement
LINENO(x)		built-in function
LINESIZE(expression)		option of OPEN statement

Keyword	Abbreviation	Use of Keyword
LIST		option of GET or PUT statement
LOCATE		statement
LOG(x)		built-in function
LOG2(x)		built-in function
LOG10(x)		built-in function
LOW(x)		built-in function
MAIN		option of OPTIONS option
MAX($x_1,x_2...x_n$)		built-in function
MIN($x_1,x_2...x_n$)		built-in function
MOD(x_1,x_2)		built-in function
MULTIPLY($x_1,x_2,x_3[,x_4]$)		built-in function
NAME(file-expression)		condition
NCP(n)		option of ENVIRONMENT attribute
NOCHECK		statement
NOCHECK[(name-list)]		condition prefix
NOCONVERSION	NOCONV	condition prefix
NOFIXEDOVERFLOW	NOFOFL	condition prefix
NOFLOW		statement
NOFORMAT		option of %CONTROL statement
NOLOCK		option of READ statement
NOMAP[(arg-list)]		option of OPTIONS attribute
NOMAPIN[(arg-list)]		option of OPTIONS attribute
NOMAPOUT[(arg-list)]		option of OPTIONS attribute
NOOVERFLOW	NOOFL	condition prefix
%NOPRINT		listing control statement
NORESCAN		option of %ACTIVATE statement
NOSIZE		condition prefix
NOSTRINGRANGE	NOSTRG	condition prefix
NOSTRINGSIZE	NOSTRZ	condition prefix
NOSUBSCRIPTRANGE	NOSUBRG	condition prefix
%NOTE		preprocessor statement
NOUNDERFLOW	NOUFL	condition prefix
NOWRITE		option of ENVIRONMENT attribute
NOZERODIVIDE	NOZDIV	condition prefix
NULL		built-in function
OFFSET[(area-name)]		attribute
OFFSET(x_1,x_2)		built-in function
ON		statement
ONCHAR		built-in function, pseudovariable
ONCODE		built-in function
ONCOUNT		built-in function
ONFILE		built-in function
ONKEY		built-in function
ONLOC		built-in function
ONSOURCE		built-in function, pseudovariable
OPEN		statement
OPTIONS(list)		attribute, option of ENTRY and PROCEDURE statements
ORDER		option of BEGIN and PROCEDURE statements
OTHERWISE	OTHER	clause of select-group
OUTPUT		attribute, option of OPEN statement
OVERFLOW	OFL	condition, condition prefix
P 'picture specification'		format item
PAGE		format item, option of PUT statement
%PAGE		listing control statement
PAGESIZE(w)		option of OPEN statement
PARMSET(parameter)		preprocessor built-in function
PASSWORD(password-specification)		option of ENVIRONMENT attribute
PENDING(file-expression)		condition
PICTURE	PIC	attribute
PLIRETV		built-in function
POINTER	PTR	attribute
POINTER(x_1,x_2)	PTR(x_1,x_2)	built-in function
POLY(x_1,x_2)		built-in function
POSITION (expression)	POS (expression)	attribute
PRECISION($x_1,x_2[,x_3]$)	PREC($x_1,x_2[,x_3]$)	built-in function
PRINT		attribute, option of OPEN statement

Keyword	Abbreviation	Use of Keyword
%PRINT		listing control statement
PRIORITY(x)		option of CALL statement
PRIORITY[(x)]		built-in function, pseudovariable
PROCEDURE	PROC	statement
%PROCEDURE	%PROC	preprocessor statement
PROD(x)		built-in function
PUT		statement
R(x)		format item
RANGE		option of DEFAULT statement
READ		statement
REAL		attribute
REAL(x)		built-in function, pseudovariable
RECORD		attribute, option of OPEN statement
RECORD(file-expression)		condition
RECSIZE(record-length)		option of ENVIRONMENT attribute
RECURSIVE		option of PROCEDURE statement
REDUCIBLE	RED	attribute
REENTRANT		option of OPTIONS option
REFER(element-variable)		option of BASED attribute
REGIONAL(1|2|3)		option of ENVIRONMENT attribute
RELEASE		statement
REORDER		option of BEGIN and PROCEDURE statements
REPEAT(x$_1$,x$_2$)		built-in function
REPEAT		option of DO statement
REPLY(c)		option of DISPLAY statement
REREAD		option of ENVIRONMENT attribute
RESCAN		option of %ACTIVATE statement
RETCODE		option of OPTIONS attribute
RETURN		statement, preprocessor statement
RETURNS(attribute-list)		attribute, option of PROCEDURE statement
REUSE		option of ENVIRONMENT attribute
REVERT		statement
REWRITE		statement
ROUND(x$_1$,x$_2$)		built-in function
SAMEKEY(x)		built-in function
SCALARVARYING		option of ENVIRONMENT attribute
SELECT		statement
SEQUENTIAL	SEQL	attribute
SET(locator-variable)		option of ALLOCATE, LOCATE, and READ statements
SIGN(x)		built-in function
SIGNAL		statement
SIN(x)		built-in function
SIND(x)		built-in function
SINH(x)		built-in function
SIS		option of ENVIRONMENT attribute
SIZE		condition, condition prefix
SKIP[(n)]		format item, option of GET and PUT statements
SKIP		option of ENVIRONMENT attribute
%SKIP		listing control statement
SNAP		option of ON and PUT statements
SQRT(x)		built-in function
STATEMENT		option of %PROCEDURE statement
STATIC		attribute
STATUS(x)		built-in function, pseudovariable
STOP		statement
STORAGE(variable)	STG(variable)	built-in function
STREAM		attribute, option of OPEN statement
STRING(x)		built-in function, pseudovariable
STRING(string-name)		option of GET and PUT statements
STRINGRANGE	STRG	condition, condition prefix
STRINGSIZE	STRZ	condition, condition prefix
iSUB		dummy variable of DEFINED attribute
SUBSCRIPTRANGE	SUBRG	condition, condition prefix
SUBSTR(x$_1$,x$_2$[,x$_3$])		built-in function, pseudovariable
SUM(x)		built-in function

Keyword	Abbreviation	Use of Keyword
SYSIN		name of standard system input file
SYSPRINT		name of standard system output file
SYSTEM		option of ON or DECLARE statements
TAN(x)		built-in function
TAND(x)		built-in function
TANH(x)		built-in function
TASK		attribute, option of OPTIONS option
TASK[(task-name)]		option of CALL statement
THEN		clause of IF statement
%THEN		clause of %IF statement
TIME		built-in function
TITLE(element-expression)		option of OPEN statement
TO		option of DO statement, option of repetitive input/output specification
TOTAL		option of ENVIRONMENT attribute
TP(M|R)		option of ENVIRONMENT attribute
TRANSIENT		attribute
TRANSLATE($x_1,x_2[,x_3]$)		built-in function
TRANSMIT(file-expression)		condition
TRKOFL		option of ENVIRONMENT attribute
TRUNC(x)		built-in function
U		option of ENVIRONMENT attribute
UNALIGNED	UNAL	attribute
UNBUFFERED	UNBUF	attribute, option of OPEN statement
UNDEFINEDFILE (file-expression)	UNDF (file-expression)	condition
UNDERFLOW	UFL	condition, condition prefix
UNLOCK		statement
UNSPEC(x)		built-in function, pseudovariable
UNTIL		option of DO statement
UPDATE		attribute, option of OPEN statement
V		option of ENVIRONMENT attribute
VALUE		option of DEFAULT statement
VARIABLE		attribute
VARYING	VAR	attribute
VB		option of ENVIRONMENT attribute
VBS		option of ENVIRONMENT attribute
VERIFY(x_1,x_2)		built-in function
VS		option of ENVIRONMENT attribute
VSAM		option of ENVIRONMENT attribute
WAIT		statement
WHEN(generic-descriptor-list)		option in GENERIC declaration
WHEN		clause of select-group
WHILE		option of DO statement
WRITE		statement
X(w)		format item
ZERODIVIDE	ZDIV	condition, condition prefix

PL/C RESTRICTIONS

PL/I allows a programmer to define and use any valid name and can distinguish from the *context* of a name whether it is a keyword or a user-name. PL/C, however, contains *reserved* words that are not permitted as labels or identifiers, as follows:

ALLOCATE	ELSE	IF	RETURN
BEGIN	END	NO	REVERT
BY	ENTRY	NOCHECK	REWRITE
CALL	EXIT	NOFLOW	SIGNAL
CHECK	FLOW	NOSOURCE	SOURCE
CLOSE	FORMAT	ON	STOP
DCL	FREE	OPEN	THEN
DECLARE	GET	PROC(EDURE)	TO
DELETE	GO	PUT	WHILE
DO	GOTO	READ	WRITE

The following PL/I features are *not available* in PL/C:

ADDR	EMPTY	NULL	SELECT
AREA	EVENT	OFFSET	SET
BASED	FREE	POINTER	STRINGSIZE
CONNECTED	LEAVE	POSITION	UNTIL
CONTROLLED	LIKE	REGIONAL	VSAM
DEFINED	LOCATE	REPEAT	

IBM 360/370 PROGRAM CHECKS

A clean program compilation is no insurance of a clean program execution. A bug or invalid data may cause a program to attempt an operation that the CPU cannot execute. For such an error, the program is terminated and the Supervisor prints the error diagnostic. IBM OS systems print only a code as a clue to the precise error, as

COMPLETION CODE SYSTEM = 0Cn

where n is the error termination code. The following is a list of these program checks or error codes for IBM 360 and 370 computers using DOS and OS.

1. Operation Exception—an attempt to execute an invalid machine operation.
2. Privileged-operation Exception—an attempt to execute a "privileged instruction" that only the Supervisor is permitted to execute.
3. Execute Exception—an error concerned with the EX machine code that should never occur in a PL/I program.
4. Protection Exception—an attempt to move data into the protected Supervisor area or into a partition for another program.
5. Addressing Exception—an attempt to reference an address outside of available storage.
6. Specification Exception—a machine instruction that violates a rule of its use, such as incorrect boundary alignment.
7. Data Exception—an attempt to perform decimal arithmetic on a field containing invalid data (valid data is 0–9 and sign). The most common cause of this error is failure to initialize an accumulator to zero. Another cause is an incorrect subscript value that references an arithmetic field outside of an array or a blank arithmethic input field.
8. Fixed-point-overflow Exception—a calculated binary value is too large to be contained in a register.

9. Fixed-point-divide Exception—an attempt to divide a binary field by zero.

A. Decimal-overflow Exception—a decimal value is too large. Normally, the PL/I compiler generates machine code that truncates this value on the left, causing a FIXEDOVERFLOW error.

B. Decimal-divide Exception—an attempt to divide a decimal value by zero.

C. Exponent-overflow Exception—a floating-point value exceeds 10^{75}.

D. Exponent-underflow Exception—a floating-point value is less than 10^{-78}.

E. Significance Exception—a floating-point add or subtract has caused a zero fraction; all significant digits are lost, and subsequent computations may be meaningless.

F. Floating-point Divide Exception—an attempt to divide a floating-point value by zero.

10, 11, 12, 13, 40, 80—these program checks are concerned with virtual storage processing and would not normally be caused by your program.

The PL/I and PL/C compilers generate code that protects storage as much as possible. Error codes 1, 2, 4, 5, and 6 may occur in advanced programs that use subscripts for array processing; an invalid subscript attempts to move or add data to an area outside of the referenced array, causing unpredictable results.

APPENDIX E

IBM 360/370 CODE REPRESENTATION

Dec.	Hex	BCDIC	EBCDIC(1)		ASCII	EBCDIC Card Code	Binary
0	00	NUL			NUL	12-0-1-8-9	0000 0000
1	01	SOH			SOH	12-1-9	0000 0001
2	02	STX			STX	12-2-9	0000 0010
3	03	ETX			ETX	12-3-9	0000 0011
4	04	PF			EOT	12-4-9	0000 0100
5	05	HT			ENQ	12-5-9	0000 0101
6	06	LC			ACK	12-6-9	0000 0110
7	07	DEL			BEL	12-7-9	0000 0111
8	08				BS	12-8-9	0000 1000
9	09				HT	12-1-8-9	0000 1001
10	0A	SMM			LF	12-2-8-9	0000 1010
11	0B	VT			VT	12-3-8-9	0000 1011
12	0C	FF			FF	12-4-8-9	0000 1100
13	0D	CR			CR	12-5-8-9	0000 1101
14	0E	SO			SO	12-6-8-9	0000 1110
15	0F	SI			SI	12-7-8-9	0000 1111
16	10	DLE			DLE	12-11-1-8-9	0001 0000
17	11	DC1			DC1	11-1-9	0001 0001
18	12	DC2			DC2	11-2-9	0001 0010
19	13	TM			DC3	11-3-9	0001 0011
20	14	RES			DC4	11-4-9	0001 0100
21	15	NL			NAK	11-5-9	0001 0101
22	16	BS			SYN	11-6-9	0001 0110
23	17	IL			ETB	11-7-9	0001 0111
24	18	CAN			CAN	11-8-9	0001 1000
25	19	EM			EM	11-1-8-9	0001 1001
26	1A	CC			SUB	11-2-8-9	0001 1010
27	1B	CU1			ESC	11-3-8-9	0001 1011
28	1C	IFS			FS	11-4-8-9	0001 1100
29	1D	IGS			GS	11-5-8-9	0001 1101
30	1E	IRS			RS	11-6-8-9	0001 1110
31	1F	IUS			US	11-7-8-9	0001 1111
32	20	DS			SP	11-0-1-8-9	0010 0000
33	21	SOS			!	0-1-9	0010 0001
34	22	FS			"	0-2-9	0010 0010
35	23				#	0-3-9	0010 0011
36	24	BYP			$	0-4-9	0010 0100
37	25	LF			%	0-5-9	0010 0101
38	26	ETB			&	0-6-9	0010 0110
39	27	ESC			'	0-7-9	0010 0111
40	28				(	0-8-9	0010 1000
41	29				)	0-1-8-9	0010 1001
42	2A	SM			*	0-2-8-9	0010 1010
43	2B	CU2			+	0-3-8-9	0010 1011
44	2C				,	0-4-8-9	0010 1100
45	2D	ENQ			-	0-5-8-9	0010 1101
46	2E	ACK			.	0-6-8-9	0010 1110
47	2F	BEL			/	0-7-8-9	0010 1111
48	30				0	12-11-0-1-8-9	0011 0000
49	31				1	1-9	0011 0001
50	32	SYN			2	2-9	0011 0010
51	33				3	3-9	0011 0011
52	34	PN			4	4-9	0011 0100
53	35	RS			5	5-9	0011 0101
54	36	UC			6	6-9	0011 0110
55	37	EOT			7	7-9	0011 0111
56	38				8	8-9	0011 1000
57	39				9	1-8-9	0011 1001
58	3A				:	2-8-9	0011 1010
59	3B	CU3			;	3-8-9	0011 1011
60	3C	DC4			<	4-8-9	0011 1100
61	3D	NAK			=	5-8-9	0011 1101
62	3E				>	6-8-9	0011 1110
63	3F	SUB			?	7-8-9	0011 1111
64	40		Sp	Sp	@	no punches	0100 0000
65	41				A	12-0-1-9	0100 0001
66	42				B	12-0-2-9	0100 0010
67	43				C	12-0-3-9	0100 0011
68	44				D	12-0-4-9	0100 0100
69	45				E	12-0-5-9	0100 0101
70	46				F	12-0-6-9	0100 0110
71	47				G	12-0-7-9	0100 0111
72	48				H	12-0-8-9	0100 1000
73	49				I	12-1-8	0100 1001
74	4A		¢	¢	J	12-2-8	0100 1010
75	4B	.	.	.	K	12-3-8	0100 1011
76	4C	□)	<	<	L	12-4-8	0100 1100
77	4D	[	(	(	M	12-5-8	0100 1101
78	4E	<	+	+	N	12-6-8	0100 1110
79	4F	‡	|	|	O	12-7-8	0100 1111
80	50	& +	&	&	P	12	0101 0000
81	51				Q	12-11-1-9	0101 0001
82	52				R	12-11-2-9	0101 0010
83	53				S	12-11-3-9	0101 0011
84	54				T	12-11-4-9	0101 0100
85	55				U	12-11-5-9	0101 0101
86	56				V	12-11-6-9	0101 0110
87	57				W	12-11-7-9	0101 0111
88	58				X	12-11-8-9	0101 1000
89	59				Y	11-1-8	0101 1001
90	5A		!	!	Z	11-2-8	0101 1010
91	5B	$	$	$	[	11-3-8	0101 1011
92	5C	*	*	*	\	11-4-8	0101 1100
93	5D	]	)	)	]	11-5-8	0101 1101
94	5E	;	;	;	¬ ^	11-6-8	0101 1110
95	5F	Δ	¬	¬	_	11-7-8	0101 1111
96	60	-	-	-	`	11	0110 0000
97	61	/	/	/	a	0-1	0110 0001
98	62				b	11-0-2-9	0110 0010
99	63				c	11-0-3-9	0110 0011
100	64				d	11-0-4-9	0110 0100
101	65				e	11-0-5-9	0110 0101
102	66				f	11-0-6-9	0110 0110
103	67				g	11-0-7-9	0110 0111
104	68				h	11-0-8-9	0110 1000
105	69				i	0-1-8	0110 1001
106	6A		‖		j	12-11	0110 1010
107	6B	,	,	,	k	0-3-8	0110 1011
108	6C	%(	%	%	l	0-4-8	0110 1100
109	6D	ϒ	_		m	0-5-8	0110 1101
110	6E	\	>	>	n	0-6-8	0110 1110
111	6F	⁗	?	?	o	0-7-8	0110 1111

1. Two columns of EBCDIC graphics are shown. The first gives standard bit pattern assignments. The second shows the T-11 and TN text printing chains (120 graphics).

Dec.	Hex	BCDIC	EBCDIC(1)	ASCII	EBCDIC Card Code	Binary
112	70			p	12-11-0	0111 0000
113	71			q	12-11-0-1-9	0111 0001
114	72			r	12-11-0-2-9	0111 0010
115	73			s	12-11-0-3-9	0111 0011
116	74			t	12-11-0-4-9	0111 0100
117	75			u	12-11-0-5-9	0111 0101
118	76			v	12-11-0-6-9	0111 0110
119	77			w	12-11-0-7-9	0111 0111
120	78			x	12-11-0-8-9	0111 1000
121	79			y	1-8	0111 1001
122	7A	‡	:	:	2-8	0111 1010
123	7B	# ·	#	{	3-8	0111 1011
124	7C	@ '	@	@	4-8	0111 1100
125	7D	:	'	'	5-8	0111 1101
126	7E	>	=	=	6-8	0111 1110
127	7F	√	"	" DEL	7-8	0111 1111
128	80				12-0-1-8	1000 0000
129	81		a	a	12-0-1	1000 0001
130	82		b	b	12-0-2	1000 0010
131	83		c	c	12-0-3	1000 0011
132	84		d	d	12-0-4	1000 0100
133	85		e	e	12-0-5	1000 0101
134	86		f	f	12-0-6	1000 0110
135	87		g	g	12-0-7	1000 0111
136	88		h	h	12-0-8	1000 1000
137	89		i	i	12-0-9	1000 1001
138	8A				12-0-2-8	1000 1010
139	8B			{	12-0-3-8	1000 1011
140	8C			≤	12-0-4-8	1000 1100
141	8D			(	12-0-5-8	1000 1101
142	8E			•	12-0-6-8	1000 1110
143	8F			+	12-0-7-8	1000 1111
144	90				12-11-1-8	1001 0000
145	91		j	j	12-11-1	1001 0001
146	92		k	k	12-11-2	1001 0010
147	93		l	l	12-11-3	1001 0011
148	94		m	m	12-11-4	1001 0100
149	95		n	n	12-11-5	1001 0101
150	96		o	o	12-11-6	1001 0110
151	97		p	p	12-11-7	1001 0111
152	98		q	q	12-11-8	1001 1000
153	99		r	r	12-11-9	1001 1001
154	9A				12-11-2-8	1001 1010
155	9B			}	12-11-3-8	1001 1011
156	9C			□	12-11-4-8	1001 1100
157	9D			)	12-11-5-8	1001 1101
158	9E			±	12-11-6-8	1001 1110
159	9F			■	12-11-7-8	1001 1111
160	A0			¯	11-0-1-8	1010 0000
161	A1		~	°	11-0-1	1010 0001
162	A2		s	s	11-0-2	1010 0010
163	A3		t	t	11-0-3	1010 0011
164	A4		u	u	11-0-4	1010 0100
165	A5		v	v	11-0-5	1010 0101
166	A6		w	w	11-0-6	1010 0110
167	A7		x	x	11-0-7	1010 0111
168	A8		y	y	11-0-8	1010 1000
169	A9		z	z	11-0-9	1010 1001
170	AA				11-0-2-8	1010 1010
171	AB			∟	11-0-3-8	1010 1011
172	AC			⌐	11-0-4-8	1010 1100
173	AD			[	11-0-5-8	1010 1101
174	AE			≥	11-0-6-8	1010 1110
175	AF			●	11-0-7-8	1010 1111
176	B0			○	12-11-0-1-8	1011 0000
177	B1			1	12-11-0-1	1011 0001
178	B2			2	12-11-0-2	1011 0010
179	B3			3	12-11-0-3	1011 0011
180	B4			4	12-11-0-4	1011 0100
181	B5			5	12-11-0-5	1011 0101
182	B6			6	12-11-0-6	1011 0110
183	B7			7	12-11-0-7	1011 0111

Dec.	Hex	BCDIC	EBCDIC(1)	ASCII	EBCDIC Card Code	Binary
184	B8			8	12-11-0-8	1011 1000
185	B9			9	12-11-0-1-9	1011 1001
186	BA				12-11-0-2-8	1011 1010
187	BB			⌐	12-11-0-3-8	1011 1011
188	BC			¬	12-11-0-4-8	1011 1100
189	BD			]	12-11-0-5-8	1011 1101
190	BE			¥	12-11-0-6-8	1011 1110
191	BF			—	12-11-0-7-8	1011 1111
192	C0	?	{		12-0	1100 0000
193	C1	A	A	A	12-1	1100 0001
194	C2	B	B	B	12-2	1100 0010
195	C3	C	C	C	12-3	1100 0011
196	C4	D	D	D	12-4	1100 0100
197	C5	E	E	E	12-5	1100 0101
198	C6	F	F	F	12-6	1100 0110
199	C7	G	G	G	12-7	1100 0111
200	C8	H	H	H	12-8	1100 1000
201	C9	I	I	I	12-9	1100 1001
202	CA				12-0-2-8-9	1100 1010
203	CB				12-0-3-8-9	1100 1011
204	CC		♪		12-0-4-8-9	1100 1100
205	CD				12-0-5-8-9	1100 1101
206	CE		Ψ		12-0-6-8-9	1100 1110
207	CF				12-0-7-8-9	1100 1111
208	D0	!	}		11-0	1101 0000
209	D1	J	J	J	11-1	1101 0001
210	D2	K	K	K	11-2	1101 0010
211	D3	L	L	L	11-3	1101 0011
212	D4	M	M	M	11-4	1101 0100
213	D5	N	N	N	11-5	1101 0101
214	D6	O	O	O	11-6	1101 0110
215	D7	P	P	P	11-7	1101 0111
216	D8	Q	Q	Q	11-8	1101 1000
217	D9	R	R	R	11-9	1101 1001
218	DA				12-11-2-8-9	1101 1010
219	DB				12-11-3-8-9	1101 1011
220	DC				12-11-4-8-9	1101 1100
221	DD				12-11-5-8-9	1101 1101
222	DE				12-11-6-8-9	1101 1110
223	DF				12-11-7-8-9	1101 1111
224	E0	‡	\		0-2-8	1110 0000
225	E1				11-0-1-9	1110 0001
226	E2	S	S	S	0-2	1110 0010
227	E3	T	T	T	0-3	1110 0011
228	E4	U	U	U	0-4	1110 0100
229	E5	V	V	V	0-5	1110 0101
230	E6	W	W	W	0-6	1110 0110
231	E7	X	X	X	0-7	1110 0111
232	E8	Y	Y	Y	0-8	1110 1000
233	E9	Z	Z	Z	0-9	1110 1001
234	EA				11-0-2-8-9	1110 1010
235	EB				11-0-3-8-9	1110 1011
236	EC		◄		11-0-4-8-9	1110 1100
237	ED				11-0-5-8-9	1110 1101
238	EE				11-0-6-8-9	1110 1110
239	EF				11-0-7-8-9	1110 1111
240	F0	0	0	0	0	1111 0000
241	F1	1	1	1	1	1111 0001
242	F2	2	2	2	2	1111 0010
243	F3	3	3	3	3	1111 0011
244	F4	4	4	4	4	1111 0100
245	F5	5	5	5	5	1111 0101
246	F6	6	6	6	6	1111 0110
247	F7	7	7	7	7	1111 0111
248	F8	8	8	8	8	1111 1000
249	F9	9	9	9	9	1111 1001
250	FA					12-11-0-2-8-9	1111 1010
251	FB				12-11-0-3-8-9	1111 1011
252	FC				12-11-0-4-8-9	1111 1100
253	FD				12-11-0-5-8-9	1111 1101
254	FE				12-11-0-6-8-9	1111 1110
255	FF		EO		12-11-0-7-8-9	1111 1111

HEXADECIMAL and DECIMAL CONVERSION

Hexadecimal and Decimal Integer Conversion Table

HALFWORD								HALFWORD							
BYTE				BYTE				BYTE				BYTE			
BITS: 0123		4567		0123		4567		0123		4567		0123		4567	
Hex	Decimal	Hex	Decimal	Hex	Decimal	Hex	Decimal	Hex	Decimal	Hex	Decimal	Hex	Decimal	Hex	Decimal
0	0	0	0	0	0	0	0	0	0	0	0	0	0	0	0
1	268,435,456	1	16,777,216	1	1,048,576	1	65,536	1	4,096	1	256	1	16	1	1
2	536,870,912	2	33,554,432	2	2,097,152	2	131,072	2	8,192	2	512	2	32	2	2
3	805,306,368	3	50,331,648	3	3,145,728	3	196,608	3	12,288	3	768	3	48	3	3
4	1,073,741,824	4	67,108,864	4	4,194,304	4	262,144	4	16,384	4	1,024	4	64	4	4
5	1,342,177,280	5	83,886,080	5	5,242,880	5	327,680	5	20,480	5	1,280	5	80	5	5
6	1,610,612,736	6	100,663,296	6	6,291,456	6	393,216	6	24,576	6	1,536	6	96	6	6
7	1,879,048,192	7	117,440,512	7	7,340,032	7	458,752	7	28,672	7	1,792	7	112	7	7
8	2,147,483,648	8	134,217,728	8	8,388,608	8	524,288	8	32,768	8	2,048	8	128	8	8
9	2,415,919,104	9	150,994,944	9	9,437,184	9	589,824	9	36,864	9	2,304	9	144	9	9
A	2,684,354,560	A	167,772,160	A	10,485,760	A	655,360	A	40,960	A	2,560	A	160	A	10
B	2,952,790,016	B	184,549,376	B	11,534,336	B	720,896	B	45,056	B	2,816	B	176	B	11
C	3,221,225,472	C	201,326,592	C	12,582,912	C	786,432	C	49,152	C	3,072	C	192	C	12
D	3,489,660,928	D	218,103,808	D	13,631,488	D	851,968	D	53,248	D	3,328	D	208	D	13
E	3,758,096,384	E	234,881,024	E	14,680,064	E	917,504	E	57,344	E	3,584	E	224	E	14
F	4,026,531,840	F	251,658,240	F	15,728,640	F	983,040	F	61,440	F	3,840	F	240	F	15
8		7		6		5		4		3		2		1	

TO CONVERT HEXADECIMAL TO DECIMAL

1. Locate the column of decimal numbers corresponding to the left-most digit or letter of the hexadecimal; select from this column and record the number that corresponds to the position of the hexadecimal digit or letter.

2. Repeat step 1 for the next (second from the left) position.

3. Repeat step 1 for the units (third from the left) position.

4. Add the numbers selected from the table to form the decimal number.

EXAMPLE	
Conversion of Hexadecimal Value	D34
1. D	3328
2. 3	48
3. 4	4
4. Decimal	3380

To convert integer numbers greater than the capacity of table, use the techniques below:

HEXADECIMAL TO DECIMAL

Successive cumulative multiplication from left to right, adding units position.

Example: $D34_{16} = 3380_{10}$

```
D =    13
      x16
      208
3 =  + 3
      211
      x16
     3376
4 =  + 4
     3380
```

TO CONVERT DECIMAL TO HEXADECIMAL

1. (a) Select from the table the highest decimal number that is equal to or less than the number to be converted.
   (b) Record the hexadecimal of the column containing the selected number.
   (c) Subtract the selected decimal from the number to be converted.

2. Using the remainder from step 1(c) repeat all of step 1 to develop the second position of the hexadecimal (and a remainder).

3. Using the remainder from step 2 repeat all of step 1 to develop the units position of the hexadecimal.

4. Combine terms to form the hexadecimal number.

```
           EXAMPLE
  Conversion of
  Decimal Value        3380

  1.  D               -3328
                          52

  2.  3                 -48
                           4

  3.  4                  -4

  4.  Hexadecimal       D34
```

DECIMAL TO HEXADECIMAL

Divide and collect the remainder in reverse order.

Example: $3380_{10} = X_{16}$

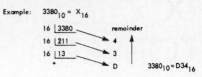

$$3380_{10} = D34_{16}$$

POWERS OF 16 TABLE

Example: $268,435,456_{10} = (2.68435456 \times 10^8)_{10} = 1000\ 0000_{16} = (10^7)_{16}$

16^n	n
1	0
16	1
256	2
4 096	3
65 536	4
1 048 576	5
16 777 216	6
268 435 456	7
4 294 967 296	8
68 719 476 736	9
1 099 511 627 776	10 = A
17 592 186 044 416	11 = B
281 474 976 710 656	12 = C
4 503 599 627 370 496	13 = D
72 057 594 037 927 936	14 = E
1 152 921 504 606 846 976	15 = F

Decimal Values

CONVERSION OF DATA FORMATS

A PL/I statement may assign data of one format to a field defined in a different format. The compiler generates special code to handle the conversion of formats. Some conversions are invalid or may generate unexpected results. The following table lists all possible conversions. For each assignment example, assume that Bit means a field defined as BIT, Char means a field defined as CHARACTER, Pic as PICTURE, and Arithmetic means a field with the attributes DECIMAL or BINARY, and FIXED or FLOAT.

ASSIGNMENT STATEMENT	CONVERSION
1. Bit = Char;	Converts characters 0 and 1 to bits 0 and 1. All other characters are invalid (CONVERSION error).
2. Bit = Pic;	Converts the Picture field to a Fixed Binary value, then to a bit string.
3. Bit = Arithmetic;	Converts the Arithmetic field to a Fixed Binary value, then to a bit string.
4. Char = Bit;	Converts bits 0 and 1 to characters 0 and 1.
5. Char = Pic;	Valid assignment (the Picture editing characters are also assigned).
6. Char = Arithmetic;	Converts to decimal value with decimal point. Invalid under the Subset—first convert Arithmetic to Picture, then Picture to Character.
7. Pic = Bit;	Converts bit string to Fixed Binary, then to Picture.
8. Pic = Char;	Character string must contain valid numeric data—digits 0–9, decimal point, and sign only. Invalid under the Subset (CONVERSION error).
9. Pic = Arithmetic;	Valid—common statement to edit arithmetic values for printing.
10. Arithmetic = Bit;	First converts bit string to binary.
11. Arithmetic = Char;	The character string must contain valid numeric data as in 8. Invalid under the Subset (CONVERSION error).
12. Arithmetic = Pic;	Valid—common statement to convert input amounts to arithmetic format.

CONVERSION OF DATA FORMATS.

EQUIVALENT DATA FORMATS IN ASSEMBLER, COBOL, AND FORTRAN

Assembler Format:	PL/I Format:
Character (C)	CHARACTER
Binary (B)	BIT
Zoned (Z)	PICTURE
Packed (P)	DECIMAL FIXED
Halfword (H)	BINARY FIXED (15)
Fullword (F)	BINARY FIXED (31)
Floating-Point (E, D, and L)	DECIMAL FLOAT
COBOL Format:	PL/I Format:
PICTURE X DISPLAY	CHARACTER
PICTURE 9	PICTURE
COMPUTATIONAL-3	DECIMAL FIXED
COMPUTATIONAL	BINARY FIXED
COMPUTATIONAL-1 and -2	DECIMAL FLOAT
FORTRAN Format:	PL/I Format:
INTEGER	BINARY FIXED REAL
REAL	DECIMAL FLOAT REAL
COMPLEX	DECIMAL FLOAT COMPLEX
LOGICAL	BIT

INDEX